Deindustrialisation and the Moral Economy in Scotland since 1955

Deindustrialisation and the Moral Economy in Scotland since 1955

Jim Phillips, Valerie Wright and Jim Tomlinson

EDINBURGH
University Press

Edinburgh University Press is one of the leading university presses in the UK. We publish academic books and journals in our selected subject areas across the humanities and social sciences, combining cutting-edge scholarship with high editorial and production values to produce academic works of lasting importance. For more information visit our website: edinburghuniversitypress.com

© Jim Phillips, Valerie Wright and Jim Tomlinson, 2021,2023

Edinburgh University Press Ltd
The Tun – Holyrood Road
12 (2f) Jackson's Entry
Edinburgh EH8 8PJ

First published in hardback by Edinburgh University Press 2021

Typeset in 10.5/13pt Sabon by
Manila Typesetting Company

A CIP record for this book is available from the British Library

ISBN 978 1 4744 7924 0 (hardback)
ISBN 978 1 474479257(paperback)
ISBN 978 1 4744 7926 4 (webready PDF)
ISBN 978 1 4744 7927 1 (epub)

Contents

Figures and Tables

Acknowledgements

Research for this book was conducted at the University of Glasgow with support from the Leverhulme Trust, funder of a thirty-six-month project that began in April 2017, 'Employment, Politics and Culture in Scotland', RPG-2016-283. We thank the Trust for its support.

Research was undertaken at Dundee Central Libraries, Glasgow Caledonian University Archives, the Mitchell Library, Glasgow, the National Archives at Kew, the National Library of Scotland, the National Records of Scotland, Renfrewshire Libraries' Heritage Centre, Paisley, the University of Dundee Archive Services, the University of Glasgow Archives and Library, the University of Strathclyde Archives and Special Collections, and the University of the West of Scotland Special Collections. Many thanks to all who work in these archives and libraries.

The book is also based on materials drawn from the three localities examined in Part II of this book: the Fairfield Heritage Centre in Govan, Glasgow; the Johnstone History Museum, adjacent to Linwood in Renfrewshire; and the Timex History Group at the Douglas Community Centre in Dundee. We are grateful to everyone involved in these three places, where we received warm and friendly hospitality on numerous visits.

Our greatest debt is to the women and men whose oral testimonies contributed to our analysis. Most are former industrial workers or family members of former industrial workers. We thank those from Fairfield, Linwood and Timex whom we interviewed, and those from Caterpillar who were interviewed by our colleague Ewan Gibbs. We thank Ewan for sharing these interviews with us and for the many valuable conversations we have had with him on deindustrialisation and the moral economy in Scotland. We also thank Mona Bozdog who provided us with transcripts of testimonies from former Timex employees interviewed within the Generation ZX (X) Project at Abertay University, Dundee.

Discussions at various conferences, seminars, workshops and public events helped us to develop the book's content and conclusions. We thank the organisers of and participants in the following: the Annual Scottish Maritime History Conference at the Mitchell Library, Glasgow, October 2017; the European Social Science History Conference, Queen's University Belfast, April 2018; the British Universities Industrial Relations Association Seminar at Westminster Business School, June 2018; the Factory Occupations in British Labour History Workshop, Newcastle University, June 2018; 'After the Factory: women, gender and deindustrialisation in European perspective', University of Glasgow, September 2018; the Scottish Oral History Centre Seminar Series, University of Strathclyde, January 2019; the Economic History Society Annual Conference at Queen's University, Belfast, in April 2019; the Modern British Studies Conference, University of Birmingham, July 2019; and the Oral History Society Annual Conference, University of Swansea, July 2019.

Thank you, finally, to our work colleagues at the University of Glasgow. Economic and Social History Work in Progress meetings at Lilybank House provided a collegial and critical forum for testing and sharpening our analysis.

Abbreviations

AEEU	Amalgamated Engineering and Electrical Union
AEU	Amalgamated Engineering Union
AUEW	Amalgamated Union of Engineering Workers
BL	British Leyland
BMC	British Motor Corporation
BSC	British Steel Corporation
BSR	Better Sound Recordings Ltd
CBI	Confederation of British Industry
COSLA	Convention of Scottish Local Authorities
CPGB	Communist Party of Great Britain
DEA	Department of Economic Affairs
FDI	Foreign Direct Investment
GCUA	Glasgow Caledonian University Archives
GCPH	Glasgow Centre for Population Health
GFC	Great Financial Crash
IDS	Industry Department for Scotland
ILO	International Labour Organisation
NCB	National Coal Board
NCR	National Cash Register
NDLB	National Dock Labour Board
NUM	National Union of Mineworkers
NUMSA	National Union of Mineworkers Scottish Area
OECD	Organisation for Economic Cooperation and Development
PSA	Peugeot-Citroen
SNP	Scottish National Party
STUC	Scottish Trades Union Congress
TGWU	Transport and General Workers' Union
THG	Timex History Group
UCS	Upper Clyde Shipbuilders

Introduction

On 3 June 1966, workers at the British Motor Corporation (BMC) commercial vehicle plant in Bathgate, West Lothian, began an unofficial strike. They were acting in support of their workplace shop stewards and local union officials, who were attempting to negotiate a substantial pay increase with BMC management. The grievance was substantial: a fundamental disparity of £3 a week between earnings at Bathgate and BMC factories in the English West Midlands.[1] The next afternoon, 4 June, a group of Bathgate shop stewards presented themselves at St Andrews House in Edinburgh, the administrative centre in Scotland's capital of the UK government's Scottish Office, twenty miles away. The stewards demanded an audience with Willie Ross, Secretary of State for Scotland in the Labour government. Ross was not present, although in any case could not have met the stewards. Doing so might have inferred encouragement of unofficial strike action; the government's view was that industrial disputes could only be resolved through established union–management dialogue and procedures.[2] The unofficial strike and the appeal to the Secretary of State for justice were measures of serious workforce frustration. Management had agreed to discuss the pay claim with union representatives after a one-day unofficial strike three weeks earlier, but no progress had materialised. The new stoppage was more protracted. Involving all 3,500 of the plant's workers, it ended after thirteen days when management agreed to a pay conference

1 'Strike for parity at BMC works', By Our Own Correspondent, *The Guardian*, 4 June 1966, p. 14.
2 National Records of Scotland (NRS), SEP 4/2923, Godden to Scott, 6 June 1966.

involving stewards as well as union officials.[3] This resulted in both a local pay increase and a small narrowing of the differential between West Lothian and West Midlands workers. Pay parity across BMC was eventually established – after further collective action – in 1972.[4]

The Bathgate dispute of 1966 highlights the chief contours of the history of deindustrialisation in Scotland which are analysed in this book. In economic and employment terms, industry contracted over a much longer period than is commonly understood. Job losses in most sectors were incremental and pre-dated the high-profile closures of mines and factories in the 1980s. Employment in industrial units generally peaked ten, fifteen, or even twenty years before this. The BMC plant, later owned by British Leyland, exemplified this history. Its closure, in stages from 1982 to 1986, is associated with the broader acceleration of industrial job losses in Scotland after the election in 1979 of Margaret Thatcher's Conservative governments.[5] It was referenced in The Proclaimers' 'Letter from America', which drew parallels between factory closures in the 1980s and the Highland Clearances of the eighteenth and nineteenth centuries.[6] What can be forgotten with this interpretation is that the Bathgate plant was itself established to offset the impact of industrial job losses in the 1950s and 1960s. Opened in 1961, its workforce was drawn from industries where employment was in the process of falling significantly in West Lothian, as elsewhere in Scotland, notably coal, the railways and textiles.

The shrinkage of these older industrial 'staples' was tolerated and even encouraged by government policy, which sought to promote more rapid economic growth through promoting the manufacturing of commercial vehicles and other engineering products in export and consumer goods markets. Manufacturing enterprises such as BMC were incentivised through government grants and loans to locate in areas of above-average unemployment. Workers at Bathgate had expectations of progress cultivated by this policy-driven process of industrial restructuring. Communities in West Lothian and elsewhere accepted the loss of employment in the staples on the understanding that new enterprises

---

3 'Bathgate Pay Talks', *Financial Times*, 12 May 1966, p. 22, and 'BMC Scots strike ends – Pay talks on Monday', By Our Labour Staff, *Financial Times*, 16 June 1966.
4 Catriona L. MacDonald, *The Shopfloor Experience of Regional Policy: Work and Industrial Relations at the Bathgate motor plant, c.1961–86* (University of Glasgow, PhD thesis, 2013), pp. 230–2.
5 MacDonald, *Shopfloor Experience of Regional Policy*, pp. 234–6.
6 The Proclaimers, 'Letter From America', *This Is the Story* (Chrysalis Records, 1987).

would offer greater stability and economic reward. Pay disparity between Scotland and England was one way in which these expectations were compromised. Labour governments were more popular in Scotland than Conservative governments, and more trusted by working-class voters on the issue of economic security. This explains why the stewards – representatives of the ex-miners, ex-railwaymen and ex-textiles employees who worked at Bathgate – wanted to speak to Ross about the injustice of their position.

CONTENT AND FOCUS

In this book deindustrialisation is presented as the central feature of Scotland's economic, social and political history since the 1950s, when employment peaked in shipbuilding and metals along with coal and textiles. Deindustrialisation was occurring across Britain and elsewhere in Western Europe, but nevertheless had distinct political effects in Scotland. The organisational focus for Conservatives in Scotland was the Unionist Party, until the establishment in 1965 of the Scottish Conservative and Unionist Party. At the 1955 general election Conservative and Unionist candidates won a combined 49.7 per cent of votes cast throughout the UK. In Scotland Unionists won 50.1 per cent of the votes. At every subsequent general election, however, the Unionist and then Conservative and Unionist share of votes was lower in Scotland than England: by 2.5 per cent in 1959, 14 per cent in October 1974 and more than 20 per cent in 1987. Unionist and then Conservative and Unionist candidates won fewer votes in Scotland than Labour candidates in every general election after 1959 until 2017. Labour's vote share in Scotland generally matched or exceeded its vote share in England in general elections from 1945 to 2010, and it was unambiguously Scotland's eminent political force from 1959 until 2007, when the Scottish National Party (SNP) won the Scottish Parliamentary election and for the first time formed the Scottish Government.

Various forces contributed to these long-term electoral changes. Social policy was important. The growth of state intervention in housing provision and education from the 1950s contributed to greater appreciation of collective action in pursuit of public welfare. Labour was the electoral beneficiary of this.[7] Upward social mobility took place in Scotland as

---

7 Steven Kendrick and David McCrone, 'Politics in a Cold Climate: The Conservative Decline in Scotland', *Political Studies*, 37 (1989), pp. 589–603, with electoral data at p. 590.

elsewhere in the UK, but newly middle-class Scots retained greater support for government action in defence of economic and social security. This narrowed the appeal in Scotland of Thatcher's individualist politics in the 1980s.[8] Party activism and the charisma of particular Labour and then SNP politicians had an impact too, generally contrasting in favourable terms with Conservative and Unionist leaders.[9] Thatcher herself was enormously unpopular in Scotland.[10] She was abused by opponents in Scotland – most notably at Hampden Park during the 1988 Scottish Cup final – in offensive gender and national terms,[11] and her policies united disparate parties and interests in Scotland against the Conservative and Unionist Party.[12] Cultural trends were also significant with writers, artists and musicians – among them The Proclaimers – highly influential in articulating Scottish distinctiveness in terms of social solidarity. Literary scholars struggled over decades to establish Scottish literature and its position within the curricula of English literature departments at universities in Scotland. Campaigning for a Scottish Parliament in the face of the self-evident democratic deficit of the Thatcher years was an extension of this deeper cultural and political project.[13]

The Scottish Parliament established in 1999 was nevertheless a product of deindustrialisation. Economic insecurity arising from lost industrial employment was a constant presence in Scottish political debates from the 1960s onwards. A labour movement campaign was important in generating broader support for political-constitutional change. This was led by the Scottish Trades Union Congress (STUC), which argued for devolution from the early 1970s. A Parliament in Edinburgh would match Scotland's status as a historic nation with the substance of administrative and legislative statehood. National political renewal would serve as precursor to enhanced collective economic security. After Labour's plans for a Scottish Parliament were halted in 1979, the spectacular

8 Lindsay Paterson, *Education and the Scottish Parliament* (Edinburgh: Dunedin Academic Press, 2005), pp. 21–7; *Scottish Education in the Twentieth Century* (Edinburgh: Edinburgh University Press, 2003), pp. 130–54.
9 Ewen A. Cameron, *Impaled upon a Thistle: Scotland since 1880* (Edinburgh: Edinburgh University Press, 2008), pp. 263–319.
10 David Torrance, *'We in Scotland': Thatcherism in a Cold Climate* (Edinburgh: Birlinn, 2009).
11 Ewan Gibbs, '"Civic Scotland" vs Communities on Clydeside: Poll Tax Non-Payment c. 1987–1990', *Scottish Labour History*, 49 (2015), pp. 86–106.
12 James Mitchell, *The Scottish Question* (Oxford: Oxford Scholarship Online, 2014), pp. 187–215.
13 Scott Hames, *The Literary Politics of Scottish Devolution – Voice, Class, Nation* (Edinburgh: Edinburgh University Press, 2019).

mismanagement of industrial and economic change by Thatcher's governments provided the devolution campaign with renewed impetus. The
STUC helped to convene the Scottish Constitutional Convention in the
late 1980s. Civic bodies, local authorities, cultural organisations and
non-Conservative mainstream political parties were brought together,
all pressing for devolution. The Labour government elected in 1997 had
a clear mandate to establish the Scottish Parliament, and did so after a
public referendum, in 1997.

The argument that deindustrialisation shaped devolution was made by
one of the authors in 2008, in a book focusing on industrial politics in
the 1960s and 1970s.[14] This book deploys a longer chronological sweep
and a broader empirical base. The phased nature of deindustrialisation is
carefully delineated. Three distinct periods are identified. The Bathgate
plant was established during the first phase, from the mid-1950s to the
mid-1960s, when policy accommodated the shrinkage of the staple industries – coal, metals, ships, textiles – and the growth of new manufacturing
enterprises. In the second phase, from the mid-1960s to the late 1970s, the
speed of restructuring decelerated. New investment stagnated and governments were compelled to protect working-class economic security by stabilising employment in the staples. There was new hope especially for coal
mining and shipbuilding. The third phase, from the election of Thatcher's
governments to the mid-1990s was characterised by the accelerated loss of
employment across all industrial sectors, with no meaningful policy effort
to protect working-class economic security.

The book uses unpublished documentary sources from a range of
industrial sectors that have not been examined together before. Car manufacturing and shipbuilding feature alongside coal mining, dock work,
and watch-making and electronics assembly production. New ground
is also established in conceptual terms. A moral economy framework is
adopted to explain popular understanding of industrial and employment
restructuring. This is adapted in part from E. P. Thompson's famous
moral economy of the plebeian English crowd of the eighteenth century,
which attempted to resist changes associated with liberalisation and
industrialisation where these confounded existing customs, rights and
securities. Thompson's important contributions were published in the
1960s and 1970s.[15] A second and less familiar influence on the book's

---

14 Jim Phillips, *The Industrial Politics of Devolution: Scotland in the 1960s and
    1970s* (Manchester: Manchester University Press, 2008).
15 E. P. Thompson, *The Making of the English Working Class* (London: Gollancz,
    1963) and 'The Moral Economy of the English Crowd in the Eighteenth Century',
    Past and Present, 50 (1971), pp. 76–136.

moral-economy framework is Karl Polanyi, whose account of industrialisation, *The Great Transformation*, was published during the Second
World War. Polanyi argued that industrialisation as a process heightened the influence of market forces, abstracting economic life from
social obligations and cultural expectations. Reform movements in the
nineteenth and twentieth centuries emerged and evolved principally with
the aim of re-establishing the social basis of economic activity. Popular
notions of justice and morality were central to these movements and
their demands.[16]

This book shows that in post-Second World War Scotland there was
a working-class moral economy, consisting of customs and expectations
that were rooted in the worlds of employment and industry. Economic
security was prioritised, along with an obligation on policy-makers and
industrialists to obtain the consent of workers and communities affected
when significant restructuring was proposed. The workers' moral economy co-existed with a social-democratic policy-making moral economy
that accepted the state's obligation to maintain high levels of employment. This was superseded in the 1980s by a Thatcherite moral economy, emphasising the values of personal responsibility and a limited role
for the state in stimulating employment provision or industrial activity.
Workers in Scotland tolerated changes to industrial employment where
their longer-term economic security was protected, and when their
trade union and political representatives were involved in managing the
restructuring. The Bathgate strike of 1966 illustrated how the management of deindustrialisation contributed to working-class moral economy
feeling. Disinvestment in established industry had been accepted because
it was accompanied by the growth of alternative forms of employment,
particularly in assembly goods manufacturing. The expectation of secure
and well-rewarded work at the new plant was confounded, however, by
the BMC practice of pay disparity. The working-class moral economy
was embedded in a specifically Scottish national setting. Hence the frustrated Bathgate workers appealed for justice to the Secretary of State for
Scotland.

The working-class moral economy also shaped the politics of many
Scottish electors who were not manual employees. This influenced
the broader anti-Conservative turn in Scottish politics noted earlier.
Upwardly mobile as well as middle-class electors along with manual
workers viewed deindustrialisation as a harm, corroding communal as

16 Karl Polanyi, *The Great Transformation: the Political and Economic Origins of
Our Time* (Boston, MA: Beacon Press, 1944).

well as individual security. A cross-class coalition of electors regarded the Labour Party as a more sensitive manager of deindustrialisation than the Conservative and Unionist Party. It is important to reiterate that the movement in popular opinion away from Conservatism in Scotland in the 1980s did not begin in this decade. Rather it was embedded in the working-class moral-economy interpretation of deindustrialisation since the 1950s. Public sector professionals in education, local government and the health services were adversely affected in Scotland by government spending cuts in the 1980s, which had a negative impact on manual workers in a range of industrial as well as service occupations. Both middle-class and working-class Scots were offended in moral as well as material terms by Thatcherism. The rapid loss of industrial jobs and related increase in unemployment was characterised as repugnant and unjust, contributing to the further marginalisation of Conservatism in Scotland.[17]

The book links political and industrial changes through a two-part integration of themes and case studies. Part I elaborates understanding of deindustrialisation in Scotland from the mid-1950s to the mid-1990s: in longer historical and global terms in Chapter 1; within the moral-economy framework in Chapter 2; and as a phased and protracted process in Chapter 3. Deindustrialisation and the moral economy are analysed in Part I through close reading of developments in Fife, West Lothian and Lanarkshire, where established employment in coal mining and textiles incrementally contracted as these sectors were gradually overtaken in their importance by engineering and other forms of manufacturing, along with public services. Major industrial initiatives in the 1950s and 1960s were secured through UK government regional policy: the various factories clustered in Fife's New Town of Glenrothes, the commercial vehicle assembly plant at Bathgate, and the Caterpillar earthmoving equipment plant at Uddingston, Lanarkshire. Part II develops the analysis with chapter-length case studies. These show the presence and evolution of moral-economy expectations and activism in both established and new industrial activity: shipbuilding from the Upper Clyde, with close study of Fairfield shipyard in Govan, in Chapter 4; motor manufacturing, with examination of the car plant at Linwood in Renfrewshire, in Chapter 5; and watch-making and electronics subassembly, viewed through the life of Timex in Dundee, in Chapter 6. These cases are familiar in the sense of being well known, but in this

---

17 Catriona M. M. Macdonald, *Whaur Extremes Meet: Scotland's Twentieth Century* (Edinburgh: John Donald, 2009), pp. 243–5.

book are subject to major reinterpretations, using the moral economy and deindustrialisation frameworks along with new empirical evidence.

The three cases in Part II cumulatively demonstrate the working-class moral economy of deindustrialisation in action. Gender and class were central to the process of industrial and political transition. Skilled manual male employment and identity were challenged by industrial restructuring in the 1950s and 1960s, particularly where diversification involved multinationals with semi-skilled labour processes and intensive managerial supervision of production. New manufacturing activity also encompassed a greater range of job opportunities for women, whose overall share of industrial employment increased from the 1950s to the 1980s. Skilled male expectations were central to the working-class moral economy; managing these expectations was a vital component of the social-democratic policy-making moral economy. Men accepted lost employment in coal mining and shipbuilding because of the promise of greater collective security through the growth of assembly goods manufacturing. Their household-provider role was diluted but remained intact until the 1980s. Perceptions of social injustice arising from industrial job loss and the political illegitimacy of economic change therefore became more acute and more widely held after 1979.

A shorter Part III completes the book with a chapter-length analysis of deindustrialisation since the mid-1990s. Deindustrialisation continued, albeit at a slower pace than in the 1980s. This reinforces the value of seeing the contraction of industry as a process rather than an event. The influences of deindustrialisation and the moral economy remained live. Any characterisation of early twenty-first-century Scotland as post-industrial was inaccurate. Work and politics were still mediated by the structures and institutions, including trade unions, of industrial society. The SNP government's approach resembled more closely the social-democratic policy-makers' moral economy than the Thatcherite variant. Popular understanding of economic and social activity was still measured against norms and expectations that were developed in the working-class moral economy of industrial society. Scotland's divergence politically from England continued to widen, ever more evident in the referenda on Scottish Independence in 2014 and UK membership of the European Union in 2016, and in various Scottish Parliament and UK General Elections.

The book is based on a wide range of sources. It engages with social science and historical literature on the economy, 'high' politics, working-class culture, labour and gender, as well as specialist writings on the economy, industrial relations, and the selected industries with their distinct

employment cultures. Fresh perspective is drawn from interviews conducted with ex-employees and family members of ex-employees in the
selected industries. These interviews follow the life-course approach
and shape the book's emphasis on popular understanding of political and economic changes from the 1950s. These interviews are integrated with unpublished material in UK government, industry and trade
union archives. The STUC archive at Glasgow Caledonian University
has been a particularly rich resource, along with materials on each of
the three case studies compiled by academic researchers in the 1970s
and 1980s, located in the University of Glasgow archives (Upper Clyde
Shipbuilders), the Mitchell Library, Glasgow (Linwood), and with the
Timex History Group in Dundee.

Part I

Understanding Deindustrialisation

1

Deindustrialisation as a Historical and Global Phenomenon

The term deindustrialisation emerged into political and academic debate in Britain in the 1970s.[1] It gained resonance through suggesting that something profound, even threatening, was occurring in society, resulting from changes in the structure of the economy. The underlying assumption was that dividing up economies into broad sectors, such as agriculture/industry/services, is important in understanding economic and social change. This approach long pre-dated the 1970s, being established in pioneering 'political arithmetic' literature by the late seventeenth century. Understanding of such divisions has gradually been reworked over time: refined, extended and contested, and a whole range of connotations attached. Understanding the history of these shifting meanings helps us to think more effectively about modern debates concerning the 'deindustrial', a term that only makes sense as a perceived alternative system and/or stage to the 'industrial'.

This chapter examines the longer-run evolution of deindustrialisation as an historical and global phenomenon that economic thinkers, actors and policy-makers have attempted to make sense of. The first part traces the idea of the economy as constituted by different sectors, showing

---

1 The term had previously been used in other contexts, notably in relation to India and Germany, as discussed further below. In the Indian case, the trend seems to be confirmed by modern historians' analysis of India's national accounts, suggesting a fall in the share of workers in Indian industry throughout almost all the period of the Raj: S. Broadberry and B. Gupta, 'The historical roots of India's service-led development: a sectoral analysis of Anglo-Indian productivity differences, 1870–2000', *Explorations in Economic History*, 47 (2010), p. 269. In the German case, the term was used for the idea that to prevent future aggression, Germany should be subject to deindustrialisation: F. Gareau, 'Morgenthau's Plan for Industrial Disarmament in Germany', *Western Political Quarterly*, 14 (1961), pp. 517–34.

how the centrality of one sector, industry, became dominant in understandings of economic and social change from the eighteenth century to the twentieth century. The second looks at the emergence of ideas that diagnosed a supposed transition to a new kind of non-industrial society. Various terminologies were attempted to characterise the outcome of this shift, most notably the 'service economy' and the 'post-industrial society'. The third part examines the impact of Thatcherism on deindustrialisation in the 1980s. It shows that the policies of Margaret Thatcher's Conservative governments in the 1980s accelerated rather than initiated deindustrialisation. The fourth part looks at the broader global debate about deindustrialisation in the early twenty-first century. Even as industrial *output* continued to expand across the world, the proportion of workers in the industrial sector, argued below to be the crucial definition of recent deindustrialisation, declined in many countries. The International Labour Organisation (ILO) suggested that we may have passed the peak of the proportion of the world's population engaged in industry in 2014.[2] Scotland's deindustrialisation can then be seen as specific and conjunctural, but also as a part of a long-running and widely experienced phenomenon.

ECONOMY AND INDUSTRY

A tripartite division of the economy can be found in the work of William Petty, often regarded as the founder of national income accounting. In 1672 Petty wrote: 'There is much more to be gained by Manufacture than by Husbandry, and by Merchandize than Manufacture'.[3] This analysis derived from his attempt to explain the relative economic strengths of England, France and the Netherlands. Petty's threefold division drew upon the work of Dutch analysts, and reflected the recognition (however grudging) of the success of the Dutch economic 'model'. His emphasis on the role of merchanting also, of course, reflected the Netherlands' extraordinary strength in international trade, which was the cause of much jealousy in England and France.[4]

---

2 ILO, ILOSTAT database, retrieved from data.worldbank.org. The figure for 2014 was 23.2 per cent, down to 22.8 per cent in 2019.
3 C. Hull, ed., *The Economic Writings of Sir William Petty* (Cambridge: Cambridge University Press, 1899), p. 256.
4 S. Schama, *The Embarrassment of Riches: An Interpretation of Dutch Culture in the Golden Age* (London: Collins, 1987), pp. 254–6, 259–60. J. Appleby, *Economic Thought and Ideology in Seventeenth-Century England* (Princeton: Princeton University Press, 1978).

Over the succeeding two centuries the emergent discipline of classical political economy talked a great deal about industry and rather less about services. When it did discuss the latter much of what was said was framed by questions about the productiveness, or otherwise, of services. Productiveness was itself a complex term. Classical economists were not united in answering the question, productive of *what*? Tax revenue? Employment? Capital accumulation? So the discussion of the economic role of services became embedded in often very abstract debates about productiveness and value, with classical economists adhering to some version of the labour theory of value.[5] Illustrative of this kind of linkage was Adam Smith, who wrote that there were two types of labour:

> the former produces a value, may be called productive, the latter, unproductive. Thus the labour of a manufacturer (i.e. an industrial worker) adds generally to the value of the materials, which he works upon, that of his own maintenance, and of his master's profit. The labour of a menial servant, on the contrary, adds to the value of nothing.

Smith was nevertheless wrestling with this, adding the argument later in the same passage that the labour of the menial servant 'has its value, and deserves its reward'.[6] Karl Marx, of course, had his own version of the labour theory of value, in which productiveness meant the production of surplus value. Marx was above all a theorist of industrial capitalism, so it is perhaps unsurprising that his account of non-industrial activities was fragmented and ambiguous.[7] But the terminology of 'productiveness'. which, at least in some formulations, treated industrial activity as more productive than other forms, was to cast a long shadow. It famously led Soviet economists to seek to treat only industrial production as valuable ('material balances'), and more broadly left a legacy of scepticism about the 'value' of services. This was evident in the Labour

---

5 J.-C. Delaunay and J. Gadrey, *Services in Economic Thought: Three Centuries of Debate* (2nd edn; Boston: Kluwer, 1992), pp. 7–29.

6 Adam Smith, *The Wealth of Nations* (Oxford: Oxford University Press, 1976), Vol. 1, Book II, Ch. 3, p. 330. Note that Smith describes merchants as productive (Vol. 1, Book II, Ch. 5, p. 362), and describes the appellation of 'unproductive' as 'humiliating' (Vol. 2, Book IV, Ch. 9, p. 664), the context being his critique of French philosophers who designate all non-agriculturalists as unproductive.

7 For Marx and industrial capitalism, see K. Tribe, *The Economy of the Word: Language, History and Economics* (Oxford: Oxford University Press, 2015), pp. 171–254. Delaunay and Gadrey seek to make sense of Marx's formulations: *Services in Economic Thought*, pp. 31–55.

Prime Minister Harold Wilson's revealing reference to the dangers of the 'candy floss' economy in the 1960s.[8]

Classical political economy remained predominant in the mid-nineteenth century, when John Stuart Mill wrestled with these matters. He pointed out the problems of the conventional equation of 'productive' with the production of material objects, stressing that 'All the labour of all the human beings in the world could not produce one particle of matter. To weave broadcloth is but to re-arrange, in a peculiar manner, the particles of wool . . .' He sought to rescue at least some services from being 'stigmatised' as unproductive, wanting to rescue the term from its association with wasteful or worthless.[9] Such efforts were soon to be overtaken by a bigger shift in economic thinking, commonly characterised as the neo-classical revolution. This undermined all the debate about 'productiveness' and value as linked to the character of the activity producing economic goods, in favour of the view that 'value' should be imparted to any kind of commodity only by the demand for that commodity. In this version of the world, how much labour was embodied in a commodity, and whether it took the form of a tangible, physical entity, were irrelevant considerations.[10] Many economists continued to be closely concerned with the analysis of manufacturing and other industrial sectors,[11] but at the most abstract level of economic theory there was nothing inherently 'special' about industry. Paradoxically, this shift in economic theory was taking place at a time when industry was seen as more important than ever in the 'real world', above all because of its perceived centrality to the two great intertwined projects of the nineteenth and twentieth centuries, nation building and economic prosperity.

The idea that industrialisation was the key to prosperity arose in the wake of the industrial revolution in Britain, which was seen by many as the harbinger of modernity. For Hobsbawm, 'The Industrial Revolution marks the most fundamental transformation of human life in the history of the world recorded in written documents'.[12] This formulation became

8 For the 'Candy floss economy': Parliamentary Debates, Fifth Series, Commons, Vol. 696, Col. 1552, 18 June 1964.
9 John Stuart Mill, *Principles of Political Economy*, *People's Edition* (London: Longmans Green, 1896), p. 55.
10 Delaunay and Gadrey, *Services in Economic Thought*, p. 64.
11 Alfred Marshall, *Industry and Trade: A Study of Industrial Technique and Business Organisation; And of their Influences on the Conditions of Various Classes and Nations* (London: Macmillan, 1919).
12 Eric J. Hobsbawm, *Industry and Empire* ((London: Weidenfeld & Nicolson, 1968), p. 1.

the common sense of most historians and, more importantly, was embedded in the beliefs of rulers of most existing or fledgling nation states by the middle of the nineteenth century.[13] In the broadest terms, industrialisation has been integral to the creation and persistence of most nation states, and in the nineteenth century all the ascending powers sought to industrialise. Britain, of course, was the 'first industrial nation', but its rivals, most obviously the USA and then Germany, sought to follow suit. Friedrich List, who analysed the possibilities for both countries, famously founded a genre of 'national political economy' whose central concern was how these countries could industrialise in the face of the competition from the British pioneer.[14] His objection to free trade was clear: 'a nation which has an agrarian economy and is dependent upon other countries (for its manufactured goods) can . . . stimulate the establishment of industries by means of a protective tariff . . . Such a country . . . will greatly increase its productive power in the future.'[15] These were not just the concerns of theorists. Alexander Hamilton, the first US Secretary of the Treasury from 1789 to 1795, was the key political actor seeking to transform the new republic's economy. Like the leaders of all 'late industrialisers', Hamilton was happy to deploy all means, legal or otherwise, to gain the knowledge of new industrial processes.[16] In Germany, famously, the state played a key role in industrialisation. Even before unification in 1870, 'the rulers of the German states were expected by their subjects to take an active part in fostering the economic growth of their territories'.[17] After unification, the linking of growth to industrialisation was even more important, and Germany became synonymous with a nation-building project centred on state-guided industrialisation.[18]

What did the process of industrialisation involve, beyond faster economic growth? O'Rourke and Williamson distinguished the spread of manufacturing, their main concern, from a focus on industrialisation as part of a process of structural change. Manufacturing as an economic activity spread from Western Europe through much of the rest

13 E. Gellner, *Nations and Nationalism* (Oxford: Basil Blackwell, 1983), pp. 19–38.
14 D. Levi-Faur, 'List and the political economy of the nation state', *Review of International Political Economy*, 4 (1997), pp. 154–78.
15 List, cited in Levi-Faur, 'List', p. 167.
16 D. Ben-Atar, 'Alexander Hamilton's Alternative: technology policy and the report on manufactures', *William and Mary Quarterly*, 52 (1995), pp. 389–414.
17 W. O. Henderson, *The Rise of German Industrial Power 1834–1914* (London: Temple Smith, 1975), p. 71.
18 A. Gerschenkron, *Economic Backwardness in Historical Perspective* (Cambridge, MA: Harvard University Press, 1962).

of the world, with 'Golden Age' peaks in the 1960s and early 1970s.[19] Structural change, above all the decline of the proportion of the working population in agriculture, historically the overwhelmingly largest activity of human populations, was central to this shift. Even countries that became rich initially in large part because of agricultural development, such as Australia, Argentina and Denmark, saw the numbers in agriculture shrink as a corollary of the fast expansion of output accompanied by rapid rises in rural productivity. And these countries were *necessarily* exceptional, because their prosperity largely derived from expanding demand in industrialising countries. The belief that industrialisation was central to national prosperity (and security) continued to be powerful through the twentieth century. Perhaps most famously it was embodied in the extraordinary Soviet industrialisation effort from 1928, but importantly also in the efforts of the 'Asian Tigers' later in the twentieth century. More broadly in the post-1945 world, many poor countries saw their development as requiring 'import substitution industrialisation', echoing the arguments of List from the previous century.[20]

In Britain, the shift out of agriculture long pre-dated the late eighteenth century, the conventional starting point in over-simplified accounts of the industrial revolution. Before the mid-nineteenth century the data a highly inexact, but the best estimates available, shown in Table 1.1, suggest how early the proportion of those employed in agriculture began to fall.[21] The shift into secondary and tertiary occupations was related to this. The growth of secondary occupations – industrial in other words – was striking even before 1710, and emphasises how much the changes we link to the industrial revolution involved switches in *types* of industrial jobs rather their increase.

A historical account of the centrality of industrialisation to 'modernity' has to be accompanied by the recognition that a simple stage theory based on the statistical predominance in turn of agriculture, industry and services can be highly misleading. As Hartwell emphasises, industrialisation in Britain was accompanied and indeed greatly facilitated by the growth of services in transport and communication, in finance, and

19 Kevin O'Rourke and Jeffrey Williamson, eds, *The Spread of Modern Industry to the Periphery since 1871* (Oxford: Oxford University Press, 2017), pp. 1–3.
20 Ha-Joon Chang, *Kicking Away the Ladder: Development Strategy in Historical Perspective* (London: Anthem, 2003).
21 The early census used occupational distinctions, but these paralleled the three sectors: E. Wrigley, 'The PST System for Classifying Occupations', Cambridge Group for the History of population and Social Structure, paper 20, at www.geog.cam.ac.uk/research/projects/occupations/abstracts/, accessed 25 April 2019.

Table 1.1 Structural change in employment in England, 1600–c.1817 (percentage of males)

	1600	c. 1710	c. 1817
Primary	71	50.8	39.4
Secondary	21.0	37.2	42.1
Tertiary	8.0	12.0	18.4
Male population aged 15–64 (000s)	1,242	1,576	2,910

Source: E. A. Wrigley, *The Path to Sustained Growth. England's Transition from an Organic Economy to an Industrial Revolution* (Cambridge: Cambridge University Press, 2016), p. 71.

in retail and wholesale trade. 'The essential link between services and industry ensured the expansion of both, and complementarity explains the rapid growth of even those services (like retail trade) whose productivity only increased slowly'.[22]

Three important points emerge from Table 1.2. First, the long-run decline of agriculture was fastest in the decades immediately before 1913, and thereafter the sector was too small to influence changes in the labour force later in the twentieth century. This is an especially important point in comparison with most of the rest of Western Europe, where the agricultural labour shrinkage was rapid after 1945, and made a major contribution to the various 'economic miracles' in those countries during the three decades after the war. It is also noticeable that after 1924 the decline in agricultural employment is broadly paralleled by that in mining, emphasising how the weight of employment in that sector – especially in coal – had grown by the First World War. Second, there was a marked growth of public and professional services, especially from the Second World War onwards. This is perhaps the most dramatic index of a shifting labour market, with the emergence of mass employment requiring high levels of formal education, a trend with cultural and social as well as economic implications. The advance of public sector services, notably in health and education, was connected to another new element of economic and political organisation in the twentieth century: the growth of state expenditure and the development of tax regimes to finance this growth. Third, the employment share of

22 R. Hartwell, 'The service revolution: The growth of services in the modern economy', in C. Cipolla, ed., *The Fontana Economic History of Europe, III: The Industrial Revolution* (London: Fontana, 1973), p. 367. Hartwell's broad conclusion stands, despite the fact that the data he uses, derived from P. Deane and W. Cole, *British Economic Growth, 1688–1959* (Cambridge: Cambridge University Press, 1962), pp. 141–4, probably exaggerate the scale of service expansion.

Table 1.2 Sectoral shares of labour in Britain, 1856–1973

	1856	1873	1913*	1924	1937*	1951	1964	1973
Agriculture, fishing and forestry	29.6	21.4	10.4	8.1	5.6	5.6	4.1	2.9
Mining and quarrying	3.6	4.1	6.2	6.2	4.1	3.7	2.6	1.5
Manufacturing	32.5	33.5	32.3	32.9	31.7	35.1	36.1	34.7
Construction	4.0	4.8	4.9	4.5	6.0	6.9	8.5	8.7
Gas, electricity and water	0.1	0.2	0.7	1.1	1.3	1.6	1.7	1.4
Transport and communication	4.1	5.6	8.0	8.6	7.7	8.1	7.5	7.5
Commerce	20.8	24.7	29.3	29.2	34.0	23.4	24.5	25.4
Public and professional services	5.3	5.7	7.9	9.4	9.9	16.6	15.0	18.0

Source: R. Matthews, C. Feinstein and J. Odling-Smee, *British Economic Growth 1956–1973* (Oxford: Clarendon Press, 1982), pp. 223–4.
* For 1913 and 1937 the authors often supply two estimates: in these cases, the figure here is simply the mean of those two figures, rounded up.

manufacturing, industry's largest sector, was remarkably stable from the 1850s to the 1930s. The move during and after the Second World War to a much more distinctly industrial economy is rightly emphasised by Edgerton.[23] Viewed from the perspective of the early 1970s, analysts like Matthews et al. could reasonably believe that the decline from 1964 onwards was just a return to the long-term level, after a wartime 'blip'.[24] With the benefit of hindsight we know they were wrong in this interpretation. From the mid-1960s the trend in manufacturing employment, and because of its weight in the total, the whole of industry, was unambiguously downwards. Figure 1.1 shows that the employment share of the service (tertiary) sector passed 80 per cent by the 2000s, with the industrial (secondary) sector well below 20 per cent.

The primary sector is mainly agriculture and mining; the secondary sector, mainly manufacturing and construction; the tertiary sector, services.

23 David Edgerton, *The Rise and Fall of the British Nation* (London: Allen Lane, 2018).
24 R. C. O. Matthews et al., *British Economic Growth, 1856–1973* (Oxford: Oxford University Press, 1982), pp. 221, 225. It is therefore unsurprising that they do not discuss deindustrialisation, except in a footnote reference to the need to distinguish employment from output trends (p. 220).

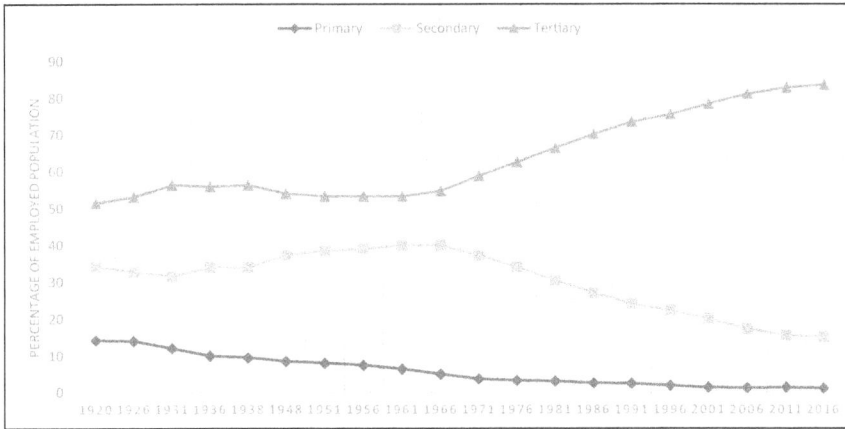

Figure 1.1 UK sectoral employment levels, 1926–2016
Source: ONS, Long-term trends in UK employment: 1861 to 2018 (London: ONS, 2019). No measurements were made between 1938 and 1948 because of the Second World War.

Beyond industrial society?

While 'deindustrialisation' was not significant in public discussion until the 1970s and 1980s, the idea that some economies were beginning to move beyond the industrial stage has a much longer history. A key author in beginning the analysis of 'post-industrial' society was A. G. B. Fisher, although he did not deploy this terminology. In *Clash of Progress and Security*, published in 1935, he started from the paradox that while many commentators in Australia and New Zealand believed their countries' futures depended upon an indefinite expansion of their rural populations, what was actually happening was a growing urban population fed from an increasingly efficient agriculture. His conclusion was both general and clear: 'to complain about the world-wide drift to the towns is to complain that the whole world is growing richer.'[25] Fisher identified the human dilemma of structural economic change, encapsulated in his book's title. Tensions were inevitable, he argued, because changes associated with rising incomes and prosperity involved incidence of insecurity. 'Material progress means change, and change frequently inflicts much inconvenience and suffering upon individuals directly affected.' After discussing the shifts in demand and supply that shaped the growth of prosperity, Fisher analysed how resistance to change can be reduced and its resultant insecurities mitigated. In particular, and again acting as

25 A. G. B. Fisher, *Clash of Progress and Security* (London: Macmillan, 1935), p. vi.

a precursor to much modern discussion, he stressed the importance of education in allowing people to adjust to the demand for new skills as new types of employment expand.[26]

Fisher saw structural change as following three 'stages', echoing much older, Enlightenment-era thinking, but also feeding forward into many subsequent accounts. So there was a 'primary producing stage', when agricultural and pastoral occupations were most important; a 'manufacturing or industrial or secondary producing stage', the beginning of which in Britain he conventionally dated to the end of the eighteenth century; and 'a "tertiary" stage (which) begins in the twentieth century'. Fisher did not claim enormous novelty for his arguments, noting that 'It has been a well-known feature of modern economic development that the proportion of total population engaged in "tertiary" production has been rapidly growing', and he cited both Census data and secondary sources for this trend since 1920, in both the USA and UK.[27] Broad ideas about tertiary growth were indeed in general circulation among economists in the 1930s. Keynes, for example, wrote that 'as wealth increases, both primary and manufactured products play a smaller relative part in the national economy compared with houses, personal services and local amenities.[28] Another key figure was Colin Clark, a pioneer of national income accounting, but with a broad interest in structural change that marked him out from others working on constructing such accounts.[29] His *Conditions of Economic Progress*, drafted in the late 1930s, was influential in post-1945 concerns with economic development and growth in a Cold War context.[30] It fed into Kuznets' foundational text on *Modern Economic Growth*, which stressed the importance of structural change, especially shifts in the composition of *output* towards industry, while noting the rising share of labour in services in a number of countries.[31]

Concern about structural change was expressed in a number of registers in the 1960s. The post-Second World War revolution in international economic statistics fed into the first detailed comparative analyses of the rise of the service sector, with Lengelle's Organisation

26 Fisher, *Clash*, pp. 7, 66–8, 204.
27 Fisher, *Clash*, pp. 25–8, 30–1.
28 John Maynard Keynes, 'National self-sufficiency', in John Maynard Keynes, *Collected Writings*, Vol. XXI (London: Macmillan, 1971), p. 238.
29 For national income accounting and Clark's role: Tribe, *Economy of the Word*, pp. 89–107.
30 C. Clark, *The Conditions of Economic Progress* (2nd edn; London: Macmillan, 1953), especially Chapter V, 'The Flow of Labour to Tertiary Production'.
31 S. Kuznets, *Modern Economic Growth* (New Haven, CT: Yale University Press, 1966). Kuznets also emphasised structural change *within* sectors.

for Economic Cooperation and Development (OECD) study. This noted that OECD countries were in very different phases of their development, and so industry played widely varying roles, but that among the richest countries, especially in north America, the trend from industry to services was unmistakable, and that Western Europe overall would follow the same trajectory over the next decades. On the productivity issue the report was inconclusive, noting the diversity of productivity performance across service sectors within countries, and also divergences between sectors across countries.[32]

The productivity impact of the sectoral shift became a huge issue in ensuing decades, because of the possible implication of an inevitable slowing down in overall growth as the economy shifted to greater reliance on services. This issue was addressed at a theoretical level by Baumol, who argued that it was inherently difficult to improve productivity in many areas of the service sector. He used an example that became famous: the thirty-minute Mozart quartet, which would take two hours of labour to provide whether performed in 1700 or 1965. Baumol also pointed to the growing weight of health and education within the service sector, and again emphasised the difficulties of raising productivity where a service required personal contact.[33] This question about the productivity implications of service expansion has continued to be central to the work of economists and economic historians, who are concerned with economic growth, with Broadberry's work being particularly important for Britain.[34]

Baumol's approach to the service sector emphasised the supply-side aspects, with low productivity growth in services compared with industry inescapable because of less dramatic technological possibilities. This contributed to the funnelling of more and more workers into the former activity. Shifting emphasis to the demand side allows for a more optimistic interpretation. This suggests that the income elasticity

32 M. Lengelle, *The Growing Importance of the Service Sector in Member Countries* (Paris: OECD, 1966), pp. 18–20.
33 W. Baumol, 'Macroeconomics of Unbalanced Growth: The Anatomy of Urban Crisis', *American Economic Review*, 57 (1967), pp. 415–26; W. Baumol, 'Health Care, Education and the Cost Disease: A Looming Crisis for Public Choice', *Public Choice*, 77 (1993), pp. 17–28.
34 Stephen Broadberry, *Market Services and the Productivity Race, 1850–2000: British Performance in International Perspective* (Cambridge: Cambridge University Press, 2006); and 'The rise of the service sector', in Roderick Floud, Jane Humphries and Paul Johnson, eds, *The Cambridge Economic History of Modern Britain Vol. II 1870 to the Present* (Cambridge: Cambridge University Press, 2014), pp. 330–61.

of demand is lowest for agricultural products (food), higher for tangible industrial goods, and highest for services. Thus rising incomes are seen as closely allied with sectoral shifts.[35] This broad idea has a well-established pedigree and is crucial to many accounts of long-run sectoral change, and implies a rather more benign process at work than where the emphasis is on supply-side *constraints*. Baumol's work emerged in the USA of the 1960s, when new concern with the 'service sector' was highly evident. This may be linked to the fact that, as one author wrote, 'The United States is now pioneering in a new stage of economic development. During the period following World War II the country became the world's first "service economy" – that is, the first nation in which more than half of the employed population is not involved in the production of food, clothing, houses, automobiles, or other tangible goods'.[36]

The sense of epochal shift was evident elsewhere in the 1960s in the sociological debate about the 'post-industrial society'. This was influenced by economists such as Clark, but also by sociological thinking about the 'future of work', especially among French Marxist and neo-Marxist thinkers concerned with the existence and character of the working class. Their concern was not so much with the immediate economic and social consequences of the loss of industrial jobs, but with the future of the working class as an agent of revolutionary change.[37] Analysts associated with the Labour Party in Britain were likewise concerned from the 1950s onwards about the perceived erosion of its social base within the 'traditional' working class. The perceived rise of the 'affluent worker', believed to exhibit less collectivist impulses, was regarded as a substantial threat to Labour's electoral future.[38] By the 1970s there was broader pessimism that the very transformation of industrial structure, and especially the decline of the industrial working

35 E. A. Wrigley, *Path to Sustained Growth: England's Transition from an Organic Economy to an Industrial Revolution* (Cambridge: Cambridge University Press, 2016), pp. 74–86; A. Wren, ed., *The Political Economy of the Service Transition* (Oxford: Oxford University Press, 2013), p. 3.
36 V. Fuchs, *The Service Economy* (New York: NBER, 1968), p. 1; the key figure cited in support of this contention was that service employment in the USA had grown from approximately 40 per cent in 1929 to over 55 per cent in 1967 (p. 30).
37 A. Touraine, *The Post-Industrial Society: Tomorrow's Social History: Classes, Conflict and Culture in the Programmed Society* (London: Wildwood House, 1974). This was first published in French in 1969.
38 Lawrence Black, *The Political Culture of the Left in Affluent Britain, 1951–64* (Basingstoke: Palgrave Macmillan, 2003), pp. 124–54.

class, meant long-term decline for the party. This concern was articulated by figures on Labour's left, notably Eric Hobsbawm. His *Forward
March of Labour Halted* was a stand-out of writing in this genre.[39]
Psephologists were by no means universally convinced by these arguments, but their appearance in strong form in the mid-1970s coincides,
as noted above, with the emergence of public discussion of deindustrialisation, and helped animate that discussion.[40]

Structural change had implications for gender as well as class. The
potentially radical impact on the gender composition of the workforce
was recognised. Mingelle's OECD study was unambiguous: the expansion of services favoured women's employment even although this was
not uniform across all service sub-sectors.[41] A more emphatic iteration of
such claims was later made by Delaunay and Gadrey: 'The social prominence of men over women, once a pillar of the traditional social structure, is a thing of the past, largely as the result of the rise of the services
sector and its reliance on a female labour force'.[42] Whether patriarchy
has been decisively uprooted, and whether this has occurred 'largely' by
virtue of employment change, is doubtful. The rise of the service sector
has nevertheless transformed women's labour market experience across
much of the world.[43] Not all theorists of 'post-industrialism' have direct
political concerns or much concern with their gendered implications.
A central text was the American sociologist Daniel Bell's *The Coming
of Post-industrial Society*. His focus was on the changing structure of
occupations, and he saw the decline in industrial work, pioneered in the
USA, as leading to a fundamental change in social structure. For him,
the future was one of especially rapid growth of services in the form
of health, education, research and government, leading to the creation
of a 'new intelligentsia' and the 'pre-eminence of the professional and
technical class'. So, while drawing on ideas that had come to have wide

39 Eric Hobsbawm, 'The Forward March of Labour Halted?' in Martin Jacques and
   Francis Mulhern, eds, *The Forward March of Labour Halted?* (London: Verso,
   1981), pp. 1–19; the lead article in this collection first appeared in *Marxism
   Today* in 1978.
40 I. Crewe, 'Labour force changes, working class decline and the Labour vote:
   social and electoral trends in postwar Britain', in F. Piven, ed., *Labor Parties
   in Postindustrial Societies* (Oxford: Oxford University Press, 1991), pp. 20–46.
41 Lengelle, *Growing Importance*, pp. 21–2.
42 Delaunay and Gadrey, *Services in Economic Thought*, p. 1.
43 Sara Horrell, 'Living standards in Britain 1900–2000: Women's century?'
   National Institute Economic Review (2000), pp. 62–77.

circulation by the end of the 1960s, Bell was also a precursor to much later discussions about the 'information society'.[44]

Many of those who have written about 'the rise of the service economy' or the coming of 'post-industrial society' have attached broadly positive connotations to this shift, in contrast to those who speak of 'deindustrialisation', with its common sense of a damaging and even dangerous historical turn. Somewhere between these poles of argument have been the political scientists who debate the 'political economy' of the service transition.[45] This literature is especially useful because of its focus on the labour market effects of the expansion of services, and the implications these have for political allegiances. In particular, it points to the dilemma arising in a political economy characterised by the growth of low productivity and often publicly funded employment. The reconciliation of demands for egalitarian wage structures and expectations of full employment with political constraints on taxation and state expenditure becomes much harder to achieve.[46]

Deindustrialisation became a live issue in Britain in the 1970s, just as the 'Golden Age' boom ended with a rapid surge in global oil prices, sometimes referred to as OPEC 1, and the first significant economic recession since the Second World War.[47] In 1974 the *Sunday Times* ran a series of articles by the economists Bacon and Eltis, which argued that 'Britain's difficulties . . . largely result from a structural shift away from industry since 1962'. Bacon and Eltis followed these articles with a book, which claimed that the unwelcome move out of industry was the result of an excessive growth of the 'non-marketed sector' of the economy: the alleged culprit, in other words, was the state, with government services provided in kind 'crowding out' private investment in manufacturing. While drawing on classical economic theory, this intervention was part of the broad attack on the public sector, which became central to British politics in the 1970s. Bacon and Eltis were Thatcherites, or at least proto-Thatcherites.[48] From a socialist position, by contrast, the Labour government's Secretary of State for Industry, Tony Benn, lamented in

---

44 D. Bell, *The Coming of Post-industrial Society: A Venture in Social Forecasting* (London: Heinemann, 1974).
45 Wren, *Political Economy of the Service Transition*.
46 T. Iversen and A. Wren, 'Equality, employment and budgetary restraint: the trilemma of the service economy', *World Politics*, 50 (1998), pp. 507–46.
47 Though the recession was far less serious in output and employment loss than those of the 1980s, 1990s and 2000s, it was accompanied by very high inflation. Peaking at 25 per cent in 1975, this stimulated a moral panic.
48 R. Bacon and W. Eltis, *Britain's Economic Problem: Too Few Producers* (London: Macmillan, 1976).

April 1975 the 'devastating trend to contraction of British industry'. In his budget speech that same month Denis Healey, the Chancellor of the Exchequer, explicitly used the word 'deindustrialisation', defined as a 'steady loss of jobs and factory capacity year after year'. Healey's statement included this passage:

> But from now on we must do everything in our power to ensure that our exports of manufactures increase faster than our imports and not the other way round. We must preserve and improve our international competitiveness – a word that covers many things other than just relative wages and prices. It comprises the quality and availability of industrial capacity and of skilled manpower, and the efficiency, the originality and the vitality of our industrial management. It includes, above all, the ability to deliver on time. In all these respects there is a vast task of regeneration ahead of us. We must reverse the process of deindustrialisation – of a steady loss of jobs and factory capacity year after year – which my right hon. Friend the Secretary of State for Industry described so convincingly in a recent article.[49]

Benn not only pioneered the use of the term deindustrialisation, but also called explicitly for the 'reindustrialisation' of Britain. In his key Cabinet paper opposing the terms of the famously contentious International Monetary Fund loan to Britain in 1976, he called for an alternative strategy of import and exchange controls that would underpin a strategy 'necessary to allow us to re-industrialise so that we can emerge strong again at the end'.[50]

Benn's approach was rejected by his Cabinet colleagues. But more generally the Labour government viewed industrial production and employment as the best guarantor of working-class economic security. A series of policy interventions notably renewed investment in the nationalised coal sector and the taking into public ownership of shipbuilding, along with the 'rescue' of Chrysler UK, underlined this priority. The detailed implications of this approach and their Scottish particularities are examined in later chapters. The use of the term deindustrialisation by politicians of the left was linked to a belief that industry, especially manufacturing, was central to the growth performance of the economy, both because of the importance of the sector for productivity, and for the balance of payments, the position of which at this time was widely

49 Parliamentary Debates, Fifth Series, Commons, Vol. 890, Col. 288, 15 April 1975; 'Tony Benn writes about industrial policy', *Trade and Industry* (London: HMSO, April 1975).
50 The National Archives, Kew (TNA), CAB 129/193/7, CP (76) 117, Secretary of State for Energy, 'The real choices facing the Cabinet', 29 November 1976.

held to be a constraint on the expansion of the economy. Without using the term deindustrialisation, Nikolas Kaldor had articulated these as the key problems facing Labour in the 1960s. As economic adviser to the Labour governments from 1964 to 1970, Kaldor's major contribution was probably the Selective Employment Tax. This was geared to dis-incentivising employment in services compared with manufacturing.[51] Kaldor's influence was apparent in the approach of Ajit Singh, author in 1977 of one of the first academic articles that sought to define and deploy deindustrialisation. For him this was the inability of the economy to generate enough manufacturing exports to finance a level of imports commensurate with full employment.[52]

THATCHERISM AND DEINDUSTRIALISATION

In 1978, a landmark conference largely followed Singh and Kaldor in agreeing a macroeconomic view of the problem, linked to Britain's trad-ing performance. Frank Blackaby, editor of the resulting book, opined: 'in "deindustrialisation" we had a new label for an old problem – the relatively poor competitive performance of British manufacturing indus-try'.[53] But this macroeconomic focus, while not disappearing from debate, became less central in the early 1980s when what Rodrik calls 'employment deindustrialisation' came into new prominence.[54] This was the result of the extraordinary contraction of both employment and output in manufacturing that followed the election of the Thatcher government in 1979. There followed an unprecedented deindustrialising shock, leading to the loss of almost two million industrial jobs in the space of four years from 1979 to 1983. The scale of this deindustriali-sation led many commentators to see this as the period when deindus-trialisation began in both Britain and Scotland, and that this sudden phenomenon was the result of a deliberate policy choice by the Thatcher government.

51 Nikolas Kaldor, *Causes of the Slow Rate of Growth of the United Kingdom* (Cambridge: Cambridge University Press, 1966); J. Tomlinson, *The Labour Governments 1964–70: Vol. 3 Economic Policy* (Manchester: Manchester University Press, 2004), pp. 132–4, 225–6.
52 A. Singh, 'UK industry and the world economy: a case of deindustrialisation?' *Cambridge Journal of Economics*, 1 (1977), pp. 113–36.
53 Frank Blackaby, ed., *De-industrialisation* (London: Heinemann, 1979), p. 268. For other discussions of the 1970s: T. Sherif, *A De-industrialized Britain* (London: Fabian Society, 1979).
54 D. Rodrik, 'Premature deindustrialisation', *Journal of Economic Growth*, 21 (2016), pp. 2–4.

Neither of these propositions is true. On the timing of deindustriali-sation, as the data in Table 1.2 and Figure 1.1 made clear, the decline of industrial employment in the UK began in the 1950s, and in manufactur-ing in the 1960s. A broadly similar pattern is evident in Scotland, noted in the final section of this chapter and examined in detail in Chapter 3. Admittedly there was a rapid acceleration of the problem, and the Thatcher governments – in vivid contrast to their Labour predecessor – took no meaningful action to protect or stimulate industrial employ-ment. Different industrial policies were also accompanied from 1979 by a different moral interpretation of economic security and its hazards, as Chapter 2 demonstrates. In the narrower sphere of intentions, however, there is no evidence to support the contention that Thatcher's govern-ment envisaged – and far less welcomed the prospect – that their policies would shape an across-the-board contraction of the industrial sector. Typical of the approach to this issue was a Thatcher speech given in the 1979 General Election campaign in the manufacturing core of the English West Midlands:

> I want to talk about the state of industry and the state of Britain, which so largely depends upon it, and where better than Birmingham to do that. In the five years since the present government came to office, Britain has had the worst record on industrial production of any major industrial country. Our industrial growth has been a third of Italy's, a quarter of America's, half of France's and half of Japan's . . . without the wind of change the Conservatives offer, there can be no hope of halting Britain's industrial decline.[55]

There were some on the political right who believed that Britain's comparative advantage lay in the service sector, and that a tough pur-suit of free-market policies would beneficially shrink the 'bloated' indus-trial sector.[56] But there is no evidence that members of the Thatcher government or their advisers adhered to such views in the early years of Thatcher's rule. On the contrary, the views of Bacon and Eltis, that industrial production should be revived by reducing the size of the

---

55 Margaret Thatcher Foundation, Speech to Conservative rally in Birmingham, 19 April 1979, Margaret Thatcher Foundation Website (hereafter MTFW), at https://www.margaretthatcher.org/document/104026, accessed 21 December 2020.

56 Samuel Brittan, 'A lethal cure for a dubious disease', *The Times*, 29 June 1978; Samuel Brittan, 'Deindustrialisation is good for Britain', *Sunday Times*, 3 July 1980; Samuel Brittan, 'How British is the British sickness?' *Journal of Law and Economics*, 21 (1978), pp. 245–68. A historian with similar arguments is W. Rubinstein, *Capitalism Culture and Decline in Britain, 1750–1990* (London: Routledge, 1993).

public sector, was much closer to Thatcherite thinking. Also ideologically important was the work of Corelli Barnett, who argued that Britain's industrial position had been fatally undermined by an anti-industrial culture promulgated by the left, a view strongly echoed by Thatcher and ideologues like Sir Keith Joseph, her initial Secretary of State for Industry.[57] Indeed, the defence of the 'enterprise culture', which clearly embraced industrial enterprise, was a central component of Thatcherite ideology. These influences were nevertheless muddied and even contradictory. A more detailed reading of Barnett, for instance, reveals his policy prescriptions as unambiguously *anti*-Thatcherite: in pursuit of industrial regeneration, he advocated 'Prussian-style' state-led initiatives. These placed him in policy terms closer to Benn and other advocates of strong industrial interventionism policy than the market fundamentalists elected in 1979.[58]

Why, then, did the years immediately after the 1979 election see such a disastrous fall in industrial employment? Of central importance was the unplanned and unprecedented appreciation of the exchange rate of the pound. Sterling had been strengthening under the impact of North Sea Oil since 1977, but the 'monetarist' policies pursued by Thatcher's government account for most of the upward movement after 1979.[59] These policies can reasonably be labelled 'adventurist', given that they had not been thought through in anything like the depth required, and certainly not in the level of detail applied to tax policy over several years by the Conservatives in Opposition.[60] The policies were also made in wilful ignorance of the complexities of controlling the money supply, which had been revealed when the Bank of England attempted similar measures in the early 1970s.[61] The effects of the appreciation of sterling were concentrated on the industrial sectors of the economy because

---

57 Corelli Barnett, *The Collapse of British Power* (London: Eyre Methuen, 1971); *Audit of War* (London: Macmillan, 1986). Barnett, a military historian by training, was very weak on economic issues: see J. Tomlinson, 'Corelli Barnett's History: The Case of Marshall Aid', *Twentieth Century British History*, 8 (1997), pp. 222–38. For a similar line of argument from a literary historian, M. Wiener, *English Culture and the Decline of the Industrial Spirit 1850–1980* (Cambridge: Cambridge University Press, 1981).
58 D. Edgerton, 'The prophet militant and industrial: The peculiarities of Corelli Barnett', *Twentieth Century British History*, 2 (1991), pp. 360–79.
59 Martin Chick, *Changing Times: Economics, Policies, and Resource Allocation in Britain since 1951* (Oxford University Press, Oxford, 2020), pp. 324, 317–20.
60 Jim Tomlinson, 'Mrs Thatcher's Economic Adventurism', *British Politics*, 2 (2007), pp. 3–19.
61 D. Needham, *Monetary Policy from Devaluation to Thatcher, 1967–82* (Basingstoke: Palgrave, 2014).

that was where most tradeable goods came from. Squeezed exports and much cheaper imports rendered almost all of British industry unprofitable, and this was the core cause of mass redundancies in industry. In the House of Commons Thatcher conceded that 'the rapid increase in the exchange rate caused tremendous problems, particularly for industries that are exporting', but disclaimed government responsibility for this appreciation.[62] When her adviser John Hoskyns circulated an economist's paper arguing the contrary, that sterling's elevated value *was* the result of monetary policy, the response by Thatcher and key ministers was dismay and denial.[63]

This central macroeconomic problem was accompanied by other aspiration-driven policies that indirectly exerted a disproportionate squeeze on the industrial sector. One ambition with important ramifications, relating to the aim of curtailing public expenditure, was to cut the deficits of publicly owned enterprises. These were overwhelmingly industrial in character. This policy was pursued at the same time as the overall macroeconomic squeeze on the economy gravely worsened these deficits: industrial enterprises were paying more to borrow and earning less from reduced revenues. As a government paper noted, in 1981 these deficits were mounting across most public enterprises, well beyond the 'traditional loss makers.'[64] These 'traditional' losers included coal mining. In this key ideological and economic sector, the government combined a desire to cut the deficit of the National Coal Board (NCB) with a desire to break the *political* power of the National Union of Mineworkers (NUM). The 1984–5 strike was shaped above all other issues by the government's determination to remove union influence from the management of the industry.[65] The government's more generalised hostility to trade unions arguably shaped its reluctance to protect industrial jobs. The positive correlation historically between industrial employment and trade union membership meant that job losses arising from deindustrialisation eroded the scale and influence of the labour movement. This was a convenient if indirect outcome for Thatcher's

62 Parliamentary Debates, Fifth Series, Commons, Vol. 998, Col. 418, 5 February 1981.
63 Jim Tomlinson, *Managing the Economy, Managing the People: Narratives of Economic Life in Britain from Beveridge to Brexit* (Oxford: Oxford University Press, 2017), pp. 153–4.
64 TNA, CAB 134/4517, Ministerial committee on Economic Strategy, 'Nationalised Industries 1981 Investment and Financial Review', 22 July 1981.
65 Jim Phillips, 'Containing, Isolating, and Defeating the Miners: The UK Cabinet Ministerial Group on Coal and the three phases of the 1984–85 strike', *Historical Studies in Industrial Relations*, 35 (2014), pp. 117–41.

government, with unions typically much weaker in services, especially in the private sector. The erosion of union voice in workplaces – and in decisions at macro-policy level affecting particularly manual workers – reinforced a further basic tenet of Thatcherism, 'restoring' the 'right of management to manage', liberated from state regulation and the trade union 'veto'.[66] The unwillingness of government ministers to engage with union representatives on the related questions of economic security and industrial job loss was an important element of deindustrialisation's distinct political impact in Scotland, examined at various points later in this book.

As well as cutting public sector deficits, the government also wanted to reduce public spending on industrial subsidies, hitting hard at private sector industrial employment and regional support, which was mainly focused on industry.[67] Again, this did not derive from an especial animus against *industry*, but from the fact that this was the sector where most (overt) subsidies existed, following on from years of previous governments seeking to encourage industrial regeneration (subsidies to agriculture are the obvious qualification to this point), a theme developed in Chapters 2 and 3. But in a broad sense the government still favoured manufacturing. After all, one of the purposes of spending cuts was to lower taxation, including on industrial corporations, to encourage them to invest more. This general stance was combined with large explicit subsidies for multinational car companies, for example, particularly new-start operations with clearer restraints on union organisation and workplace voice.[68]

Far from welcoming the contraction of industrial employment in 1980 to 1982, therefore, the Conservatives were initially panic-struck, believing they could not win a general election with such unemployment levels.[69] But then the position changed, explaining the confidence with which miners and other groups of unionised workers were confronted by the government in the mid-1980s, and how ministers tolerated the continued acceleration of deindustrialisation. An important harbinger

66 Chris Howell, *Trade Unions and the State: the Construction of Industrial Relations Institutions in Britain, 1890–2000* (Princeton, NJ: Princeton University Press, NJ, 2005), pp. 131–73.
67 Typical of the kind of arguments put by Thatcherites was that of John Redwood, *Going for Broke: Gambling with Taxpayers' Money* (Oxford: Basil Blackwell, 1984).
68 'Company Report: Nissan UK's £800 Million Worth of Corporate Welfare', at https://www.corporate-welfare-watch.org.uk/2017/09/26/nissan-nearly-1bn-corporate-welfare/, accessed 6 November 2019.
69 Tomlinson, *Managing the Economy*, pp. 150–1.

was the 1983 General Election, where the Conservatives increased their vote share and number of seats in England – although not in Scotland – despite the mass unemployment concentrated in industrial sectors. It was apparent by this date that the upswing in the economy was centred not on industrial activity, but on a credit-fuelled boom in services. The balance of payments consequences of industrial contraction were being offset by the fall in the value of the pound, which commenced in late 1981. Attacks on the government from those who argued that industry was the key to prosperity, and that direct state action to aid industrial recovery was a necessary response, opened the way to new ideological positioning that the Conservatives found fruitful. Increasingly, proponents of industrial expansion were associated with advocacy of the kind of anti-free-market attitudes that the government rejected. Such views were evident in the government's response to criticism from the employers' organisation, the Confederation of British Industry (CBI), and to a strongly 'pro-industry' report from the House of Lords Select Committee on Overseas Trade in 1985.[70] In evidence to that Select Committee, the Chancellor of the Exchequer, Nigel Lawson, argued that, 'There is no adamantine law that says we have to produce as much in the way of manufactures as we consume . . . If it does turn out that we are relatively more efficient in world terms at providing services than at producing goods, then our national interest lies in a surplus on services and a deficit on goods.'[71]

The pre-1979 practice of favouring industry over services was visibly abandoned in the field of regional policy, where manufacturing had been stimulated in areas of relatively slow economic activity and above-average unemployment. When expenditure in this sphere was initially cut back in 1980, there was little controversy. The proposed further cuts and reforms in 1983 solicited greater disquiet, however, not least because they were presented as an attempt to 'rebalance' investment, to include services. Norman Tebbit, the Secretary of State for Trade and Industry, told the House of Commons: 'It is not immediately obvious to me at any rate that it is necessarily more virtuous or more wealth-producing to manufacture ladies' home-perm sets than to run a ladies' hairdressing salon.' Nicholas Winterton, Conservative MP for Macclesfield, close to

70 House of Lords, *Report from the Select Committee on Overseas Trade* (London: HMSO, 1985); Parliamentary Debates, Sixth Series, Lords, Vol. 468, Cols 1191–294, 3 December 1985.
71 Nigel Lawson, Oral Evidence, in House of Lords, *Report from the Select Committee on Overseas Trade*, Volume 11 (London: HMSO, 1985), p. 554.

the geographical centres of English industrialisation, was dismayed. 'My right hon. Friend [Tebbit] does not want to maintain jobs in manufacturing industry', Winterton lamented, 'he wants to open hairdressing salons instead.' Tebbit's approach – judged from the debate overall – was not based on deprecating the economic role of manufacturing, but on the belief that policy should in principle not discriminate against services. This was consistent with the view, frequently stated by Conservative ministers, that the market and not the government should determine the distribution of resources between sectors.[72]

Late in 1985, the government's record on industry came under strong attack when the House of Lords Select Committee on Overseas Trade published its report. This argued that Britain's industrial weakness had damaged the balance of payments position. Once North Sea Oil ran out, services would be unable to compensate for the deficit on manufactured goods which had appeared for the first time in 1983.[73] Lawson responded by claiming that the Select Committee had underestimated the contribution of the service sector, especially financial services, to exports.[74] But this was *not* coupled to any general claim about where Britain's comparative advantage lay. Rather, Lawson asserted, 'The Government's policy is to create the conditions in which business can thrive and prosper – manufacturers and non-manufacturers alike.' What particularly aroused the Chancellor's hostility to the Report, beyond its general gloominess about the state of the British economy, was its advocacy of greater government support for industry. Lawson characterised this offer as amounting to a 'a cocoon of subsidies'.[75] Lord Young, speaking for the government in Parliament, followed the same line. 'The creation of an enterprise culture is the most important goal we have', he argued, emphasising that this kind of encouragement, along with policies like tax cuts, applied to the whole economy, not just manufacturing. Answering the Select Committee's concern about the future consequences when North Sea Oil revenues were exhausted, Young said that 'the worst way to achieve such an adjustment [rebalancing the external trade account] would be for the state to discriminate now in favour of

---

72 Parliamentary Debates, Sixth Series, Commons, Vol. 50, Cols 846–8, 13 December 1983.
73 House of Lords, *Report from the Select Committee on Overseas Trade.*
74 Mansion House speech 1985, by Nigel Lawson, 17 October 1985, p. 1, at https://www.gov.uk/government/publications/chancellors-mansion-house-speeches-1985-1994, accessed 21 December 2020.
75 Mansion House speech 1985, p. 2. See also Parliamentary Debates, Sixth Series, Commons, Vol. 86, Cols 590–1, 13 November 1985.

one particular sector of the economy: government's "second-guessing" of economic reality has provided few benefits in the past.'[76]

Lawson and Young had made clear that, by the mid-1980s, talk of needing to mitigate 'deindustrialisation' was seen as code for calling for the revival of dirigiste 'industrial policy', and its corollary of 'picking winners', vigorously anathematised by some economists as well as government ministers. Crafts offered a qualified defence of Thatcherite policies and worried that too much focus on reviving industry would license a return to the alleged failings of pre-1979 policy.[77] A broadly similar positioning was evident in his later debate with the anti-Thatcherite economists.[78] The boom in the City of London in the 1980s strengthened the non-industrial balance of payments and so underpinned the government's position. The inadvertent favouring of the service over the industrial sector could even be presented as a far-sighted recognition of market realities. But this shifting economic context certainly did not lead to a wholesale retreat from encouragement of industry. In one of her last Commons speeches as Prime Minister, Thatcher extolled the successes of her governments. 'Our industry is better managed and better equipped than ever before – from cars to steel, to chemicals, to aerospace, to electronics. New industries are growing up and industries that scraped by under Labour are flourishing under the Conservatives. *We are seeing the re-industrialisation of Britain*' (emphasis added).[79]

Thatcher's claims in her final days as Prime Minister reinforced the political significance of manufacturing in the UK. The record of her governments had nevertheless offered substantial qualification of the long-held Conservative belief that industrial prosperity was the essence of economic and political success. Outside government circles, the diagnosis of deindustrialisation as a major problem was certainly widespread in the early 1980s. There was much debate, especially in the Labour Party,

76 Parliamentary Debates, Sixth Series, Lords, Vol. 468, Cols 1204–6, 3 December 1985.
77 N. Crafts, *Can De-industrialisation Seriously Damage Your Wealth?* (London: Institute of Economic Affairs, 1993).
78 N. Crafts, 'Deindustrialisation and economic growth', *Economic Journal*, 106 (1996), pp. 172–83; Michael Kitson and Jonathan Michie, 'Britain's industrial performance since 1960: Underinvestment and relative decline', *Economic Journal*, 106 (1996), pp. 196–212; see also Kitson and Michie, 'The De-industrial Revolution: The rise and fall of UK manufacturing, 1870–2010', in R. Floud, J. Humphries and P. Johnson, eds, *The Cambridge Economic History of Modern Britain: Vol. II, 1870 to the Present* (Cambridge: Cambridge University Press, 2014), pp. 302–29.
79 Parliamentary Debates, Sixth Series, Commons, Vol. 180, Col. 23, 7 November 1990.

about how best to respond to Thatcherite policies, particularly over the plausibility and efficacy of policies restricting imports. But the view that revived industry would promote both immediate employment expansion and longer-term prosperity did not change.[80] Alongside these political arguments there was a growing academic literature that focused attention on the scale and impact of recent industrial job losses. This literature, understandably, highlighted the social damage brought about by the dramatic contraction of industrial employment.[81] Cultural factors were also emphasised, not least in analyses of Scotland. Discussion of industrial losses focused on their impact on the existential identity as well as the material well-being of workers and communities affected. Contributors to this new strand of literature on deindustrialisation were generally unconcerned with the deeper structural changes that pre-dated the early 1980s, but they did raise a crucial longer-term issue: the linkage between industrial employment and economic welfare, particularly for working-class people with limited qualifications and skills prior to starting work. The loss of jobs in manufacturing, metals and mining was keenly felt not because of the intrinsic properties of industrial employment, although this was hinted at by some.[82] The real value of these jobs was in a sense extrinsic: they were well-paid, and regulated through union voice, which ensured a degree of workforce control and employment protection.[83]

The high unemployment and decline in manufacturing of the early 1980s also stimulated a revival of the kinds of macroeconomic arguments about their impact on growth and total employment. One of the most distinctive accounts was that of Rowthorn and Wells. While adhering to Singh's earlier definition of deindustrialisation as a problem because it undermined attempts to the combine payments balance with full employment, this new formulation saw the decline in industrial

80 J. Tomlinson, *Monetarism: Is There an Alternative?* (Oxford: Basil Blackwell, 1986), pp. 99–123.
81 R. Martin and R. Rowthorn, eds, *The Geography of Deindustrialisation* (London: Macmillan, 1986); H. Levie, D. Gregory and N. Lorentzen, eds, *Fighting Closures: Deindustrialisation and the Trade Union* (Nottingham: Spokesman, 1984); D. Rose, C. Vogler, G. Marshall and H. Newby, 'Economic restructuring: the British experience', *Annals of the American Academy of Political and Social Science*, 475 (1984), pp. 137–57.
82 Sean Damer, 'Life after Linwood? The Loss of the Cash Nexus, or, De-industrialisation in the Periphery', British Sociological Association Conference, University College Cardiff, 5–8 April 1983; John Foster and Charles Woolfson, *The Politics of the UCS Work-in: Class Alliances and the Right to Work* (London: Lawrence & Wishart, 1986).
83 Tony Dickson and David Judge, eds, *The Politics of Industrial Closure* (Palgrave London: Macmillan, 1987).

employment as largely the effect of changes in the structure of British trade. With North Sea Oil cutting oil imports, and subsidised agriculture supplying much more of the country's food, Rowthorn and Wells argued that a decline in manufacturing's trade balance, and employment level, was unavoidable. They wanted to see a revival in manufacturing output and efficiency, but regarded the decline in industrial *employment* as part of a structural change common to all industrial countries.[84]

Debates in the twenty-first century

Arguments tentatively set out in the 1980s about deindustrialisation's seriously damaging effects were remade with greater force in the twenty-first century. Economists and others pointed to a fundamental problem in the labour market. The core theme was economic welfare. Where industry had historically provided large-scale, relatively stable and well-paid employment to workers with little formal education, the new service-dominated economy offered less to those without extensive educational qualifications. The result was a growing polarisation of the labour market between those who could take up the growing number of well-paid and relatively secure jobs in such areas as professional services, health care and education, and those whose lack of qualifications confined them to poorly paid and often precarious employment.[85]

These changes were detected in a range of rich countries, including Australia and the USA.[86] The deindustrialisation debate in the USA had pessimistic beginnings in the early 1980s. There was a degree of panic about the perceived shortcomings of the US economy, especially in comparison with Japan. A sense of economic failure generated a variety of responses, including an important new literature on deindustrialisation. Like that in Britain, this literature was preoccupied with recent employment loss in industry, but was distinct in exploring the migration of jobs from the 'rust-belt to the sun-belt', from northeastern USA to the south and southwest. Deindustrialisation reflected the impact of capital flight, as businesses sought lower wages and less robust union

84 R. Rowthorn and J. Wells, *Deindustrialisation and Foreign Trade* (Cambridge: Cambridge University Press, 1987).
85 M. Goos and A. Manning, 'Lousy and Lovely Jobs: The rising polarisation of work in Britain', *Review of Economics and Statistics*, 89 (2007), pp. 118–33; Guy Standing, *The Precariat: The New Dangerous Class* (London: Bloomsbury, 2011).
86 J. Borland and M. Coelli, 'Labour market inequality in Australia', *Economic Record*, 92 (2016), pp. 517–47.

organisation. Low-tax and deregulated labour market offers from 'business-friendly' state 'booster' governors in the south and west were an important 'pull' factor.[87] It was gradually appreciated, however, particularly by historians, that this process was also international, driven by the class imperatives of capitalism to secure 'green' and hence more compliant labour.[88] Historical perspective has been especially valuable in shaping Gordon's analysis of the USA. This has combined a pessimistic view about the recent growth trajectory of the US economy with longer-term optimism about the impact of occupational change on the experience of work. While recognising the recent process of polarisation, for the long term he offers a threefold typology of work that is 'physically difficult and taxing', 'physically not challenging but repetitive and boring', and, third, 'nonroutine cognitive' work, deemed pleasant. He argues that in the century to 1970 there was a shift from the first to the second of these. After 1970 the third type of job grew rapidly, and the ratio of the 'physically difficult and taxing' to nonroutine cognitive jobs shifted from 7.9 in 1870 to 2.1 in 1940 to 0.1 in 2010. Gordon calls this 'one of the great achievements of American growth over the past fourteen decades'. This has the great merit of linking the rather grand notions of long-run historical structural change to major shifts in the everyday pains and pleasures of work,[89] although it plainly glosses over the fate and the struggles of those still labouring in 'physically not challenging but repetitive and boring' occupations that characterise much of the casualised and exploitative work scenarios that commonly apply in the USA and many other economies in the twenty-first century.[90]

In the 2000s, the issue of deindustrialisation became enmeshed in analyses that also framed manufacturing job losses in terms of globalisation.

---

87 The most important American work was Barry Bluestone and Bennett Harrison, *The Deindustrialisation of America: Plant Closings, Community Abandonment, and the Dismantling of Basic Industry* (New York: Basic Books, 1982). For the context of this work see Barry Bluestone, 'Foreword', in Jefferson Cowie and Joseph Heathcott, eds, *Beyond the Ruins: The Meanings of Deindustrialisation* (Ithaca, NY: Cornell University Press, 2003).

88 Jefferson Cowie, *Capital Moves: RCA's Seventy-Year Quest for Cheap Labor* (New York: New Press, 2001).

89 R. Gordon, *The Rise and Fall of American Growth: The US Standard of living since the Civil War* (Princeton, NJ: Princeton University Press, 2016), p. 257.

90 Gabriella Alberti, Ioulia Bessa, Kate Hardy, Vera Trappman, Charles Umney, 'In, Against and Beyond Precarity', *Work, Employment and Society*, 32.3 (2018), pp. 447–57.

It was a problem in both developed and developing economies.[91] The debate in the USA was reignited by evidence of a speeding-up of the long-run trend to industrial job loss: a return to a concern with *employment* deindustrialisation. There was much debate about the causes of this acceleration, and in particular how far it was the consequence of Chinese imports into the USA.[92] The USA had, of course, been the 'pioneer' of deindustrialisation, but increasingly there was evidence that the decline in employment in this sector was evident across the globe. In the early twenty-first century, despite the global rise in industrial output, especially in China, the proportion of workers in industry was stagnating or falling in many countries. Rodrik emphasised that this contraction was happening to countries at much earlier stages of development and at lower incomes than had historically been normal, suggesting that 'premature deindustrialisation' was blocking what previously had been the key route to development for poor countries.[93]

While (state-led) industrial development had dominated in East Asia, including China, the problem of an absence of industrial employment was a particular worry for India, where national economic growth had accelerated from the 1980s, largely on the back of the growth of the service sector.[94] The question of how far this growth pattern was sustainable, and in particular how far the labour market could absorb the growing numbers of poorly educated workers *outside* industry, was central to debate about the country's economy.[95] In China itself, the 13th Plan (2016–20) envisaged a small fall in the share of the labour force in industry, and ILO data indicated that such a fall began in 2017, from a

91 F. Tregenna, 'Deindustrialisation: An issue for both developed and developing countries', in J. Weiss and M. Tribe, eds, *The Routledge Handbook of Industry and Development* (New York: Routledge, 2015), pp. 97–113.

92 D. Autor et al., 'The China syndrome: labor market effects of import competition in the United States', *American Economic Review*, 103 (2013), pp. 2121–68; R. Lawrence and L. Edwards, 'US Employment Deindustrialisation: Insights from history and international experience', Petersen Institute for International Economics, Policy Brief (Washington, DC: Petersen Institute, October 2013).

93 Rodrik, 'Premature deindustrialisation'; N. Haraguchi, C. Cheng and E. Smeets, 'The importance of manufacturing in economic development: has this changed?' *World Development*, 93 (2017), pp. 293–315.

94 B. Bosworth and S. Collins, 'Accounting for growth: comparing China and India', *Journal of Economic Perspectives*, 22 (2008), pp. 45–66; Broadberry and Gupta, 'The historical roots'.

95 A. Amiapu and A. Subramanian, 'Manufacturing or services? An Indian illustration of a development dilemma', Working Paper 409 (Washington, DC: Centre for Global Development, 2015).

level of around 28 per cent.[96] But in many other countries the trend was less the outcome of design and more of circumstance. In a fashion parallel to the enrichment of agrarian exporters like Australia, Argentina and Denmark, in the first great globalisation from the 1870s to the early 1910s, many countries had commodity export booms based on the rapid rise in Chinese demand for food and raw materials arising from its breakneck growth rates and urbanisation.[97] Brazil is one example where the growth in export of primary products, especially to China, has led to the decline in the relative economic role of industry. But China also competed with the industrial products of other developing economies as well as the developed, and this constrained their route to industrial expansion.[98]

Deindustrialisation has therefore clearly been a global as well as an historical phenomenon. The process in Scotland is examined in detail in the chapters that follow this one. Scotland's experiences in some respects have been distinct. In common with much of the UK, Scotland suffered from significant loss of industrial employment between the two world wars, especially in the 'staple' trades established in their importance in the nineteenth century: coal, metals, textiles, heavy engineering and ships. Scotland then experienced a notable industrial expansion prior to and during the Second World War, which continued in the period of reconstruction that followed. So, when Scottish industrial employment reached its peak in the mid-1950s, the level of that employment was exceptionally high by historic standards in the country, and by the standards of most of the advanced industrial countries.[99] It also had a particularly vulnerable composition within its industrial employment. This was concentrated in sectors that were to suffer more shrinkage than the industrial average over the next decades: coal mining, shipbuilding and textiles especially, which are discussed in detail in Chapters 2 and 3.

---

96 See https://data.worldbank.org/indicator/SL.IND.EMPL.ZS, accessed 21 December 2020. It is notable how far some Chinese cities are mirroring a common Western pattern of deindustrialisation followed by 'cultural-led' regeneration: J. Zheng, 'The "Entrepreneurial State" in "Creative Industry Cluster" Development in Shanghai', *Journal of Urban Affairs*, 32 (2010), pp. 143–70.

97 Australia perhaps most strikingly did well in both periods, with some continuity in the products exported between the two periods, such as wool.

98 A. Wood and J. Mayer, 'Has China deindustrialised other developing countries?' *Review of the World Economy*, 147 (2011), pp. 325–50.

99 C. Feinstein, 'Structural change in the developed countries in the twentieth century', *Oxford Review of Economic Policy*, 15 (1999), pp. 35–55.

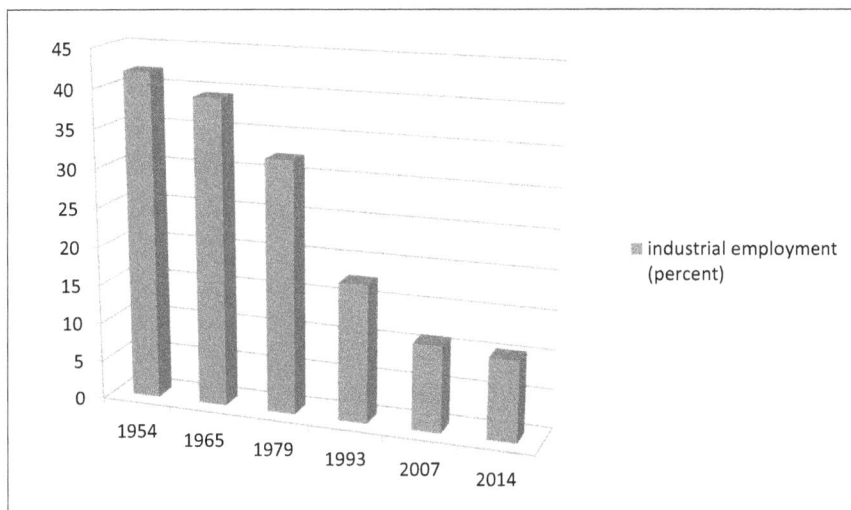

Figure 1.2 The decline of industrial employment in Scotland since the 1950s
Sources: *Digest of Scottish Statistics*: Scottish Economic Statistics, 1960, 1966.

This process of deindustrialisation, the loss of industrial jobs and the rise of a polarised service sector, has fundamentally affected the distribution of economic welfare and economic security in the country, with profound implications for the lives of Scots. But, as this chapter has argued, 'industry' was never a neutral, descriptive term for a particular type of economic activity. It always carried connotations of progress, modernity and effective nationhood. These connotations have been strongly present in Scotland, so that intertwined with the welfare effects of deindustrialisation have been cultural, economic and political consequences. Scotland's economic history had embedded a widespread notion of the country as an 'industrial nation'. National identity strongly featured industry and industrial employment. This became an important aspect of the response to deindustrialisation.[100]

100 For 'industrial nation', see Olive and Sydney Checkland, *Industry and Ethos: Scotland 1832–1914* (2nd edn; Edinburgh: Edinburgh University Press, 1989); W. W. Knox, *Industrial Nation: Work, Culture and Society in Scotland, 1800–present* (Edinburgh: Edinburgh University Press, 1999); and, on parallel lines, John Foster, 'A Proletarian Nation?', in A. Dickson and J. Treble, eds, *People and Society in Scotland, Vol. III, 1914–90* (Edinburgh: John Donald, 1992), pp. 201–41.

CONCLUSION

Deindustrialisation was a long-term phenomenon, widely experienced across first-mover industrial economies in the twentieth century and apparent even in later developing economies in the twenty-first century, including China. The shifts from primary to secondary to tertiary sectors were not evenly encountered, however; they were accelerated in some cases by state intervention, and slowed or even reversed in others, such as the movement back into primary production in economies where secondary development was disincentivised by the demand for raw materials from richer countries.

Employment data by sector in the UK show particular patterns of early onset deindustrialisation. In shipbuilding and coal mining the process was in train from the 1920s onwards, although this was delayed by the Second World War. This contributed to a stabilisation of industry, as military production leant heavily and understandably on coal and ships, along with metals, heavy engineering and textiles. These were Scotland's nineteenth-century staples. Chapter 3 itemises their common contraction in employment terms from the 1950s onwards, within a broader UK pattern where younger forms of manufacturing – geared primarily to satisfying emerging consumer markets – were encouraged by public policy as well as private investment. Deindustrialisation became a concern for economists in the 1970s as the restructured industrial order appeared to stagnate. There were significant pressures on the balance of payments, and concerns that the shift towards services would inhibit further economic growth. In the 1980s the negative implications of deindustrialisation for economic welfare were identified. This reflected an important change in the management of deindustrialisation that can be attributed to the election of Thatcher's Conservative governments in 1979. Thatcher and her ministers were not responsible for initiating deindustrialisation, or even willing it to happen. Deindustrialisation, to reiterate, was a phenomenon with deep historical roots, and the Thatcher government elected in 1979 did not desire mass unemployment. But when its monetarist misadventure triggered the rapid acceleration of industrial job loss, the government took no effective remedial action. The effects of this process were especially pronounced in Scotland, as the rest of this book demonstrates.

2

The Moral Economies of Deindustrialisation

The working-class moral economy of deindustrialisation in Scotland is the analytical core of this chapter. The moral-economy perspective has enriched historical analysis of industrial politics. It has been immensely valuable in explaining the reasoning and activism of workers and trade unionists who believed that employers and policy-makers were illegitimately disturbing or dismantling an agreed economic or workplace order. Viewing the erosion of manual employment and changing working-class organisation through the twin frameworks of deindustrialisation and the moral economy has marked an important transition in historical interpretation out of older and arguably dead-end narratives of economic decline and trade union defeat.[1]

The Scottish working-class moral economy comprised a set of assumptions that were informed by actual regulations as well as informal rules. In this it resembled the moral economy of E. P. Thompson's eighteenth-century English plebeian crowd, which resisted changes running counter to existing customs and expectations.[2] Scottish working-class activists from the 1950s were defending their 'intelligible moral order', to paraphrase Tim Strangleman, following Thompson's New Left comrade, Raymond Williams, in examining popular responses to deindustrialisation.[3] In Scotland this moral order had two fundamentals: changes in economic life and workplace organisation had to be negotiated with the

---

1 Jim Tomlinson, 'De-Industrialization not Decline: A New Meta-Narrative for Post-War British History', *Twentieth Century British History* 27.1 (2016), pp. 76–99.
2 Thompson, 'Moral Economy of the English Crowd'.
3 Tim Strangleman, 'Deindustrialisation and the Historical Sociological Imagination: making sense of work and industrial change', *Sociology*, 51 (2017), pp. 466–82.

trade union and political representatives of workers and communities affected; and any restructuring proposed would only be acceptable if communal economic security was protected.

Working-class moral economy thinking interacted with policy-making. This was also guided by moral considerations, as David Marquand has shown.[4] Two distinct policy-making moral economies can be observed. Social democrats and 'One Nation' Conservatives and Unionists advanced a 'solidaristic' moral economy from the 1940s to the 1970s. This positioned industrial change as a prerequisite of faster growth and improved living standards. The Scottish Trades Union Congress (STUC), the institutional guardian of the working-class moral economy, accepted the logic of this diversification and regularly affirmed a readiness to support the promotion of 'science-based' industry as a means of generating greater economic growth.[5] A broadening of the national economy's industrial foundations was seen as a corrective to the narrow reliance on the staple industries. This had severely compromised working-class economic security in the 1920s and 1930s, with mass unemployment accompanying major slumps in the global demand for exports of Scottish-produced coal, textiles, locomotives and ships. A greater mixture of activities, with more consumer goods sold into UK and European markets, would also narrow the economic gap with England. In this respect the strategy was successful. Scottish gross domestic product per capita increased from 87.7 per cent of the UK level in 1962 to 91.1 per cent in 1966–73 and then 96 per cent in 1973–9.[6] This incomplete process of convergence was nevertheless slow and frustrating for the labour movement and workers. A different policy-making moral economy was advanced by Thatcherites from the late 1970s, committed to economic liberalisation and the autonomy of private capital. Society was characterised as a market, populated by individuals and their families with duties to be enterprising and flexible. Collective customs introduced or nurtured during the solidaristic period were annulled, and reluctant participants in this new moral world obliged to modify their

4 David Marquand, *Mammon's Kingdom: An Essay on Britain, Now* (London: Allen Lane, 2014).
5 Glasgow Caledonian University Archives (GCUA), STUC General Council, Economic Committee, Report of Trade Union Conference, 7 March 1962.
6 Peter Scott, 'Regional development and policy', in Roderick Floud and Paul Johnson, eds, *The Cambridge Economic History of Modern Britain: Volume III, Structural Change and Growth, 1939–2000* (Cambridge: Cambridge University Press, 2004), pp. 332–67, with detail at p. 338.

behaviour. This represented a major assault on the working-class moral economy.

The interplay of these three moral economies is examined in this chapter. The structure is chronological, shaped by three distinct phases of deindustrialisation in Scotland from the mid-1950s to the mid-1990s. Periodisation can be 'fuzzy': there were continuities across the chronological frontiers marked out here in terms of government policy and labour movement activism. But there were unmistakable transitions in employment structure, which are detailed in Chapter 3. The first phase was the 'long' decade from the mid-1950s to the late 1960s, with labour and capital moving from the staples to engineering and assembly goods manufacturing. During the second phase, from the late 1960s to the late 1970s, it became clear that growth in these new sectors was not being sustained. Workers pressed policy-makers into stabilising employment in the staples. Restructuring was not reversed, but significantly slowed down, and economic security was strengthened. Labour movement pressure on the employment question was accompanied by demands for Scottish Home Rule, with a Parliament in Edinburgh seen as valuable means of protecting the distinct interests of workers in Scotland. A third phase followed from 1979, with Thatcherite policy overseeing the acceleration of capital flight, job losses and the closure of mines along with mills and factories in all industrial sectors. This transgressed the working-class moral economy. Scotland's political divergence from England, already apparent in the 1960s and 1970s, with stronger support generally for Labour among Scottish voters, became entrenched. Support for Conservatism and Unionism, and the unreformed political-constitutional structures of the UK, fell significantly, with the SNP consolidating its position in the centre-left and becoming Labour's chief electoral rival. At the 1987 general election the share of votes won by Conservative and Unionist candidates was lower in Scotland than England by more than 20 per cent. The government's reckless management of deindustrialisation influenced the establishment in 1989 of the Scottish Constitutional Convention. Fittingly, this gathering of various non-Conservative political forces, local authorities and civic organisations was coordinated by the STUC. The Convention's work led to the establishment of the Scottish Parliament in 1999.[7]

---

7 James Mitchell, *The Scottish Question* (Oxford: Oxford University Press, online, 2014), Chapter 10, 'Here's to the Next Time'.

EMPLOYMENT PEAKS IN THE STAPLES AND THEN MANUFACTURING, C. 1955–66

The moral-economy analysis of deindustrialisation has been influenced by the writings of Karl Polanyi as well as E. P. Thompson and Raymond Williams.[8] Thompson and Williams drew on a long tradition of writing that saw the British industrial revolution as a social and moral catastrophe.[9] Key figures were the Hammonds and R. H. Tawney, the Christian socialist. Their line of argument inferred 'a Fall of Man', before which human society had been dominated by a Christian-inspired morality, and afterwards had come an amoral individualism.[10] Thompson's English crowd model could be read as continuing this dichotomy, though with a certain ambivalence.[11] The implications of such a dichotomy are unhelpful to historical understanding. A key target of Tawney and Thompson's polemics is Adam Smith. Suggesting that Smith's political economy is 'amoral' is entirely unhelpful. Smith was concerned with examining how an economy driven by individual striving could be reconciled with a moral society. His writings were therefore profoundly moral. This highlights a fundamental truth in the examination of historical moral economies. We are always faced with *competing* moralities rather than morals and their absence.

Polanyi's approach was set out in *The Great Transformation* of 1944. Rogan argues that this provided a 'more convincing account of the intellectual history of political economy than Tawney before him or Thompson after him', not least by recognising Smith as a 'moral economist'.[12] Polanyi argued that industrialisation in the eighteenth and nineteenth centuries had been accompanied by the unleashing of market

---

8 See Ewan Gibbs, 'The Moral Economy of the Scottish Coalfields: Managing Deindustrialization under Nationalization, c. 1947–1983', *Enterprise and Society*, 19.1 (2018), pp. 124–52; Strangleman, 'Deindustrialisation and the Historical Sociological Imagination'.

9 Stefan Collini, 'The Literary Critic and the Village Labourer: "Culture" in Twentieth-Century Britain: The Prothero Lecture', *Transactions of the Royal Historical Society*, 14 (2004), pp. 93–116.

10 Stefan Collini, 'Moral mind: R. H. Tawney', in *English Pasts: Essays in History and Culture* (Oxford: Oxford University Press, 1999), pp. 177–94.

11 Donald Winch, 'Mr Gradgrind and Jerusalem', in Stefan Collini, Richard Whatmore and Brian Young, eds, *Economy, Polity and Society: British Intellectual History 1750–1950* (Cambridge: Cambridge University Press, 2000), pp. 243–66.

12 Karl Polanyi, *The Great Transformation: The Political and Economic Origins of Our Time* (Boston, MA: Beacon Press, 1944); T. Rogan, *The Moral Economists: R. H. Tawney, Karl Polanyi, E. P. Thompson, and the Critique of Capitalism* (Princeton, NJ: Princeton University Press, 2017), pp. 57, 87–91.

mechanisms and competitive forces. This disruption of human cooperation undermined economic security among the mass of the population.
A delayed social reaction followed, from the late nineteenth century,
as economic actors protected themselves from market insecurity in
different forms. Government regulation was important, often an ameliorative response to revolutionary movements and working-class political organisation. Market-shaped economic change modified by social
intervention was characterised by Polanyi as the 'double movement'.
Intervention was often guided by 'counter-movement' coalitions, which
included policy-makers and representatives of organised workers. This
was evident in the UK in the final years of the Second World War, just
as *The Great Transformation* was published. Governments sought to
re-embed economic activity in a strengthened social framework, answering working-class criticisms of mass unemployment during the 'Hungry
Thirties'. The new economic environment also reflected the long-run
influence of a social-democratic critique of unemployment and under-
employment, with roots in the Edwardian era. Concerns about the sup-
posedly demoralising effects of casual labour had framed the reforms of
the 1906–14 Liberal governments, including the institution of employment exchanges to match vacancies with unemployed workers.[13]

The moral framing of employment, an activity that citizen-subjects
were obliged to undertake, was strongly prevalent in policy-making
from the mid-1940s onwards.[14] The Churchill coalition's White Paper,
Employment Policy, set the governing agenda until the 1970s.[15] It
offered protection from unemployment so long as workers changed
jobs as national priorities shifted.[16] Margaret Thatcher's copy of
Employment Policy highlights this expectation. Sentences outlining the
necessity of occupational mobility are underlined or flagged in different
coloured pencils: the future Prime Minister revisited the document several times while developing her arguments for labour market flexibility.[17] This qualified re-embedding of economic life was consolidated by

13 Noel Whiteside, 'Casual Employment and Its Consequences: A Historical
   Appraisal of Recent Labour Market Trends', *Historical Studies in Industrial
   Relations*, 40 (2019), pp. 1–26, with details on Edwardian reforms at pp. 17–21.
14 Guy Standing, *Work after Globalization: Building Occupational Citizenship*
   (London: Edward Elgar, 2009), pp. 1–9.
15 Jim Tomlinson, *Managing the Economy, Managing the People: Narratives of
   Economic Life in Britain from Beveridge to Brexit* (Oxford: Oxford University
   Press, 2017), pp. 139–40.
16 *Employment Policy*, Cmd 6527 (London: HMSO, 1944).
17 *Employment Policy*, annotated copy, pp. 13, 19–20, accessed 14 March 2017,
   www.margaretthatcher.org/document/110368.

the Labour government elected in 1945. The coal industry was nationalised, along with the railways, road transport and the utilities of water
and gas. Workers in these sectors enjoyed new protections against dismissal and their unions had a stronger 'voice' on various bargaining
questions. The double movement did not, however, mean an end to
class conflict. Counter-movement coalition partners articulated different
moral economies with distinct social aims. In the coal industry there
remained substantial industrial tension.[18] In the private sector, better
working conditions were obtained through collective action, but these
were reluctantly conceded by employers and policy-makers, particularly
Conservatives in Churchill's coalition before 1945 and his government
from 1951 to 1955.[19] Problems were evident too in the docks, the classic
site of casual employment and target of social-democratic reformers.
The National Dock Labour Scheme of 1947 provided workers with a
weekly guaranteed wage, but registered men had to attend every morning and afternoon from Monday to Friday with an eleventh shift oblig-
atory on Saturday mornings too.[20] This heavy workload was aggravated
because ports were significantly busier in the 1940s and 1950s than they
had been in the 1920s and 1930s. A series of unofficial strikes ensued.
These had different causes, but a common theme was collective opposition to the disciplines of 'full' employment. Dockers appreciated their
newly acquired economic security and valued the Scheme because it put
their union representatives on a more equal footing with employers.
The daily obligation to work – or report for work even when the port
was quiet – was nevertheless an unwelcome departure from established
employment culture.[21]

   The electoral effects of economic change were undramatic in Scotland
until the 1960s.

18 Norman Dennis, Fernando Henriques and Clifford Slaughter, *Coal Is Our Life:
    An Analysis of a Yorkshire Mining Community* (London: Tavistock, 1969),
    pp. 9–10, 15–17, 26–33, 56–63.
19 Geoffrey G. Field, *Blood, Sweat and Toil: The Remaking of the British Working
    Class, 1939–45* (Oxford: Oxford University Press, 2011), pp. 79–128, 299–334;
    Justin Davis-Smith, *The Attlee and Churchill Administrations and Industrial
    Unrest, 1945–55: a study in consensus* (London: Pinter, 1990).
20 Gordon Phillips and Noel Whiteside, *Casual Labour: The Unemployment
    Question and the Port Transport Industry* (Oxford: Oxford University Press,
    1985), especially pp. 250–60.
21 Jim Phillips, 'Class and Industrial Relations in Britain: The "long" mid-century
    and the case of port transport, 1920–1970', *Twentieth Century British History*,
    16.1 (2005), pp. 52–73.

Table 2.1 Vote shares (as percentage) of Labour and Unionist parties in Scotland at UK general elections

	Labour	Unionist
1945	47.6	41.1
1950	46.2	44.8
1951	47.9	48.6
1955	46.7	50.1
1959	46.7	47.2
1964	48.7	40.6
1966	49.9	37.7

Source: Steven Kendrick and David McCrone, 'Politics in a Cold Climate: The Conservative Decline in Scotland', *Political Studies*, 37 (1989) (electoral data at p. 590).

Table 2.1 shows that Labour's vote share was consistently high. The vote share of Unionist Party candidates incrementally increased after 1945, as anti-Labour supporters were gradually absorbed from the shrinking Liberals. In 1955 the Unionist Party won a thin majority of all votes cast, securing thirty-six out of seventy-one Scottish seats. The coincidence of this high Unionist Party vote share and peaks of employment in established forms of industry is important. A significant drop in the absolute and relative volume of employment in the staple industries was followed by a substantial movement in Scotland away from Conservativism and Unionism, evident in the wide margin of Labour's victories in 1964 and 1966, when it took forty-three and then forty-six of the seventy-one constituencies.

There were, of course, multiple explanations for Labour's ascendancy in the 1960s. Stephen Kendrick and David McCrone identified the critical factor as falling support for Conservatism and Unionism among collectivist-inclined working-class voters.[22] More recently, Malcolm Petrie emphasised the intersection of ideology and policy. Confidence in Conservatism and Unionism among individualist-minded voters fell from the late 1950s. Particularly within the middle class there were concerns that Conservative governments since 1951 had eschewed income tax and public expenditure cuts. Tories had further destabilised the relative privileges of middle-class voters by retaining Labour's welfare state and nationalisation policies along with full employment and dialogue with trade unions. Conservative and Unionist support gradually seeped in the late 1950s to the Liberals, critics of nationalisation and the welfare

22 Kendrick and McCrone, 'Politics in a Cold Climate', pp. 589–603.

state, and from the mid-1960s to the SNP, which opposed 'centralisation' under Tory as well as Labour governments in London, offering a strong appeal to 'libertarianism', according to Gordon Wilson, a later leader.[23] Catriona Macdonald points out that the SNP capitalised on the formation in 1965 of the Scottish Conservative and Unionist Party, which, more embedded in UK structures, found difficulty in presenting itself as an effective guardian of Scotland's distinct economic and social interests.[24] Younger voters socialised after the Second World War were less deferential than their elders and correspondingly open to competing anti-Conservative alternatives, whether the modernisation rhetoric of Labour or the new appeal of nationalism.[25] James Mitchell shows that Labour in office from 1964 was highly adept at articulating a modernisation agenda that accommodated the emergent interest among younger Scots in national identity. Willie Ross, Secretary of State for Scotland, was a key figure. His achievements included the establishment of the Highlands and Islands Development Board, which successfully encapsulated Labour's projection of the future with a defence of the old.[26]

Within this varied pattern of influences, changes in employment contributed to the political choices of Scottish voters. The contraction of Scottish-owned shipbuilding and metals, coupled with the nationalisation of coal and the railways, narrowed the everyday influence on working-class voters of Scottish capital, the Unionist-supporting business leaders like the Colvilles of Lanarkshire and the Lithgows of the Clyde.[27] Detailed employment data are analysed in Chapter 3. Here it can be noted that employment in coal mining halved in the 1960s and fell in the other staples, albeit less precipitously. This created anxiety among manual-worker Tories, pushing many of their number towards Labour. At the same time economically liberal Unionist activists were disturbed by the Macmillan government's strategy of industrial diversification, because this involved the state-subsidised growth of new manufacturing employment. This process had problematic longer-term features across the UK, according to Huw Beynon. Embedded linkages in industrial

---

23 Malcolm Petrie, 'Anti-socialism, liberalism and individualism: Rethinking the alignment of Scottish politics, 1945–1970', *Transactions of the Royal Historical Society*, 28 (2018), pp. 187–217.
24 Macdonald, *Whaur Extremes Meet*, pp. 222–3.
25 Cameron, *Impaled upon a Thistle*, pp. 266–7.
26 Mitchell, *Scottish Question*, pp. 141–55.
27 John Foster, 'The Twentieth Century, 1914–1979', in R. A. Houston and W. W. J. Knox, eds, *The New Penguin History of Scotland* (London: Penguin, 2001), pp. 417–93, with details at pp. 455–7.

communities between home and employment were disrupted, contributing to the greater commodification of labour, reducing its social and collectivist content. Looser workforce control over employment was consolidated by the Redundancy Payments Act, introduced by Harold Wilson's Labour government in 1965. This removed an important class barrier to labour market 'flexibility' by easing the financial transition to new employment. Social democracy in the 1960s thus enabled neoliberalism in the 1980s, Beynon argues.[28] Policy-makers were promoting larger value-added manufacturing production and employment. This would deliver more rapid growth and higher living standards. Start-ups were promoted through regional grants and loans, buttressed by public investment in the local authority housing, which comprised a vital element of the emergent industrial communities. Labour's broad approach was set out in the *National Plan* of 1965, supplemented by *The Scottish Economy* with its significant sub-title, *A Plan For Expansion*.[29]

The process of restructuring was exemplified by two establishments: Caterpillar earthmoving equipment in Uddingston, Lanarkshire; and BMC commercial vehicles in Bathgate, West Lothian. The transition out of staple industry was accentuated in the case of Caterpillar because a mining village, Tannochside, was cleared to house the plant.[30] This opened in 1956 at the mid-point of colliery closures that ended mining in the adjacent Blantyre–Cambuslang–Hamilton–Uddingston conurbation. In this narrow corridor of Lanarkshire, 3,200 miners were made redundant between 1950 and 1964.[31] Caterpillar diminished the impact of the coal job losses, employing around 2,500 at its peak in 1968.[32] The adult children of former employees and union representatives at

28 Huw Beynon, 'After the Long Boom: Living with Capitalism in the Twenty-First Century', *Historical Studies in Industrial Relations*, 40 (2019), pp. 187–221, with details at pp. 194–5.

29 Department of Economic Affairs, *The National Plan*, Cmnd 2764 (London: HMSO, 1965); The Scottish Office, *The Scottish Economy, 1965 to 1970: A Plan For Expansion*, Cmnd 2864 (Edinburgh: HMSO, 1966).

30 NRS, DD 10/380, 'US Tractor Firm Picks Lanarkshire Site. Employment for 1500 Workers', *The Scotsman*, 16 January 1956, clipping; and Scottish Home Department, Note for Under Secretary of State, Note on Company and Tannochside Project, 21 August 1959.

31 These calculations are based on the employment peaks and closure dates of five collieries: Blantyreferme 1 and 2 (1), Blantyreferme 3 (2), Hamilton Palace (3), Thankerton (4), and Bothwell Castle (5). This information is detailed in Miles K. Oglethorpe, *Scottish Collieries: An Inventory of the Scottish Coal Industry in the Nationalised Era* (Edinburgh: Royal Commission on the Ancient and Historical Monuments of Scotland, 2006).

32 NRS, SEP 2/49, 'Strike by 1100 at Tannochside', *Glasgow Herald*, 12 June 1968.

the plant, interviewed by Ewan Gibbs, emphasise localised 'ownership' and raised collective expectations in Uddingston. This was the working-class moral economy in action. Caterpillar acquired obligations to the community that the local authority built around the plant, with new housing for workers moving to the area from Glasgow and elsewhere.[33] At Bathgate, private-industry growth was also predicated on substantial public investment, including the provision of housing. Young communities developed in the New Town of Livingston and the older settlements of Armadale, Blackburn and Whitburn. In the early 2010s the Workers' Educational Association conducted a programme of public events to capture local memories of the commercial vehicle plant. The confluence of new employment and housing opportunities, especially for younger workers with children, was an important theme in these testimonies. Jim Bilsborough moved to a three-bedroom house in Blackburn from a room and kitchen in Glasgow with his wife and two children: 'new job, new house'. 'It was opportunity, opportunity, opportunity', said Guthrie Aitken, aged nineteen, when starting with BMC as it commenced manufacturing trucks in October 1961.[34] Tractor production followed from September 1962. A labour force of 5,600 was projected in April 1961, compensating for heavy local losses in mining.[35]

The labour movement in Scotland supported industrial diversification but offered substantial moral-economy criticisms of Macmillan's Conservative government. These criticisms were translated into effective labour activism, qualifying Beynon's implied claim that working-class security degenerated continuously from the 1960s. Resistance was directed by the STUC, to which most British-wide unions in Scotland were affiliated, including the National Union of Mineworkers (NUM), the Amalgamated Engineering Union (AEU) and the Transport and General Workers' Union (TGWU). The STUC had two central moral-economy criticisms of the government's approach to industrial restructuring: the growth and employment 'gap' between Scotland and England was not being narrowed quickly enough; and private industry was receiving public subsidy with no requirement to accept wider social

---

33 John Slaven, Interview with Ewan Gibbs, STUC Offices, Woodlands, Glasgow, 5 June 2014; and Helen Knight, Interview with Gibbs, Tannochside Miners' Welfare, 20 January 2017.

34 *Bathgate Once More: The Story of the BMC/Leyland Truck and Tractor Plant, 1961–86*, compiled and edited by Elizabeth Bryan (Edinburgh: Workers' Educational Association, 2012), p. 6.

35 NRS, SEP 4/1661, BMC, Note of Meeting held in Ministry of Labour, Scottish Headquarters, Glasgow, 24 August 1960.

obligations. The challenge of bridging the growth gap was reinforced in the year from February 1962, when unemployment in Scotland jumped from 85,366 to 136,030.[36] This stemmed from a change in government policy designed to curb inflationary pressures evident in the south of England and the Midlands. Spending cuts and interest rate increases sucked demand out of the economy and pushed Scottish workers into unemployment.[37] The STUC argued that policy-makers were unjustly penalising Scottish workers.[38]

Diversification had its business champions, among them John Toothill, Chairman of the electronics group Ferranti in Scotland. Toothill identified Scotland's structural-political disadvantages within the UK as fact. His 1961 report was published by the Scottish Council for Development and Industry, a lobbying body comprised primarily of manufacturers and local authority representatives.[39] Toothill argued for improved transport, housing, and educational infrastructure to stimulate 'science'-based industry. The report recommended that incentives be directed to economic 'growth points' instead of stabilising employment in older and more congested urban-industrial settings.[40] Toothill had an important political impact. The Conservative government's soft support for its state-interventionist agenda, antagonising individualist-cum-libertarian Unionist voters and pushing them towards the Liberals, has already been noted.[41] The report's distaste for defending established industry and workers also alienated trade unionists. Additional social distance resulted from what the STUC saw as continued private-industry neglect of social considerations. An important grievance was the reluctance of incoming multinationals to recognise trade unions.[42] Caterpillar had a long anti-trade union history in the USA from its establishment in the mid-1920s. It accepted the right of the United Automobile Workers to industry-wide bargaining only in 1958. Until that point the union had

---

36 NRS, SEP 10/312, Ministry of Labour, Monthly Report on the Main Features of the Employment Position in Scotland, February 1963.
37 Tomlinson, *Managing the Economy*, pp. 188–9.
38 Phillips, *Industrial Politics of Devolution*, pp. 119–29.
39 Peter L. Payne, 'The Scottish Council (Development and Industry)', in Michael Lynch, ed., *The Oxford Companion to Scottish History* (Oxford: Oxford University Press, 2001), pp. 574–5.
40 Committee of Inquiry appointed by the Scottish Council (Development and Industry) under the Chairmanship of J. N. Toothill, *Report on the Scottish Economy* (Edinburgh: Scottish Council, 1961).
41 Petrie, 'Anti-socialism', p. 213.
42 B. Knox and A. McKinlay, 'Working for the Yankee Dollar: US Inward Investment and Scottish Labour, 1945–1970', *Historical Studies in Industrial Relations*, 7 (1999), pp. 1–26.

been required to win recognition on a plant-by-plant basis.[43] Caterpillar likewise opposed union recognition at Uddingston. This was only over-turned by a lengthy strike in the winter of 1960–1, examined in Chapter 3. It was also 'galling', the STUC's term, that Toothill recommended the granting of public money to unregulated private firms while remaining 'silent' on the redundancy and community abandonment arising from restructuring.[44]

The STUC organised a Conference on Scotland's Economy, held in St Andrew's Halls, Glasgow, on 18 February 1962. It issued an advance statement highlighting Scottish disadvantage: one-tenth of the UK pop-ulation, but one-fifth of the unemployed, lived in Scotland. The con-ference was attended by 1,400 delegates from sixty-two unions and trades councils, along with Labour MPs and invited observers, includ-ing members of the Scottish Council for Development and Industry. Alex Moffat, NUMSA (Scottish Area) President, outlined the failings of NCB strategy. Mines were closed on economic grounds; redundant miners were transferred to other mines, which became less economic as a result. It was incumbent on the government to intensify the direction of private industry to coalfield areas. Moffat was followed to the speak-ing podium by Jack Service, of the Confederation of Shipbuilding and Engineering Unions (Clyde Area), and John Irvine, of the Iron and Steel Confederation.[45] The conference unanimously passed a motion, shaped in moral-economy terms, setting out the case for stronger direction of industrial location and activity, with recipients of government subsidy compelled to respect their acquired social responsibilities.[46]

Labour movement pressure pushed the government towards lim-ited policy changes. There was no action on democratic oversight of regional policy-aided firms, but in 1963 new investments in transport and social infrastructure plus increased spending on regional assistance were promised. This was a guarded acknowledgement that Scotland's economic problems were distinct, although the Conservative govern-ment insisted that it was embarked on a *regional* intervention, with a

43 Stephen Franklin, *Three Strikes: Labor's Heartland Losses and What They Mean for Working Americans* (New York: Guilford Press, 2001), pp. 90–1.
44 GCUA, STUC General Council, Economic Committee, 28 December 1961; General Council Press Statement, 10 January 1962; Economic Committee, Report of Trade Union Conference, 7 March 1962.
45 GCUA, STUC General Council, Organisation Committee, 5 January 1962.
46 GCUA, STUC General Council, Resolution for Conference, 18 February 1962.

parallel approach being taken in northeast England.[47] The Labour government pursued a more dynamic approach, overseeing the sixteen-fold increase in real terms of regional policy incentives across the UK from 1962/3 to 1969/70. This was perhaps the decisive influence in narrowing Scotland's GDP per capita gap with England.[48] The stimulation of employment was strategic, advancing the government's drive to more rapid economic growth.[49] But it also reflected labour movement activism in protecting working-class economic security. In June 1965 the STUC's Economic Committee put the case for more active intervention in a meeting with Harold Wilson, the Prime Minister, and several Cabinet ministers at the House of Commons. The STUC delegation was led by Alex Kitson of the TGWU, who framed the issue by referring to a speech made by Wilson to the STUC in April 1964, when Leader of the Opposition. This speech contrasted the 9 per cent growth of employment in England and Wales from 1951 to 1963, the 'wasted' Tory years,[50] with just 3 per cent growth in Scotland. In these years, the STUC noted in an advanced memorandum for the meeting, the number of males in employment in Scotland fell by 33,000, where it increased by 933,000 in England and Wales. The number of women in work in Scotland grew by 48,000 in this period, less than half – in proportional terms – the addition of 989,000 in England and Wales. To summarise, employment had stagnated in Scotland while growing by 1.9 million in England and Wales. Wilson accepted that Scotland needed 'a New Deal' and referred to the 'record number' of Industrial Development Certificates for new production sites already granted since the election. Growth was not being experienced evenly, however. The government's fuel policy, with more intensive use of oil and atomic energy, was contributing to the further erosion of employment in mining. Bill McLean of the NUMSA told Wilson that measures to provide alternatives for redundant miners were inadequate, citing recent closures in Central Fife. Others from the STUC side urged the necessity of another big industrial relocation, to follow BMC and the Rootes car plant at Linwood, opened

---

47 Scottish Development Department, *Central Scotland: Programme for Development and Growth*, Cmnd 2188 (London: HMSO, 1963); 'White Papers Soon on North', *The Times*, 31 October 1963.
48 Scott, 'Regional development and policy'.
49 Jim Tomlinson, *The Labour Governments, 1964–70: Volume 3: Economic policy* (Manchester: Manchester University Press, 2004), pp. 85–7.
50 The Labour Party, *Twelve Wasted Years* (London: Labour Party, 1963).

in 1963, expressing hopes that Ford would situate a new facility planned for later in 1965 in Scotland.[51]

The government appeared both sympathetic and responsive. A build-up of assisted industrial development followed shortly afterwards in the New Town of Glenrothes, just a few miles from the Central Fife coalfield.[52] There was major disappointment, however, in September 1965, when Ford intimated that it would not be establishing a new site after all. This troubled the STUC, with officials querying the government's commitment to narrowing the economic gap with England. This emerging tension was further evident when Willie Ross, Secretary of State for Scotland, discussed coalfield employment in October 1965 with NCB officials and a joint NUMSA–STUC delegation. Scottish national imperatives were abundantly clear in this counter-movement gathering, as the NCB shared the NUM ambition for state intervention to stabilise coalfield security. Union representatives emphasised the urgency of bringing 'new industries' to Fife, the Lothians and Lanarkshire, 'to provide alternative jobs for miners displaced from work'. There were divisions within this counter-movement. The NCB was offering redundant Scottish miners transfers to English collieries. This offended union officials in national as well as class terms: 'The wholesale migration of Scottish miner [sic] to the South would not be accepted as an alternative.' Ross agreed 'that there must be no further acceleration of Scottish pit closures', emphasising that securing more advance factories in the coalfields was a priority.[53]

STABILISATION AND THE PROTECTION OF WORKING-CLASS ECONOMIC SECURITY, C. 1966–78

The labour movement in Scotland became more active in its defence of economic security from the mid-1960s onwards. Developments in the coalfields were highly influential. Generational change was important. Miners who entered the world of employment in the 1940s were

---

51 The National Archives, Kew (TNA), EW 8/294 'Meeting between PM and his colleagues and representatives of the STUC', 2 June 1965, appendix F; GCUA, STUC Economic Committee, Advanced Memorandum for meeting with Prime Minister, 2 June 1965 and Report of a Meeting with the Prime Minister, 2 June 1965.
52 David Cowling, *An Essay For Today: Scottish New Towns*, 1947–97 (Edinburgh: Rutland Press, 1997).
53 GCUA, STUC Economic Committee, Report of a Meeting with the Secretary of State for Scotland, St Andrew's House, Edinburgh, 29 October 1965.

more vigilant in defending the working-class moral economy than their elders.[54] This generational shift reflected differences in formational 'concrete', with contrasting experiences and expectations derived from early working life.[55] For younger miners, the pit closures of the 1950s jarred with the promises of full employment and stability under nationalisation. Older miners were more sanguine, tending to measure post-1945 progress positively against the conflict and privation of the 1920s and 1930s. A similar transition was taking effect in other parts of the labour movement. Jimmy Milne was born in Aberdeen in 1921 and started his working life just before the Second World War, in Hall Russell shipyard. Milne joined the Communist Party of Great Britain (CPGB) in 1939 and served as Secretary of the Aberdeen Trades Council from 1948 until his appointment as STUC Deputy General Secretary in 1969. In 1975 Milne succeeded James Jack, born in 1910, as General Secretary. Alex Kitson was born in the same year as Milne, in Kirknewton, Midlothian. His early working experiences in Edinburgh included delivering milk by horse-drawn cart from St Cuthbert's Cooperative Society in Fountainbridge. There he befriended Tam – or Sean – Connery, whose retained sympathies for workers were apparent in his support for the Fairfield shipyard experiment, discussed in Chapter 4. Kitson joined the Labour Party and was elected General Secretary of the Scottish Commercial Motormen's Union in 1959, which he led into a merger with the TGWU in 1971, by which point he was also a leading advocate of devolution.[56] In the 1960s Kitson served on the STUC General Council with others born shortly after the First World War. Bill McLean, from a Lanarkshire mining family, joined the CPGB and advanced through the NUMSA, was elected General Secretary in 1968 while serving continuously on the STUC General Council from 1961.[57]

Milne and McLean both witnessed the significant contraction of employment in the industries where they started working life, shipbuilding and coal mining, just as working-class economic security more broadly was improving in the 1950s. This shaped their sharp approach

---

54 Jim Phillips, 'Economic Direction and Generational Change in Twentieth Century Britain: The Case of the Scottish Coalfields', *English Historical Review*, 132 (2017), pp. 885–911.

55 Karl Mannheim, 'The Problem of Generations', in Karl Mannheim, *Essays on the Sociology of Knowledge* (London: Routledge & Kegan Paul, 1952), pp. 276–322.

56 Ian MacDougall, *Voices From Home and Work* (Edinburgh: Mercat Press, 2000), pp. 1–67.

57 STUC, *81st Annual Report*, The Music Hall, Aberdeen, 17–21 April 1978 (Glasgow: STUC, 1978), Obituary, W. McLean, p. 394.

in dealings with UK policy-makers, including Wilson's Labour government. Influenced by the CPGB's 'Popular Front' legacy of the late 1930s and 1940s, Milne and McLean were accustomed to building cross-party 'progressive' alliances. The Popular Front was constructed in the 1930s on a British basis but had particularly important Scottish features. Its leading advocate was Willie Gallacher, Communist MP for West Fife. One of its legacies was support from Communists in Scotland for the Scottish Covenant of the 1940s, a cross-class movement that briefly campaigned for a Parliament in Edinburgh.[58] Milne and McLean, operating in this tradition on a Scottish as well as a British basis, were broadly supportive of Labour in office. They nevertheless proffered frank criticism where policy or inaction jeopardised the employment conditions and wages of Scottish workers. Similar vigilance was maintained by Kitson and other non-Communists, notably Lawrence Daly. Born in 1924, Daly was a Fife miner who left the CPGB in 1956 and joined Labour. He was elected NUMSA General Secretary in 1965 and then NUM General Secretary in 1968.[59]

Wilson's government was re-elected in March 1966, the summit of Labour's electoral popularity in the twentieth century in Scotland. Its share of 49.9 per cent was followed by an incremental loss of support to the SNP, which won 5 per cent of votes in 1966, 11.4 per cent in 1970 and then 21.4 per cent in February 1974 followed by 30.6 per cent in October 1974. The SNP took votes from the Tories as well as Liberals, but its pluralist appeal was such that much of its progress in urban constituencies in central Scotland was at Labour's expense.[60] This was partly because Labour's economic management from the summer of 1966 was queried by many working-class voters, including trade unionists. As in the early 1960s, inflationary pressures arose from rapid economic growth in England's southern and central regions. Labour's remedy, reprised from the Conservative repertoire, was a major programme of public expenditure cuts and increases in indirect taxation and the rate of borrowing.[61] The 'July measures' adopted in 1966 were opposed forcefully by trade unionists across the UK.[62] The STUC had a distinct critique, however,

58 Cameron, *Impaled upon a Thistle*, pp. 277–9.
59 Jean McCrindle, Obituary, Lawrence Daly, *The Guardian*, 30 May 2009.
60 Cameron, *Impaled upon a Thistle*, pp. 289–319.
61 Tomlinson, *Managing the Economy*, pp. 218–22.
62 Andrew Thorpe, 'The Labour Party and the Trade Unions', in John McIlroy, Nina Fishman and Alan Campbell, eds, *British Trade Unions and Industrial Politics: Volume Two: The High Tide of Trade Unionism, 1964–79* (Aldershot: Ashgate, 1999), pp. 133–49, with details at pp. 136–7.

focusing on the unfair punishment inflicted on Scottish workers who were liable to suffer the most from measures that threatened industrial and public sector employment, which were proportionately larger in Scotland. Unemployment moved quickly upwards in Scotland, from 60,000 in August 1966 to 67,000 in September, 78,000 in November and then almost 89,000 in January 1967. The official unemployment benefit claimant rate in Scotland topped 4 per cent, above the whole Great Britain average of 2.6 per cent.[63] McLean and Kitson were part of an STUC Economic Committee delegation that met Wilson in Downing Street in late November 1966, the Prime Minister accompanied by James Callaghan, the Chancellor of the Exchequer, Michael Stewart, the First Secretary of State for Economic Affairs, Ray Gunter, the Minister of Labour, plus Ross. The STUC officials stated that the July measures had severely compromised the government's stated employment goals. The proposed target of 130,000 new jobs in Scotland by 1970, set out in the *National Plan* and the Scottish *Plan For Expansion*, had become far more distant. Wilson fell back on his government's pre-July track record of opening advance factories.[64]

The July measures shifted the Scottish labour movement's diagnosis of the economic problems facing Scotland. The issue of deindustrialisation was explicitly identified. Economic insecurity, measured in unemployment, was characterised as more pronounced in Scotland than elsewhere in the UK. The government's deflation of the economy aggravated two key problems: a slowdown in the rate of start-ups; and disinvestment-cum-contraction among existing outfits. The STUC's Economic Committee drew attention to these problems in 1968 and 1969 when examining regional patterns of unemployment. These are shown in Table 2.2.

In all areas of Scotland unemployment exceeded the Great Britain average. The comparative success story, Dundee and Tayside, was predicated on the strong presence of multinationals. In late 1966 the second and third largest employers in the city were National Cash Register (NCR) and Timex, each US-owned. NCR, makers of cash registers and electronic equipment, employed 4,048; Timex, producing watches, employed 3,173.[65] Higher unemployment, especially in west central

63 GCUA, STUC, For Information of General Council members, Unemployment in Scotland, 9 January 1967.
64 GCUA, STUC Economic Committee, Report of a Meeting with the Prime Minister, 10 Downing Street, 28 November 1966.
65 TNA, BT 177/2686, Miss McGhee (Office for Scotland) to Miss Hodkinson, 'Information for brief on Dundee', 29 November 1966.

Table 2.2 Unemployment rates (as percentage) in planning regions of Scotland

	October 1968	October 1969
Aberdeen and northeast	3.2	3.4
Dundee and Tayside	2.6	2.7
Edinburgh	3.0	3.2
Glasgow*	4.3	4.2
Falkirk and Stirling	3.6	3.7
Scotland	3.6	3.7
Great Britain	2.4	2.5

Source: GCUA, STUC Economic Committee, October Unemployment Figures, 14 November 1969.
* Glasgow includes Ayrshire, Lanarkshire, Dunbartonshire and Renfrewshire.

Scotland, reflected the slower pace of industrial diversification. An AEU delegation had reported to the STUC Economic Committee in February 1967, detailing the accumulated loss of 6,000 jobs in the Glasgow area in the preceding fifteen months. This included the redundancy of 1,700 workers at the US-owned Singer sewing machine works in Clydebank following the July measures. Further attrition losses in the Glasgow area could 'not possibly be absorbed'.[66]

Timex continued to grow in the 1970s, but NCR shrunk rapidly from 1971 after unsustainably expanding to complete the one-off task of adapting cash registers for decimalisation. This contraction reflected a broader trend. NCR and Singer were two of many multinationals 'in retreat'. In 1971 the STUC and constituent unions noted 'the dangers of "runaway" companies', particularly for women employed in the making of electrical components.[67] Total employment in foreign-owned factories peaked in 1975, but growth by the late 1960s was already too slow to offset the aggregate loss of jobs in Scotland. Hence the overall fall in manufacturing employment from 1968, which proved permanent.[68] The Scottish labour movement viewed this with alarm, especially as it coincided with publication of government plans for further rundown of coal production and employment. *Fuel Policy* in November 1967 projected that coal's market share would drop from 58 per cent in 1966 to 34 per cent in 1975, with employment across the UK industry to be more

66 GCUA, STUC Economic Committee, Meeting with AEU delegation, 28 February 1967.
67 GCUA, STUC Women's Advisory Committee, Secretary's Report, 26 August 1971 and STUC Women's Advisory Committee, Minutes, 14 June 1972.
68 Neil Hood and Stephen Young, *Multinationals in Retreat: the Scottish Experience* (Edinburgh: Edinburgh University Press, 1982), pp. 5–6, 30–7, 101–13.

than halved, from 425,000 to 195,000.[69] Ministry of Power officials estimated that coal industry employment in Scotland would drop from 36,000 at the end of 1967 to 24,700 by March 1971, to 15,000 in 1975 and 8,000 in 1980.[70]

Here is a crucial point of departure in Scotland's deindustrialisation path. Employment in coal was stabilised, dropping more slowly to 29,000 in 1972 before tapering to 24,000 in 1975 and 20,000 in 1980. Exogenous shock was a factor. Oil became both politically and economically unreliable. The OPEC-instigated price jump in 1973 meant the end of cheap oil and recast coal as a relatively cheap and predictable source of energy. But the mobilisation of miners in defence of their jobs was vital too. Michael McGahey, elected President of the NUMSA in 1967, refused to accept further closures unless two moral-economy criteria were strictly observed: the local workforce and its representatives had to agree; and alternative employment with comparable pay and conditions had to be put in place. McGahey and McLean blocked or delayed individual closures until miners could be transferred to other pits within daily travel distance, and only on the further condition that there was stability in earnings. The NUMSA also worked hard with the NCB, its counter-movement ally, to ensure a stronger market for coal. The Labour government was pushed to exert pressure on the South of Scotland Electricity Board to accept coal as the primary fuel at new power stations, notably the giants of Longannet in West Fife and Cockenzie in East Lothian. Miners also mobilised for improved coal industry pay, with unofficial strikes in 1969 and 1970 prefiguring the national strikes of 1972 and 1974 that secured hefty increases, restoring the miners' relatively strong position in the earnings 'league' of manual workers.[71]

McGahey and the NUMSA also energised the Home Rule politics of the labour movement in Scotland. At the 1968 STUC annual meeting McGahey introduced a motion in favour of a Scottish Parliament. This was a logical extension of existing STUC thinking, that policy-making privileged the English southern and central core. Lowering overall UK demand in times of over-expansion had strangled more fragile growth in Scotland, under both Conservative and Labour governments. McGahey argued that a Scottish Parliament could be used to influence the redirection of policy in Scotland to fit the distinct priorities of manual workers

69 Ministry of Power, *Fuel Policy*, Cmnd 3428 (HMSO, 1967), pp. 36, 71.
70 TNA, EW 7/826, Secretary State Brief, Colliery Closures, November 1968.
71 Jim Phillips, *Scottish Coal Miners in the Twentieth Century* (Edinburgh: Edinburgh University Press, 2019), pp. 199–219.

in Scotland.[72] The debate within the STUC lasted for three years but was eventually resolved in favour of a Scottish Parliament. The election of a Conservative government with Edward Heath as Prime Minister in 1970 influenced this outcome. Heath wanted to end subsidies for 'lame duck' companies and industries. Ministers allowed unemployment to increase significantly, moving upwards across the UK from 2.7 per cent in the summer of 1969 to more than 4 per cent in 1971.[73] In Scotland the problem was more acute still. Joblessness among men rose from 5.7 per cent in the first quarter of 1970 to 8.2 per cent in the third quarter of 1971.[74] In February 1972 the STUC convened a Scottish Assembly on Unemployment at the Usher Hall, Edinburgh, inviting several hundred representatives of mainstream political parties, local authorities and business organisations as well as trade unions. The Assembly endorsed the call for a Scottish Parliament, to promote industrial activity and social justice through a more thorough-going regional policy effort.[75] The Conservative government was shaken and ultimately defeated by the miners' strikes of January–February 1972 and March 1974. Between these coal crises the government also bowed to workers on the Upper Clyde, an episode examined in Chapter 4. In moral-economy terms the Upper Clyde Shipbuilders' (UCS) work-in rejected Heath's attempt to dis-embed industrial activity from the social needs of the workers and communities involved. The work-in was led by a group of stewards, among them Jimmy Reid, born in 1932, and Jimmy Airlie, born in 1936.[76] With fellow Communists and others in the NUMSA and the STUC, Airlie and Reid defended the working-class moral economy, and supported the argument that the failings of UK policy-making could be corrected through a Scottish Parliament.[77]

Moral-economy factors also applied in defence of steel industry employment, which in 1972 was comparable in scale to coal mining. The STUC saw the delicate situation facing steel in terms of 'acute

72 STUC, *71st Annual Report*, The Beach Ballroom, Aberdeen, 18 April 1968 (Glasgow: STUC, 1968), pp. 398–401.
73 Tomlinson, *Managing the Economy*, pp. 145–8.
74 Frank Herron, *Labour Market in Crisis: Redundancy at Upper Clyde Shipbuilders* (London: Macmillan, 1975), p. 16.
75 GCUA, STUC General Council, Scottish Assembly on Unemployment, 14 February 1972, Charter of Proposals for the Scottish Assembly, and List of Speakers.
76 W. W. Knox and A. McKinlay, *Jimmy Reid: A Clyde-built man* (Liverpool: Liverpool University Press, 2019); Terry Pattinson, Obituary: Jimmy Airlie, *The Independent*, 11 March 1997.
77 Phillips, *Scottish Coal Miners*, pp. 172–87.

under-investment' in the deep-water ports and production plant required for scale economies in transport of ore and completion of materials.[78] This criticism was echoed by the Scottish Council for Development and Industry and the respective Clyde and Forth Port Authorities. In 1970 and 1971 the Scottish Council published a two-part prospectus for investment in sea and land transport infrastructure, plus new steel works. The *Oceanspan* model, drafted by William Lithgow, the Lower Clyde shipbuilder, proposed stronger links between Scotland's west and east coasts across a regenerated industrial belt. Steel and manufacturing industries would be stabilised with ore and other raw materials brought from the Atlantic via the Irish Sea and processed into goods for Western European markets across the North Sea. The centrepiece would be a combined ore terminal and steel works at Hunterston in Ayrshire. Heath discussed *Oceanspan* in January 1972 with John Davies, Secretary of State for Trade and Industry, Gordon Campbell, Secretary of State for Scotland, and Sir William McEwan Younger, Chairman of the Conservative and Unionist Party and an industrial brewer who sat on the Scottish Council's Executive. Lithgow and Younger had a distinctly Scottish critique, asserting that the misapplication of UK-level state intervention and public ownership had influenced Scotland's industrial difficulties since the Second World War. The nationalisation of coal in the 1940s and then iron and steel in the 1960s, both under Labour governments they emphasised, had reduced *Scottish* control of vital resources.[79] The formulation of the publicly owned British Steel Corporation (BSC) was a particular sore for these Unionist business leaders, eliminating the direct economic influence of an important fragment of Scottish privately owned industry.[80]

No immediate commitment to the protection of steel was offered by the Conservative government. This troubled the STUC, which restated the case for Scottish steel in separate talks with Davies and Lord Melchett, Chairman of BSC, in October 1972. The moral-economy basis for protecting employment in the sector was set out. BSC proposals for closing open hearth operations would likely cost 7,500 of the existing 26,000 jobs in Scotland over the next five years. This could be tolerable if 'alternative' employment were available. In the labour market conditions that

---

78 GCUA, STUC Economic Committee, 24 October 1972.
79 Jim Phillips, 'Oceanspan: Deindustrialisation and Devolution in Scotland', *Scottish Historical Review*, 84 (2005), pp. 63–84.
80 Foster, 'Twentieth Century', pp. 474–6.

applied such an outcome was improbable. The special obligations of the publicly owned BSC were emphasised:

> It would be iniquitous if a private firm decided to move out of an area almost solely dependent on it and public opinion would undoubtedly be violently opposed to such a plan. It is doubly iniquitous that a Corporation which is state owned and thereby responsible to the state which, let us not forget, is comprised of every man and woman who has voted or ever will vote, should be allowed to promote such a policy which will bring economic hardship and serious social discontent.[81]

James Jack and seven other STUC officers, including Bill McLean, met Melchett at the Caledonian Hotel in Edinburgh. Jack referred to the difficult employment position in Scotland since 1967, with 105,000 jobs created but 156,000 lost. Melchett was asked to bring forward the development of a deep-water ore terminal at Hunterston and questioned about apparent plans to concentrate production at Ravenscraig in Lanarkshire. Melchett was not optimistic about Hunterston, but emphatic that Ravenscraig would continue to serve only as the 'main' and not 'sole' producer in Scotland.[82]

The provision of alternative employment as precondition of steel's contraction was lifted directly from the mode of resistance deployed in the coalfields. New steel works were never established at Hunterston. Return on a very high investment would be minimised by huge excess capacity in world production and the unexpected fall in demand that followed the global economic recession, accentuated as this was by the oil-price surge. A new ore terminal was nevertheless agreed in 1973, and its construction completed under the Labour government elected in 1974, which also stabilised steel industry employment. The annual average rate of job loss in iron and steel was significantly slower than in coal from 1959 to 1968, roughly 1.6 per cent per annum compared with 5.7 per cent per annum. The effectiveness of subsequent action is clear: the annual average rate of steel industry job loss fell to just 1.2 per cent between 1968 and 1973.[83] In October 1974 there were still more than 25,000 steel workers in Scotland. The Labour government accepted the need for more regional aid in steel communities before further rational-

---

81 GCUA, STUC Economic Committee, Notes for Meetings with Davies and Melchett, October 1972.
82 GCUA, STUC General Council, Report of a Meeting with Lord Melchett, Caledonian Hotel Edinburgh, 27 October 1972.
83 The Scottish Office, *Scottish Abstract of Statistics*, 4 (Edinburgh: HMSO, 1974), Table 80.

isation. Government strategy in 1978 acknowledged this, and related difficulties in the sector to the externalities of over-supply and sinking global demand.[84] Even in these increasingly difficult conditions the rate of job loss rose only slightly, to 2.3 per cent per annum on average between 1973 and 1978.[85]

The position on steel reflected the Labour government's broader commitment to economic security in heavy industry as private sector growth continued to stall. Significant initiatives were *Plan For Coal*, an investment programme agreed by industry unions and the NCB, which had positive effects especially in the Lothians and Fife,[86] and the nationalisation of shipbuilding in 1977, which consolidated the victory of the UCS work-in through safeguarding production and employment on the Clyde.[87] It was no coincidence that Labour's popularity grew in Scotland after 1974. This was against the movement of opinion away from Labour in England. Recent research emphasises the emergence in England from the 1960s of popular individualism, which became an even more potent force in the 1970s. This was not necessarily a harbinger of Thatcherism, but plainly pointed towards the creeping rejection in England of collective action as the basis of social improvement.[88] Collective and specifically working-class consciousness was markedly strengthening in the opposite direction in Scotland, despite convergence in occupational and social structures with England. From 1974 to 1992 the volume of Scottish citizens self-identifying as working class increased from 68 to 74 per cent.[89]

Labour's position in Scotland was admittedly checked by the SNP in the late 1960s and early 1970s. Economic insecurity contributed to high-profile SNP victories in Westminster by-elections in industrial constituencies. These came in 1967 in Hamilton, close to the shrunken South Lanarkshire coalfield, and in 1973 in Govan, at the heart of the

84 *British Steel Corporation: The Road to Viability*, Cmnd 7149 (London: HMSO, 1978).
85 The Scottish Office, *Scottish Abstract of Statistics*, 12 (Edinburgh: HMSO, 1981), Table 9.3.
86 James R. Cowan, 'National Coal Board: Scottish Area in the 1980s', *Mining Technology*, 62 (January 1980), pp. 20–1.
87 Lewis Johnman and Hugh Murphy, *Shipbuilding in Britain: a political economy of decline* (Exeter: University of Exeter Press, 2002), pp. 208–10.
88 Jon Lawrence, *Me, Me, Me? The Search for Community in Post-War England* (Oxford: Oxford University Press, 2019); Emily Robinson, Camilla Schofield, Florence Sutcliffe-Braithwaite and Natalie Thomlinson, 'Telling Stories about Post-war Britain: Popular Individualism and the "Crisis" of the 1970s', *Twentieth Century British History*, 28.2 (2017), pp. 268–304.
89 Macdonald, *Whaur Extremes Meet*, pp. 244–5.

threatened Upper Clyde shipbuilding sector. In the second of two UK General Elections in 1974 the SNP won eleven seats and came second to Labour in thirty others. The nationalist case was buoyed by the discoveries of major new fields in the North Sea Oil sector. SNP campaigning from March 1973 characterised the resource as 'Scotland's oil'. In fiscal terms, oil held transformational potential, neutralising the argument that independence would automatically reduce aggregate wealth and average standards of living in Scotland. Labour's case against independence involved showing Scots that their economic security was improved through the transfer of resources to Scotland from England. Cash transfers funded regional policy and greater net public expenditure per head of population in Scotland than in England. Oil fundamentally challenged the assumption that Scotland was a net beneficiary of the Union.[90] Scottish nationalists have argued that the Labour government elected in 1974 sought to minimise the benefits of oil, to subvert political support in Scotland for independence. A memorandum written for the government in 1974 by its Economic Adviser in Scotland, Gavin McCrone, has often been cited in this connection.[91] This concluded that an independent Scotland deriving the entire receipts of North Sea Oil tax revenue would move from a deficit in public finances – income versus expenditure – to a substantial surplus. But McCrone also emphasised the highly problematic implications of Scotland becoming an independent nation with a strong and escalating petrocurrency. Manufacturing exports from Scotland would be severely curtailed, contributing to the substantial elimination of industrial employment. Oil would be no guarantor of economic security for working-class Scots.[92]

Mining union representatives in Scotland feared that oil would supplant coal in the generation of electricity. They saw North Sea development as threatening rather potentially enhancing Scotland's autonomy. The oil was controlled by multinationals granted licences for exploration and production under the Conservative government before 1974. Willie Clarke, a member of the NUMSA executive, speaking at the 1978 STUC, said, 'It is not Scottish oil, it is not British oil, until it is nationalised; it belongs to the monopolies, and the monopolies will determine

90 Chick, *Changing Times*, pp. 331–5.
91 Christopher Harvie, *Fool's Gold: the Story of North Sea Oil* (Harmondsworth: Penguin, 2004), pp. 250–1.
92 Gavin McCrone, 'The Economics of Nationalism Re-examined', February 1974, www.oilofscotland.org/mccronereport.pdf, accessed 26 August 2020.

the rate of extraction'.[93] Labour in office responded carefully to these concerns. Two policy innovations were made. First, the government established the British National Oil Corporation with headquarters in Glasgow. Publicly owned, this was directly involved in exploration and exploitation. Second, a dedicated levy on North Sea profits, the Petroleum Revenue Tax, was introduced in 1975. Labour was criticised by nationalists for appropriating and squandering a Scottish resource, but at least in the 1970s oil revenues contributed to the government's broader approach of defending economic security in all parts of the UK.[94] This also involved minimising unemployment and stabilising the balance of payments through vigorous defence of industrial activity and employment: keeping manual workers in jobs, and maximising external earnings through exports.[95]

The personal backgrounds of Labour ministers were important in framing this approach. Such insight is often overlooked in the literature as political history, which tends to differentiate prominent Labour figures by their positioning within 'left–right' or 'militant–moderate' spectra.[96] Bruce Millan was Minister of State at the Scottish Office from 1974 to 1976 and then appointed Secretary of State for Scotland in 1976 by the new prime minister, James Callaghan. Millan usually features in historical accounts because he became a European Commissioner in 1988, triggering a by-election in Glasgow Govan won by Jim Sillars of the SNP.[97] But Millan's career also encompassed a vital role in Labour's protection of economic security in Scotland, helping to establish the Scottish Development Agency (SDA) in 1975 with a responsibility for cultivating industry.[98] His protection of manual employment in Scotland was surely informed by his early life in pre-Second World War Dundee, where mother worked in a jute mill and father in a shipyard. Millan promoted

93 STUC, *81st Annual Report*, pp. 620–1.
94 Harvie, *Fool's Gold*, pp. 209–13.
95 M. Artis, D. Cobham and M. Wickham-Jones, 'Social democracy in hard times: the economic record of the Labour government 1974–79', *Twentieth Century British History*, 3 (1992), pp. 39–53.
96 See various contributions to John Callaghan, Steven Fielding and Steve Ludlum (eds), *Interpreting the Labour Party: Approaches to Labour Politics and History* (Manchester: Manchester University Press, 2003), and Dianne Hayter, *Fightback! Labour's traditional right in the 1970s and 1980s* (Manchester: Manchester University Press, 2005).
97 Cameron, *Impaled upon a Thistle*, p. 342.
98 Peter Payne, 'Scottish Development Agency', in Lynch, *Oxford Companion to Scottish History*, pp. 575–6.

the government's SDA agenda with Eric Varley, Secretary of State for Industry, who was born in the Derbyshire coalfields at the bottom of the inter-war depression and followed his father into mining.[99]

Labour won by-elections in two industrial constituencies in 1978, Hamilton and Glasgow Carscadden, and in a third, Berwick and East Lothian, where there was a substantial population of coal miners. This prefigured two important expressions of electoral opinion in 1979: the referendum on the government's proposed establishment of a Scottish Parliament, and the UK general election. The referendum has been characterised as a defeat for Labour, punishment by Scotland's electorate for the government's alleged mismanagement of the economy.[100] This perspective is problematic. The government's devolution plans were sabotaged by George Cunningham, ex-patriate Fifer and Labour MP for Islington South and Finsbury, who secured an amendment where a Parliament would only be established if endorsed in a referendum by 40 per cent of the entire electorate. In March 1979 32.5 per cent of the electorate voted 'Yes' for the Parliament, 30.4 per cent 'No', and 37.1 per cent did not vote at all.[101] This result was not clear-cut. An outdated electoral roll included 500,000 persons who could not vote, owing to infirmity or illness. If they had been excluded the 40 per cent target would have totalled 1,284,754, just 31,252 more than the votes won by the devolution campaign.[102] Above-average support for devolution was recorded in the three counting areas with the largest concentrations of industrial employment: Central, Fife and Strathclyde. This reflected the long-established trade union call for a Parliament in Edinburgh to strengthen working-class economic security, reiterated at the 1977 annual gathering of the STUC.[103] From this perspective the referendum outcome was hardly a negation of Labour's position in Scotland, which was further vindicated by the general election result

99 Brian Wilson, 'Bruce Millan, 1927–2013, Obituary', *The Guardian*, 25 February 2013; Geoffrey Goodman, 'Eric Varley, 1932–2008, Obituary', *The Guardian*, 29 July 2008.

100 T. M. Devine, *The Scottish Nation, 1700–2000* (London: Allen Lane, 1999), p. 591.

101 Henry Drucker and Gordon Brown, *The Politics of Nationalism and Devolution* (London: Longman, 1980), pp. 120–1.

102 Vernon Bogdanor, *Devolution in the United Kingdom* (Oxford: Oxford University Press, 1999), pp. 188–91.

103 STUC, *80th Annual Report*, The Pavilion, Rothesay, 18–22 April 1977 (Glasgow: STUC, 1977), pp. 794–5.

less than two months later. The SNP, threatening Labour in 1974, lost
nine MPs. Labour increased its vote share in Scotland from 36 per cent
in October 1974 to 41.5 per cent. This was 5 per cent higher than its
share in England. Collective action in defence of individual and communal security retained a significantly greater mandate in Scotland than in
England. The Conservatives had also lost support to the SNP between
1970 and October 1974 and regained some of this in 1979, but with
31.4 per cent of votes in Scotland was still 10 per cent behind Labour.
Thatcher's House of Commons majority of fifty was based on ground
won largely in England.

THATCHERISM AND THE WORKING-CLASS MORAL ECONOMY AFTER 1979

Whether Thatcherism amounted to a coherent ideology can be contested, but it was underpinned by a set of moral beliefs. As Thatcher
herself put it in 1976, the main issue was not material but 'moral . . .
where the State is too powerful, efficiency suffers and morality is
threatened'.[104] Thatcher believed that moral conduct was encouraged
by maximising the self-reliance and autonomy of individuals and
their families. The 'over-mighty' state was the main threat to achieving this end. This 'market fundamentalist' approach was the basis of
an alternative policy-making moral economy. The 'solidaristic' model
was attacked: various collective customs were revoked and reluctant
individuals and groups were coerced into modifying their behaviour.[105]
Central aims of the 'adventurist' macroeconomic policy, examined in
Chapter 1, were reduced taxation and public expenditure. The biggest
change to the tax regime was the shift from direct taxation to indirect
taxation. This widened inequality substantially. With public expenditure no overall cut was attained. This was owed to the 'ring-fencing' of
resources for military and law and order, political commitments on the
NHS and pensions, and the impact of recession.[106] There were, however, big cuts in industrial and regional subsidies, and in the allowable
deficits of nationalised industries. These adversely affected industrial
employment but were represented as removing expenditures that were

104 MTFW, Speech to Zurich Economic Society, 14 March 1977, at https://www.
      margaretthatcher.org/document/103336, accessed 21 December 2020.
105 Marquand, *Mammon's Kingdom*.
106 Tomlinson, *Managing the Economy*, pp. 74–80, 229–30.

not only inefficient, but also enabled a demoralising reliance on state spending and other people's taxes on the part of those employed in the supported industries.[107]

The approach to the labour market was also both moral and material. Thatcher's reading and re-reading over time of the 1944 *Employment Policy* White Paper has been noted. Interviewed in May 1983 she claimed, 'There's far more in this White Paper that's on the side of my philosophy and my economic practice than anyone else's. And I can read you out sentence after sentence which says there's no substitute for industrial efficiency, industrial co-operation and for sound money'.[108] What seems clear from Thatcher's annotated copy of *Employment Policy* is her moralised view that workers and unions by increments had relinquished their side of the 1944 'bargain'. In this connection it is apposite that her government, re-elected in 1983, brought forward in 1985 a White Paper, *Employment*, which was explicitly characterised as bringing the 1944 document 'up-to-date'. It even quoted the earlier paper's Foreword, to the effect that government's ability to deliver employment depended especially on the 'efforts of employers and workers in industry'. Later it pinned down more specifically the perceived source of rising unemployment from the 1970s:

> Many workers, especially those in powerful unions, felt they could escape the discomfort of new ways of working and hold economic reality at bay, often by strikes or the threat of them: some behaved as though their jobs would always be there, no matter what they or anyone else did. Companies were burdened by overmanning and outdated methods.[109]

The chief practical levers of the working-class moral economy, trade union voice and state intervention to safeguard workers' rights, had been destabilised since 1979. Thatcherite policy involved strong action against the capacity of unions to affect the workings of the labour market. Employment and industrial relations reforms were reinforced by selected government attacks, most notably on coal miners, which

---

107 The governments' economic propaganda agenda was very clearly set out after being initiated in July 1979, broadening out radically after an initial focus on pay: TNA: CAB 134/4336 Ministerial Committee on Economic Strategy, E(79)37, 'Public attitudes to pay determination', 6 September 1979.

108 Interview in *The Times* 3 May 1983, cited in E. H. H. Green, *Thatcher* (London: Bloomsbury, 2006), p. 77.

109 *Employment: The Challenge for the Nation*, Cmnd 9474 (London: HMSO, 1985), para. 1.5, 2.5.

represented an ideological 'war' against the organised working class.[110] Providing management with the 'right to manage', freed from the constraints of workplace trade unionism, was a principal aim. This was another moral question, in Thatcherite terms, influenced by Friedrich Hayek, who in turn drew on the earlier arguments of W. H. Hutt and Henry Simons.[111] Hayek saw unions as monopolistic barriers to free markets. Their rights – or 'privileges' – were incrementally dismantled. The closed shop was a key target. Union membership as a condition of employment offended neoliberalism's moral-individualised view of freedom, an illegitimate attempt by unions to enforce costs on employers and employees as well as consumers. The Employment Acts of 1982 and 1988 made action to enforce the closed shop illegal.[112] Unions defended the practice as protection against free riders who accepted the benefits of membership opportunistically without sharing the costs. 'If you want a seat on the bus then you have to buy a ticket', was a common working-class moral economy rationalisation, recounted in 2018 by Tom Smith and Dave Howie, two former engineers at Timex in Dundee.[113]

In Chapter 1 the 'accidental' nature of deindustrialisation's acceleration after 1979 was demonstrated. The loss of industrial jobs was not willed by Thatcher and her ministers but nevertheless advanced their strategy of transferring authority from workers to managers. Unemployment had powerful 'demonstration effects', eroding working-class morale.[114] The changing 'rules' of engagement were only gradually appreciated by the labour movement's leadership in Scotland. An important early lesson came when STUC officials met Sir Keith Joseph, the Secretary of State for Industry, in December 1979. The STUC delegation, led by Jimmy Milne, said that 30,000 workers in Scotland had been made redundant since July. Public expenditure cuts and the abolition of exchange controls had worsened the situation, the latter encouraging

110 Jim Phillips, 'Containing, Isolating and Defeating the Miners: The UK Cabinet Ministerial Group on Coal and the Three Phases of the 1984–5 Strike', *Historical Studies in Industrial Relations*, 35 (2014), 117–41.
111 Ben Jackson, 'Neo-liberalism and the trade unions, c. 1930–1979', in Clare Griffiths, James Nott and William Whyte, eds, *Classes, Cultures and Politics: Essays on British History for Ross McKibbin* (Oxford: Oxford University Press, 2011), pp. 263–81.
112 Jim Tomlinson, *Hayek and the Market* (London: Pluto Press, 1990), pp. 87–96.
113 Tom Smith and Dave Howie, former engineering shop stewards at Timex, Dundee, Interview with Valerie Wright (VW) and Jim Phillips (JP), Dundee, 3 July 2018.
114 Ralph Miliband, *Divided Societies: Class Struggle in Contemporary Capitalism* (Oxford: Clarendon, 1989), pp. 115–66.

capital exports and reducing domestic investment. Joseph said that he wanted a 'genuine exchange of views, and not a series of monologues'. With limited self-awareness, the Secretary of State then spoke at length about the follies of state intervention, 'tried and found wanting over the last 15 years'. He asserted that it was not the government's responsibility to subsidise goods for which there was limited consumer demand.[115]

Joseph and the government managed deindustrialisation recklessly. The trend was accelerated by the escalation of sterling's value in international currency exchanges, noted in Chapter 1. This was exacerbated by the petrocurrency effect of North Sea Oil revenues.[116] In metal manufacturing the average annual rate of job loss from 1973 to 1978 of 2.3 per cent all but trebled to 6.3 per cent between 1978 and 1983. Those employed across all forms of metal manufacturing numbered 32,000 in 1980 but only 26,000 in 1982.[117] This drop was precipitated by a lengthy dispute in the winter of 1979–80, where BSC workers rejected a pay offer and unsuccessfully resisted cuts proposed by their new Chairman, Sir Ian MacGregor, a Scots-born US business manager and aggressive advocate of Thatcherite managerial sovereignty.[118] Joseph's interventions in the dispute encapsulated the new approach. A House of Commons debate was initiated by Alec Jones, Labour MP for Rhondda, on the motion that Joseph's salary as Secretary of State be reduced by £10,000. Joseph's reply was moralistic, emphasising the duty of the state to reduce financial commitments to an allegedly inefficient industry. He minimised the government's responsibilities to the workers facing redundancy and offered little hope of action to stimulate employment in the communities affected.[119]

Towards the end of 1980 the STUC came to recognise the permanent character of the structural changes that government policy was shaping. In November its Economic Committee met George Younger, Secretary of State for Scotland, along with Alex Fletcher, Under-Secretary of State for Scotland and responsible for economic and industrial matters, and Gavin McCrone, Economic Adviser to the Scottish Office. In a notable

---

115 GCUA, STUC General Council, Report of Meeting with Sir Keith Joseph, 10 December 1979.
116 William Keegan, *Britain without Oil* (Harmondsworth: Penguin, 1985), pp. 31–4, 108–10.
117 *Scottish Abstract of Statistics*, 12 (Edinburgh: HMSO, 1983), Table 9.3.
118 Charlie McGuire, '"Going for the Jugular": The Steelworkers' Banner and the 1980 National Steelworkers' Strike in Britain', *Historical Studies in Industrial Relations*, 38 (2017), pp. 97–128.
119 Parliamentary Debates, Fifth Series, Commons, Vol. 975, 13 December 1979, 1562–678, with Joseph speech at 1574–88.

and early trade union use of the term, Milne characterised the problem as 'serious deindustrialisation', beyond the disturbing enough rise
of mass unemployment: 'The likely effect of this would be that when
the recession is over, there would be precious little left of industry in
Scotland.' Government policy was the diametrical opposite of what the
situation required, with public expenditure cuts strangling production
and employment at British Railways, British Leyland, BSC and British
Shipbuilders. Fletcher asserted that industry would recover more quickly
if inflation could be squeezed out of the economy.[120] This was the central defence offered by the government during this intense period of
industrial job loss. The moralised narrative persuaded many of those
not directly involved that inflation was serious enough to warrant a
large increase in unemployment that might in the longer term slow the
upward movement of prices.[121]

The STUC pushed the deindustrialisation question further, hosting
a Scottish Convention on Unemployment at the University of Glasgow
the following month, December 1980. This resembled the coalition
assembled in 1972, with participants from the Convention of Scottish
Local Authorities (COSLA) and the Scottish Council for Development
and Industry as well as mainstream political parties. But this time the
Conservative representatives, led by the party's Chairman in Scotland,
Michael Ancram, explicitly repudiated the labour movement's analysis
of deindustrialisation and prescription for safeguarding economic security. The STUC's pre-circulated memorandum, 'Scotland in 1980', saw
the situation as market and policy failure, with the government allowing
'the near mystical "market forces" to work their alchemy on the dying
body of the British economy and somehow restore it to life'. A route
to economic safety was available, through reduced borrowing costs,
increased public investment and renewed exchange controls. Ancram
rejected this agenda, restating the intention to control inflation while
encouraging enhanced productivity and competitiveness. The same gulf
of understanding was apparent in a further counter-movement meeting
on unemployment with the government in January 1981. Milne told
Younger that those present, representatives of the STUC, COSLA and
the Scottish Council, agreed on four measures to reduce industrial contraction: increased selective assistance to manufacturers, reduced interest rates, public spending rises and protection of UK producers through

120 GCUA, STUC Report of a Meeting between the Economic Committee and
George Younger, 7 November 1980.
121 Tomlinson, *Managing the Economy*, pp. 187–8.

import controls. Younger said this agenda was false: other remedies could only be sought once the 'battle' against inflation had been won.[122]

The government's distinct approach to deindustrialisation extended to a more fatalistic attitude than that of its Labour predecessors to factory closures and multinational abandonment of Scotland. The ending of production at the Linwood car plant in 1981 was a key episode. Tolerated by Joseph and his colleagues, where it had been resisted by Labour ministers in 1975–6, this features in Chapter 5. Two other closures are noteworthy, the Bathgate commercial vehicle plant, which proceeded in three discernible stages from 1982 to 1986, and Caterpillar in 1987. These demonstrated that the working-class moral economy, while challenged by Thatcherism, was not dismantled altogether. Burnished by its assault from hostile policy-makers and disinvesting employers, it survived and shaped Scotland's distinct political pathway subsequently. At Bathgate the publicly owned British Leyland (BL) resolved to sell the tractor half of the plant in January 1982, responding to the pressures imposed by the government's cash limits. The 2,500 tractor workers anticipated redundancy and protested by occupying the plant. Family and community links shaped a remarkable parallel occupation in Bathgate, mainly by female workers, at Plessey Capacitors. Plessey, one of the UK's largest electronics firms, had gradually contracted in the town from a peak of 2,400 employees in 1973 to just 330 in December 1981, when it announced that closure would take place in March 1982.[123] The Plessey workers were influenced by the resistance at BL, and occupied their factory too. BL and Plessey each secured an interim interdict compelling the occupiers to withdraw. Both protests ended with the further loss of employment. A successor was found for Plessey, Arcotronics, providing eighty jobs for another year. The 2,500 tractor production jobs were lost entirely. BL workers organised a further occupation in the summer of 1984, this time resisting closure of the trucks division, where roughly 2,000 were still employed. Family and community solidarities were again evident, this time with miners at Polkemmet Colliery in nearby Whitburn, defending their jobs in the great strike against pit closures.[124]

122 GCUA, STUC, Scotland in 1980'; Report and Proceedings at the Scottish Convention on Unemployment, 8 December 1980; Report of a Meeting on Unemployment in Scotland, 7 January 1981.
123 Patricia Findlay, 'Resistance, Restructuring and Gender: The Plessey Occupation', in Tony Dickson and David Judge, eds, *The Politics of Industrial Closure* (Basingstoke: Macmillan, 1987), pp. 70–96.
124 West Lothian Trade Union Council, *Unity Is Strength: West Lothian Memories of the Miners' Strike, 1984–85* (West Lothian TUC, 2015).

This second BL occupation bought the workers time, with another two years of employment before closure in 1986.[125]

These and other occupations in the 1980s were geared to protecting a relatively small number of jobs. The Plessey example is illustrative in this respect: seven jobs out of eight were lost in eight years from 1973 before the firm announced its departure from Bathgate. This illustrates the broad trend examined in Chapter 3: deindustrialisation proceeded gradually rather than suddenly. Closures and occupations were nevertheless important politically and culturally, contributing to a powerful narrative of resistance – against both Thatcherism and economic insecurity – that took root in Scotland in the 1980s.[126] Engineering workers at Timex occupied their plant in Dundee in 1983, unsuccessfully opposing the ending of watch-making in the city, but resisting compulsory redundancies and defending trade union voice. This moral-economy victory is examined in Chapter 6, and prefigured the occupation at Caterpillar which, in the general election year of 1987, was central to the construction of the anti-Thatcherite resistance narrative. In September 1986 the multinational had agreed a new programme of regional aid with the UK government, worth £8 million, to develop a new bulldozer, the D6H. Caterpillar executives said that more than £50 million of the firm's own money would also be invested, promising stable employment for Uddingston's 1,300 workers until 1991. Malcolm Rifkind, the Secretary of State for Scotland, claimed this news as vindication for his government's backing of industrial 'winners'. Rifkind and the government were therefore severely embarrassed by what followed. On Friday 9 January 1987 Uddingston management contacted the Industry Department for Scotland (IDS) at the Scottish Office with information that Caterpillar's leadership in Illinois had decided to close the plant, along with two others in the USA.[127] Caterpillar's global capacity exceeded demand. Work undertaken at Uddingston could be accommodated within Caterpillar factories in Belgium and France, but the opposite was not true, a deciding factor in closing the Scottish site.[128] The decision was made public the following Wednesday, 14 January. Local Caterpillar management

---

125 *Bathgate Once More*, p. 45.
126 Andy Clark, '"There is nothing here for us and nothing for the future": Deindustrialisation and the dynamics of workplace occupation, 1981–1982', *Labour History Review*, forthcoming.
127 NRS, SEP 4/4693, Secretary of State's Visit to Caterpillar, 19 September 1986, and G. R. Wilson, IDS, 9 January 1987.
128 Charles Woolfson and John Foster, *Track Record: The story of the Caterpillar occupation* (London: Verso, 1988), p. 41.

communicated the news via a press conference, an affront to moral-economy expectation that disinvestment on this scale first be discussed with union representatives to find ways of preserving the economic security of those affected.[129]

Caterpillar was protecting its market share internationally against an emergent Japanese rival, Komatsu, through a radical restructuring of global operations. From 1981 to 1991 its international payroll was cut from 83,455 to 55,950, and there were lengthy disputes in the USA where labour costs were reduced, and established union rights violated. Long-time employees with a record of union activism were targeted for dismissal as the multinational adopted a 'low-road' response to globalisation.[130] In Scotland, workers occupied the Caterpillar plant to defend their jobs and the equipment, characterised as property of the community rather than the multinational. The occupiers were led by men and women in their thirties and forties, whose parents had exchanged employment in the coal, steel and textile industries for work in multinational engineering. They acknowledged that Caterpillar was the factory's legal owner, but in moral-economy terms, pointing to the hefty investment of public money over three decades, felt it belonged to the people of Lanarkshire.[131] There was cross-generational investment in the occupation. The protectors of the plant included a group of sixty-one teenagers from Uddingston and surrounding settlements who signed a petition to Queen Elizabeth. This called on the sovereign to intervene to keep the factory open. 'We Need a Future', it read. The lead petitioner was Joanne Farrell, aged fourteen, who later wrote to the Prime Minister with four of her friends, making the same request for action to safeguard the factory and their generation's economic future.[132]

John Brannan, convenor of the factory's stewards, was asked about the legality of the occupation on its thirtieth anniversary. 'As far as we were concerned the laws and the rules were broken when Caterpillar decided to close it [the plant]'.[133] The occupation drew explicitly on

129 Jean Stead, 'Rifkind finds Caterpillar closure "extraordinary"', *The Guardian*, 15 January 1987.
130 Franklin, *Three Strikes*, pp. 8–9, 40–1, 89–107, 251–3, 276.
131 Ewan Gibbs and Jim Phillips, 'Who Owns a Factory? Caterpillar Tractors in Uddingston', *Historical Studies in Industrial Relations*, 39 (2018), pp. 111–37.
132 NRS, SEP 4/4573, 'A Petition From Caterpillar Worker Children', no date but probably March 1987; and SEP 4/4574, Jacqueline Donnelly (13), Denise Donnelly (15), Joanne Farrell (14), Wendy McAuley (14) and Julie Moore (13) to Mrs Thatcher, no date but probably April 1987.
133 John Brannan interviewed by Sharon Frew, STV News, 29 January 2017, at https://www.youtube.com/watch?v=-JD1qoklpNs, accessed 5 December 2019.

resistance motifs that were generated in the second phase of deindustrialisation. The determination to fight from within the factory, as occupiers, was a conscious echo of the UCS work-in. Foster and Woolfson
saw three distinct parallels between the two episodes: the geographi-
cally and politically 'remote' nature of industrial disinvestment; a free
market-defending Conservative government powerless to protect industrial employment; and strong workplace trade unionism mobilising a
broader political movement in defence of working-class security.[134] A
fourth similarity can be added. As with the UCS crisis, the Caterpillar
occupation moved the political mood in Scotland further away from
Conservatism and Unionism. Representatives of the older Unionist business elite in Scotland were mortified. Viscount Weir, of the Weir Group
of industries, wrote to Rifkind, 'horrified', arguing no Caterpillar equipment should be bought by the government or used in completion of any
public contracts.[135] Rifkind and Thatcher recognised the likely political
consequences of closure, but their ideological commitment to market
forces and the autonomy of private capital inhibited their capacity for
meaningful action.[136] The 1987 general election was held six weeks after
the end of the occupation. While re-elected across the United Kingdom
with a majority in the House of Commons of 102, the Conservative government lost eleven of its twenty-one seats in Scotland. Six constituencies switched from Conservative to Labour: Aberdeen South, Edinburgh
Central and Edinburgh South, plus three in west-central Scotland
where industrial employment had eroded significantly since 1979:
Cunninghame West, in North Ayrshire; Renfrew West and Inverclyde,
incorporating the shipyard towns of Greenock and Port Glasgow; and
Strathkelvin and Bearsden, just to the north of Glasgow, which included
a fringing of coalfield villages.[137]

Anguished post-mortems at the highest level in government followed
on Scotland's resistance to 'Thatcherism',[138] but limited adjustment in
policy-making terms resulted. Arguments about the 'democratic deficit' were made more forcefully by the government's many opponents in
Scotland after 1987. These included increasing numbers of non-manual

134 Woolfson and Foster, *Track Record*, pp. 263–5.
135 NRS, SEP 4/4570, Viscount Weir to Rifkind, 22 January 1987, and Bryan
    Grieve to Michael Forsythe (sic), 19 January 1987.
136 Andrew Gamble, *The Free Economy and the Strong State: The Politics of
    Thatcherism* (Basingstoke: Macmillan, 1994).
137 Cameron, *Impaled upon a Thistle*, pp. 320–40.
138 TNA, PREM 19/2481, A. Dunlop to PM, 'Enterprise Scotland', 2 September
    1988; B. Griffiths and J. O'Sullivan, 'Scotland', 28 July 1987.

workers, particularly those in the public sector. Teachers, doctors, nurses, social workers and housing officers were all burdened with additional workloads, managing the adverse social effects of deindustrialisation.[139] While Thatcherite ambitions to reduce public expenditure overall were thwarted, the government's anti-public sector rhetoric appeared to alienate many engaged in the teaching and medical professions in Scotland.[140] The working-class moral economy duly acquired many middle-class adherents in Scotland. Narratives about the immorality and class injustice of Thatcherism were reinforced by the poll tax crisis from 1988 to 1990, when socially regressive changes to local authority funding were established in Scotland one year before their introduction in England and Wales. In this new political tide, the STUC brought together the Scottish Constitutional Convention to establish the ground for a future devolved Parliament in Edinburgh.[141] The Conservatives unexpectedly retained their ten seats in Scotland in the 1992 general election and even regained Aberdeen South, aided by a movement of support from Labour to the SNP, but were wiped out completely in New Labour's landslide in 1997. This was followed by the establishment of the Scottish Parliament in 1999. These later electoral developments were related to the survival of the working-class moral economy and are analysed in Chapter 7.

At Caterpillar, tensions had arisen as the occupation extended into a second and then a third month. The engineering union leadership feared sequestration of its funds if the occupiers ignored an interim interdict to end the action. Its executive officer responsible for seeking a resolution was Jimmy Airlie, one of the UCS work-in's leading protagonists. Airlie had an unenviable task, which he pursued with great moral courage, earning mounting unpopularity among the occupiers and their supporters. Generational as well as political-industrial differences were apparent, as some of the younger occupiers bemoaned the alleged unwillingness of older union officials to fight. Airlie negotiated an ending that provided Caterpillar employees with substantially improved exit terms: redundancy was deferred for six months and came with enhanced financial provisions. The STUC had an important role in securing this difficult ending, accepted reluctantly by the occupiers and their stewards, indicating that Scottish national and working-class solidarities were strained but not ruptured.[142] An unusually well-supported

139 Macdonald, *Whaur Extremes Meet*, p. 245.
140 Paterson, *Scottish Education in the Twentieth Century*, pp. 130–54.
141 Gibbs, '"Civic Scotland" vs Communities on Clydeside', pp. 86–106.
142 CGUA, STUC General Council, 1 April and 6 May 1987.

private–public retraining initiative was put in place: the Caterpillar Working Group, coordinated by Strathclyde Regional Council.[143] The operations of this Group were monitored closely by the STUC, which had been instrumental in its formation. John Brannan, one of the leading occupiers, was appointed to the Group. Labour movement pressure compelled Caterpillar to accept some obligations to the workforce and the communities around the plant. The firm contributed substantially to the costs of job-searching and retraining. By September 1987 some 300 workers had registered for HGV training, with 120 started by August. Many workers nevertheless found re-entry to the labour market difficult. The chief executive of the Working Group reported in June 1988, nine months after closure, that 49.3 per cent of the 1,300 had found another job. Among weekly wage-earners it was slightly less: 46.5 per cent. Few of those in new employment were engaged at their former level of skill or grade, and few were working as productively or efficiently as at Caterpillar. The sense of communal injustice was emphasised: 'The loss of this quality industrial complex to the region is greater than just the reduction of 1,238 jobs, severe though this is.'[144]

This transgression of the moral economy was not forgotten in Lanarkshire. Gibbs has interviewed three generations of workers in Lanarkshire about their experiences and memories of deindustrialisation. The ending of production at Caterpillar is an important theme in the testimonies provided by members of the youngest of these generations, born in the later 1960s, who had looked to the factory and other industrial units for their longer-term security. Two of these interviews stand out. John Slaven's father and mother both had Caterpillar jobs for many years. John expected to work there too but the closure compelled him to leave for London and employment in the railways. The occupation, which his mother was involved in, shaped John's political development. He joined the Labour Party and became a trade union activist, employed by the STUC in the late 2010s. Bill McCabe was slightly older, following his grandfather – a former coal miner – and father plus older brother into Caterpillar in the early 1980s. Bill used the opportunity of retraining, which he emphasised had only been secured through determined collective action by the occupiers. This led him into employment in North Sea Oil and then insurance, where he remained involved in

143 NRS, SEP 4/4574, G. R. Wilson, IDS, Note for Secretary of State for Scotland, 21 April 1987.
144 GCUA, STUC General Council papers, Strathclyde Regional Council Economic and Industrial Committee, Caterpillar Working Party, Report by Chief Executive, 17 June 1988.

trade union activism. John and Bill developed politically in the 1980s, retaining a commitment to working-class economic security through collective action and state intervention.[145]

CONCLUSION

A solidaristic moral economy, shared by One Nation Tory and Labour policy-makers, emphasised the importance in Scotland of industrial diversification from the 1950s. This would provide growth and improved living standards and narrow the economic 'gap' with England. Public money was used to encourage and smooth this transition. Labour governments in the 1960s and 1970s were recognised in Scotland as more reliable exponents than Conservative governments of policy interventions to protect working-class security. This was reflected in a movement of electoral support from Conservativism and Unionism to Labour that lasted until the 2000s. The solidaristic policy-making moral economy interacted with the working-class moral economy, which had two central components, individual/communal security and popular consent, as prerequisites of significant changes to employment structures and conditions. Popular expectations of future stability were shaped by policy-making diversification. People in industrial communities accepted the shrinkage of jobs in the staple trades in exchange for a more sustainable future in manufacturing goods for consumer markets. When it appeared that this promise could not be fulfilled, as new-growth manufacturing stalled in the later 1960s and 1970s, the labour movement demanded that employment in the staples be stabilised.

The interaction of these two moral economies had a significant Scottish Nation dimension. Polanyi's concept of the counter-movement coalition can be applied here: a cross-class alliance existed of actors with an interest in embedding economic life more firmly within social needs. In Scotland there were tensions within this coalition, primarily of class, between workers' representatives and policy-makers. There was disagreement, for example, on the question of how public money should be used, with the STUC frustrated by the limited regulation of private-sector companies that secured government funding. The government's reluctance to regulate the behaviour of such employers more firmly was a factor in the labour movement's support for a Home Rule Parliament in Edinburgh. The miners were central to this mood, with devolution of

145 Ewan Gibbs, *Coal Country: The Meaning and Memory of Deindustrialisation in Post-war Scotland* (London: University of London, 2021, pp. 146–7, 184).

policy on economic and industrial as well as social matters understood as a potentially powerful antidote to deindustrialisation in the 1970s.

The working-class moral economy was destabilised in the 1980s by Conservative governments. Thatcherism was an alternative moral-economy form of policy-making. It privileged control of public expenditure, seeing inflation as immoral, and in industrial politics elevated the right of managements to manage, freed from the influence of trade unionism. Thatcherites were reckless in their administration of deindustrialisation. Job losses accelerated and there were no effective means willed or applied to arrest the increase in working-class insecurity. This was deeply unpopular in Scotland. The democratic deficit – a UK government with limited Scottish mandate – reinforced the widely held perception of gross social injustice. This consolidated Scotland's distinct political path away from Conservatism and the unreformed Union.

3

Scotland and the Age of Deindustrialisation

The age of deindustrialisation is an apt title for this chapter, which analyses the details of employment change in Scotland from the mid-1950s to the early 1990s. The process was long-running, with complex gender and class dimensions. Chapter 2 showed how the shrinkage of employment in the staples of coal, metals, shipbuilding and textiles was encouraged by policy-makers. It was accepted in the working-class communities affected because government regional assistance was used to build up engineering and assembly goods manufacturing in central Scotland, as in parts of northern England and South Wales. This restructuring was governed through the interaction of the contrasting policy-making and working-class moral economies.

Industrial and employment changes were gendered and had important implications also in class terms. Shifts in the gender distribution of employment were especially pronounced in engineering and assembly goods, and in the coalfield areas where regional assistance was concentrated. Part-time hours featured in the growth of these opportunities for female employees. Women organised in unions and acting through the STUC sought to enhance the status of female employment in the face of employer intransigence and policy-making indifference. Incremental improvements were made by the 1970s, but recurrent demands for enhanced nursery provision and maternity employment rights remained unfulfilled. Restructuring threatened skilled male working-class identity, historically situated within established sectors of mining, shipbuilding, metals and heavy engineering. This identity privileged autonomy from managerial supervision and employer control, and the value of craft-based production. Autonomy and craft were both challenged by the new production regimes of lighter engineering and assembly goods, where there was strong emphasis on tight supervision of standardised or semi-standardised manufacturing. There was a 'culture clash' between skilled tradition and the requirements of the new employers, many of whom, particularly those from the USA, were reluctant to recognise trade unions. Workers nevertheless asserted collective strength in the new units, winning workplace bargaining rights that helped to secure improved wages and employment conditions. The culture of autonomous and skilled labour was instrumental to these advances, especially in Lanarkshire, where the Clydesider tradition had a compelling subjective influence on working-class identity and activism.

The analysis is developed thematically. The first part examines three distinct phases of deindustrialisation. These map on to the moral-economy transition periods explored in Chapter 2. The changing distribution of industrial employment by gender as well as sector is emphasised, using Ministry of Labour and then Department of Employment data published by the Scottish Office. The careful manner of deindustrialisation's management from the mid-1950s to the late 1970s is demonstrated through detailed examination of the Fife, West Lothian and Lanarkshire coalfield economies. This is contrasted with the effects of the reckless oversight of deindustrialisation from 1979 by the Thatcher governments. The second part examines new opportunities for women, with details again from the coalfield economies, using Population Census data and material from government and trade union archives. The third part examines the challenges confronting skilled working-class men. The frustrations of multinational employment and assembly production are illustrated by the cases of Caterpillar and Bathgate which were introduced in Chapter 2.

DEINDUSTRIALISATION IN SCOTLAND: A PHASED PROCESS

There were major losses of industrial jobs in Scotland after the election of Margaret Thatcher's Conservative government in 1979.[1] Writing in January 1987 about Caterpillar's threatened abandonment of its earth-moving equipment factory at Uddingston, Andrew Cornelius of *The Guardian* observed that in the short period since 1980 roughly one-half of manufacturing capacity and employment in the UK had been lost.[2] As

---

1 Tomlinson, 'Mrs Thatcher's Macroeconomic Adventurism'.
2 Andrew Cornelius, 'No notice or conscience: how Caterpillar bulldozed through its closure', *The Guardian*, 16 January 1987.

Chapters 1 and 2 have shown, however, deindustrialisation had a longer pedigree. The Thatcher years represent not so much a starting point – or even an ending point – but a distinct phase of a process that commenced in the mid-twentieth century and has not yet been completed in the third decade of the twenty-first century. There were three distinct phases of deindustrialisation from the later 1950s to the early 1990s, set out in Figure 3.1. The later history is examined in Chapter 7.

In the first phase the UK government actively promoted industrial diversification. Regional assistance built up lighter industries in central Scotland, as in parts of northern England and South Wales. This approach continued into the second phase and was broadly successful, narrowing the wealth gap between Scotland and England, as noted in Chapter 2. Economic welfare was broadly maintained in the first and second phases of deindustrialisation. One measure of this is the growth of membership of unions affiliated to the STUC, which peaked in the late 1970s, two decades after the summit of total industrial employment. This is shown in Table 3.1. STUC-affiliated membership was probably lower than overall union membership in Scotland. In the 1950s and 1960s union density – the portion of the workforce organised by trade unions – was higher in Scotland by an unknown margin than the STUC's

Phase	Economic features	Alternatives for redundant industrial workers
Managed change, c. 1955–67	Peak of employment in the staples; regional policy: growth of assembly manufacturing and inward investment	Engineering; electronics; consumer goods industries
Careful stabilisation, c. 1968–79	Peak of employment in manufacturing; stabilisation of staples through public investment	Public sector; other manufacturing
Reckless acceleration, c. 1979–96	Rapid loss of all industrial employment, especially 1980–2; disinvestment in public sector industry; sustained rise in unemployment and hidden unemployment	Public and private sector services; education and training

Figure 3.1 The phases of deindustrialisation in Scotland, c. 1955–96

Table 3.1 Employment in Scotland (000s) and Scottish Trades Union Congress membership (000s), 1959–96

	1959	1968	1978	1988	1996
Total employment	2,183	2,200	2,067	1,911	1,981
Industry share	45.2%	43.1%	38.3%	28.3%	21.5%
STUC membership	776.5	827.2	1,033.9	910.9	670.6
STUC 'density'	35.6%	37.6%	50.0%	47.7%	33.9%

Sources: *Digest of Scottish Statistics*, 16 (October 1960), Tables 29 and 30; *Scottish Abstract of Statistics*, 1 (1971), Tables 43a, 45 and 47; *Scottish Abstract of Statistics*, 10 (1981), Table 9.3; *Scottish Abstract of Statistics*, 18 (1989), Tables 9.2 (a) and (b); *Scottish Abstract of Statistics*, 26 (1998), Table 6B3; STUC, *Annual Reports*, 1959, 1968, 1978, 1988; industry share is construction plus coal plus manufacturing.

affiliated membership as a portion of the workforce.[3] This probably remained the case in the 1970s. Union density across the UK peaked in 1980, at 54.5 per cent. It is reasonable to assume by dint of its distinct employment structure – relatively more industry and public sector jobs – that union density in Scotland was higher than this, although Table 3.1 indicates that the STUC only just captured 50 per cent of the workforce in 1978. Growth in the 1970s reflected a recruitment effort undertaken among tertiary sector workers, especially those in public services, meaning that union membership was growing faster among female than male employees. Union density among women workers in Britain increased from 31.2 per cent in 1970 to 39.9 per cent in 1980.[4]

Table 3.2 shows the broad trends in industrial employment from 1959 to 1996.

Manufacturing employment remained stable in the first phase of deindustrialisation. The contrasting position of coal-mining employment, which more than halved, is stark. The largest coalfield territory in production and employment terms after nationalisation in 1947 was Fife, where 23.3 per cent of employed men in 1961 were miners. The rate of subsequent job losses in coal in Fife was high: about 65 per cent from 1961 to 1971 as opposed to about 55 per cent across Scotland from 1959 to 1968. Just 10.1 per cent of working men in Fife were still in coal by 1971. The erosion of employment in the staples from the late 1950s

---

3 Angela Tuckett, *The Scottish Trades Union Congress: The first 80 years* (Edinburgh: Mainstream, 1986), p. 358.
4 Chris Wrigley, *British Trade Unions Since 1933* (Cambridge: Cambridge University Press, 2002), pp. 18–19.

Table 3.2 Employment in industrial sectors (000s) (as a percentage of total employment) in Scotland, 1959–96

	1959	1968	1978	1988	1996
Coal	85	36	21	6	1
Manufacturing	741.4 (34.0)	728.3 (33.1)	609 (29.5)	408 (21.4)	314 (15.6)
Metals manufacture*	56.5	47.5	38	–	–
Construction	162.3	185.5	163	126	111
All industry	988.7 (45.2)	949.8 (43.1)	793 (38.3)	540 (28.3)	426 (21.5)
Total employment	2,183	2,200	2,067	1,911	1,981

Sources: *Digest of Scottish Statistics*, 16 (October 1960), Tables 29 and 30; *Scottish Abstract of Statistics*, 1 (1971), Tables 43a, 45 and 47; *Scottish Abstract of Statistics*, 10 (1981), Table 9.3, *Scottish Abstract of Statistics*, 18 (1989), Tables 9.2 (a) and (b); *Scottish Abstract of Statistics*, 26 (1998), Table 6B3; Miles K. Oglethorpe, *Scottish Collieries* (Edinburgh: RCAHMS, 2006), p. 20.
* Metals manufacture is a subdivision within manufacturing.

was keenly felt, and initially resisted by the workers and communities affected. It became accepted because apparently sustainable alternative sources of employment and economic security were established through regional policy. This kept the all-industry share of male jobs high in coalfield territories despite the reduction of mining employment. In Fife 44 per cent of men were working in industrial categories in 1971, slightly above the national Scottish average for men and women in 1968 shown in Table 3.2. The shrinkage of coal in employment terms was offset by the growth of other industrial sectors, engineering especially, in and around the New Town of Glenrothes. This was built to house families of miners, many of whom moved eastwards from Lanarkshire, attracted by a major new colliery, Rothes, which opened in 1957. Geological difficulties and extreme flooding caused the closure of Rothes in 1962,[5] but a local labour market crisis was averted. A range of industrial employers were attracted to the town through regional policy,[6] including US multinationals such as Hughes Electronics. The population of Glenrothes increased from 1,682 in 1951 to 27,335 in 1971, and then 32,747 in 1981.

5 Robert S. Halliday, *The Disappearing Scottish Colliery* (Edinburgh: Scottish Academic Press, 1990), pp. 49–77.
6 Cowling, *Scottish New Towns*, pp. 29–30.

About 65 per cent of male jobs and 55 per cent of female jobs in the town in 1971 were in industrial categories.[7]

A similar trend was evident in Lanarkshire, Scotland's pre-eminent coal economy until the 1940s, although the movement away from mining was both earlier and more pronounced. Census data assembled by Ewan Gibbs show that coal's employment share among males in the county dropped from 15.5 per cent in 1951 to 9.3 per cent in 1961 and then 2.8 per cent in 1971. But employment in metals was stable, dropping only slightly from 18 per cent of male jobs in 1951 to 16.2 per cent in 1971. Crucially, however, the share of male jobs in engineering steadily *increased* under the impact of multinational plant openings: from 9.9 per cent in 1951 to 19.4 per cent in 1961 and 25.6 per cent in 1971. Despite the heavy loss of coal jobs, the combined three-sector employment share among men thereby held steady at 43.4 per cent in 1951, 44.9 per cent in 1961 and 44.6 per cent in 1971.[8] In 1969 the *Financial Times* noted the impact of investment on manufacturing employment in Lanarkshire since 1964, reflecting – although this was not acknowledged – the significant increase in regional incentives overseen by the Labour government elected in that year. A total of 138 firms had begun manufacturing in Lanarkshire since 1945, with fifty of these established in the most recent five-year period. since 1964. The post-1945 investors had employed 38,000, around 40 per cent of all workers in manufacturing industry in Lanarkshire. Their presence had helped preserve security as coal's significance as an employer diminished.[9] In West Lothian the Bathgate commercial vehicle plant symbolised the same shift in male employment from coal to engineering. In 1951 roughly 30 per cent of the county's male workers, just over 7,000 in total, were in coal mining. By 1971 coal still enjoyed a significant share, 12.6 per cent, of male jobs, but as in Fife the absolute level of employment in the industry had more than halved. Job losses in mining were outnumbered by those gained at the commercial vehicle plant. In 1971 nearly 4,000 men in West Lothian – 14.7 per

7 General Register Office (Scotland), *Census 1961: Scotland. Volume Six: Occupation, Industry and Workplace. County Tables: Dundee, Clackmannan and Fife* (Edinburgh: HMSO, 1966), Table 3; General Register Office (Scotland), *Census 1971: Scotland. Economic Activity. Part Two: County Tables* (Edinburgh: HMSO, 1975), Table 3.
8 Gibbs, *Coal Country*, Table 1.1.
9 'Lanarkshire woos news industry as the last pits close', by Andrew Hargrave, *Financial Times*, 16 October 1969, p. 33.

cent of employed males – were working in engineering.[10] The memories of former BMC and BL workers compiled in the early 2010s offer
a vivid depiction of the plant as a site of labour intensity and diversity. Guthrie Aitken recalled stocking the 20,000 parts that comprised
a single tractor, the assembly of which involved input from a lengthy
list of personnel with distinct job titles and roles: estimators, inspectors,
mechanics, field engineers, design engineers, tool grinders, production
grinders, engine rectifiers, machine operators, cab trimmers, pipe fitters,
boiler men and slip men. BMC also employed hundreds of men and
women in non-engineering roles, providing additional opportunities for
those displaced by industrial restructuring. Alex Bennie left his job in
the railways, which contracted in the same way as coal, and started as a
fireman in the commercial vehicles plant in 1964.[11] Only a small number
of female employees were recruited at the site initially, mainly in clerical
work, with up to a hundred shorthand typists sought in August 1960.
Gendered restrictions applied: BMC expressed a preference in dialogue
with the Ministry of Labour for single women, although if such were in
limited supply in West Lothian 'married women would be accepted'.[12]

In deindustrialisation's second phase, 'careful stabilisation', employment in coal and other staples continued to fall, but more slowly than in
the 1960s. This was related in Chapter 2 and enforced the working-class
moral economy. The pattern shifted again – with an acceleration of job
losses in all industrial categories – after 1979, as Table 3.2 demonstrates.
One exception to this trend was dock work. Employment in this sector –
in Scotland as elsewhere in the UK – remained relatively stable from the
1940s until the early 1960s. For much of that period a large majority
of dockworkers were employed in ports that were registered under the
National Dock Labour Scheme. This was operated by the National Dock
Labour Board (NDLB), which sought to decasualise work in the face of
the intermittent demand for labour. Table 3.3 shows how the numbers
employed under this scheme changed from the introduction of the Board
in 1947 to its abolition in 1989. Census data, more comprehensive in
scope, show a similar trend, with numbers employed in the 'big 4' ports
of Aberdeen, Dundee, Glasgow and Leith falling from 5,835 in 1951

---

10 General Register Office (Scotland), *Census 1951: Scotland. Volume Four:
   Occupations and Industries. County Tables* (Edinburgh, 1956), Table 13; and
   Census 1971: Scotland. Economic Activity. Part Two, County Tables (Edinburgh:
   HMSO, 1975), Table 3.
11 *Bathgate Once More*, pp. 13–25.
12 NRS, SEP 4/1661, BMC. Note of Meeting held in Ministry of Labour, Scottish
   Headquarters, 24 August 1960.

Table 3.3 Dockers in registered ports in Scotland, 1947–88

1947	6,603
1950	6,432
1955	6,402
1960	5,393
1965	4,333
1970	3,041
1975	1,883
1980	1,573
1988	721

Source: National Dock Labour Board, Reports and Accounts, 1947 to 1989
(London: NDLB).

to 2,130 in 1971. There were parallel falls in smaller ports, with a few
exceptions such as the expansion at Grangemouth.[13]

The significant disrupter in the docks in the 1960s and 1970s was
technological innovation: the introduction of 'roll-on, roll-off' ferries
and, more significantly, the adoption and rapid spread of containerisa-
tion of cargoes.[14] This transformed the scale of demand for dock labour
as well as the nature of the job. Occupational knowledge and manual
dexterity became less important; employers secured tighter control over
loading and unloading.[15] The labour intensity of the sector was vastly
reduced, and in a fairly short period, as shown in Table 3.3. This was
contrary to the general experience of manual workers in 'traditional'
sectors in the late 1960s and 1970s, examined in Chapter 2. Job security
in coal mining and shipbuilding was stabilised by government action in
this period, responding to trade-union pressure.

13 General Registry Office, Edinburgh, *Census 1951: Scotland. Volume Four:*
   Occupations and Industries. County Tables (Edinburgh: HMSO, 1956), Table 6;
   and *Census 1971: Scotland. Economic Activity* (Edinburgh: HMSO, 1975),
   Table 3.
14 Marc Levinson, *The Box: How the Shipping Container Made the World Smaller*
   and the World Economy Bigger (Princeton, NJ: Princeton University Press,
   2008); F. Broeze, *The Globalization of the Oceans: Containerization from the*
   1950s to the Present (St Johns, Newfoundland: International Maritime History
   Association, 2002), p. 237, emphasises the global impact on employment, with,
   for example, numbers on the US East Coast falling from 51,000 in 1952 to
   15,000 in 1972. Scotland was also affected by the long-run shift in Britain's
   trade towards Europe, which favoured ports closest to Europe in southern and
   eastern England.
15 David F. Wilson, *Dockers: The impact of industrial change* (London: Collins,
   1972).

The experiences of dockers then converged with those of other manual workers in the third phase of deindustrialisation, after 1979. Until this point trade unions had fought hard to sustain the Scheme, which was administered locally by boards with joint employer–union representation. Reduced numbers of dockers were negotiated with the workers, rather than imposed on them. But numerous younger ports expanded, including container terminals, outside the control of the Board. These included the Scottish ports of Peterhead, Montrose and Cairnryan.[16] The Scheme offended Thatcher's moral economy. She told the Cabinet in 1984 that dockers in NDLB-regulated ports enjoyed 'extraordinary privileges' in job security and pay, asserting that almost one-third of their number were surplus to 'the genuine requirements of their industry'. This discussion took place during the great miners' strike in defence of jobs and communities. Potential parallel action by dockers threatened the government's strategy for defeating the miners. Proposals to scrap the Scheme were shelved, to keep the peace and the important movement of goods flowing, including, of course, vital stocks of imported coal.[17] The government's defeat of the striking miners both symbolised and intensified Thatcherism's assault on the working-class moral economy. This assault was motivated primarily by the goal of removing union voice from the industry.[18] Pits closed after the strike without workforce consultation and there was no meaningful government action to protect economic security in the coalfields or other localities shorn of industrial employment. In Fife coal's share of male employment, from 6.9 per cent in 1981, fell to 3.1 per cent in 1991.[19]

In the ports the Dock Labour Scheme was abolished in 1989, ending joint regulation and guaranteed income for dockers.[20] Redundancies and a rapid increase in unemployment followed. In Dundee only twenty-five of the ninety dockers employed when the NDLB was dismantled found

16 *Scotsman*, 13 April 1989, 'Dockers out in cold as times and tolerance levels change'.
17 TNA, CAB 130/1268, Cabinet Ministerial Group on Coal, Minutes, 11 and 16 July 1984.
18 Phillips, *Scottish Coal Miners*, pp. 241–51.
19 General Register Office (Scotland), *Census 1981: Scotland. Volume One, Fife Region* (Edinburgh: HMSO, 1982), Table 13; General Register Office for Scotland, *1991 Census. Report for Scotland. Part Two, Fife Region* (Edinburgh: HMSO, 1993), Table 79.
20 Department of Employment, *Employment in the Ports: The Dock Labour Scheme*, Cm. 664 (London: HMSO, 1989); Peter Turnbull, Charles Woolfson and John Kelly, *Dock Strike: Conflict and Restructuring in Britain's Ports* (Aldershot: Avebury, 1992).

employment with the new company that provided stevedoring in the port, which employed a total of thirty workers.[21] Ian MacDougall's interviews with Leith dockers detailed the highly negative effects encountered by the labour force: intermittent work and incomes; reduced union influence; a creeping increase in workplace hazards; and a loosening bond between community and job as industrial changes were accompanied by rehousing and gentrification.[22] These local experiences were reflected in the broader trend across the ports in Scotland and the UK. Managerial sovereignty exerted downward pressure on wages in the 1990s, and the intensification of work contributed to an increase in injuries and fatalities.[23]

Industrial job losses and a sustained rise in officially measured unemployment after 1979 were accompanied by a substantial growth of hidden joblessness. As redundant workers withdrew from economic activity altogether, there was a related and marked increase in those registered with the state as 'permanently sick'. In Fife 2.7 per cent of adult males were in this category in 1981. This rose to 5.7 per cent in 1991 and then 7.1 per cent in 2001.[24] In Glasgow 'permanent sick'-ness among all adults increased even more quickly, from 3 per cent in 1981 to around 9 per cent in 1991. Most of these people were neither evading work nor claiming benefits that they were not entitled to. Instead, they were acting rationally in the absence of available job opportunities, incentivised by the benefits system. They could claim incapacity benefits while in receipt of occupational pensions if these came 'early' in connection with redundancy payments. Their benefits were not means tested, and the earnings of other household members were unaffected. The approach of Conservative governments in the 1980s and 1990s is worth brief elaboration. Political pressure arising from the growth of unemployment was eased by repeated massaging downwards of the headline levels of unemployment, partly by removing redundant workers from economic activity.[25] This deception was conjured by paying

---

21 Turnbull, Woolfson and Kelly, *Dock Strike*, p. 185.
22 Ian MacDougall, *Voices of Leith Dockers: Personal Recollections of Working Lives* (Edinburgh: Mercat Press, 2001).
23 Peter Turnbull and Victoria Wass, 'The Greatest Game No More – Redundant Dockers and the Demise of "Dock Work"', *Work, Employment and Society*, 8.4 (1994), pp. 487–506.
24 General Register Office for Scotland, *Scotland's Census 2001. Key Statistics for Council Areas and Health Boards across Scotland* (Edinburgh: HMSO, 2003).
25 Ruth Levitas, 'Fiddling while Britain burns? The "Measurement" of unemployment', in Ruth Levitas and Will Guy, eds, *Interpreting Official Statistics* (London: Routledge, 1996), pp. 45–65.

relatively generous redundancy payments to some groups of workers, and encouraging registration for incapacity benefits rather than unemployment pay, while the government was simultaneously making radical cuts to the relative value of unemployment benefit.[26] The effect was a 'truly astonishing' rise in the number of men on incapacity benefit in the UK, trebling from around 400,000 to 1.2 million between the early 1980s and the mid-1990s.[27]

The 'real' level of unemployment in Glasgow among adults in the 1980s – adding the 'permanently sick' to those officially registered as unemployed – was therefore consistently in the region of 22 to 25 per cent, about 6–8 per cent above the UK average. The 'real' level of unemployment in the Scottish coalfields was likewise high. In 1991 it ranged from 21.2 per cent in Fife to 30 per cent in Ayrshire, via 28.7 per cent in Lanarkshire. It was lower in the Lothians, at 16 per cent, although still above the UK average of 14.9 per cent.[28] The average age of a coal miner in 1984 was 38.[29] This underlines the economic and social costs of coalfield deindustrialisation,[30] with the loss of manual employment shared by workers in other sectors, including women. Those living in ex-coalfield territories still experienced relative economic and social disadvantage in 2019,[31] but the extent of degeneration can be exaggerated. Community cohesion was probably enhanced as gender inequalities gradually narrowed. Ideologically and politically, mining communities were stronger in the late 1980s, more united, *even as the mines closed*, than they had been thirty years previously. This owed much to the survival of the working-class moral economy examined in Chapter 2. It was

26 Christina Beatty and Stephen Fothergill, 'The diversion from "unemployment" to "sickness" across British regions and districts', *Regional Studies*, 39 (2005), pp. 837–54; Anthony Atkinson and John Micklewright, 'Turning the screw: benefits for the unemployed, 1979–1988', in Anthony Atkinson, ed., *Poverty and Social Security* (London: Harvester Wheatsheaf, 1989), pp. 125–57.

27 Beatty and Fothergill, 'The diversion', p. 839.

28 Christina Beatty and Stephen Fothergill, 'Labour Market Adjustment in Areas of Chronic Industrial Decline: The Case of the UK Coalfields', *Regional Studies*, 30 (1996), pp. 627–40.

29 National Coal Board, *Report and Accounts, 1983/4* (London: NCB, 1984), pp. 18–19.

30 Andrew Perchard, '"Broken Men" and "Thatcher's Children": Memory and Legacy in Scotland's Coalfields', *International Labor and Working Class History*, 84 (2013), pp. 78–98.

31 Christina Beatty, Steve Fothergill and Tony Gore, *The State of the Coalfields 2019* (Sheffield Hallam University and the Coalfields Regeneration Trust, 2019), at https://www.coalfields-regen.org.uk/research-and-reports, accessed 21 October 2019.

evident in the consolidation of centre-left voting patterns in the 2000s and 2010s, which are analysed in Chapter 7.[32]

GENDER AND DEINDUSTRIALISATION

The distribution of employment between women and men in Scotland altered from the 1950s to the 1970s in industrial sectors, as the staples were superseded by new manufacturing. The shifting patterns of women's employment in Scotland are set out in Table 3.4.

During the period of managed restructuring, from 1959 to 1968, women's employment in manufacturing increased in absolute terms. The real growth area in this phase, however, was in public sector services, up by around a third. The relative importance of manufacturing and public services in women's employment was reversed during the second phase, a trend emphatically reinforced in the third. Women's employment opportunities were negatively affected by the flight of multinational capital, although in the 1970s a further and more pronounced growth of public sector service jobs offset manufacturing losses. Hence the combined manufacturing and public services share was barely unchanged: 54.7 per cent in 1968 and 54.0 per cent in 1977. The scale and share of public sector service employment for women was maintained in the 'reckless' years of Thatcherism, while female jobs in manufacturing were drained in the decade to 1987 with lasting effects. The resilience of women's public sector service employment in Scotland was reflected in Table 3.1, showing that the STUC 'reach' only fell slightly in the 1980s. Some of this employment was at least indirectly caused by deindustrialisation, with public servants managing the social wounds of unemployment and poverty. If Thatcher's ambition of shrinking the state was unrealised, this was in part because of the new demands made on welfare services by increased industrial job losses.[33]

Table 3.2 exhibits a net loss of 272,000 jobs from 1959 to 1988. Table 3.4 shows a net gain of 119,000 jobs for women in the same period. Table 3.5 reinforces the impression that deindustrialisation contributed to a modest rebalancing of the labour market, which enabled women to acquire a slightly increased share of employment, including in manufacturing. Jobs in manufacturing generally paid better wages, it is worth emphasising, than service roles with equivalent entry

32 Jim Phillips, 'The Meanings of Coal Community in Britain since 1947', *Contemporary British History*, 32.1 (2018), pp. 39–59.
33 Tomlinson, *Managing the Economy*, pp. 74–80, 229–30.

Table 3.4 Women employed in Scotland (000s) (percentage of female employment), including selected sectors, 1959–96

	1959	1968	1977	1987	1996
All sectors	752	825	873	871.1	1,006
Manufacturing	234.4	241.8	194	132.8	97 (9.6)
	(31.1%)	(29.3)	(22.2)	(15.2)	
Public services*	155.2	209.4	277.5	281.9	384 (38.1)
	(20.6)	(25.4)	(31.8)	(32.4)	

Sources: *Digest of Scottish Statistics*, 16 (October 1960), Tables 29 and 30; *Digest of Scottish Statistics*, 34 (October 1969), Tables 39 and 40; *Scottish Abstract of Statistics*, 10 (1981), Table 9.3, *Scottish Abstract of Statistics*, 18 (1989), Tables 9.2 (a) and (b); *Scottish Abstract of Statistics*, 26 (1998), Table 6B3.
* Education, medical and public administration.

Table 3.5 Women's share of manufacturing employment in Scotland, 1959–96

Year	Share (%)
1959	28.9
1968	32.3
1977–8	31.9
1987–8	32.5
1996	30.1

Sources: As Table 3.2.

qualifications. Women broadly retained this share of manufacturing jobs in Scotland, just less than one in three, through the second and third phases of deindustrialisation, although the absolute number of females in industrial jobs was falling.

Table 3.6 highlights the changing employment profile of women in industry from 1959 to 1987. The prolonged importance of the food, drink and tobacco sector is plain. This sector accounted for about one-fifth of women's manufacturing jobs in 1959, 1968 and 1977, and it was more resilient than others in the third phase of deindustrialisation. In 1987 about a quarter of surviving female manufacturing employment was in food, drink and tobacco. Clothing and footwear was likewise steady from the 1950s to the 1970s, with a slightly increasing share of female manufacturing jobs in the second and then the third phases of deindustrialisation, rising from 10.5 per cent in 1959 to 15.9 per cent in 1987 before shrinking in the 1990s. Table 3.6 also demonstrates the significant distributional shift of employment from textiles to engineering and electrical goods that took place in the first phase of deindustrialisation,

Table 3.6 Women employed in selected manufacturing sectors in Scotland (000s) (percentage of total employed females), 1959–87

	1959	1968	1977	1987	1996
Textiles	65.8 (8.9)	54.3 (6.6)	33 (3.8)	17.3 (2.0)	11.6 (1.1)
Food, drink and tobacco	44.9 (6.0)	47.6 (5.7)	40 (4.6)	33.1 (3.8)	20.2 (2.0)
Engineering and electrical goods	32.2 (4.3)	47.2 (5.7)	42 (4.8)	27.1 (3.1)	21.9 (2.2)
Clothing and footwear	24.7 (3.3)	27.1 (3.3)	29 (3.3)	21.1 (2.4)	12.4 (1.2)

Sources: As Table 3.2.

in the 1960s, and was consolidated in the second phase, in the 1970s, despite concerns articulated by the STUC and others as multinationals down-scaled or abandoned operations in Scotland. Textiles remained the primary industrial sector for women's employment in Scotland in 1968, but its lead over engineering and electrical goods had become marginal.

The manufacturing workforce was constructed through collective action by employers and policy-makers, who encouraged recruitment of female school-leavers and older women whose children had attained school age. The STUC Women's Advisory Committee in 1970 was advised by government officials that 'special campaigns' were being run in Aberdeen and Dundee, along with the designated New Town of Cumbernauld in North Lanarkshire, to help mothers 'return' to 'the employment field'. These initiatives were replicated in two other New Towns, East Kilbride in South Lanarkshire along with Glenrothes. An effort was made to smarten up employment exchanges, which would-be workers were reluctant to visit, given their 'unfortunate "dole" image'.[34] Part-time and shift work were available in many industrial sectors and became core features of the labour process in new factories operated by US firms in engineering.[35] This can be viewed positively, helping women to combine paid work with childcare, shopping, cleaning and other vital tasks of social reproduction. Arguably, gendered inequalities in the division of domestic labour were being recognised rather than legitimised. A narrative of women's paid work as amounting to secondary-value activity, less important than men's, was nevertheless consolidated. The

34 GCUA, STUC Women's Advisory Committee, Secretary's Report, 6 May 1970.
35 W. W. Knox and A. McKinlay, 'American Multinationals and British Trade Unions', *Labor History*, 51.2 (2010), pp. 211–29.

STUC Women's Advisory Committee attempted to challenge this, pursuing legislative protection of the employment rights of pregnant women and young mothers in the late 1960s and early 1970s. The Committee advanced the progressive claim of a female manual career, calling for an entitlement to time off work to attend antenatal classes and then three months of maternity leave. Robert Carr, Secretary of State for Employment in Edward Heath's Conservative government, asserted that public opinion was not ready for this. Women having 'family' were expected to take several years off from paid employment outside of the home. Collective bargaining, Carr said, would be a more appropriate avenue than legislation for trade unionists seeking these new rights, enabling women to have direct influence over any arrangements that emerged.[36]

The trade union movement more broadly, including the STUC, was slow to respond to the new agenda of workplace gender equality. For women trade unionists in Scotland the trend to greater parity in pay was stymied directly by the difficulties in comparing work done predominantly by women with work done predominantly by men, and indirectly, with the continuing salience of gendered assumptions about the domestic division of labour. Nursery education was pushed by the STUC as a parental right in the late 1970s, but also a trade union and employment rights issue.[37] Deficiencies in childcare remained significant through the third phase of deindustrialisation and beyond, underlining the structural obstacles facing women in the labour market. In an STUC seminar on Women in the Labour Market in 1988 the absence of non-statutory nursery provision was characterised as a 'scandal' inhibiting female workers from moving into full-time employment.[38]

The national Scottish trends in female employment were observable in the changing coalfield economies of Fife, West Lothian and Lanarkshire. Table 3.7 highlights Fife. Two features unarguably stand out: the major expansion in combined forms of engineering, which exceeded the losses in textiles; and the centrality of public services, the growth of which contributed to a clear shift in the gender distribution of paid work. The ratio of males to females in employment in Fife was 2.6 to 1 in 1961 but just 1.5 to 1 in 1981, and 1.17 to 1 in 1991.

36 GCUA, STUC Women's Advisory Committee, Secretary's Report, 3 June 1971.
37 GCUA, STUC General Council, Resolution on Equal Pay, 11 March 1970; STUC, Conference on Nursery School and Nursery Provision, 30 August 1978, Draft Programme.
38 GCUA, STUC Joint General Council/Women's Committee Seminar, October 1988.

Table 3.7 Women employed in selected sectors in Fife (percentage of total employed females), 1951, 1961 and 1971

	1951	1961	1971
Food, drink and tobacco	964 (3.1)	950 (2.7)	1,390 (2.8)
Engineering	625 (2.0)	400 (1.1)	4,930 (9.9)
Textiles	4,324 (14.0)	3,000 (8.6)	2,500 (5.0)
Clothing and footwear	800 (2.6)	440 (1.3)	1,770 (3.6)
Public services*	5,005 (16.2)	8,180 (23.5)	11,810 (23.8)
Total employment	30,954	34,820	49,600

Sources: General Register Office (Scotland), *Census 1951: Scotland. Volume Four: Occupations and Industries. County Tables* (Edinburgh: HMSO, 1956), Table 13; GRO, *Census 1961 Scotland. Occupation, Industry and Workplaces. County Tables* (Edinburgh: HMSO, 1966), Table 3; GRO, *Census 1971: Scotland. Economic Activity. Part Two, County Tables:* (Edinburgh: HMSO, 1975), Table 3.
* Education, medical and public administration.

Overall female employment in Fife grew by 42 per cent from 1961 to 1971. A total of 32 per cent of women employed in 1971 were in industrial categories, above the national Scottish average of 26 per cent.

Table 3.8, reproducing *Population Census* data assembled by Gibbs, shows a similar pattern of changing female industrial employment in Lanarkshire.

The shrinkage of jobs for women in textiles resembled that of dwindling male employment in mining. The growth of engineering more than absorbed the textiles losses for women, so that the three-sector manual share highlighted by Gibbs – textiles plus clothing and engineering – peaked in 1971. The precipitous loss to 1981, more than half, can be attributed in part to the gradual contraction of industry in the 1970s, compounded by the sudden accelerating effects of Thatcherism

Table 3.8 Female employment in Lanarkshire (as percentage of female jobs), selected industrial sectors, 1951–81

	Textiles	Engineering	Clothing	Combined three-sector share
1951	3,820 (8.1)	4,226 (8.9)	2,760 (5.8)	22.8%
1961	4,070 (7.1)	8,548 (15.0)	3,320 (5.8)	27.9%
1971	2,200 (2.8)	15,290 (19.5)	3,560 (6.5)	28.8%
1981	1,000 (1.2)	6,920 (8.6)	4,040 (5.0)	14.8%

Source: Ewan Gibbs, *Coal Country: The Meaning and Memory of Deindustrialisation in Post-war Scotland* (London: University of London, 2021), Table 1.2.

in 1980–1. The shrinkage of textiles in Lanarkshire was matched in West Lothian, where it dropped from about 11 per cent of women employed in 1951 to only 2.1 per cent in 1971. This was balanced by a growth in clothing manufacture, an insignificant force in 1951 but the third largest industrial sector for women in 1971, some 6.1 per cent of female jobs. Food, drink and tobacco also grew rapidly, to 7.1 per cent of female jobs in 1971 from 1.9 per cent in 1951. The largest industrial sector for women in West Lothian was the same in 1971 as 1951: electrical engineering, up in absolute terms from 850 or so jobs to nearly 1,400, and only down marginally in job share terms, from 11.9 to 9.4 per cent. Plessey Capacitors, one of the largest electronics firms in Britain and a near neighbour of BMC Bathgate, was the key actor. In 1967 Plessey acquired TCC, a local electronics firm operating since the 1940s. As noted in Chapter 2, employment at Plessey peaked in 1973 at around 2,400.[39] The most marked change in female employment in West Lothian, as in Fife, was the enhanced presence of the public sector. The combined share of women's jobs in education, local government and health services increased from 23.8 per cent in 1951 to 28.7 per cent in 1971. In these two decades employment of women in West Lothian increased by 50 per cent in health services, trebled in education and quadrupled in local government.[40]

Regional policy was vital to the growth of female jobs in the coalfields. A telling episode came in the winter of 1967–8, following a disastrous fire in East Fife at Michael Colliery, Scotland's largest. Nine miners died early in the morning of 9 September 1967, and major damage was sustained to the pit's underground workings. The NCB's Scottish officials proposed investing around £4 million to bring Michael back into profitable operation, retaining two-thirds of the colliery's workforce of 2,184. This was over-ruled by the NCB Chairman, Alfred Robens, who was operating within the Labour government's target of a smaller coal share in the UK energy market.[41] The government responded to moral-economy pressure from the miners' union representatives by investing heavily in the further diversification of Fife's industrial economy. The special incentives for attracting industry to Glasgow were extended to Glenrothes, five

---

39 MacDonald, *Shopfloor Experience of Regional Policy*, p. 26.
40 *Census 1951: Scotland. Volume Four: Occupations and Industries. County Tables*, Table 13; and *Census 1971: Scotland. Economic Activity*, Table 3.
41 Jim Phillips, 'The Closure of Michael Colliery in 1967 and the Politics of Deindustrialization in Scotland', *Twentieth Century British History*, 26.4 (2015), pp. 551–72.

miles from Michael.[42] Burroughs Machines, the US computer manufacturer, was persuaded to operate in Glenrothes from 1971 in a £4 million factory built and funded in full by the UK government.[43] Burroughs indicated that 1,000 workers would be recruited.[44] This target was never reached, unsurprisingly, given the 'retreat' of the multinationals. By the end of 1974 Burroughs nevertheless employed 160 women and 270 men in Glenrothes.[45] Of more lasting value was the arrival in East Fife in 1969 of Distillers Company (Ltd), employing 1,000 workers by 1973.[46] The blending and bottling plant in Leven, just two miles from Michael, provided further opportunities for women. It was part of the longer-term stability in food, drink and tobacco, and was still operating in 2020.

The success of deindustrialisation's management prior to 1979 can be measured in the fact that the rate of employment among married women in coalfield areas was higher than in Scotland as a whole.[47] Women's wages contributed to the solidarity of the strike in 1984–5, sustaining the struggle in households without male wages.[48] This changing material position was reflected in the progressive turn in gender relations in the coalfields. The process was incremental and unnoticed by many outwith mining communities. Female strike activists partly disguised this pre-strike improvement, it has recently been argued, to secure greater sympathy and hence practical support from feminists in non-coal metropolitan areas.[49] Coalfield women lost heavily with the acceleration

---

42 NRS, SEP 4/57, I. R. Duncan, Regional Development Division, St Andrew's House, to A. H. J. Herpels, EEC Social Affairs Division, 21 September 1971.
43 NRS, SEP 4/3869, W. Mackenzie, Regional Development Division, Burroughs Machines: background note, 23 December 1970.
44 NRS, SEP 4/57, Regional Development Division, St Andrew's House, Note for Lady Tweedsmuir's Visit to Glenrothes on 2 March 1971.
45 NRS, SEP 4/57, Glenrothes Development Corporation, Progress Report, Quarter Ended 31 December 1974.
46 NRS, CB 360/14/1, National Coal Board, Scottish North Area, Statement showing the deployment of manpower from Michael Colliery, 12 February 1968; and SEP 4/2334, Miss M. J. Alexander, Regional Development Division, 'The Closure of Michael Colliery and Industrial Development in the Leven Area of Fife', 19 October 1970.
47 *Census 1961: Scotland. Volume Six, Occupation, Industry and Workplace*, Table 1, Population in Employment by Areas of Residence and Workplace; *Census 1981: Scotland. Regional Reports. Volume One, Fife*, Table 13; *1991 Census. Part Two, Fife Region*, Table 79.
48 Jim Phillips, *Collieries, Communities and the Miners' Strike in Scotland, 1984–85* (Manchester: Manchester University Press, 2012), pp. 119–22.
49 Florence Sutcliffe-Braithwaite and Natalie Thomlinson, 'Women's Activism during the Miners' Strike: Memories and Legacies', *Contemporary British History*, 32.1 (2018), pp. 78–100.

of deindustrialisation that followed the strike's defeat. Coal jobs disappeared, and so did manual jobs in other categories, especially in the manufacturing firms where women had been employed since the 1960s. At BL in Bathgate, women had gained access to higher-status work in engineering positions in the late 1970s and early 1980s. A similar pattern was evident at the Linwood car plant, examined in Chapter 5. Collective action was important, with AEU representatives at BL supporting female engineering apprenticeships.[50] The loss by women of industry-sector jobs after 1979 was arguably the decisive factor in consolidating the long-term position of economic and social disadvantage in the ex-coalfields.[51] In Fife the female share of the falling market in manufacturing jobs fell from 36.5 per cent in 1981 to 30.6 per cent in 1991. This was sharper and further than the national trend, detailed in Table 3.5.[52] Burroughs withdrew from Glenrothes in 1982, its difficult competitive position aggravated by the increased exchange rate and rising borrowing costs that were central to the government's reckless management of deindustrialisation.[53]

CLASS TENSIONS AND DEINDUSTRIALISATION: CATERPILLAR AND BATHGATE

The changing structures of industrial employment from the late 1950s onwards were accompanied by class tension at workplace level. This was especially marked in plants operated by US multinationals. Gibbs notes that such firms employed 82,600 workers in Scotland in 1972, 56,700 of them in the Glasgow Planning Region, which encompassed Lanarkshire. US multinationals were responsible across Scotland that year for 26.5 per cent of employment in mechanical engineering, 39.5 per cent in electrical engineering, and 45.6 per cent in instrument engineering.[54]

The US-owned Caterpillar earthmoving vehicle plant at Uddingston was among the largest of these ventures. It will be remembered from

50 *Bathgate Once More*, pp. 30–1.
51 Mike Foden, Steve Fothergill and Tony Gore, *The State of the Coalfields: Economic and social conditions in the former mining communities of England, Scotland and Wales* (Sheffield Hallam University and the Coalfields Regeneration Trust, 2014), pp. 13–26.
52 *Census 1981: Scotland. Regional Reports. Volume One, Fife*, Table 13; *1991 Census. Part Two, Fife Region*, Table 79.
53 NRS, SEP 4/3869, 'Burroughs closing Glenrothes', *The Scotsman*, 2 March 1982, clipping; Parliamentary Debates, Commons, Sixth Series, Vol. 20, Col. 376, 24 March 1982.
54 Gibbs, *Coal Country*, p. 42.

Chapter 2 that this was constructed in the mid-1950s on the site of a mining village, Tannochside, as coal mining was eradicated in the Hamilton–Bothwell–Blantyre conurbation. Industrial transformation was accepted in Lanarkshire as a means of strengthening economic resilience. John Brannan, convenor of the stewards in 1987, joined Caterpillar as a young man in the mid-1960s. His father was a coal miner. This reinforced the many family connections at the plant between mining and engineering and underlines the theme of generational transition evident at various points in the age of deindustrialisation.[55] Bill McCabe, a Caterpillar shop steward before his twentieth birthday, was also from a mining background. He followed his father, uncle and brothers into the engineering plant.[56] For the Brannans, the McCabes and apparently many other families, the switch from mining to engineering was nevertheless problematic. In the 2010s coal jobs and collieries were remembered as valuable social resources, reluctantly exchanged for the promise of a better future.[57]

Family and community connections stimulated expectations of a rewarding future. In its Uddingston publication, *The Earthmover*, Caterpillar claimed in the 1960s to be a model employer in Scotland, asserting that safety, training and welfare were prioritised at the plant.[58] Caterpillar certainly offered attractively paid work in a safe environment. By August 1959, when the firm's US President from Illinois, Harman S. Eberhard, belatedly visited Uddingston to confer 'official' opening status, the plant employed 1,750 workers.[59] Caterpillar was nevertheless reluctant to recognise wider obligations to employees and their communities. The firm opposed trade union recognition and sought to impose a labour regime that alienated skilled engineering workers. These men privileged the values of craft skill and autonomy from managerial supervision. In political terms they saw their interests as distinct from and sometimes in opposition to those of their employer. As AEU members

---

55 John Brannan, Interview with Ewan Gibbs at University of the West of Scotland Hamilton campus, 21 February 2017.
56 Bill McCabe, Interview with Ewan Gibbs, Tannochside Miners' Welfare, 20 January 2017.
57 'Policy Forum: 30 years after the Caterpillar Occupation: Trade Unions in Past, Present and Future', University of the West of Scotland, 2017, at https://hml.helix.uws.ac.uk/Play/12131, accessed 21 December 2020; Janet Burrows, Interview with Ewan Gibbs, Tannochside Miners' Welfare, 20 January 2017.
58 NRS, SEP 2/49, *The Earthmover: A Monthly Newspaper for Caterpillar People at the Glasgow Plant*, 10.2 (1957).
59 'Scots Tractor Plant Opened', From Our Own Correspondent, *Financial Times*, 25 August 1959, p. 10.

they wore badges bearing the three words 'EDUCATE, ORGANISE, CONTROL'. For craftsmen at Caterpillar, control was the central issue as they struggled for union recognition. This was won in 1961 after a nine-week strike, triggered in November 1960 when plant management dismissed two AEU activists, Alexander Cumming and William Selkirk.[60]

This dispute was part of a larger pattern of conflict in US-owned factories in Scotland in the 1950s and 1960s. The 'frontier of control', Carter Goodrich's memorable phrase from the 1920s, was usually the focus of contestation.[61] McKinlay and Knox have identified the existence of an industrial culture clash in multinational plants. This reflected intense class conflict and arose from mismatched expectations. US employers, in Scotland for its lower wage environment and access through the European Free Trade Agreement to West European consumer markets, had reckoned on employing a 'green' or compliant workforce. This would facilitate enforcement of no-union agreements, consolidating the lower-cost advantage of operating in Scotland. Scottish engineering workers were offended by these assumptions and fought to assert their traditions of skilled labour and union autonomy in the new plants.[62] The Gibbs interviews with former Caterpillar stewards are replete with memories of this culture clash. Jim McRobbie asserted that the 'Americans have a different way of thinking from us', and recounted various tactics adopted by Caterpillar workers. These were lifted directly from the Clydesider repertoire of resistance, which is explored further in Chapters 4 and 5. Foremost was the practice of effort rationing. McRobbie was also adamant about the centrality of trade unionism and adversarial bargaining: 'you need to fight for what you get'.[63]

The culture clash narrative at Caterpillar was derived from the collective origin story of the recognition strike. The AEU's national officials were pushed in the winter of 1960–1 by Uddingston members to intervene. John Boyd, of the union's national executive council, threatened to spread the dispute to Caterpillar's other UK-based plant, at Birtley on Tyneside, if recognition was not granted at Uddingston. The injustice of the position – as well as its illogicality – was underlined by the fact that

---

60 'AEU Challenge to US Firm', *The Guardian*, 21 December 1960.
61 Carter Goodrich, *The Frontier of Control* (London: Pluto Press, 1975; first published 1920), with foreword and additional notes by Richard Hyman.
62 Knox and McKinlay, 'Working for the Yankee Dollar'.
63 Jim McRobbie, Interview with Ewan Gibbs, Viewpark Community Centre, 12 December 2016.

the AEU already had workplace bargaining rights at the Tyneside plant.[64] William Carron, AEU President, told reporters that he was disappointed with the multinational. Having won recognition with British-owned engineering firms, his union was now fighting the battle over again, this time with US employers. Fourteen separate recognition struggles had taken place since the Second World War involving US firms and AEU members, reporters noted. The union had won eleven of these struggles.[65] Caterpillar was pressurised further as Carron submitted an official complaint to the US ambassador and sought solidarity action by engineering unions in the USA. 'For the normally peace-loving AEU to fight a battle on this scale is a rare occurrence', commented *The Guardian*'s Industrial Staff.[66] Caterpillar sought a strategic retreat: the sacked men, Cumming and Selkirk, were re-employed; and the firm agreed to recognise full-time AEU officers but not workplace stewards. This partial recognition strategy was unsuccessful: the stewards incrementally established a position of strength, securing plant-level bargaining rights.[67] This outcome was part of the labour movement's strengthening position in Scotland in the first and second phases of deindustrialisation. Few US firms were able to withstand calls for recognition and collective bargaining in Scotland in the 1960s. IBM at Greenock, notorious or renowned according to interpretation, was unusual in this respect. It purchased this 'right to manage' through provision of greater job security, promotion opportunities and pay rewards than applied in other US-owned firms operating in Scotland.[68]

Moral-economy tensions remained live at Caterpillar throughout the 1960s and 1970s. The firm continually challenged union rights in the workplace. In June 1968 the dismissal of a shop steward was reversed only following strike action involving 1,100 dayshift and 650 nightshift

64 'Threat to Extend Strike at Scottish Caterpillar', From Our Labour Correspondent, *Financial Times*, 9 December 1960, p. 11.
65 'AEU's Quarrel with US Group', By Our Labour Correspondent, *Financial Times*, 21 December 1960, p. 9.
66 'Tractor Men win fight for union recognition', *The Guardian*, 7 January 1961.
67 W. W. Knox and A. McKinlay, '"Organizing the unorganized": union recruitment strategies in American transnationals, c. 1945–1977', in G. Gall, *Union Organizing: Campaigning for trade union recognition* (London: Routledge, 2003), pp. 19–38 with Caterpillar material at pp. 30–3.
68 Knox and McKinlay, '"Organizing the unorganized"', pp. 21–9; Pavlos Dimitratos, Ioanna Liouka, Duncan Ross and Stephen Young, 'The multinational enterprise and subsidiary evolution', *Business History*, 51 (2009), pp. 401–25.

workers.[69] This followed a major expansion in the mid-1960s, lifting employment above 2,000.[70] John Gillen, who started at the plant in the 1960s, recalled that his generational peers gradually superseded their elders in the factory. John Brannan joined at the same time, and likewise remembered that he and the other 'daft young boys' assumed control of union organisation from older trade unionists who he felt had become slightly complacent in their relations with the company after 1960–1. Defending union rights in the factory required relentless struggle. Gillen recorded various kinds of conflict, from stoppages arising from pay and work-organisation disputes, to aspects of an autonomously run social life, including a bookmaking operation in the factory.[71]

Class tensions in West Lothian were different from those at Caterpillar. Union recognition was not contested by BMC, but workers still felt under-valued. This was partly a reflection of the skill composition of the workforce. Only 10 per cent of those initially recruited were skilled: the fitters, turners, millers and other craftsmen who were deployed in the tool rooms. The majority, 70 per cent, were semi-skilled. BMC management told Ministry of Labour officials in 1960 that 'the work does not require a fine degree of manual manipulation'.[72] Former workers remember wages along with employment conditions and welfare amenities as attractive in comparison with those that applied elsewhere in the local economy.[73] At the same time, however, pay levels were below the rate enjoyed by the firm's employees in the industry's English Midlands core.[74] The same problem was evident at Linwood and regional policy motor plants in northern England and South Wales in the 1960s.[75] The pay disparity issue surfaced dramatically with the three-week unofficial strike in June 1966 examined in this book's introduction. Many workers were frustrated but also encouraged. Parity remained an objective

69 NRS, SEP 2/49, 'Strike by 1100 at Tannochside', *Glasgow Herald*, 12 June 1968, clipping.
70 NRS, DD 10/380, 'Caterpillar to Expand Again', *The Scotsman*, 19 August 1964, clipping.
71 John Gillen Interview with Ewan Gibbs, University of the West of Scotland Hamilton campus, 21 February 2017; Brannan, Interview.
72 NRS, SEP 4/1661, BMC: Note of meeting held in Ministry of Labour, Scottish Headquarters, 24 August 1960.
73 *Bathgate Once More*, pp. 33–4.
74 Catriona L. MacDonald, 'Scotland's Affluent Workers? Pay, Stability and the Struggle for Parity at the Bathgate Motor Plant'. *Scottish Labour History*, 48 (2013), pp. 95–115.
75 Jon Murden, 'Demands for Fair Wages and Pay Parity in the British Motor Industry in the 1960s and 1970s', *Historical Studies in Industrial Relations*, 20 (2005), 1–27.

for the workforce through the later 1960s and was eventually attained in 1972 after a nine-week strike.[76] BMC employees secured an average increase of 30 per cent, bringing them in line with average earnings across the industry.[77] This achievement was accompanied by a similar trend to parity won through collective action by motor industry workers in northern England and south Wales.[78]

There was another structural problem at Bathgate: lay-offs and short-time working. This confounded expectations of stable and rewarding employment, particularly among workers who had moved there, such as migrants from the coalfields of Lanarkshire and Fife. The STUC and workforce union representatives frequently raised it as a problem: while the UK government pushed BMC to operate in West Lothian, there was no related action to incentivise the movement of components suppliers. The company was over-reliant on stocks brought by road from the West Midlands. Interruptions could arise from production or labour problems in the West Midlands, or heavy weather, especially in the winter, which was a frequent occurrence in the early snow-filled months of 1963. The difficulty of 'crossing the Shap', the high Cumbrian peak of the old A6 connecting Scotland with England, became lodged in West Lothian memory as a primary explanation for the plant's longer history of production difficulties. Catriona L. MacDonald, interviewing former Bathgate workers in the early 2010s, was struck by the frequent reassertion of this narrative, applied to stoppages that occurred long after the completion of the M6 in the later 1960s.[79]

In April 1963 the Conservative government's Secretary of State for Scotland, Michael Noble, visited Bathgate. Workplace union representatives told him that the supply shortfall was the most pressing problem at the plant.[80] In the summer of 1964 the Scottish Office privately noted that the plant was facing a loss of £2 million in the year to July, requiring 1,300 completed vehicles per week to break even, but achieving only 1,000. Components shortages were indeed the key, contributing to escalating overtime costs. Strangely, however, the officials characterised this as a problem of 'inefficient labour' rather than managerial-cum-organisational deficiency. Representatives of the workforce saw the matter differently. An eight-strong delegation, including members of the

76 MacDonald, *Shopfloor Experience of Regional Policy*, pp. 230–2.
77 *Bathgate Once More*, p. 42.
78 MacDonald, 'Scotland's Affluent Workers?'
79 MacDonald, *Shopfloor Experience of Regional Policy*, p. 195.
80 NRS, SEP 4/1661, Report of Secretary of State for Scotland visit to East Kilbride and Bathgate, 17 April 1963.

AEU, the TGWU and the National Union of Vehicle Builders, arrived unannounced on Friday 12 June at St Andrews House. The delegation was an early expression of Scottish working-class moral economy protest, appealing to the Secretary of State for Scotland about the suspension from employment by BMC of 450 workers on the vehicle assembly line because components were in short supply. These workers, the union delegates asserted, were meeting the costs of BMC's managerial incompetence. They sought an inquiry by the Secretary of State into the motor industry in Scotland. This was deftly avoided by Noble and Edward Heath, President of the Board of Trade, although it was quietly noted that Rootes at Linwood was obtaining a larger share of its components in Scotland than BMC.[81]

Moral-economy tensions remained evident at Bathgate in the mid-1960s. The chief issue was unchanged: employment insecurity caused by supply difficulties and short-run market fluctuations. Workforce representatives again presented themselves unannounced at St Andrews House in December 1965, seeking an audience with Ross, who was not present. The delegation was received instead by Scottish Office Regional Development Department and Ministry of Labour officials. The stewards stated that adverse weather had delayed the delivery of components from the West Midlands to Bathgate once more, resulting in large-scale lay-offs. The position was not one of dispute between labour and management in West Lothian. The stewards urged the government to push component makers to establish operations in Scotland.[82] Ross styled himself as a firm defender of Scottish interests, to protect living standards in Scotland and the political integrity of the UK.[83] He would have been alarmed, therefore, when STUC officials felt compelled to intervene in bolder terms. James Jack, STUC General Secretary, visited Bathgate with four of his officials in November 1965 at the invitation of AEU workplace representatives. The workers told Jack that BMC's management was 'notorious' in the industry for failing to stock more than a single day's components.[84] Jack told Ross afterwards that the workers 'maintain they are treated as no more than "casual labour"'. In working-class moral economy terms this was an instructive phrase,

81 NRS, SEP 4/2923, Michael Noble to Edward Heath, 16 June 1964, and Heath reply, 6 July 1964.
82 NRS, SEP 4/2923, Miss J. M. Alexander, RDD, note of meeting with delegation to St Andrews House, 1 December 1965.
83 Alvin Jackson, *The Two Unions: Ireland, Scotland, and the Survival of the United Kingdom, 1707–2007* (Oxford: Oxford University Press, 2012), pp. 275–8.
84 GCUA, STUC Economic Committee, 2 September and 2 December 1965.

calling attention to the unacceptable injustice of irregular employment. The same expression was used by workers at the Linwood car plant, which the STUC officials had also investigated. At both sites, union representatives felt 'that at top management level there was an "anti-Scottish attitude"'.[85]

BMC managers claimed that poor productivity at Bathgate was the real problem, pointing to a rash of unofficial strikes since 1961. The Ministry of Labour accepted a direct request from Bathgate stewards for an official investigation. This was held at Bathgate under the auspices of the Motor Industry Joint Labour Council, chaired by Jack Scamp, a well-known industrial relations 'trouble-shooter'. Scamp focused on lay-offs and short-time working. Between 1961 and 1966 there had been 117 separate unofficial stoppages, only one of which was related to pay. The majority were caused by disagreements on working hours and conditions. In the same period there had been sixteen instances of lay-offs or short-time working: seven were ascribed by Scamp to managerial failure to stock enough components and the other nine to unofficial strikes in the West Midlands that had cut supply. BMC managers said that lay-offs or short-time working in such circumstances were normal practice in the motor industry. Union representatives responded that this attitude indicated the company's serious failure to understand the industrial culture of central Scotland, specifically the workforce's expectations of 'stable employment and a forty-hour week'. These competing positions could not easily be resolved, although there were signs that BMC was adjusting its expectations and behaviour. Scamp was assured that the firm was committed to working more closely with unions at plant level, through regular meetings with a Joint Shop Stewards Committee, and late in 1965 had upped the value of component stocks from £3.3 million to £4.5 million. This was possibly a response to the damaging 'casual labour' label levelled by stewards and the STUC.[86]

Harmony was not established entirely. A new challenge emerged in September 1966, which would also disfigure employment at Linwood: large-scale redundancy. The problem at each site reflected the impact on consumer demand of the government's anti-inflationary 'July measures', discussed in Chapter 2. BMC responded to the unfavourable market conditions by reducing its labour costs. The firm employed a total of 130,000 and resolved to make 9,828 – over 7.5 per cent – redundant. But the share of Bathgate workers being shaken out was more than

85 NRS, SEP 4/2923, Jack to Ross, 15 February 1966.
86 MacDonald, *Shopfloor Experience of Regional Policy*, pp. 85–7, 122–3.

double this: at least 850 out of 5,009 employees. This news was relayed insensitively to the West Lothian workforce via a management circular issue from BMC headquarters in the West Midlands, with the added insult that after the redundancies there would still be no guarantee of a five-day working week for those retained.[87] At a mass meeting David Wilson, AEU plant stewards' convenor, highlighted the injustice in stark terms. Referring to the deteriorating labour market situation, he said, 'It is criminal to send workers out when there is only the labour exchange for them'.[88] Wilson and other workforce representatives briefed STUC officials on the crisis. Two moral-economy elements were emphasised: the injustice of redundancy in Scotland as a remedy for over-heating in England; and the pay disparities that meant short-time workers in the Midlands on a three-day week earned the same as those in West Lothian on a four-day week. Bill McLean of the STUC promised the Bathgate representatives that these concerns would be raised directly with the government,[89] and they were, in a meeting with Michael Stewart, First Secretary of State for Economic Affairs in late September, and in talks with Wilson and several Cabinet ministers at Downing Street in late November, as noted in Chapter 2. Tam Dalyell, Labour MP for West Lothian, also intervened. He told Lord Hughes, Under-Secretary of State for Scotland, that Bathgate workers were being unfairly treated by BMC. Dalyell pointed out that Bathgate produced commercial vehicles primarily for export markets but was paying for BMC's lost domestic car sales. By April 1967 just over 500 of the redundant workers had found alternative employment, but a significant minority – more than 300 men – had not. Their predicament was accentuated by the heavy local job losses in coal mining detailed earlier in this chapter.[90]

Employment at Bathgate was stabilised in the second phase of deindustrialisation. The Labour government's protection of economic security in industrial communities from 1974 was emphasised in Chapter 2 and is a central theme in Chapters 4 and 5. This effort included the quasi-nationalisation in 1975 of BL, the employer at Bathgate after

87 '1,000 to go at Bathgate', From Our Own Correspondent, *Financial Times*, 15 September 1966, p. 1.
88 'BMC adamant on redundancy plan', By Our Labour Correspondent, *Financial Times*, 16 September, p. 15.
89 GCUA, STUC Economic Committee, Meeting with Trade Union Representatives from BMC Bathgate, 16 September 1966.
90 NRS, SEP 4/2400, BMC redundancies: note by K. R. Cooper, Ministry of Labour, to Prime Minister's Private Secretary, 16 September 1966; Note of meeting between Tam Dalyell MP and Lord Hughes, 20 September 1966; Ministry of Labour, BMC Redundancy, 19 April 1967.

BMC merged with Leyland Motors in 1968. Problems at Bathgate now assumed a different pattern. Low-pay grumbles were articulated by workers comparing their wages, not with those of BL employees in England but those of their neighbours and friends at other factories in West Lothian, said to be earning between £10 and £15 more each week in the late summer of 1978. BL management implied that the issue was low productivity at Bathgate, claiming that hefty investment – £45 million over three years in new machinery in the tool rooms at the plant – had not led to increased output, which was running at around 65 per cent of target. Jim Swann, the engineering workers' lead steward at the plant, said the target was unrealistic as a five-week strike ensued. Productivity improved in the next six months, according to Scottish Office officials, briefing the new Conservative government's Industry Minister in Scotland, Alec Fletcher, in May 1979. This had been the result of an attendance scheme negotiated by the firm with the engineering union, but a proposed expansion of production and employment had not yet taken place.[91]

CONCLUSION

The closures of the commercial vehicle operation at Bathgate in 1984 and the Caterpillar plant at Uddingston in 1987 were examined in Chapter 2. Each violated the working-class moral economy of deindustrialisation. They were separate but linked episodes in the acceleration of industrial job loss in the 1980s, which represented a distinct phase in the age of deindustrialisation, when the process was grievously mismanaged by the Conservative governments. This was highly evident in falling levels of women's employment in industry. Across Scotland the combined female employment share in four key manufacturing sectors – textiles, engineering, food/drink/tobacco and clothing/footwear – fell from 16.5 per cent in 1977 to 11.3 per cent in 1987. Women continued in the 1980s to occupy a significant share of manufacturing employment, but this was a shrinking portion of a contracting labour market. Public sector employment did not fully offset these manufacturing job losses but nevertheless became even more important for women in the later 1980s. Trade union membership, presented here as a proxy of employee

---

91 NRS, SEP 4/5608, various press clippings from August and September 1978, and note on British Leyland – Scottish Operation, for Alec Fletcher, meeting West Lothian Constituency Labour Party, 31 May 1979.

welfare, also fell, reinforcing the sense that deindustrialisation was not beneficial for women as workers.

The position had been different in the 1950s, 1960s and 1970s. During these decades economic change was managed carefully, with an emphasis on the security of industrial workers and their communities. There was a redistribution of industrial job opportunities from men to women. The extent of this ought not to be exaggerated. More men than women occupied industrial jobs in 1979. Structural obstacles to women attaining greater equality included the depressingly entrenched poverty of nursery provision. This was tolerated by policy-makers and employers because of gendered assumptions about the division of domestic labour between women and men. Securing continuity of employment for women during pregnancy and young motherhood was not a priority for policy-makers. Women's disproportionately large dependence on part-time work and wages persisted. The gender gap at least in opportunity if not reward nevertheless narrowed. Diversification of Scotland's industrial economy provided women in the 1960s and 1970s with jobs that had not been available to them in the 1940s and 1950s. These offset the losses in textiles, the key industrial sector for women's employment until the 1950s. The growing number of women with jobs in engineering was especially marked in the changing coalfield economy in Fife. There was long-run stability in another important manufacturing area, food/drink/tobacco, responsible for roughly one female manufacturing job in five in Scotland in the 1950s and 1960s and one female manufacturing job in four in the 1970s and 1980s. But broader social changes cannot be overlooked, including the consolidation of public sector services in the 1960s and 1970s, which were the largest areas of female employment in Scotland and in Fife.

The expansion of engineering contributed positively to changes in employment in Lanarkshire and West Lothian too. As textiles contracted women found more attractive jobs in the new engineering factories. This was positive, contributing to a convergence of economic growth rates and living standards between Scotland and England, but there were significant social costs, encapsulated in the cases of Caterpillar and Bathgate. In Lanarkshire the US multinational employer was hostile to trade unionism and extremely reluctant to share authority with workforce representatives. This transgressed the Clydesider expectations of the skilled engineers. At the commercial vehicle plant in West Lothian the issues were slightly different although similarly reflective of frustrated working-class expectations: there was less scope than anticipated for the exercise of skilled labour, and economic security was compromised by wages below the national industry average and the incidence of large-scale redundancy. Collective action at both Caterpillar and Bathgate improved the position, with a stronger union voice and greater continuity of employment. This progress was part of a broader pattern across Scotland in the later 1960s and 1970s, as coal miners, steel and shipbuilding workers also won greater stability. These gains were consolidated by the Labour government elected in 1974. Like the Labour government before it in the 1960s, this administration managed the difficult process of deindustrialisation carefully, with working-class economic security a key priority.

Part II

The Politics of Deindustrialisation

4

Fairfield, Govan:
Shipbuilding and the Scottish Nation

Deindustrialisation was a shared female and male working-class experience. Chapter 3 showed that women lost heavily in employment terms from the contraction of industry in the 1970s and 1980s. Male experiences of deindustrialisation were nevertheless distinct, as the examination of Fairfield shipyard in Govan in this chapter demonstrates. On Clydeside the employment culture of shipyard workers was formed in the peculiar production regime of the industry. Male workers privileged earnings and craft skill along with their autonomy from managerial supervision and employer control. This intersectional class-cum-gender identity was transmitted across generations, with emphasis on learning the craft and the politics of 'being a Clydesider' in the workplace. The male grip on shipyard employment was never shaken, even during the pronounced labour shortages of the Second World War.[1] Fairfield, which opened in the 1890s and remains a site of industrial production in the early 2020s, showcases the continuous construction and reconstruction of this culture. Deindustrialisation threatened employment at the yard in each of the three phases identified in Part I of this book. The erosion of shipbuilding employment was a significant feature of the first phase, in the decade or so from the mid-1950s. Skilled men were, however, able to find alternative employment with the growth of new engineering facilities on Clydeside, notably the Linwood car plant examined in Chapter 5. Social and political crises punctuated the second phase, as employment alternatives dwindled. The Clydesider culture was an important resource in helping the workforce to resist closure of the

---

1 Hugh Murphy, '"From the Crinoline to the Boilersuit": Women Workers in British Shipbuilding during the Second World War', *Contemporary British History*, 13.2 (1999), pp. 82–104.

yard on two separate occasions, in 1965 and 1971. The outcome of these crises strengthened working-class moral economy feeling on the Clyde, and the expectation that trade union organisation and state intervention could advance communal security. This helped the workers to mitigate unattractive features of the third phase, including the erosion of union voice and the overall volume of shipyard employment.

The first part of this chapter examines the key ingredients of the Clydesider culture, using oral history testimonies from workers who began their employment careers as young men in Fairfield in the late 1960s and early 1970s. They owed this start in industrial employment to the success of older men in preserving the yard, and their testimonies reflect gratitude on this account. Analysis then moves to the long crisis of the second phase of deindustrialisation on the Clyde. In 1965 Fairfield entered and was then taken out of receivership when the Labour government assisted a reconstruction of ownership and production. This intervention, known as the 'Experiment', is explored in the second part of the chapter. The Experiment involved a relaxation of some craft practices. There was greater scope for union voice and influence, raising the esteem and expectations of manual workers, and apparent improvements in productivity resulted. The Experiment ended when Labour government policy compelled Fairfield to join the UCS grouping in 1968. The third part of the chapter focuses on UCS. The new combine was unstable financially because of losses inherited from its second largest constituent after Fairfield, the John Browns yard in Clydebank, acquired in building the *QE2*. Liquidation at UCS was avoided in 1969 when the workforce agreed to substantial redundancies, roughly one in five of those employed. The concession was made in return for investment from the government, and on the understanding that the labour market would be sufficiently buoyant for redundant men to obtain equivalent jobs elsewhere.

These moral-economy expectations of a sustainable future were transgressed by Edward Heath's Conservative government, elected in 1970. Unemployment was allowed to escalate, weakening the labour market prospects of redundant UCS men. The government then refused UCS requests for credit guarantees, despite a healthy order book, pushing the firm into liquidation in June 1971. The Experiment had emboldened Clydesider identity. A stronger sense of ownership consciousness provided the campaign to defend the yards in 1971 with decisive moral force. The novel tactic of a work-in, devised by the joint stewards' committee representing men from each of the yards, cast the government as irresponsible wreckers and forced a major policy U-turn. Further subsidy was granted in 1972, preserving roughly three jobs in four. This was a working-class moral economy victory, with large-scale employment maintained at three of the yards, including Fairfield. The work-in also highlighted the apparent inadequacy of unreformed political structures in the UK. The stewards mobilised a large cross-class and cross-party alliance within Scotland against the alleged failure of decision-makers in Westminster to accommodate the distinct economic and social interests of workers and businesses on the Clyde. The failure of the market, emphasised strongly by shipyard workers and their union representatives, was recognised when the Labour government nationalised the industry following its election in 1974, which is examined along with the yard's post-1979 history in the fourth and final part of the chapter.

FAIRFIELD AND THE CLYDESIDER CULTURE

Men who began their working lives in Fairfield in the late 1960s and early 1970s have positive memories of the shipbuilding industry. They recount the camaraderie and solidarity of the yard, emphasise the value of their earnings as workers derived from skilled employment, and speak positively about the role of trade union organisation in strengthening individual and collective economic security. These are blended, however, with an acknowledgement that employment in the yard was often difficult, with men labouring sometimes in heavy weather outdoors, and it was potentially hazardous. Welfare amenities were rudimentary. The term 'critical nostalgia', used to characterise individual and collective memory of valuable but lost social resources, feels apt when making sense of Fairfield narratives and the Clydesider employment culture.[2]

The skilled male employment culture had deep historical roots in Glasgow's emergence as a shipbuilding hub in the nineteenth century. A crucial turning point was the establishment of trade unions to organise workers against exploitative employment practices that pitted groups of workers against each other in order to keep wage rates low.[3] Craft skill was privileged as a means of protecting workers within this environment, where trade union efforts to enforce collective bargaining were resisted by employers in the 1920s and 1930s. The distinct and indeed conflicting interests of workers and employers on the Clyde were continually

---

2 Alastair Bonnett, *Left in the Past: Radicalism and the Politics of Nostalgia* (London and New York: Bloomsbury Press, 2010).
3 Irene Maver, *Glasgow* (Edinburgh: Edinburgh University Press, 2000), pp. 113–20, 203–5.

reinforced by the employment practices of the leading shipbuilders, who released workers on the completion of orders. Memories of long-term unemployment and under-employment in the 'Hungry Thirties' were transmitted to younger workers, and influenced the mobilisation against deindustrialisation in the 1960s and 1970s. Stronger union voice and greater social protection from the state reinforced the Clydesider identity in the 1940s and the 1950s. This was the Polanyian double movement in action. The embedding of economic life in a richer foundation of social relationships and priorities was reflected in various ways in the shipyards, not least in languages of class and resistance deployed by workers' representatives. Jimmy Reid, communist, skilled engineer and union steward in John Browns, frequently counterpoised the 'rat race' of competitive capitalism with the 'human race', of which trade unionism and working-class political organisations were central features.[4] Gendered language was central to the discourse as well as the performance of this male culture. Interviewed for Thames Television's *This Week* in 1972 by Jonathan Dimbleby, Reid said that workers protecting industrial employment through collective action were exhibiting their social essence 'as men'.[5]

Reid was part of a social movement against the loss of industrial employment. Returning to a concept introduced in Chapter 2, the process of deindustrialisation challenged but also reinforced the workforce's 'intelligible moral order' on the Clyde. Policy-makers in the first phase of deindustrialisation, in the decade roughly from 1957 onwards, viewed shipyard rationalisation and modernisation as essential to improved international competitiveness. Such restructuring was resented by workers but broadly accepted until the mid-1960s in terms of the working-class moral economy. Employment in shipbuilding fell overall from its Clydeside peak in 1957–8, but alternatives for male as well as female workers in engineering and other industrial sectors were developing. The onset of crisis at Fairfield in 1965 coincided with a slowing of the growth of other employment sectors on Clydeside. It was for this reason that further closures and redundancies were resisted, especially after the serious escalation of male unemployment in the winter of 1970–1.[6]

4 W. W. J. Knox and A. McKinlay, *Jimmy Reid: A Clyde-Built Man* (Liverpool: Liverpool University Press, 2019).
5 'Jimmy Reid Unlimited', *This Week*, Thames Television, directed by Tom Steel, first broadcast 11 May 1972.
6 John MacInnes, 'The deindustrialisation of Glasgow', *Scottish Affairs*, 11 (1995), pp. 73–95.

Men who started at Fairfield during or immediately after the long crisis of the late 1960s and early 1970s were interviewed for this book. Without exception they were proud of the yard and the anti-deindustrialisation resistance that had given them the opportunity to work there. The components of Clydesider identity were itemised in their testimonies. This status required the acquisition of manual craft skill. In the shipbuilding industry across the UK in the 1960s around two-thirds of those manually employed were skilled workers. On the Upper Clyde at the time of the work-in the skilled share of employment was slightly higher, at around 71 per cent.[7] White-collar workers and unskilled male cleaners were not considered 'Clydesiders' and neither were female workers. There were further distinctions between metal workers 'in the black trades' and those engaged in 'fitting out' operations, such as carpenters, plumbers and electricians. Within the 'black trades' there were rivalries between caulkers, platers and welders. Alan Glover started in the early 1970s. 'I didnae want to be a caulker burner', he recalled. 'Erm, that's like being a drummer in a band, you don't want to be the drummer in a band, you want to be the lead guitarist . . . or the singer, right'. For him welders 'were the royalty'.[8] The platers and caulkers were nevertheless part of the 'band', having worked 'on the tools', learned their trade through time-served apprenticeship and become skilled men.[9] Reinforcing the elevated status of shipbuilding men was the comparatively 'good' money earned in the industry. Tam Brady, born in 1960, chose a welding apprenticeship in Fairfield in 1976 on £27 a week over a job as an electrician at £16 a week.[10] Alan estimated that his father, also a welder in Fairfield, was paid 'basically double' that of comparable workers in other local trades. This paid for a family holiday to Spain in 1969.[11]

Along with apprenticeship-based skills and high earnings, the Clydesider identity comprised intangible qualities, notably the presumed masculine attributes of resilience and responsibility. These would be recurrent rhetorical motifs of the anti-deindustrialisation resistance, with Reid and Jimmy Airlie, another prominent Clyde yard steward, contrasting the 'responsibility' of job-protecting workers with the 'irresponsibility' of Conservative policy-makers who tolerated the escalation

7 Frank Herron, 'Redundancy and Redeployment from UCS, 1969–1971', *Scottish Journal of Political Economy* 19.3 (1972), pp. 231–51, with detail at p. 235.
8 Alan Glover, Interview with VW, East Kilbride, 23 September 2017.
9 Glover, Interview.
10 Tam Brady, Interview with VW, Paisley, 20 September 2017.
11 Glover, Interview.

of manual employment loss.[12] This was a legacy of shipbuilding's brutal labour process, which applied across the sector at UK level. Boilermakers were laid off when a vessel was launched, unless another was already on order, and fitting out tradesmen were likewise made redundant on completion of their work. A study of the Swan Hunter yard in Wallsend on the Tyne in the 1960s noted that collective consciousness of such injustice was important in shaping workplace and broader social attitudes. Craft divisions were marked, but a common skilled-worker inheritance was prevalent across occupations. This shared 'tradesmen's' identity was transmitted from older workers to younger men born after the Second World War.[13] A similar process was observable on the Clyde, where a distinct moral order of the yard, codified informally, was reproduced and transmitted inter-generationally. Older men taught new entrants 'how to behave themselves' and be responsible workers, which meant becoming good tradesmen, avoiding bad influences and excessive alcohol consumption.[14]

This education showed men how to be 'Clydesiders', privileging personal integrity and honesty, along with obligations to workmates. It helped them survive the arduous labour involved. For Alan, coming of age in the shipyard was a formative experience that has guided him through life. He recalled his entry to the shipyard as a rite of passage:

> like walking into Dante's Inferno, right [. . .] my father was a welder in the shipyards, my Uncle George was a welder in the shipyards. And the foreman said to me, what's your name, son, and I says, Alan Glover, and he said, erm, what one's your dad, Jimmy or George? And I says, Jimmy. He went, I can kick . . . sorry . . . your dad can kick the crap out of me, but I bet you I can kick the crap out of you. And I went, I doubt it, I can kick the crap out my dad. Now, I couldn't. But right away, the light bulb went on, and I thought, you'll need to be smart in here, son, right.[15]

12 *UCS 1* (Cinema Action, 1971), 22 minutes, black and white. This film is included in *Tales from the Shipyard: Britain's Shipbuilding Heritage on Film* (London: British Film Institute), DVD, 2011.
13 Richard Brown and Peter Brannen, 'Social Relations and Social Perspectives amongst Shipbuilding Workers – A Preliminary Statement: Part One', *Sociology*, 4.1 (1970), pp. 71–84; and 'Part Two', *Sociology*, 4.2 (1970), pp. 197–211; R. K. Brown, P. Brannen, J. M. Cousins and M. L. Samphier, 'The Contours of Solidarity: Social Stratification and Industrial Relations in Shipbuilding', *British Journal of Industrial Relations*, 10 (1972), pp. 12–41.
14 Alex Wright, Interview with VW, Paisley, 29 August 2017.
15 Glover, Interview.

Quickness of mind and verbal violence were learned strategies for deal-ing with the yard's rigours. But Alan, conscious of contemporary mores in the late 2010s, and specifically concerns about workplace bullying, defended his mentors:

> And the best one, erm, and people talk about reverse psychology, erm, Willie McClellan was his name, he was a welding foreman, but his nick-name was The Hook. And he looked like, when I saw the video for the, Pink Floyd's Another Brick in the Wall, the, Teacher, Leave Us Alone, that's what he looked like. Tall, stooped, with a big Roman nose. And his language was atrocious, erm, but he would always abuse you, mentally, like, you're a long haired, useless hippy B. You'll never be able to tie your father's boot-laces, you're crap, you're this, you're that. And if you don't do this, you're gonna get this punishment. And yet, in a perverse way, he was educating you, to push you, and push you, and . . . I always remember him. In fact, years later, after I'd left the shipyard, or into a launch, and Willie was retired, and he was there. And I introduced him to two of my colleagues, and he turned round and says to them, my god, my worst nightmare has appeared, right. But that's the way the man was, he actually cared about a lot of the appren-tices. He didnae show it, though.

Other ex-workers shared Alan's view that verbal abuse from older colleagues 'toughened you up'. This is remembered in positive terms by Alex Wright, born in Paisley in 1956, who also started in Fairfield in 1971 and likewise attributed his moral foundation to daily contacts with older workers:

> But Fairfield has taken me from a boy to a man. And that's how it's for-mative. [. . .] Because you have, you had, going in there as a fifteen and sixteen-year-old, to learn off the men that came from a similar background to you. [. . .] As I say, I couldn't speak up more highly about the working-class environment that, not, I just didn't grow up in, but also worked in. Because I looked up to they guys. [. . .] You know, that was a great place to grow up. Although it was tough at times, and you got your leg pulled mercilessly. It was a great place to actually grow up, and just kind of toughen up a bit. The men were once apprentices themselves, and went through the same sort of kind of, almost it's like growing pains in some respect, you know.[16]

Tam, who was raised in Cranhill, ten miles east of Govan, made a sim-ilar observation about formational influence. Starting work at Fairfield from school 'made me the person that I am today and [. . .] Govan like an awful lot of institutions like that, whether it be the shipyards,

16 Wright, Interview.

steelworks or whatever, they make the men.'[17] This recalled Reid's often-quoted aphorism, articulated during the UCS work-in, that on the Clyde men were built along with the ships.[18] The presence of the 'cultural circuit', an oral history concept where individual memory reflects and also consolidates predominating narratives, is readily apparent.[19]

Apprenticeships were served partly in the training school and prefabrication shed at Fairfield, but Alan related 'real' learning to time spent on ships under construction, under the tutelage of older men:

> I remember a big guy, Jimmy Port, erm, and it was up on the deck, and it was a wee, tiny space. And this man, he was probably about six foot, erm, he probably weighed about thirteen, fourteen stone. And I think most of the guys that were welders or plater/shipwrights, could have got a job in the circus as contortionists . . . because . . . and he would show you how to get into these wee spaces, and right, move your shoulder this way, and move. It, it was amazing. Or even maybe if you were maybe not welding a job right, and they would say, look, I'll show you a better way to do this. So there was a lot of guys who kind of mentored you.[20]

Intergenerational exchanges were reciprocal. As Alex suggests, it was important for younger workers to 'look after' the older men who had educated them:

> So if you were, if you were, let's call it an old chap near retirement, a young man at that time would say, look, Tommy, let me get that. You're not going up that ladder, and you're not doing this. The younger men tended to look after the older men, and all that.[21]

The process of intergenerational teaching was not just technical, as Alan states:

> It moulded me in a lot of beliefs, my political beliefs, my beliefs about my fellow man as well. And educated me, because it sparked interest with certain things, with just people I spoke to, my dad being one of them, but others as well.

17 Brady, Interview.
18 John Foster and Charles Woolfson, 'How Workers on the Clyde Gained the Capacity for Class Struggle: the Upper Clyde Shipbuilders' Work-In, 1971–2', in John McIlroy, Nina Fishman and Alan Campbell, eds, *British Trade Unions and Industrial Politics. Volume Two: The High Tide of Trade Unionism, 1964–79* (Aldershot: Ashgate, 1999), pp. 297–325.
19 Alistair Thomson, 'Anzac Memories: Putting popular memory theory into practice in Australia', in Robert Perks and Alistair Thomson, eds, *The Oral History Reader* (London: Routledge, 1998), pp. 300–10.
20 Glover, Interview.
21 Wright, Interview.

Even guys that I worked with. So, I could sum it up and say, it's the best university in the world, personally. That's, that's the way I would round it up. [. . .] And I, I've said it many a time, and I've said it many . . . and I'm not an idiot, I'm not a genius, but I'm not an idiot, and I'm pretty well-read. And I put a lot back to that, it's as simple as that.[22]

Learning in this way from trusted elders was a central political component of the Clydesider identity, reinforcing the emphasis on workforce autonomy from managerial supervision. This identity was mobilised to protect employment and economic security during the long crisis at Fairfield that commenced in 1965.

THE EXPERIMENT

In October 1965 the Fairfield Shipbuilding and Engineering Company Limited entered receivership. The firm was short of working capital and had £5.5 million in liabilities with £560,000 due to creditors. It also had an order book worth £32 million, however, a crucial factor in the Labour government's decision to support the yard's continuation.[23] This was achieved through a pioneering exercise in industrial reconstruction. The government took a 50 per cent stake in the new firm, Fairfield (Glasgow) Limited.[24] State investment was dependent on substantial changes to production methods and business organisation, with emphasis on work study and industrial partnership. The new management structure was led by Sir Iain Stewart, a Unionist-supporting businessman who had been pressing policy-makers for several years on the theme of industrial partnership. He characterised industrial performance generally, and in shipbuilding especially, as retarded by adversarial relations between management and workers. He lamented what he saw as the careless wastage of skill arising from uncoordinated redundancies, labour hoarding and the reluctance – among managers and workers – to engage in retraining and redeployment across crafts and whole sectors.[25]

Stewart persuaded George Brown, Secretary of State for Economic Affairs, and his officials at the Department of Economic Affairs (DEA), notably Derek Palmar, of the Experiment's potential merits. They

22 Glover, Interview.
23 TNA, EW 27/118, Note of Meeting in Chancellor of the Exchequer's Room, Treasury, 29 October 1965.
24 TNA, EW 27/118, Conclusions of a Meeting in First Secretary's Room, DEA, 6 December 1965.
25 TNA, LAB 10/2358, Sir Iain Stewart to Major William Whitelaw, Parliamentary Secretary, Ministry of Labour, 23 January 1964.

supported the aim of incentivising workers to compromise on established hierarchies of demarcation and sectionalism. In return workers and their union representatives would gain greater agency in the yard through a formalised structure of joint-industrial committees.[26] The government faced objections from the UK's largest business organisation, the CBI, which saw the initiative as 'back door nationalisation' and contravening the interests of capital and private property.[27] Established shipbuilding firms on the Clyde saw the Experiment as a specific threat to their interests: closure of Fairfield would lead to a significant slackening of the local market for skilled labour. This business frustration was reflected in a sceptical and even hostile press response in Scotland to the Experiment. The chief industrial correspondent of the *Scottish Daily Express*, Jack McGill, was among those who emphasised Stewart's limited knowledge of shipbuilding.[28] Roy Mason, Minister of State at the Board of Trade, received concerned representatives from two of the industry's business groups, the Shipbuilding Conference and the Shipbuilding Employers' Federation. They argued that workers in yards across England and Northern Ireland as well as Scotland would expect to match improved pay and conditions secured by Fairfield employees. This would lead to a 'massive increase in wage costs to the detriment of the industry's competitive position'.[29]

These free enterprise business objections underline the moral-economy basis of the Experiment, which was an important Scottish national expression of the Polanyian counter-movement coalition. Business and labour combined across the class frontier to win UK government support for an industry that was regarded as central to the identity of Clydeside and Scotland more broadly. Stewart envisaged that a degree of industrial democracy would result in more productive shipbuilding. This would provide a more stable long-term future where workers had greater employment certainty. The Board of Directors of the new Fairfield included two national trade union officials, William Carron, President of the AEU, and Andrew Cunningham, Northern District Secretary of the General and Municipal Workers' Union. The AEU

26 TNA, EW 27/118, D. J. Palmar, Brief for meeting between the First Secretary (Brown), Chancellor (Callaghan) and President (Jay), 22 November 1965.
27 TNA, BT 291/119, V. I. Chapman, Board of Trade, Fairfield: Concerns in CBI, 8 December 1965.
28 Jack McGill, *Crisis on the Clyde* (London: Harper Collins, 1973), p. 14.
29 TNA, BT 291/119, Note of a Meeting between Minister of State and representatives of Shipbuilding Conference and Shipbuilding Employers' Federation, 8 December 1965.

also invested £50,000 in the experiment.[30] This reinforced Fairfield' claim to a new approach based on partnership between management and labour. Other Board members included Professor Ken Alexander of the University of Strathclyde's Department of Economics, and Sir Jack Scamp, the industrial relations 'trouble-shooter' who chaired the Ministry of Labour investigation at the BMC plant at Bathgate in 1966.[31]

The Experiment was consistent with the social-democratic policy-making moral economy. Brown and the DEA thought a revitalised Fairfield could serve as a 'proving ground' for work study, productivity, retraining and redeployment across the whole shipbuilding industry.[32] The DEA over-ruled objections from the Treasury. James Callaghan, Chancellor of the Exchequer, discussed his misgivings about saving the yard with Lord Cromer, Governor of the Bank of England, who favoured closure.[33] In a cross-departmental meeting of ministers and officials Callaghan suggested that the government could only intervene where 'serious economic and social loss would be entailed'. He doubted that such a condition applied, but other ministers disagreed, suggesting that 'formidable political and psychological repercussions on Clydeside and throughout Scotland would be bound to result from closing Fairfield'. Crucially, perhaps, T. D. Haddow, Permanent Secretary at the Scottish Office, reported that the Bank of Scotland, a major creditor, regarded Fairfield as 'a good enterprise' and 'profoundly hoped' it would remain in business'.[34]

The Scottish national counter-movement characteristics of the Experiment were evident in *The Bowler and the Bunnet*, an energetic documentary feature directed and presented by Sean Connery.[35] The international film star, whose early working life in Edinburgh had involved employment in the city's St Cuthbert's Cooperative Society, appeared for no fee. He was 'keen to promote the experiment', asserting that the 'loss of shipbuilding will turn Scotland into an industrial desert

---

30 *The Daily Record*, 5 May 1966.
31 Sydney Paulden and Bill Hawkins, *Whatever Happened at Fairfield?* (London: Gower Press, 1969), pp. 197–9.
32 Harold Wincott, 'The State's Role in Industry', *Financial Times*, 11 January 1966.
33 TNA, T 224/660, I. P. Bancroft, note of phone conversation, Chancellor and Governor, 1 November 1965.
34 TNA, EW 27/118, Note of Meeting in Chancellor of the Exchequer's Room, Treasury, 29 October 1965.
35 *The Bowler and the Bunnet*, written and researched by Clifford Hanley, directed and presented by Sean Connery (Sean Connery, Scottish Television, 1967), 36 minutes, black and white; the film is included in *Tales From the Shipyard*.

for an entire generation'. The film was shown on Scottish Television and Stewart arranged for screenings in London in November 1967, attended by a lengthy list of politicians, industrialists, trade unionists, journalists and show business personalities.[36] Connery was shown travelling around Govan by public bus and the shipyards on a delivery bicycle, all the while setting out the case for setting aside the class differences in industry symbolised in the film's title. Throughout the film he wore the democratic bunnet. The cast mirrored this pluralistic perspective. Stewart featured along with Oliver Blanford, General Manager, and Jim Houston, the Director of Productivity Services. The first full-time trade union convenor in the yard, Alec McGuinness, spoke to camera along with Jimmy Airlie and several workers. Tensions and misgivings were articulated. Airlie said, 'I had my doubts' about the Experiment, wondering if it was all a 'confidence trick', while conceding that 'some of the things they've done have been quite good'. One worker referred to the novelty of the Experiment, asserting 'its all very well in theory but you can't build ships with theory', and another expressed himself in the straightforward language of class conflict: 'quite frankly I don't trust bosses'.

The working-class moral economy rationale for the Experiment was nevertheless plain. The STUC leadership saw the threatened closure of a modernised shipyard as market failure in vivid terms, given the £32 million order book. The direct loss of 3,000 jobs in this circumstance could not be tolerated, and STUC officials were worried about the implications for potentially thousands of other workers in the complex local-regional supply chain on Clydeside that fed Fairfield. Concerns about Stewart's prominent Unionist politics and the risk of relaxing workplace union rules were set aside by STUC officials, whose priority was defending economic security on the Clyde. Workers reported that employers in other Upper Clyde yards were using the crisis to 'get tough' with employees.[37] Alex Kitson, Chairman of the STUC, advised the DEA and the Scottish Office in early December that national officials of all of the unions involved would participate in talks geared to making the Experiment successful.[38]

36 TNA, EW 27/132 DEA file, Fairfield, I. M. Stewart to Mr Dell [Edmund, Under Secretary of State, DEA], February to April 1966, 30 October 1967 with invite to view *The Bowler and The Bunnet* at the Mayfair Hotel, Starlight Cinema, Berkeley Square, on 20 November 1967.
37 GCUA, STUC Economic Committee, 4 November and 2 December 1965.
38 TNA, EW 27/118, D. J. Palmar, note to J. C. Burgh, 3 December 1965.

Working-class moral economy feeling on the Clyde was encouraged by the Experiment. Improved productivity was a key objective, but this would not be achieved at the cost of employment security. Surplus labour created by new methods would be redeployed. Stewart used mass meetings of Fairfield workers at the Lyceum cinema in Govan to communicate the changes in employment practices that such transformation would require. He spoke about 'the drawing up of a new rule book for Fairfield, eliminating restrictive practices and modernising those traditional habits which I know you regard as part of your heritage'. In return workers would attain 'guaranteed employment and guaranteed continuity of income'. This novel route to economic security would be protected through industrial partnership, as union representatives negotiated the necessary changes on equal footing with management.[39] Davie Torrance, a draftsman and shop steward in the yard from 1968 to 2001, cites this aspect of the Experiment as having a positive legacy:

> But Fairfield Glasgow experiment was the thing [. . .] Changin' the way they worked and havin' Joint Production Committees and asking guys, 'right, how can we improve this job?' But first of all you've got to guarantee the guys that they're not goan tae get paid aff. [Laughter] That's whit demarcation was about, but it wis nothin tae dae wi, it was protectin your particular job ye know [. . .] but that was the *main thing*, guaranteed employment, ye could sit down and say 'this is stupid, why are we doin it this way, why don't we do it that way'.

The emphasis on union voice in managing production influenced the growth of ownership consciousness among Fairfield workers. This shaped their response to the liquidation of UCS in 1971. Collective self-confidence in their capacity to produce ships was bolstered by their involvement in strategic discussions from 1966 to 1968 at Fairfield.[40]

The new production techniques were guided by comprehensive training for shop stewards and foremen who were sent 'back to school', with residential courses on measured day working, for instance, at Esher in Surrey in 1967.[41] Speaking to camera in *The Bowler and the Bunnet*, Blanford asserted that 'we need to make this into a kind of university where people learn and teach'. This represented a different approach

---

39 TNA, LAB 10/2358, Sir Iain Stewart, speech at the Lyceum Cinema, Govan, 27 December 1965.
40 David Torrance, Interview with VW, Old Kilpatrick, 4 October 2017.
41 Mitchell Library, Glasgow (ML), UCS 2/1/9, Minutes of Directors' Meetings, 1967–1971, 21 April 1966; UCS 2/28/14, clippings file, *The Times*, 5 May 1966; *The Daily Record*, 6 May 1966.

to workforce education from the shipyard 'university' depicted within working-class moral-economy narratives, where learning was an informal feature of daily interaction. Blanford was talking about formalised training, to be extended to the apprentices with a new school being built. Yet workers did not accept all changes unquestioningly. Wage rates continued to be a source of tension in the implementation of measured day working.[42] This was predictable, given the Clydesider emphasis on protecting and enhancing earnings. There were three notable strikes in 1966 and 1967, the men having 'lost patience' waiting for productivity rates to increase and result in higher wages.[43] Ken Alexander's study of the Experiment acknowledged the frustrations facing workers as they adjusted to a new regime.[44] The desired resource of 'mutual trust' between managers and workers was difficult to establish; adversarial relations had deep roots on the Clyde. Eventually in June 1967 the delayed measured day work scheme went into action. This had 'immediate effects' in terms of efficiency and productivity with workers' rates increasing by up to 10d an hour. This was a significant jump, equivalent roughly to an extra £2 on weekly earnings in the range of £25 to £35, depending on overtime.[45]

The Experiment ended in 1968 when Fairfield was absorbed into Upper Clyde Shipbuilders.[46] In 1965 the government had appointed the Geddes Committee to consider how British shipbuilding could become more competitive. This recommended a strategy of regional grouping, to attain scale economies and greater efficiencies in labour utilisation.[47] Douglas Jay, President of the Board of Trade, had assured Sir Reay Geddes in 1965 that the Experiment would not pre-empt any recommendations his committee might make on the future structure of the industry on the Clyde,[48] and there was no scope for Fairfield continuing outwith the UCS group. This makes it difficult to appraise the

42 ML, UCS 2/1/8, Minutes of Directors' Meetings, 1959–1966, 10 February 1966, 'Wages Policy'; 21 April 1966, 'work study'.
43 ML, UCS 2/1/9, Minutes of Directors' Meetings, 1967–1971, 16 June 1966; 6 October 1966, 17 November 1966, 18 May 1967.
44 K. J. W. Alexander and C. L. Jenkins, *Fairfield: a Study of Industrial Change* (London: Allen Lane, 1970), pp. 112–13.
45 ML, UCS 2/1/9 Minutes of Directors, 20 April 1967.
46 TNA, LAB 10/3174, UCS Employment Charter, 1967; and Hepper to A. S. Marre, Ministry of Labour, 28 November 1967; ML, UCS 2/1/9, Minutes of Directors' Meetings, 7 August 1967.
47 ML, UCS 2/1/8 Minutes of Directors' Meetings, 1959–1966, 2 August 1965; *Shipbuilding Inquiry Committee, 1965–1977. Report*, Cmnd 2937 (London: HMSO, 1966).
48 TNA, BT 291/121, Jay to Geddes, 10 January 1966.

Experiment's impact on productivity. Palmar's final report as govern-
ment-appointed Director on the Board emphasised that ships had been
completed according to schedule, industrial relations had been good,
and the basis of future productivity improvements firmly established.
He concluded that the Experiment's aims had been achieved.[49] Fairfield
joined three other yards in UCS: Connells of Scotstoun, Stephens of
Linthouse, and John Browns in Clydebank. Given the business rivalries
and resentments evident when the Experiment was established, the combination was not harmonious at board level.[50] Stewart did not remain
long on the new board, which paid limited attention to work study and
productivity experiments. He saw this as a missed opportunity and continued to write letters to broadsheet newspapers asserting that abandoning the Fairfield methods would be detrimental for shipbuilding and
British industry.[51] The UCS Employment Charter of January 1968 set
aside the Experiment's advances on work study, confirming that national
procedures on pay and conditions would be retained and applied in each
of the group's yards, including Fairfield. The Charter reiterated labour
flexibility, mobility and security with unions obtaining a guarantee of no
redundancies for two years.[52] This would be severely tested as the new
group faced a succession of increasingly serious financial difficulties.

UCS AND THE WORK-IN

UCS teetered on the brink of liquidation because of insufficient working
capital. UCS only survived this crisis after politically complex talks in
May and June 1969 in Glasgow, which involved the firm's directors,
government ministers and officials, industry and workplace union representatives, local Unionist and Labour MPs, and the STUC.[53] Moral-
economy considerations predominated, with Alex Kitson of the STUC
speaking for many in querying the prolonged use of public money to
support private enterprise. He argued that greater public control –
including the possibility of nationalisation – should accompany greater

49 TNA, FV 36/10, The Shipbuilding Industry, Note of Meeting, 25 March 1968;
    and FV 36/11, Fairfield (Glasgow) Limited: Final Report by Government
    Director, 27 February 1968.
50 ML, UCS 2/1/9, Minutes of Directors, 5 December 1967 and 6 February 1968.
51 Iain Stewart, 'Industrial strength: where Britain has gone astray' *The Times*,
    10 April 1974, p. 22; and 'Shipyard nationalisation' *The Times*, 6 August 1974,
    p. 13.
52 TNA, LAB 10/3174, UCS Employment Charter, 1967.
53 GCUA, STUC General Council, Special Meeting, 7 May 1969.

public investment. The government's shipbuilding policy was steered by Anthony Wedgwood Benn, Minister of Technology, before his radical personal and political re-engineering as Tony Benn in 1970. Wedgwood Benn opposed nationalisation and was sceptical about the long-term prospects of UCS. He was especially scathing about management at John Browns, which had accumulated substantial losses in building the *QE2* for Cunard, launched in September 1967. DEA officials saw the luxurious liner's expensive legacy as a 'major factor' in UCS's predicted liquidation. UCS management were paying for the 'mistakes of their predecessors'.[54] Ministers were advised by their officials that liquidation could result in an increase of male unemployment in the Glasgow travel-to-work area of 8.5 per cent, up from 6.1 per cent in February 1969.[55] Wedgwood Benn worried that the disappearance of shipbuilding from the Upper Clyde would damage the integrity of the UK and the Labour Party's popularity in Scotland. Criticism bordering on 'recrimination' from Stewart and other ex-Fairfield managers would follow, along with workers' demands for nationalisation.[56]

Willie Ross, Secretary of State for Scotland, faced intensifying pressure from the Scottish labour movement over the stagnation of employment growth in the late 1960s. As examined in Chapters 2 and 3, this difficulty hung over the UCS crisis. In March 1969 STUC officials met Ross, Wedgwood Benn and Roy Mason, Minister of Power, in the House of Commons. James Jack, STUC General Secretary, spoke about the important and welcome growth of the electronics industry, with fifty-plus firms operating in Scotland, but noted also the worrying 'extent to which decisions intimately affecting the people' were being taken 'in board rooms out of the British Isles'. Remote decision-making, with insufficient government control, meant that employment growth in new manufacturing was not balancing losses sustained in 'contracting industries'. Stabilisation of these older sectors was therefore essential. While Wedgwood Benn was non-committal, Ross asserted that he 'was always keen and willing to champion Scotland's cause both inside and outside the Cabinet'.[57] A few weeks later Ross told Wedgwood Benn that the government's response to the crisis at UCS had to include the preservation

54 TNA, EW 7/1456, A. J. Cody, DEA, Brief for Secretary of State, 28 February 1969.
55 TNA, EW 7/1456, D. M. O'Brien, UCS background notes for Economic Policy Committee, 5 May 1969.
56 TNA, EW 7/1456, UCS, Memo by Wedgwood Benn, 29 April 1969.
57 GCUA, STUC, Economic Committee meeting with Government Ministers, House of Commons, 19 March 1969.

of mass employment at each of its yards. The closure of Clydebank, and even heavy redundancies there, 'would be quite intolerable'.[58]

The government's Ministerial Committee on Economic Policy examined the UCS problem at length. The minutes of the decisive meeting on 6 May show that a majority of those present, including Harold Wilson, the Prime Minister, were concerned about the social costs of mass redundancy that would follow liquidation. This would have grave implications for Clydeside and inflict reputational damage on British shipbuilding. A grant of £3 million was extended to UCS. In Wilson's words this would 'increase the efficiency and reduce the surplus manpower'. A major caveat was inserted, however.[59] UCS directors were required to reduce their labour commitments by around one-fifth.[60] In August 1969 just over 400 were made redundant on a last-in, first-out basis. Larger redundancies were then secured on a voluntary basis. From May 1970, hourly-paid manual workers with less than two years' service were invited to leave, with four weeks' severance pay. From July 1970 hourly-paid manual workers with up to five years' service could exit, with four weeks' severance pay plus statutory benefits that those with less than two years' service were not entitled to. From mid-August 1970 those in the clerical, administrative and technical grades were also permitted to leave, with statutory redundancy plus between five and eight weeks' pay depending on length of service. Along with natural wastage this phased programme reduced the workforce from 10,800 in August 1969 to 8,400 by June 1971.[61] This reconstruction was presented by government ministers and UCS management as establishing a viable future for remaining employees. Trade union representatives believed that employment alternatives would be available for the redundant men. The security of the affected workers and communities was seemingly being prioritised, with the government upholding its obligations to those affected by deindustrialisation.[62]

The moral-economy position was then ruptured by Edward Heath's Conservative government, elected in June 1970. The new government

58 TNA, EW 7/1456, Ross to Wedgwood Benn, 30 April 1969.
59 TNA, EW 7/1456, Cabinet Ministerial Committee on Economic Policy, 6 May 1969.
60 University of Glasgow Archives (UG), UCS 5/1/2, Upper Clyde Shipbuilders, Minutes of Meetings of UCS Directors, 6 and 11 June 1969.
61 Herron, 'Redundancy and Redeployment from UCS', p. 233.
62 GCUA, STUC, General Council, Report of a Meeting with the Rt Hon. Anthony Wedgwood Benn, Minister of Technology, and the Rt Hon. William Ross, Secretary of State for Scotland, Board of Trade Offices, Glasgow, 12 January 1970.

was committed to withdrawing state aid for so-called industrial 'lame ducks'. In December 1970 John Davies, the Secretary of State for Trade and Industry, resolved that no further credit would be extended to UCS. Gordon Campbell, the Secretary of State for Scotland, accepted this.[63] The government was also prepared to tolerate rising unemployment without ameliorative policy responses. The jobless rate jumped nationally across the UK from 2.7 per cent in June 1970 to more than 4 per cent twelve months later.[64] This negated Wedgwood Benn's rescue plan, particularly as the situation was more acute in Glasgow, with male unemployment rising from 6.8 per cent in the first quarter of 1970 to 10.5 per cent in the third quarter of 1971. At the end of 1969 there were 3,000 job openings available for 21,000 unemployed males in Glasgow; by June 1971 there were only 642 vacancies with 35,000 men out of work.[65] Acknowledging the difficulties confronted by the redundant UCS workers in this deteriorating macroeconomic situation, the Department of Employment and Productivity commissioned an investigation of how individuals and communities dependent on 'declining industries' could be better supported, perhaps through redesigned regional policy. This was directed by Frank Herron of the University of Glasgow's Department of Economic and Social Research.[66]

The field work for Herron's study commenced as UCS entered liquidation in June 1971. A sample of 400 hundred redundant UCS workers was constructed based on the employer's occupational categories. Three hundred and twenty-eight were eventually interviewed. Two in three were skilled men from the finishing trades: plumbers and painters, electricians, joiners and polishers, or engineers and fitters. Only 6 per cent were skilled men from the shipbuilding trades. There were two explanations for this. First, UCS was moving towards greater standardisation of ship design, eliminating some of the craft labour associated with bespoke fitting-out operations. Second, it was believed that men with finishing skills were better equipped than others to adapt to occupational change.[67] The same assumption was held by observers of the industry on the Tyne, but in reality, shipbuilding workers with ostensibly transferable skills were historically reluctant to seek employment in

63 TNA, PREM 15/697, Upper Clyde Shipbuilders, 21 December 1970.
64 Tomlinson, *Managing the Economy*, pp. 145–8.
65 Herron, *Labour Market in Crisis*, p. 16.
66 TNA, LAB 110/33 Department of Employment; UCS redundancy; research University of Glasgow, S. J. Pickford, 24 May 1973, and A. B. Martin, 25 June 1973.
67 Herron, *Labour Market in Crisis*, pp. 12, 24.

other sectors.[68] Herron now detected an attitudinal shift. Many of the ex-finishing tradesmen from UCS were willing to work in another industry. They had internalised the policy-makers' moral economy entreaties for workers to be flexible and apply their skills, with some adaptation, in different environments. This accentuated the frustration and insecurity of their post-UCS employment experience. More than a quarter had found work that was less skilled, and 32 per cent received a wage cut of more than £4 a week in their first post-UCS job. The skilled men were especially frustrated, two-thirds reporting that they faced 'special disadvantages' when seeking work outside shipbuilding. They asserted that employers in other sectors did not recognise the extent of their skills: painting work in housebuilding was more varied, for example, than was believed to be the case in the shipyards.[69]

A related problem was unemployment. Among those interviewed 12 per cent had been unemployed continuously, with another 37 per cent out of work on two or more occasions. On average, a former UCS worker was unemployed for 36.9 per cent of the time between redundancy and interview. Further redundancy post-UCS was very common. Age aggravated this and other difficulties: those aged forty to forty-nine had on average been unemployed for 40.8 per cent of the period and those aged fifty to fifty-nine for 51.8 per cent.[70] In the economic circumstances of Clydeside, the policy-makers' moral-economy offer was not being fulfilled: workers were punished rather than rewarded for giving up jobs in established industries. The case of an ex-Fairfield fitter, born in 1928, encapsulated the survey's broad narrative of displaced and downwardly mobile redundant workers. He had left in May 1970 after twenty years with a lump sum of £100. Unemployed for eight out of thirteen months after redundancy, his earnings in intermittent jobs had been 10 per cent lower than at UCS.[71] With three daughters and three sons under the age of sixteen the fitter had been unable to provide for his family. 'It has shattered my plans', he said, using a bike instead of a car and relying on social security benefits to pay for his children's shoes.[72]

UCS entered liquidation on 14 June 1971, a week before the fitter was interviewed. Across the four yards 8,500 men faced the potential

68 Brown et al., 'The Contours of Solidarity', p. 20.
69 Herron, 'Redundancy and Redeployment', pp. 233–6, 245, 248.
70 Herron, *Labour Market in Crisis*, pp. 56–7, 81, 94, 164.
71 UG, GB 248, Social and Economic Research, Fitter, born 1928, interviewed 21 June 1971.
72 Herron, *Labour Market in Crisis*, p. 177.

precarity that he described, including 2,575 at Fairfield.[73] The immediate trigger was the government's refusal to extend credit to cover debts of £28 million, despite the order book being worth an estimated £87 million and an operational profit forecast for 1972.[74] This was comparable, in proportional terms, to the Fairfield order book of £32 million in October 1965, when the Labour government supported the Experiment. The Conservative government's decision was taken with full knowledge that this would 'incontestably add to the problems of the area, and will be a blow to confidence'.[75] These contrasting Labour and Conservative responses to financial crises in the shipyards contributed significantly to the political narrative and broader social memory in Scotland of deindustrialisation. The erosion of popular support for Unionism and Conservatism was embedded in the Heath government's apparent indifference to working-class economic security, symbolised by its willingness to tolerate the loss of production and employment on the Upper Clyde. The leaked 'Ridley memo' was an important pillar of this narrative. Written in 1969 by Nicholas Ridley, whom Heath appointed Under-Secretary of State at the Department of Trade and Industry in 1970, this stated that a government 'butcher' should dismember UCS and sell its assets cheaply to yards on the Lower Clyde. Ridley became a reviled figure: 'Scots on the Clyde', wrote Tam Dalyell in his obituary, 'were never so glad to see the back of any minister' when Heath removed him from office in 1972.[76]

The redundancy programme of 1969–70 had increased the average age of the UCS workforce. More than half of those who left were under the age of forty. More than half of those who remained were at least forty, and 30 per cent were at least fifty.[77] They knew that re-employment after redundancy was less likely with increased age. This was probably an important factor in generating resistance to closure. This was led by the joint shop stewards committee drawn from the four yards. A broad-based Scottish national counter-movement coalition was constructed and mobilised. The core moral-economy argument advanced by the stewards was that the government's adherence to market forces

73 UG, GB 248, ACCN 3613/1/1, Sir Robert Smith Diary, 15 June 1971.
74 Phillips, *Industrial Politics of Devolution*, pp. 90–2, Knox and McKinlay, *Jimmy Reid*, p. 99.
75 TNA, PREM 15/697, Burke Trend to the Prime Minister, 9 June and 12 June 1971.
76 Tam Dalyell, 'Obituary: Lord Ridley of Liddesdale, 1929–1993', *The Independent*, 6 March 1993.
77 Herron, *Labour Market in Crisis*, pp. 22, 58–9.

was both illogical and unjust. The order book showed demand for UCS products. Closure would inflict avoidable social costs on the communities of the Upper Clyde. 'We refuse to accept the philosophy that economics control men', argued Jimmy Reid; 'men must and shall control economics.'[78] The stewards embarked on a rigorous lobbying of government at Westminster. On 14 June a delegation, accompanied by STUC officials, met John Eden, Minister of Industry. Sammy Barr, a union convenor at Fairfield, said that the workers refused to accept the ending of shipbuilding on the Upper Clyde. Four hundred UCS workers travelled to Westminster on 16 June to support their stewards who met the Prime Minister. Reid told Heath there was no interest on the Upper Clyde for a selective 'reconstruction' of the industry, an approach the government was thought to favour. All four yards had to be kept open and the workforce retained intact.[79] Jimmy Airlie's famous summation proved prophetic: 'This government will be moved far more quickly than the men of the Clyde.'[80] The STUC supported the stewards in articulating the urgency of defending all four yards. A delegation led by Jimmy Milne and Alex Kitson told the Prime Minister on 21 June that the 'breaking up of the UCS complex' would not be tolerated in Scotland.[81]

The government ignored these entreaties. Davies appointed a small committee of four business leaders, mocked on the Clyde as 'the wise men', to make recommendations on the future of UCS. This committee reported on 29 July, recommending closure of the Clydebank and Scotstoun yards, with the redundancy of 4,000 men. Davies outlined the government's intention to adopt this course of action on the same day, with Airlie and other stewards following his statement from the public gallery in the House of Commons.[82] The stewards immediately put into action plans that they had developed for a novel form of resistance. A strike, placing the workers outside the yards and weakening their capacity to prevent the liquidation, would have been counter-productive. Instead, a work-in was conceived, accompanied by a demand for

78 Cinema Action, *UCS 1*.
79 TNA, PREM 15/697, Note for the Record. Minister for Industry's Meeting with Shop Stewards from UCS, 14 June 1971, and Note for the Record, 16 June 1971.
80 *The Times*, 17 June 1971.
81 TNA, PREM 15/697, Note for the Record. Prime Minister's Meeting with STUC Delegation, 21 June 1971.
82 Parliamentary Debates, Fifth Series, Commons, Vol. 822, Cols 791–801, 29 July 1971.

nationalisation.[83] The work-in commenced on Friday 30 July. Workers and their representatives assumed practical ownership of their yard and jobs, pledging to finish fourteen ships that were at various stages of construction. The emphasis on production was highly political. In their rhetorical interventions, Reid and other stewards frequently restated the centrality of industriousness to Clydesider identity. Reid's well-known 'no bevvying' speech was delivered in John Browns on 31 July.[84] This repeatedly contrasted the responsible workers who were defending jobs with the irresponsible policy-makers in Whitehall and Westminster who were destroying jobs. Foster and Woolfson's pioneering discussion showed that it was part of a practised rhetorical strategy, building support for the work-in by establishing the cultural and material seriousness of its intent.[85]

The stewards obtained a second hearing with the Prime Minister in his House of Commons office on 28 July 1971, as the government prepared to confirm the closure of Clydebank and Scotstoun. Reid warned Heath about the dangers of squandering the Clyde's heritage of skilled work and high-quality production, setting out the political and constitutional dimensions of the employment crisis. There 'was a need', he argued, 'for tangible, practical help for Scotland'. Airlie claimed that closure of the two yards would be so politically damaging that 'the Government will not be able to govern Scotland'.[86] The stewards carefully aligned the work-in with opposition to rising unemployment in Scotland. At a march in Glasgow on 18 August 1971 in support of the yards, estimated to have attracted 80,000 people, Reid said that 'we started fighting for jobs, and in a matter of days we knew we were fighting for Scotland and the British working-class movement'.[87] The counter-movement coalition in Scotland of labour, employers, MPs and civic leaders was gathered against market forces and Westminster decision-makers, whom Reid famously characterised as 'faceless men', remote physically and socially from the yards. In a private meeting with Heath in Glasgow in September Reid focused on the government's distance from the people

83 UG, DC 65/1, *UCS – the fight for the right to work*, by Alex Murray, Secretary, Scottish Committee, Communist Party of Great Britain (no date, presumed 1971).

84 Polly Toynbee, 'Takeover? No, it's a work-in, say Clydesiders', *The Observer*, 1 August 1971, p. 2.

85 John Foster and Charles Woolfson, *The Politics of the UCS Work-In: class alliances and the right to work* (London: Lawrence & Wishart, 1986), p. 200.

86 TNA, PREM 15/1242, Note of a Meeting with UCS Shop Stewards held at the House of Commons on 28 July 1971.

87 Knox and McKinlay, *Jimmy Reid*, p. 119.

whose lives were adversely affected by policy decisions.[88] Socialist and counter-cultural as well as trade union support for the work-in followed. A bouquet of roses and a cheque for £5,000 came from Yoko Ono and John Lennon. Other supportive campaigners included Frank Field of the Child Poverty Action Group, and the Institute for Workers' Control. Field's analysis of the social security costs of closure alone, rising to £20 million over the first three years, was published by the Institute in its 'social audit'. This critiqued in moral-economy terms the narrow financial criteria applied by the government when establishing the 'viability' of an industrial enterprise.[89]

Behind this visible and vigorous public campaigning, the work-in was a complex operation. The role of the official liquidator, Robert Smith, in maintaining supplies, cash to creditors and wages to workers, was underestimated at the time and has often been forgotten since.[90] He interacted carefully and effectively with the stewards, despite inauspicious beginnings at the start of the work-in. A group of stewards at Linthouse told him on 30 July, the Friday, that he was not welcome in any of the yards. On Sunday evening, 1 August, Smith visited by invitation the Great Western Road home of David McNee, Chief Constable of the City of Glasgow Police. McNee advised Smith to arrive at Linthouse the following morning with a squad of police officers. Smith saw this as unnecessary and declined the offer. His instincts were correct. Early on 2 August, two stewards met Smith at the Linthouse gate and took him to the UCS offices. Several minutes later a group of stewards arrived and apologised to Smith for his treatment on the previous Friday. They confirmed that Smith would not be impeded in going about his business in any of the yards. This underlined the commitment of the UCS stewards to the 'responsible' preservation of property and public order.[91]

Smith learned later that the stewards' change in attitude was a result of Jimmy Airlie's intervention. Airlie had still been in London on Friday 30 July after attending the House of Commons on the preceding afternoon. Back in Glasgow and hearing about the bad-tempered meeting between the stewards and Smith, Airlie demanded that the liquidator

---

88 TNA, PREM 15/1242, Note for the Record: Prime Minister's Visit to Glasgow, 13 September 1971.
89 UG, DC 65/50, UCS: *The Social Audit: A Special Report by the Institute for Workers' Control*, Pamphlet Number 26 (Nottingham: IWC, no date).
90 Knox and McKinlay, *Jimmy Reid*, pp. 100–2.
91 UG, GB 248, ACCN 3613/1/1, Sir Robert Smith Diary, 30 July to 2 August 1971.

be welcomed on the Monday.[92] Smith's achievements were substantial. Deep into the work-in, in December 1971, he was providing wages for 7,300 workers still officially employed at UCS. Only 933 men, 243 from Fairfield, had been made redundant. The fundraising effort marshalled by the stewards was immensely important, but provided maintenance for only about 11 per cent of those employed at the start of the work-in.[93] Six months later, in June 1972, on the near-anniversary of the firm's collapse, 6,882 men were still on Smith's payroll.[94] Smith, reflecting four decades later in conversation with Alan McKinlay, stressed that management remained in charge of the yard and that the stewards had not taken control. In this sense he described the work-in as a powerful myth that had 'enormous symbolic power'.[95] He nevertheless accepted the shop stewards' committee as a 'legitimate player' inside UCS and a pragmatic co-existence was developed.[96]

Heath's government was pressured into reversing its position. Through major state investment three of the four UCS yards were kept open and 6,000 men kept in work.[97] The work-in officially ended in October 1972 when negotiations over the acquisition of John Browns by US-owned Marathon Oil were completed. While the UCS shop stewards had not achieved their objective of saving all four yards, the work-in was a significant victory for the working-class moral economy. The perception of righteous struggle and victory in 1971–2 was central to the strengthening of Clydesider identity. Alan Glover's father was part of a large UCS delegation that petitioned MPs at Westminster, probably on 16 June 1971 as the stewards discussed the crisis with Heath. The work-in is a core element of Alan's family and personal history. In his narrative the measured and disciplined nature of the struggle was plain:

> I remember my dad going down with the big demonstration, with Jimmy Airlie, Jimmy Reid. And there was trains, there were actually trains chartered, that left Glasgow Central Station, with pipers, it was on the news, et cetera. And I remember my dad telling me that, erm, Tony Benn, the

92 UG, GB 248, ACCN 3613/1/5, clipping, Chris Baur, 'UCS: the men and the myths', *Weekend Scotsman*, 27 June 1981.
93 TNA, LAB 108/17, UCS Labour Force, December 1971.
94 UG, GB 248, ACCN 3613/1/5, Sir Robert Smith, The UCS Work-in In Perspective.
95 Smith, interview with McKinlay, quoted in Knox and McKinlay, *Jimmy Reid*, p. 129.
96 UG, GB 248, ACCN 4039, Film of Sir Robert Smith Witness Seminar, University of Glasgow, Centre for Business History in Scotland, August 2012.
97 Foster and Woolfson, 'How Workers on the Clyde Gained the Capacity for Class Struggle'.

Labour MP, he was very supportive of the, the campaign. And, erm, they were all marching down towards Downing Street, and there was agitators there, they were getting hussled, and shoved, et cetera. And Tony Benn, and Jimmy Reid, and that, says, keep the order, lads, keep the order. And they kept the order. And my dad said, as we rounded round to Downing Street, there was about twenty black marias, big police vans. Because that's what they're hoping for . . . they're hoping for people to riot, create disorder, then they can point the finger and say, look at these working-class scum, right. And they're not working-class scum. And again, if it wasn't for the likes of . . . I don't, I'm gonna be honest with you. For example, the UCS work-in, I don't think it was the politicians that, erm, saved that, the shipbuilding, it was the men. It was the men. And it was the men that not only led it, but the men believed in the fight. And I've got nothing but, erm . . . I'm getting emotional. I've got nothing but, erm, total admiration for them.[98]

Benny McGoogan joined Fairfield as a plater in 1975, becoming a full-time shop steward in 1979 and then a health and safety manager. Like Alan, Benny also learned from the men who had been involved in the work-in. His testimony drew out the working-class moral-economy view of shipyard employment as a vital communal resource that anti-deindustrialisation resistance preserved:

Ah, Big Jimmy's [Airlie] a great big guy. Brilliant . . . brilliant, the guy. [. . .] I mean, you're only a young guy, twenty-five, and here's a guy in his forties . . . you know, who's seen it, done it and bought the t-shirt. Come right through the UCS crisis . . . Along wi Jimmy Reid and all the other people. So you're, kind of, looking up to these guys . . . er, and wealth of experience. Worldly wise. Er, won't gie you bad advice. Only gie you good advice. Um, and again people like that, from the shop stewards' movement in here, we'd one focus and the focus was to keep this shipyard open. Because we all looked on it at . . . every job we've got in here . . . my job as a plater, it wasn't my job. I was only holding that temporarily until I decided that I wasn't wanting to hold that job and it was not my own but to pass it on to the generation coming behind me. So the number one priority in here for all the shop stewards and all the convenors, the joint shop stewards' committee, was to keep the shipyard open.[99]

Benny's words bear repetition and emphasis: '*It wasn't my job. I was only holding that temporarily until I decided that I wasn't wanting to hold that job and it was not my own but to pass it on to the generation*

98 Glover, Interview.
99 Benny McGoogan, Interview with VW, Fairfield Heritage Centre, 25 October 2017.

coming behind me.' This was fundamental to the articulation and defence of economic security in Scotland during the long process of deindustrialisation. The UK government – comprised of apparently unsympathetic Tory metropolitans – was forced by the collective action of workers and their supporters to relent, and part-fund the retention of shipbuilding on the Upper Clyde. Jobs were saved and other industrial communities inspired to fight to defend the 'right to work' claimed by the shipyard trade union representatives. As a 'usable past' in subsequent struggles against deindustrialisation, the work-in was without equal in late twentieth-century Scotland.[100]

NATIONALISATION AND PRIVATISATION

The work-in contributed to an important change in Labour Party policy, with Benn and others accepting the trade union argument that the shipbuilding industry should be nationalised. UCS had demonstrated the failure of private capital to marshal the resources needed for modernised production and stable employment. Capital assets per worker in the UK sector were reckoned by a UK Labour–trade union working party to be £825, but £1,000 in West Germany, £1,200 in Italy, £1,800 in Sweden and £2,800 in Japan. Nationalisation followed Labour's re-election with British Shipbuilders Plc formed in 1977.[101] This was a prime example of the Labour government's commitment to safeguard working-class security as the growth of employment in other manufacturing sectors stalled, a moral-economy process examined in Chapters 2 and 3. Working-class leaders in Scotland compelled policy-makers to reinvest in the staple industries. With the 'retreat' of multinational investors in assembly goods, shipbuilding employment on the Clyde – like mining jobs in the coalfields – became even more important.

Former workers remember the era of public ownership at Fairfield as the 'best years in the yard'. Ownership consciousness was further strengthened: 'it wis oor yard', remembers Davie Torrance. Nationalisation was accompanied by enhanced worker voice, with Joint Production Committees resembling the structures adopted during the

---

100 Michael Bailey, 'Changing Tides of Industrial Democracy: Red Clydeside and the UCS Work-In as Political Heritage', *International Journal of Heritage Studies*, 25.12 (2019), pp. 1319–88.
101 UG, DC 65/45, Nationalisation of Shipbuilding, Ship-Repair and Marine Engineering: Joint Statement, Joint Working Party, Labour Party, Trades Union Congress, Confederation of Shipbuilding and Engineering Unions, etc.

Fairfield experiment. Davie, a full-time union steward by this point, saw this joint regulation as consolidating the gains of the work-in:

> The Govan Shipbuilders [Fairfield division of the nationalised corporation] was excellent . . . because the . . . legacy carried on. But the shop stewards' committee were fully . . . [. . .] part o what . . . the production team . . . You know, we had production committees once again same as we had in Fairfield Glasgow. [. . .] And Govan Shipbuilders, right [. . .] we were still nationalised. A guy called Eric Mackie was in and he's . . . he was the understudy to Bill Gallacher . . . a couple a wild men but really, really good to work wi, I kid you not . . . Magic guys. They . . . well Mackie told us straight. He says, I . . . I'm sent here to shut yous doun, by the way. [. . .] And he says, I've just walked roond this place. He says, this place is magic. And he says, I can dae something with this place. [. . .] So him and Gallacher worked . . . with us . . . and you could knock the door and go, eh Bill, we've got a problem. Or Eric. What's the story, you know.[102]

Davie's testimony might be characterised as a counter-hegemonic view of the 1970s, insulated from the declinist narratives of union power, inefficient industry and disempowered management that tend to predominate popular memory of the decade.[103] His composed collective memory of working-class and trade union solidarity is disrupted, however, by an important dispute in the winter of 1977–8, shortly after nationalisation. The Labour government had secured a contract with the Polish government for the construction and delivery of a fleet of twenty-four military vessels, worth £110 million. Fairfield was contracted to supply ten of these, with Swan Hunter on the Tyne committed to seven and the rest shared between Caledon Robb in Dundee and Scott Lithgow on the Lower Clyde. Underlying issues in the dispute that followed were the chronic shortage of production at Govan,[104] and the absence of pay parity within British Shipbuilders. In December 1977 around 1,700 out-fitting workers at Swan Hunter enforced an overtime ban in pursuit of parity with other yards, including Fairfield. Some workers and union officials in Govan then prioritised their local welfare before solidarity with the Tynesiders by accepting the transfer of four ships from Swan

102 Torrance, Interview.
103 Andy Beckett, *When The Lights Went Out: What Really Happened to Britain in the Seventies* (London: Faber & Faber, 2009).
104 TNA, T 369/223, D. le B. Jones, Cabinet Office, to Chancellor of the Exchequer, 21 June 1977, and T 369/224, Department of Industry, Anglo-Polish Shipbuilding Deal, 26 September 1977.

Hunter.[105] Alex Wright remembers the internal union and workforce divisions at Fairfield revealed by this episode:

> And they had went out on strike, and it was quite a bad dispute. And there were boilermakers, welders, platers, like, like ourselves, and they went out on strike. And we were being told, because it was a multi-yard order, that since they went on strike, the two [sic] vessels they were contracted to build, should, they were wanting the British, the ship-owners, was wanting those ships transferred to Glasgow. This was a very heated debate. There were people that, our fellow union members in the same union as us, we shouldn't be taking those ships off them. And I remember the convenor at the time, who was the convenor at the time of the work-in, probably the second man in charge there, erm, he said, we're taking the ships here. If they don't want to build them, it'll give us extra work. And he was a CP member, he was a Communist Party member. [. . .] But he said, if they're not, there's a danger of losing the vessels to someone outwith British Shipbuilders. We have the capacity to do those vessels, and it could even be advantageous to us for recruiting staff, and for extra hours. And we took those vessels . . . and that hit the news, it hit the news positively, north of the border . . . on BBC Scotland, and such like was, oh the Govan Yard. They were like that, it was very positive how unions were changing in some respect.

The convenor was Jimmy Airlie. Alex misremembers the workers being boilermakers rather than outfitting trades, but the principle was unambiguous: in taking the ships from Tyneside, 'we were virtually breaking a strike'. The mass meeting to discuss this had been 'very heated' with 'people actually going up to the front, to cry the convenor, saying that, this is, they are fellow boilermakers, and fellow union members, and all that, we should not be accepting these ships'. It was 'a very split meeting' and the shop stewards 'literally split the hall, where if you wanted to vote for it, you went left, and if you wanted to vote against it, you went right. And even as we moved, we couldn't tell who was winning this'. The ships came to Govan and Alex 'felt for the guys down in Newcastle'.[106]

Davie Torrance was part of a Govan delegation led by Airlie that discussed the situation with union representatives in Newcastle. He offers a moral-economy defence of the decision to take the ships. The leading Tyneside representative had stated: 'Yous can take the boats if you want [. . .] So we took the boats.' Davie nevertheless concedes that 'we got shit for backstabbing. But we said, we've got an agreement [laugh].

105 *The Guardian*, 1 December 1977, p. 17; *The Times*, 3 December 1977, p. 2.
106 Wright, Interview.

That said, take the boats.'[107] Press reports indicate that the Swan Hunter stewards had in fact asked the Govan workers to black the ships.[108] Airlie stated baldly that 'it is our view that all the twenty-four vessels must, and will be built in British yards. Any barriers or problems that jeopardise all or part of that order must be removed.'[109] Airlie combined the prioritisation of local interests in Govan with a defence of the publicly owned industry in Britain more broadly. The future of British Shipbuilders would be compromised if the Polish government did not receive the contracted ships. There was the familiar Clydesider emphasis on 'responsibility' in this decision, which was noted favourably in the media, as Alex notes in his reference to BBC Scotland coverage, and evidenced in UK print reporting too. *The Guardian*'s correspondent characterised Fairfield as 'the shipyard that abolished trouble'. An unnamed trade union representative was quoted: 'we know what it's like to fight for work [. . .] I'm not criticising the lads on Tyneside but they probably have not been through what we have.'[110] Swan Hunter ultimately lost seven ships, an order worth £52 million. The four ships that came to Govan were bigger than those allotted in the original contract and undoubtedly provided more security for the Clydeside workers.[111]

The nature of the Polish contract pointed to another important shift in the 1970s. Employment stability and working-class security were increasingly reliant on producing military vessels for government contracts rather than civilian vessels for commercial operators. Alex reflects:

> In terms of getting further work towards the end of British Shipbuilders, I think you actually paid for an order. Not just the Govan Yard, but it had become part of the nationalised British Shipbuilding industry. Where they actually paid the Polish Government, the then Communist Polish Government, to build various sizes of coal vessels. And that was to, you know, for the Gdansk Yard, and such like. We found it puzzling because the Poles had their own shipbuilding industry, but it kept us busy in work. And, you know, those vessels were quite small compared to what we were doing, and we could see that, you know, our ability to compete in the marketplace was getting severely, you know, tested.[112]

107 Torrance, Interview.
108 *The Times*, 2 December 1977, p. 21.
109 *The Times*, 6 December 1977, p. 17.
110 *The Guardian*, 1 December 1977, p. 17.
111 TNA, T 369/224, Eric Varley to Prime Minister, 28 November 1977.
112 Wright, Interview.

The transition to the 1980s – the third phase of deindustrialisation identified in Chapters 2 and 3 – was therefore contentious. The Thatcher governments placed severe pressure on the working-class moral economy. Govan workers resisted, demonstrating solidarity with workers in other nationalised industries at risk. Benny McGoogan notes that 'the Thatcher government were not for the working-class'. He empathised with the great strike of 1984–5 to 'keep mines open, to keep people in jobs'. This was because mining localities are 'communities just like a shipyard. The community out there in Govan got built up around this shipyard . . . So it's the same wi a mine.' In his opinion, 'it just seemed to be every month the Thatcher government were having a go with some industry'.[113]

These changing economic and political circumstances affected the intelligible moral order of the yard. An important change for the worse identified by Benny was an ending to the practice of younger men taking a greater burden of difficult work – up ladders, welding in tight corners – from older men. In the new environment, management required intensive output from all workers.[114] Redundancy was encouraged in the early 1980s, with British Shipbuilders providing some support for workers seeking transition into alternative employment. Alex Wright trained as an HGV driver at the nationalised corporation's expense. This resembled the retraining initiatives for Caterpillar workers noted in Chapter 2, secured through collective pressure on the employer, symbolising the broader economic transition from production to services.[115] Voluntary redundancy was accepted by many in Fairfield, especially older men. They faced similar difficulties to those encountered by redundant men in 1970–1. Staying in the yard, however, was becoming less attractive, with the real value of wages falling by the mid-1980s. This was the main reason that Alex left in 1984, working as a driver for a security firm before establishing a career in financial services. Alan Glover took another route, becoming a welding inspector within the Govan yard before applying for a job at the Ministry of Defence in 1989 where he was still working in the late 2010s.

British Shipbuilders was privatised by increments from 1984. The Govan yard was sold in 1988 to the Norwegian shipping firm Kvaerner. The negative consequences of privatisation were emphasised by many former workers. Tam Brady says that Kvaerner 'came in to impose

---

113 McGoogan, Interview.
114 McGoogan, Interview.
115 Wright, Interview.

their own way o' working and they did so. And they were quite, quite authoritarian from the top down.' Five hundred men were made redundant, so that by 1990 the workforce was down to 1,600, just more than half the strength of the yard in the early 1970s. Kvaerner attempted to diminish union voice: they were 'very, very anti-union', remembers Tam, and 'if you didnae like it, tough'. A new three-shift working system was introduced in 1992, which disrupted family life and reduced overtime wages.[116] It attacked the workers' sense of being well-paid craftsmen in the Clydeside tradition. A strike against the changes was rebuffed by the firm. Those who took part were sacked and rehired on even less attractive conditions. The new environment was extremely hostile, as Tam recalls: 'The threat, and you're sacked by the way, cheerio. We were all panicking, you know, we were all flappin.' But the yard stayed open, and collective bargaining was not eradicated. Union convenors lost powers to negotiate but retained rights of consultation on various issues, which they asserted to maximum effect.[117] These were fundamentally positive motifs in the memories of those who remained as well as of those who left. In 1999 Kvaerner, facing financial difficulties, put the yard up for sale. It was acquired by BAE Systems, and has operated continuously since, mainly working on military contracts with the UK Ministry of Defence.[118]

Employment conditions changed radically from the 1980s onwards. Brian Glen entered Fairfield as an apprentice welder with his friend Alan Glover in the early 1970s, left in the 1980s and then returned in the early 2000s. Brian's optimistic narrative emphasised the positive improvements still being won by union organisation in the twenty-first century, especially in the vital area of health and safety. Superior welfare, catering and leisure facilities reinforced the continued value of union voice in the Govan workplace.[119] The yard also retained political importance in Scotland. Workers and their union representatives did not lose their capacity to use the symbolic importance of shipbuilding on the Clyde as leverage when seeking new contracts in the 2010s. Davie Torrance argues that when Kvaerner was in difficulty in 1999, he fought for a purchaser because 'it's oor yard. Employers come and go. The shop

116 Brady, Interview.
117 Alan McKinlay and Philip Taylor, 'Privatisation and Industrial Relations in British Shipbuilding', *Industrial Relations Journal*, 25.4 (1994), pp. 293–304, with detail at pp. 301–2.
118 Bobby Gordon, Interview with VW, Fairfield Heritage Centre, 5 October 2017.
119 Brian Glen, Interview with VW, Fairfield Heritage Centre, 12 October 2017.

stewards carry on.'[120] The Clydesider identity survived along with the yard. It was a life-long positive resource for those who entered the yard as young men in the 1970s. The intelligible moral order of their youth stayed with them as older men, shaping attitudes and action in subsequent workplaces. When the Ministry of Defence Office in Glasgow was threatened with closure, Alan took inspiration from the UCS work-in:

> What I did is, and I'm not allowed to do it as a civil service, I met with journalists. [. . .] But we wrote to our MPs, I made template letters up with parliamentary questions getting asked. We had total solidarity. And I kept saying to the workers in our place, we're not dead yet, right. And we won the fight, we kept the jobs in Glasgow. We're actually recruiting staff. And that, that only happened because I'm convinced of it, and I'm not, I don't say this lightly. This only happened because of the background and the upbringing I had . . . working in Govan. And even guys that I worked beside, like Alec Fairlie, he even said that, he said, that, that's the Govan coming out in you, right. [. . .] And I, I'm not, I, I don't want to sound like romantic, like a . . . Barbara Cartland story. But because of my education, in Govan . . . and my, the way my father was, and seeing the way Jimmy Reid [. . .] you know, shipbuilding's not just shipbuilding, it's a social thing. It goes beyond the shipyard. And now we're in the twenty-first century, and I've used tools that I picked up from the shipyard . . . not as a welder, but used them in my current employment. And I think that's . . . that's learning, that's learning . . . you know.

The work-in was never far from the minds of these men when discussing the lessons of the shipyard. Alan spoke warmly about mentoring younger workers, 'using the tools' picked up in the yard. Benny, Tam, Alex and Brian all described similar experiences of taking younger male workers 'under their wing' and passing on knowledge about their job and 'how to conduct yourself', just as they had learned from their elders in Govan. The Clydesider identity was still being transmitted across generations in the 2010s. This was a positive legacy of shipbuilding, 'a social thing', in Alan's words, that survived six decades of deindustrialisation. Clydesider culture bridged the incomplete passage from industrial to post-industrial society. In the 2010s it enabled workers to assuage the negative effects of deindustrialisation, such as low pay and authoritarian employers.[121]

120 Torrance, Interview.
121 Strangleman, 'Deindustrialisation', 472.

CONCLUSION

The employment culture of the Upper Clyde shipyards was challenged by deindustrialisation. Fairfield and the other yards became central sites of working-class moral-economy resistance to industrial job loss in the 1960s and 1970s. The sovereignty of market forces was challenged by the representatives of workers who faced redundancy: 'men must and shall control economics', said Jimmy Reid during the work-in. Reid's reference to the agency of men was telling. The yards were a highly masculine environment, and the defence of shipbuilding employment was unarguably geared to protecting the gender privileges of skilled male workers. The social basis of this resistance was nevertheless not entirely homogeneous. A Polanyian counter-movement coalition encompassing employers and policy-makers as well as workers was evident on the Upper Clyde. This involved clear national interests, with deindustrialisation characterised as a threat to Scotland as a whole and not just to the shipbuilding communities immediately affected. Decisive force was nevertheless provided by the culture of skilled male workers that was jeopardised by the contraction of shipbuilding. Job losses in the yards were accepted in the 1950s and early 1960s, just as they were in coal mining, on the grounds that employment alternatives, equivalent in pay and status, were both available and growing. The moral-economy calculus changed from the mid-1960s, however, as the acceleration of industrial diversification stalled. The real value of shipyard employment appreciated in labour market terms, and opposition to its further erosion stiffened.

The Labour government's intervention to support the Fairfield Experiment in 1965 raised expectations about the potential for state protection of the industry on the Upper Clyde. In emphasising the value of union voice and workforce participation in the organisation of production, the Experiment increased ownership consciousness among employees. These moral-economy expectations were central to the longevity and success of the UCS work-in six years later. The defence of economic security in an area of above-average unemployment was mobilised in the language of nation, with Scotland imperilled. But class interests were deftly interwoven. The legitimacy of private ownership and market forces was challenged and overturned. Heath's Conservative government was forced into a policy U-turn, funding capitalisation of three of the yards under reconstructed private ownership; and the Labour government, moved in large part by the work-in, nationalised the industry a few years later. The distinct approaches of Conservative and

Labour governments to the Upper Clyde contributed to the significant longer-term political shift in Scotland, apparent in the 1960s and 1970s, and consolidated in the 1980s. Conservatives – the 'faceless' Tories – became associated with unfeeling disregard for the social consequences of market forces. Labour, by contrast, was identified with a continued commitment to defending working-class economic security through the protection so far as was possible of industrial employment. Thatcher's government privatised shipbuilding. At Fairfield there were job losses and reduced trade union rights in the workplace. Collective bargaining nevertheless survived. This reflected the Clydesider identity. Working-class agency was vital in maintaining the existence of shipbuilding in Govan deep into the twenty-first century.

5

Linwood, Renfrewshire: Car Manufacturing and Scotland's Political Divergence from England

The Linwood car plant in Renfrewshire opened in 1963. It offered an important employment outlet for workers squeezed out of the contracting staple industries, including shipbuilding. Linwood was less than ten miles from the Fairfield yard in Govan. Making cars differed from building ships in three important respects. First, the labour process was organised around the mass manufacture of semi-standard products. Second, market fluctuations had a more immediate bearing on production and employment volumes. Shipyard workers were often made redundant with the launching of a vessel or conclusion of a contract, an important factor in the bowler versus bunnet culture, but motor industry employees were even more vulnerable, as firms cut payrolls in response to short-run falls in demand. Third, US ownership of Linwood under Chrysler from 1967 to 1978 shaped a distinct style of management, less formal in personal-social terms than that of the shipyards but in some ways more authoritarian. These distinct elements of production tested the Clydeside workers' moral code, which was transmitted to Linwood through the migration of workers from Glasgow and elsewhere in Clydeside. Craft culture nevertheless had agency in the plant, and was frequently asserted. Workers constructed a strong trade union organisation. Elements of social continuity were also present in the communities that developed around the plant. Migrants were accommodated in purpose-built local authority housing in Linwood and the adjacent settlement of Johnstone. Working-class social life was highly communal in these towns, pursued in clubs and bars, and in recreational facilities attached to the plant, which workers played a key role in organising. There was limited evidence of the type of home-centred social life associated with the 'affluent' workers of assembly goods manufacturing in southern England.

Linwood's history contributed to the political divergence between Scotland and England examined in Chapter 2. The car plant was established through UK regional policy. The size of the workforce fluctuated, rising to peaks of 9,000 in the late 1960s and late 1970s, with intermittent redundancies frustrating moral-economy expectations of employment stability and financial security. Chrysler threatened closure within a wider strategy of withdrawing from the UK in 1975. This was resisted by workers and their union and political representatives, who pressed the Labour government for action to preserve Linwood. As with the UCS in 1969, this involved subsidy in exchange for redundancy and the reconstruction of production, reinforcing expectations of future security. These were transgressed in 1981, when the Conservative government made no effort to prevent closure by Linwood's subsequent owner, Peugeot-Citroen (PSA). Labour's policy effort in pursuit of working-class economic security, reviewed in Chapter 2, was popular in Scotland. Linwood's closure, a significant element in the larger acceleration of deindustrialisation after 1979, contributed to the sharper fall in support for Conservatism in Scotland.

The chapter is structured in four parts. The moral-economy expectations cultivated at Linwood are examined first, and then analysis moves to employment conditions and conflicts in the plant. The Labour government's rescue of Chrysler and the plant in 1975 is detailed in the third part, followed by the Conservative government's toleration of closure in 1981.

LINWOOD AND MORAL-ECONOMY EXPECTATIONS

Rootes Motors, the original operator at Linwood from 1963, was based in the West Midlands hub of English car manufacturing, in Coventry. In the 1950s Rootes operated in an expanding consumer market. Rootes wanted to meet demand by opening a new factory in the West Midlands, but was directed instead by the Conservative government to locate in Renfrewshire.[1] Harold Macmillan, the Prime Minister, was persuaded in 1960 by John Maclay, the Secretary of State for Scotland, that 'spending generously' to locate car manufacturing in Scotland would be valuable economically and politically. Maclay's officials argued that this would help to correct Scottish historical over-reliance on a small number of industries. The presence of 'actual car manufacture' at Linwood would be

---

1 J. F. B. Goodman and P. J. Samuel, 'The Motor Industry in a Development District', *British Journal of Industrial Relations*, 4 (1966), pp. 336–65.

'a real industrial "break-through"', representing an 'essential part of the whole' strategy for Scotland's manufacturing diversification, with multiplier effects through demand for steel, components and other supplies.[2]

The Scottish Council for Development and Industry, the coalition of manufacturers and local authority officials introduced in Chapter 2, strongly supported Linwood. Timing was important. Employment in the staple industries was falling and male unemployment a public policy concern. The Scottish Council, using Ministry of Labour data, noted in April 1959 that there were 20,330 unemployed men of working age in Glasgow and 4,420 in Renfrewshire. More than 40,000 across the Clyde valley as whole were looking for work, and a growing proportion were under twenty-five years of age. The car plant would absorb a sizable portion of the jobless. Maclay and his officials emphatically endorsed this argument.[3] Rootes indicated in November 1961 to government and local authority officials that labour requirements at Linwood would build over ten years to 11,000 in car manufacturing with another 5,250 at the existing Pressed Steel facility, where vehicle bodies were already being produced, along with railway carriages.[4]

The primary role of government policy along with the promise of a new future was remembered by former Linwood employees when interviewed in the late 2010s. Ian Stobo was a logistics manager at the plant. He emphasised that 'Rootes was a political decision', reached by the government because 'work was needed in the area'. This was welcomed by people in Renfrewshire: 'we were all delighted, that was work'. But 'if it [the decision] had been left to Rootes', then the firm would have 'extended [operations in] Coventry'.[5] These foundational circumstances cultivated contrasting expectations. The employer believed that workers would be grateful enough for employment to tolerate wages below the Midlands standard. This was not so, however, with workers anticipating national industry standards. Working-class expectations were further elevated, as elsewhere in Scotland, by the involvement of public money in establishing the plant. The total start-up investment by central

2 NRS, SEP 4/1662, Scottish Home Department, Note for Secretary of State for Scotland's meeting with the Prime Minister, 16 June 1960.
3 NRS, SEP 4/1663, SCDI, Memorandum on Motor Car Manufacture in Scotland, 30 December 1959.
4 NRS, SEP 4/3991, Department of Health for Scotland, Note of a Meeting with Rootes Group and Pressed Steel, Linwood, 9 November 1961.
5 Ian Stobo, Interview with VW, Paisley, 15 November 2017.

government amounted to £23 million.[6] High volumes of a new model, the Hillman Imp, were assembled at Linwood with this support.[7] The public stake grew. A Board of Trade loan of £7.85 million in 1966 enabled increased manufacture on-site: of car bodies, engine blocks and a larger number of components.[8] The government also authorised a major change in ownership. Chrysler obtained a minority share in Rootes in 1964 and was permitted to obtain a controlling interest in 1967.[9] These changes represented progress given Linwood's initial reliance on supplies from manufacturers in the Midlands. The first Imps were built with Rootes engines made in Coventry and Sankey wheels from Wolverhampton, plus bumpers and other assorted components from Rubery Owen in Darlaston, near Walsall.[10] The value of expansion in 1966–7 was amplified by the stalling of industrial development and growth of unemployment. James Jack, STUC General Secretary, described Chrysler's acquisition of Linwood as 'very significant for Scotland. It is the best news we have had for a long time'.[11]

Public investment extended to the formation of new communities that housed the Linwood workforce. This was part of a broader pattern of housing reformation in the west of Scotland in the 1950s and 1960s, involving the movement of people from inner-city Glasgow to new-built peripheral housing schemes, notably Drumchapel to the north and Castlemilk to the south,[12] and to the New Towns of Lanarkshire, East Kilbride and Cumbernauld, plus the more distant Irvine in Ayrshire, Livingston in West Lothian and Glenrothes in Fife. Linwood's population quadrupled from 2,500 in 1961 to 10,500 in 1971, then doubled to 23,000 in 1981. Large-scale construction of local authority housing was involved,[13] with Renfrew County Council in November 1961 identifying

6 NRS, SEP 4/3991, Board of Trade, Note on aid/assistance to Rootes, no date, but probably August 1962.
7 Films of Scotland and the Rootes Group, 'Young in Heart', producer David Walsh, Glasgow Films, 1963, at https://movingimage.nls.uk/film/1480, accessed 21 December 2020.
8 TNA, FV 44/17, Agreement between Board of Trade and Rootes Pressings, 1 July 1966.
9 TNA, FV 44/17, I. J. Minett, Chrysler Group Vice President to Anthony Wedgwood Benn, Minister of Technology, 16 January 1967.
10 NRS, SEP 4/3991, N. R. Rennie, Board of Trade, Note of Visit to Linwood, 10 August 1962.
11 NRS, SEP 4/2402, clipping, 'Linwood Car Plant Set for Big New Expansion', The Scotsman, 9 March 1967.
12 Lynn Abrams, Ade Kearns, Barry Hazley and Valerie Wright, High-Rise Homes, Estates and Communities in the Post-War Period (London: Routledge, 2020).
13 Elspeth Farmer and Roger Smith, 'Overspill Theory: A Metropolitan Case Study', Urban Studies, 12 (1975), pp. 151–68.

a need for 6,500 new homes.[14] Two new housing schemes were added to the neighbouring settlement of Johnstone along with the expansion of Linwood. Local authority tenure in the Renfrew local authority area grew from 47.8 per cent of households in 1961 to 56.2 per cent in 1971 and 63.1 per cent in 1981. This easily exceeded the rate in 1981 for Glasgow of 53.9 per cent and Scotland of 54.6 per cent.[15]

A high proportion of nuclear families lived in these new schemes. Joe Reilly, who moved to Johnstone from Govan in Glasgow's inner city to work as a welder on the assembly line, remembers that Linwood workers 'all had two point five kids'. He saw this as part of an unofficial employment strategy adopted by Rootes and perpetuated by Chrysler for controlling the plant. Lost income through sick leave or even dismissal was less damaging for workers with larger families, cushioned by greater social security provision, or those with no children at all.[16] This perspective is confirmed in interviews with former employees undertaken by Cliff Lockyer and Lesley Baddon of the University of Strathclyde in 1984–5. An ex-member of the training department said, 'we were told to avoid young single men, eh they wanted steady family people'.[17] In this practice Chrysler followed other US car manufacturers, recruiting workers 'scientifically' through personnel management departments that sifted job applications to identify workers deemed compliant by family and material circumstances.[18] Joe was newly married when he started at Linwood, moving into a new local authority house. There was no realistic prospect of obtaining a similar home in Glasgow, where he and his wife were starting married life in a rented tenement flat:

> We were a young couple, and the way out of it was either to, um, move abroad, which some of my relations did or the overspill, and some of my relations had moved to Cumbernauld [seventeen miles north-east of Govan] and

14 NRS, SEP 4/3991, Department of Health for Scotland, Note of a Meeting with Rootes Group and Pressed Steel, Linwood, 9 November 1961.
15 General Register Office (Scotland), *Census 1961: Scotland. County Report: Renfrew* (Edinburgh: HMSO, 1964), Table 15; *Census 1971: Scotland. Economic Activity. County Report: Renfrew* (Edinburgh: HMSO, 1972), Table 22; *Census 1981: Scotland. Regional Reports. Volume One, Strathclyde* (Edinburgh: HMSO, 1982), Table 27; General Register Office (Scotland), *Census 1981: Scottish Summary* (Edinburgh: HMSO, 1983).
16 Joe Reilly, Interview with VW, Johnstone, 7 December 2017.
17 University of Strathclyde Archives and Special Collections (USASC), SOHC 001022, Cliff Lockyer and Lesley Baddon's conversations with workers at the former Linwood car plant, 1981–5.
18 Wolfgang Streeck, 'Through Unending Halls', *London Review of Books*, 7 February 2019, pp. 29–31.

places like that . . . and I thought, no, that's the back of beyond, used to take about two days on the bus and train to get to Cumbernauld, you know? So I opted for to get a job in Chrysler [. . .] . I thought, a brand-new house, no-one had ever lived in it, and that's for me, so that's how I ended up in Johnstone.[19]

The impression of a young community organised around the plant is reinforced by data collated by Strathclyde Regional Council in December 1975 when Chrysler was threatening to abandon Linwood. Only 12 per cent of the workforce was fifty or older, compared with over 25 per cent of the economically active male population of Strathclyde Region as a whole. Seven in ten workers lived in Linwood or neighbouring Paisley and Johnstone, and two in ten travelled daily from Glasgow. In Linwood half the employed population worked for Chrysler,[20] and locals referred to it as 'Rootesville', despite the change of ownership in 1967.[21]

The citizens of Linwood were characterised as the 'new Clydesiders' by Séan Damer. He used the term to signal the social continuities associated with industrial change. Orientations to employment and social practices at Linwood were little different from those in established industrial communities in the west of Scotland. The intensity and scale of employment in the plant provided Linwood citizens with a strong working-class identity. Leisure activities were highly communal, centred on pubs and clubs. Tellingly, many Linwood and Johnstone residents frequently visited extended family members and friends in Govan, travelling on a direct bus service also to shop, use the hairdressers and drink in the pubs.[22] The Clydesider identity examined in Chapter 4, embedded in life and work in the shipbuilding community, was therefore an important structural dimension of everyday life in Linwood too.[23] A social club at Linwood was run by employees, encompassing sports facilities that could be used by family members. Joe Reilly also remembered workers organising family trips 'doon the watter' to the seaside, children's Christmas parties and dinner dances at the social club.[24]

19 Reilly, Interview.
20 NRS, SEP 4/3996, N. J. Shanks, Scottish Office, Chrysler. Secretary of State for Scotland's meeting with representatives of Strathclyde Regional Council and Renfrew District Council, 3 December 1975; ML, TD 758/1/1, Strathclyde Regional Council, Draft Report, Chrysler: Linwood, November 1975.
21 Alex Neill and Margaret Neill, Interview with VW, Glasgow, 18 September 2017.
22 Damer, 'Life after Linwood?'
23 Lynn Abrams and Callum Brown, 'Introduction: Conceiving the Everyday in the Twentieth Century', in Lynn Abrams and Callum Brown, eds, *A History of Everyday Life in Twentieth-Century Scotland* (Edinburgh: Edinburgh University Press, 2010), pp. 1–12.
24 Reilly, Interview.

There was limited emphasis at Linwood, therefore, on the home-based leisure and changes in political attitudes associated in the 1960s with 'affluent workers' in new or growing communities in England. This was an important theme in the famous sociological survey of manual employees in the expanding town of Luton. John Goldthorpe, David Lockwood, Frank Bechhofer and Jennifer Platt rejected the hypothesis of *embourgeoisement*. Improved living standards did not result in affluent workers adopting middle-class attitudes although greater divergence within the working class was emphasised. Affluent workers in Luton were said to have adopted or developed a more instrumental orientation to employment than 'traditional' workers, privileging monetary 'extrinsic' rewards over social value-based 'intrinsic' rewards.[25] Continuities more than ruptures in patterns of social life and attitudes have been emphasised in more recent literature on class and new community formation in both English and Scottish settings. Mike Savage used the original *Affluent Worker* research notes to query whether manual employees in the archetypal English town of Luton were substantially distinct from traditional workers. He doubted the extent to which those in Luton rejected a 'solidaristic' working-class identity.[26] Jon Lawrence also revisited the *Affluent Worker* study within a broader analysis of class and community in post-Second World War England, which included a re-reading of sociological investigations of, *inter alia*, Stevenage and Cambridge. Lawrence argued that there was no straightforward or wholesale rejection of communal identity and obligation among workers in these localities. Manual working-class loyalties were loosened rather than abandoned. A pre-migration tendency to greater individualisation was nevertheless accentuated, with greater focus on home-centred social activity.[27]

New community formation was different in Scotland. Propinquity was important: Scottish New Towns were both physically and politically close to their 'parent city'. Stevenage was thirty miles from London, whereas East Kilbride was ten miles from Glasgow. As in Linwood, the young population of East Kilbride retained close connections to

25 John Goldthorpe, David Lockwood, Frank Bechhofer and Jennifer Platt, *The Affluent Worker: Industrial Attitudes and Behaviour* (Cambridge: Cambridge University Press, 1968); *The Affluent Worker in the Class Structure* (Cambridge: Cambridge University Press, 1969); *The Affluent Worker: Political Attitudes and Behaviour* (Cambridge: Cambridge University Press, 1968).
26 Mike Savage, 'Working-class identities in the 1960s: Revisiting the affluent worker study', *Sociology*, 39.5 (2005), pp. 929–46.
27 Lawrence, *Me, Me, Me?*, pp. 72–134.

family and social life along with employment in the metropolis.[28] In East Kilbride residential development included a substantial volume of houses, distinct from flats, which were equipped with gardens. This perhaps shaped a greater tendency to home-centred living than in Linwood,[29] but the prevalence of industrial employment meant that class conflict in the workplace was more overt in East Kilbride than Stevenage or Luton. Better Sound Recordings (BSR) Ltd, headquartered in the English West Midlands, was established in 1964 with regional aid as one of East Kilbride's largest industrial operations, producing turntables for record-player manufacturers. BSR was reluctant to accept moral obligations to workers and citizens in East Kilbride. It resisted calls for union recognition, which was only secured by the 1,500 mainly female workers after a very bitter and high-profile fifteen-week strike from August to November 1969. BSR tried to break the strike by bussing in a substitute workforce from distant and scattered settlements. A two-hour stoppage from 50,000 engineers across central Scotland on 2 October demonstrated support for the strikers, whose actions compelled BSR to concede recognition. Industrial relations in the factory nevertheless remained highly adversarial until its closure in 1980.[30] Working-class activism in East Kilbride was sustained into the 1970s. It included a remarkable episode of international solidarity. Workers in the town's Rolls Royce factory realised early in 1974 that they were being asked to repair engines from Hawker Hunter fighter-bombers used in Chile by General Pinochet's military forces in the coup against the elected socialist government. The Rolls Royce engineers refused to undertake this work, resisting considerable pressure from their employer to do so. The engines were eventually returned to Chile, unrepaired, in 1978. *Nae Pasaran!*, Felipe Bustos Sierra's 2018 film, positioned the East Kilbride action within the longer history of Clydeside trade unionism and socialism, reinforcing the impression that new community formation from

---

28 Peter Wilmott, 'East Kilbride and Stevenage: Some Social Characteristics of a Scottish and an English New Town', *Town Planning Review*, 34.4 (1964), pp. 307–16.

29 Lynn Abrams, Barry Hazley, Valerie Wright and Ade Kearns. 'Aspiration, Agency, and the Production of New Selves in a Scottish New Town, c.1947–c.2016', *Twentieth Century British History*, 29.4 (2018), pp. 576–604.

30 Alan McKinlay, John Boyle and William Knox, '"A Sort of Fear-Run Place": Unionising BSR, East Kilbride, 1969', *Scottish Labour History*, 54 (2019), pp. 103–25.

the 1950s to the 1970s followed a distinct path in Scotland. The 'parent city' and its labour movement politics were not left behind.[31]

Linwood's industrial politics were similarly shaped by Clydeside labour organisation and culture. Norman Buchan was elected as Labour MP for West Renfrewshire in Harold Wilson's victory of October 1964. His campaign prioritised the defence of local industrial employment. Frank Glasgow of the TGWU and Bill McLean of the AEU, joint convenors of Linwood's shop stewards, both appeared in Buchan's electoral publicity material.[32] Buchan's maiden House of Commons speech identified economic security as both advanced and imperilled by the Linwood initiative. People in their thousands had 'come from single-room housing' in Glasgow to live in 'decent three- or four-apartment houses for the first time, with all the commitments that this entails'. Such increased financial obligations could only be met, however, through continued employment at the car plant. Experience of car plant labour was already falling short of expectations. Rootes had recently responded to reduced market demand by adopting a four-day week. This could be tolerated, perhaps, in the Midlands, with its relative abundance of employment alternatives. In Renfrewshire, the position was markedly different. At the Paisley employment exchange in late 1964 there were 730 registered unemployed men, 212 at Johnstone, 418 at Barrhead and 1,411 at Greenock. In the Midlands there were 1,359 job vacancies for every 100 unemployed men, while in Scotland there were only sixty openings per 100 jobless males.[33]

WORKING IN THE FACTORY

Buchan's concerns reflected the nature of car manufacturing in the UK, which was generally responsive to cyclical markets. Linwood was accordingly ill placed to satisfy expectations of stable production. The projected employment of 16,000 was never attained. Peaks of 9,000 were reached in 1965, 1970 and 1974, followed in each case by damaging

---

31 *Nae Pasaran!*, produced and directed by Felipe Bustos Sierra (Debasers Fillums, 2018), at https://naepasaran.com/, accessed 13 July 2020.

32 University of the West of Scotland, Paisley (UWS), Norman Buchan Archive (NBA), *Election special, October 1964 – 'The Old and the New'*, Box 11/File 12 (Rootes Linwood).

33 Parliamentary Debates, Fifth Series, Commons (London: HMSO), Vol. 702, cols 398–408, 17 November 1964.

redundancy: 1,000 in September–October 1966,[34] another 1,000 by increments in 1971,[35] and more than 2,000 late in 1974. Short-time working was a recurrent, related frustration. A three-day week operated in the first quarter of 1975, pushing the STUC to argue for nationalisation to preserve economic security for those employed. Normal working resumed in June, but in September Linwood moved to a pattern of ten working days in fifteen, and a seven-day lay-off for everyone in October.[36] Barry Brown joined the assembly floor in 1970 but the 1975 crisis pushed him to accept lower paid but more reliable employment in the public sector as a painter-decorator. A family 'cannae live on three days' wages', he recalled in 2017.[37]

Redundancies tended to be concentrated in the 'Crazy K' assembly block. In separate interviews for this book, three ex-workers – Brown, Joe Reilly and Alex Neill – recalled without prompting an additional tactic used by Chrysler when facing a shortfall in market demand: breaching agreements with unions to provoke strikes. Brown remembered that a car park full of unsold vehicles was the usual harbinger of trouble. Reilly said this practice was 'blatant'. The strike-provoking repertoire included dismissing workers on contentious grounds, such as the case of a forklift driver found sleeping during a quiet nightshift, when there was no call on his services. Alex said management would speed up the assembly line, knowing this would instigate a work stoppage. In the 1970s Chrysler was usually making sixty cars an hour at Linwood. A week's production lost to a strike enabled management to move accumulated stock while making significant wage savings.[38]

Employment instability at Linwood reflected the broader trend in UK car manufacturing. Labour turnover was higher in development areas than the Midlands.[39] Rootes executives shared data with the Donovan Royal Commission on industrial relations in 1965, showing that far more 'lost time' arose at Linwood from lay-offs than unofficial strikes.[40] Redundancy pointed to the imperfections of regional assistance, geared to employment growth in market-volatile consumer sectors, and also

---

34 NRS, SEP 4/2402, Redundancy at Rootes' Factories at Linwood, Note of a Meeting at the Ministry of Technology, 11 October 1966.
35 NRS, SEP 4/2403, 'Rootes, Linwood since 1 January 1968', no date, within Ministerial correspondence, Linwood, March 1972.
36 STUC, *79th Annual Report, 1976* (Glasgow, 1976), pp. 83–4.
37 Barry Brown, Interview with VW, Paisley, 22 November 2017.
38 Neill, Interview; Brown, Interview; Reilly, Interview.
39 Goodman and Samuel, 'Motor Industry in a Development District'.
40 TNA, LAB 28/15/18, Rootes Motors Ltd, Report for Royal Commission, June 1966, Appendix E.

raised defects in macroeconomic policy. The 1966 redundancy crisis reflected the impact of the Labour government's anti-inflationary July measures, examined in Chapter 2. Linwood job losses contributed to the significant rise of Scottish unemployment in the autumn and winter that followed. Union representatives sought a negotiated pattern of short-time working to avoid redundancy, but the company instead imposed a four-day working week immediately after the summer holiday shutdown with 540 redundancies in August and another 500 in October. In discussion with STUC officials the plant stewards claimed that Rootes made the redundancies to secure greater investment from Chrysler with the US multinational uncertain about increasing its UK stake.[41]

Redundancy frustrated working-class expectations of improvement. Pay levels were a further but nuanced concern: attractive in local labour market terms, but short of national industry standards. Neill started at Linwood in 1963, moving from NCB employment at Cardowan Colliery in Lanarkshire. He earned more in the assembly block than he had as a miner. The pay differential between mining and motor industry was still apparent in the 1970s. A Lanarkshire miner who earned a weekly £22-10s before the national coal strikes of 1972 and 1974 knew Linwood assembly workers on £35 a week.[42] Data collected by the Ministry of Labour in 1968 indicated that skilled men in Linwood were earning 4d an hour more than their equivalents in Clydeside shipbuilding, a weekly premium of almost £1.[43] When Brown joined the assembly floor in 1970 he exceeded his painter-decorator's weekly wage by £14 and Reilly remembered the plant as 'one of the highest wage payers in the area'.[44] Rootes and then Chrysler were nevertheless paying Linwood employees less than workers in the West Midlands. Chrysler rationalised this disparity on two grounds: preserving harmonious relations with other engineering employers on Clydeside by limiting the relative local value of car plant wages; and compensating for the additional supply costs of operating on the 'periphery'.[45] These were claimed by Gilbert Hunt,

41 GCUA, STUC Economic Committee, Meeting with Linwood Trade Union Representatives, NUVB office Paisley, 19 September 1966.
42 Ewan Gibbs, *Deindustrialisation and Industrial Communities: The Lanarkshire Coalfields c.1947–1983*, University of Glasgow PhD, 2016, 92, 106.
43 TNA, LAB 10/2834, B. Roscoe, Rootes Motors Scotland Ltd, Linwood, 6 May 1968.
44 Brown, Interview; Reilly, Interview.
45 TNA, LAB 28/16/7, C. H. B. Cattell, Director/General Manager Rootes, Evidence to Royal Commission on Trade Unions and Employers' Associations, 7 June 1966.

Chrysler UK's Managing Director, as equivalent to double the sum received in regional assistance for running Linwood from 1963 to 1970.[46]

Policy-makers tolerated pay disparity as the price of regional policy. Unemployment was reduced in development districts and the production costs for inward investing firms were minimised.[47] The practice nevertheless offended new motor industry employees in northwest England and South Wales as well as in Renfrewshire.[48] This impressed Beynon as a central factor in workplace conflict at Ford's Merseyside plant in the late 1960s and early 1970s.[49] The earnings grievance at Linwood was at times expressed by workers in terms of Scottish particularity. A quasi-colonial narrative of resistance was articulated by some, who told news reporters that they resented their status as 'kilted coolies'.[50] Meeting Chrysler management at Linwood in 1970 Jack of the STUC said that trade unionists would not accept that industry was only viable in Scotland on the basis of 'a substantial differential in terms of earnings'. The STUC was supporting a workforce claim for parity,[51] which was won after a lengthy strike in 1972.[52] Linwood management advised the Scottish Office in 1975 that this removed the largest source of discontent at the plant. Strikes had become less frequent and were triggered by national rather than local disputes.[53]

Wage disparity and interrupted earnings through redundancy were problematic features of employment at Linwood. Another, less tangible perhaps, was the process of production. In Chapter 4 the essentials of the Clydesider skilled working-class identity were examined: autonomy from managerial supervision; exercise of craft skill; vigorous workplace trade union voice. Many at Linwood had personal or family

46 NRS, SEP 4/2403, Confidential Proof, Minutes of Evidence Taken before the Trade and Industry Sub-Committee of the House of Commons Expenditure Committee: Evidence from Gilbert Hunt, Managing Director, Chrysler (UK) Ltd, 25 October 1972.
47 Scott, 'Regional development and policy', pp. 343–57.
48 Murden, 'Demands for Fair Wages and Pay Parity'.
49 Huw Beynon, *Working for Ford: Men, Masculinity, Mass Production and Militancy* (Harmondsworth: Penguin, 1973).
50 David Wilson, 'Parity for the kilted coolies', *The Guardian*, 6 February 1972, p. 15.
51 GCUA, STUC, Report of Meeting with the Management at Linwood, 14 May 1970, and Meeting with Trade Union officials and shop stewards from Linwood, NUVB offices, Paisley, 10 August 1970.
52 Geoffrey Whitely, '6,500 car men get a £5 rise', *The Guardian*, 5 February 1972, p. 22.
53 NRS, SEP 4/3993, W. B. Kilpatrick, SEPD, Note of visit to Linwood, 2 September 1975.

employment experience in shipbuilding as well as heavy engineering and coal mining. Lockyer and Baddon's ex-Linwood interviewees in 1984–5 included men who joined the plant from the shipyards in the mid-1960s.[54] Among those interviewed for this book, Joe Reilly's narrative continually returned to the formative influence on Linwood workers' expectations and behaviour of the shipyards, while Alex Neill's previous job was in coal mining. Production at Linwood undermined and challenged two elements of the Clydesider identity: autonomy and skill.[55] In stark contrast to shipyard production, motor manufacturing entailed close managerial supervision of standardised or semi-standardised tasks. The 'works rules' were extensive and detailed. The forty-hour working week in 1965 involved Monday to Thursday day shifts from 7.45 a.m. to 4.30 p.m. with an earlier finish at 4.05 p.m. on Fridays. Lunch break was forty minutes. Security staff were permitted to conduct personal searches of employees at any time, and many activities were explicitly prohibited, notably the playing of football and gambling.[56] In 1969 across the UCS group 59 per cent of all employees, including staff and non-manuals, were skilled,[57] whereas 60 per cent at Linwood in 1975 were semi-skilled.[58]

As in the shipyards, there were skill differentials and a plurality of trade unions at Linwood representing different grades of employees. The core distinction was between the semi-skilled assemblers, the majority, who were mainly members of the TGWU, and the skilled engineers who produced parts, represented by the AEU and its successor body, the Amalgamated Union of Engineering Workers (AUEW). TGWU stewards had a very difficult task. Their members were subjected to a more alienating labour process and exhibited greater militancy in the Crazy K than engineers in the tool and component shops.[59] Linwood management tended to obscure this structural question, however, emphasising instead the pragmatic virtues of the engineers and their leading union steward, John Carty.[60] Conflict recurrently surfaced between the different groups of workers. In the 1960s engineers tried to preserve pay differentials as

54 USASC, SOHC 001012, Baddon, Interview with anonymised former Linwood worker.
55 Knox and McKinlay, 'Working for the Yankee Dollar'.
56 TNA, LAB 28/15/18, Rootes Motors Ltd, Report for Royal Commission, June 1966, Appendix L.
57 Herron, 'Redundancy and Redeployment', p. 235.
58 ML, TD 758/1/1, Strathclyde Regional Council, Draft Report, Chrysler: Linwood, November 1975.
59 TNA, FV 22/96, A. G. Manzie, 'Chrysler, Linwood', 1 April 1977.
60 NRS, SEP 4/3994, W. B. Kilpatrick, File Note, Linwood, 10 November 1975.

these gradually narrowed, and lengthy stoppages by assemblers in 1977 and 1978 caused engineers to be laid off temporarily.[61]

Union protection of sectional interests has not featured strongly in activist memories. Joe Reilly followed the Lockyer and Baddon interviewees in emphasising that divisions between workers and managers were deeply embedded in everyday life at Linwood.[62] Within this macro-class conflict workers used union organisation and the Clydesider identity to advance their influence. They protected their security by asserting a right to greater autonomy and a command of craft skill. This effort was contested strongly by Rootes and then Chrysler.[63] The existence of a 'culture clash' between craft heritage and automated assembly duly figures prominently in the historical literature.[64] Reilly's narrative was likewise organised around his struggle to exert personal agency as both assembly line welder and shop steward. Strikes were remembered as the inevitable consequence of the culture clash: 'people wouldn't take rubbish'.[65] Workers undermined managerial control through other forms of collective action. Output and effort were often rationed, these practices lifted directly from the Clydesider repertoire of resistance to raise wages.[66] Rootes as an employer at Linwood was compared favourably with BMC at Bathgate by James Jack in November 1965, more 'enlightened' in its attitude to the 'problems of industry'.[67] Linwood management nevertheless reacted over-zealously to work rationing, which they viewed as a 'fundamental breach and wrongful repudiation' of the employment contract. Sackings of unofficial strikers were administered in 1964, when a highly conflictual pattern of industrial relations was established. This included occasionally sharp internal union dissension when unofficial strikers repudiated agreements negotiated by their representatives.[68]

---

61 TNA, FV 22/96, Chrysler Linwood Dispute – Note of Discussions at Department of Industry, 2 November 1977; FV 22/96, J. E. Cammell, Chrysler Linwood Dispute, 29 June 1978.
62 USASC, SOHC 001012; Reilly, Interview.
63 Alison Gilmour, 'The Trouble with Linwood: Compliance and Coercion in the Car Plant, 1963–1981', *Journal of Scottish Historical Studies*, 27 (2007), pp. 75–93.
64 Christopher Harvie, *No Gods and Precious Few Heroes: Scotland since 1914* (Edinburgh: Edinburgh University Press, 1993), p. 151; Knox, *Industrial Nation*, pp. 272–9.
65 Neill, Interview; Reilly, Interview.
66 Alison Gilmour, *Examining the 'Hard-boiled Bunch': Work Culture and Industrial Relations at the Linwood Car Plant*, University of Glasgow PhD thesis, 2009, pp. 261–6.
67 GCUA, STUC Economic Committee, 2 December 1965.
68 'Unions may support workers' dismissal', *The Guardian*, 30 May 1964, 1.

Industrial unrest received extensive press coverage in Scotland. Workers and unions were presented as misbehaving even when managers had been the culpable party in provoking a stoppage. Alex Neill remembered challenging a *Scottish Daily Express* journalist outside a union meeting who suggested that workers were dishonouring an agreement by striking. Alex asked the journalist: 'if your boss told you you're not getting a rise for a year, and then came and said to you a week later, I want you to do more work, what would you do?'. The journalist agreed that 'oh that wouldnae be right' but 'they never made a mention of that in the paper'.[69] Workplace friction became more pronounced after Chrysler's takeover. Norman Buchan sensed early that multinational ownership would jeopardise local employment. Linwood would 'merely become a production unit'. Without research and development facilities it would be more insecure 'in the event of a recession'.[70] This anticipated the 'branch-plant syndrome' analysis of multinational retreat in the 1970s, where Scottish-located operations focused on making goods designed elsewhere were highly vulnerable.[71] The Labour government only supported Chrysler's acquisition of Rootes after other potential purchasers, including BMC, had proved unwilling, and on the further condition that the multinational promised to expand production and employment in the UK.[72]

Chrysler sold its UK operations in 1978 to PSA, but those looking back at the 1981 closure just a few years later blamed their lost employment on the US multinational. A union convenor reflected that he 'didnae think much of the American management' as 'they were always parading up and down shouting at people, shouting and "sack that man", that sort of attitude prevailed wae thim when they came in'. Another veteran stated that '[during the] Chrysler period people would say "gosh, I wish we could go back to the railway days [of Pressed Steel], those were the happy days in this place"'.[73] In the late 2010s Joe Reilly vividly recalled a curious but instructive episode when Linwood managers resolved to make the buildings cleaner. Pattern makers were asked

---

69 Neill, Interview.
70 Norman Buchan, letter to *The Glasgow Herald*, 11 June 1964.
71 Dimitratos et al., 'The multinational enterprise'.
72 NRS, SEP 4/3999, Brief for Secretary of State for Scotland's Visit to Linwood, September 1977; TNA, FV 44/17, I. J. Minett, Chrysler Group Vice President to Anthony Wedgwood Benn, Minister of Technology, 16 January 1967.
73 USASC, SOHC 001022, Lockyer and Baddon, Conversations, 1981–5; SOHC 001012 and SOHC 001002, Baddon Interviews with anonymised former Linwood workers.

to make a large effigy of a pig, to be placed in untidy areas as 'incentive' to clean up. 'Aye', asked Reilly, 'are you going to shame a Scotsman? He's more likely to hit you with the bloody thing isn't he?' Managers then offered gold Rolex watches to individuals identified as making a special effort to maintain cleanliness. Reilly was awarded a watch but 'had no respect for it. That's why I just wore it to work, you know, because of the incident with the pig.' He related this episode directly to the work culture and traditions of Clydeside: workers were not coerced by attempted humiliation, nor were their collective loyalties subverted by individualised rewards.[74]

These conflicts developed in large part from the boredom and intensity of production, particularly in the assembly block. Jeff Torrington's 1996 novel, *The Devil's Carousel*, took readers into the Centaur Cars Plant at Chimeford. Alasdair Gray pointed out in his obituary of Torrington that the novel was presented as a collection of linked stories to reflect Linwood's integrated but alienating division of labour.[75] Torrington drew creatively from his own experiences of the production line at Linwood from 1973 until 1981. He highlighted the limits of human agency in the labour process, which was controlled by the line, known as 'the Widow', and the 'Martians' of top management. The physically remorseless and morally draining exercise of task repetition in the 'Main Assembly Division', or 'MAD', was emphasised. His characters exhibited a range of responses, from class rebellion to personal and social dysfunction.[76] The experience was unbearable for some, perhaps especially for those whose previous employment had been more varied and less regimented. Alex Neill, thirteen years a coal miner, reluctantly started in the assembly block at Linwood, having entertained hopes of a job in the tool rooms:

> the worst thing about the track was, if you wanted to go to the toilet, you'd tell the foreman you needed to go to the toilet. Right. The toilet was across a big bit of the, the floor, and upstairs. There was a ladies and a gents. But the foreman would say to you, right okay, there's three away in front of you, you'll be fourth. And if they all take ten minutes [laughing] . . . you're talking over half an hour, you're waiting. Because that's the only way you'd get a break, if you went up to the toilet [laughing]. Because the track just kept going.

74 Reilly, Interview.
75 Alasdair Gray, 'Obituary: Jeff Torrington: Author of "Swing Hammer Swing!"', *The Independent*, 16 May 2008.
76 Jeff Torrington, *The Devil's Carousel* (London: Mandarin, 1997).

Neill left Linwood after three years. He found a job in production control in another factory, becoming a manager before he retired.[77] Ian
Stobo, a logistics manager, remembered that in the assembly block 'a lot
of them would probably give up just because it was so boring'. He stated
that 'there was a hell of a lot of tradesmen came to work in, erm, Rootes,
purely for the money . . . And then discovered that there wasnae, you
know, the money . . . wasn't that worthwhile [laughing]'.[78]

Trade unionism and the Clydesider identity were important enabling
factors for those who were able to accommodate the challenges of the
plant over a prolonged period. In 1977 government officials – preparing a
visit to Linwood by the new Secretary of State for Scotland, Bruce Millan –
emphasised the correlation between longevity of service and union activism. John Carty of the AUEW, convenor of the plant's stewards, born in
1936, had worked there continuously since 1961. He remained at Linwood
until his election as a full-time union officer in 1980.[79] Tommy Boyle of
the AUEW and Jimmy Livingstone of the TGWU had been employed in
the plant for fourteen years.[80] Joe Reilly worked in the 'very, very famous
crazy K' assembly block from 1971 until the plant's closure in 1981. He
was a welder and a 'snag-man', stationed at the end of the line 'catching
everything that didn't get done correctly'. His job was less repetitious than
others in the K building, but Reilly still managed semi-standardised tasks
while reading and interacting with workmates. Conversations, jokes,
singing and playing chess or draughts were everyday elements of life on
the line. This was how class-conscious Clydesiders protected themselves
mentally and morally against the numbing effects of assembly production:
'guys were quite happy to keep their brain active, if you like, while they
were doing the routine'.[81]

Alison Gilmour's close reading of a TGWU steward's diary showed
there was a collective moral code that distinguished acceptable from
unacceptable forms of individual behaviour. Acceptable forms were
those described by Reilly. Unacceptable were those that transgressed
labour solidarity and disrupted production. The most obvious of these
were repeated drunkenness, fighting and property theft.[82] The collective moral code extended to supporting workmates in legitimate dispute

77 Neill, Interview.
78 Stobo, Interview.
79 Obituary, John Carty, *The Herald*, 9 August 2001.
80 NRS, SEP 4/3999, Brief for Secretary of State for Scotland's Visit to Linwood,
    September 1977.
81 Reilly, Interview.
82 Gilmour, 'Trouble with Linwood'.

with management, including where stoppages had plainly been instigated strategically by the employer. This was as important to employees
in the car plant as it was in the shipyards. So was helping new colleagues
to learn the job and acquire the identity of a skilled industrial worker.
At Linwood women worked throughout the 1960s in the trim shops,
sewing car interiors. Moira McMillan worked in the data-processing
office, which was largely female. Her earnings exceeded those of her
husband, Pete, employed on assembly in the Crazy K. In the mid-1970s
women also entered this part of the plant.[83] The Labour government's
intervention in 1975, discussed below, accentuated the advantages of
widening opportunities for women. Reilly happily fulfilled a mentoring
role for new-start female welders:

> Prior to that, the women in the factory were all doing the trimming and the
> seats and stuff like that. The . . . I was given two young women to teach how
> to weld on the production line . . . And I always remember at teatime and we
> were all sitting there with our overalls on, and I says to them, this is going to
> create havoc with your social life. And this young woman says, why's that,
> Joe? And I said, if you're at the dancing, are you going to tell people you're
> a welder?

This important gender shift was opposed by a sullen minority of unreconstructed male workers. One complained to Baddon in 1984 that
women working on the line had told the wives of male colleagues how
much nightshift bonus they earned. Their revelations 'caused trouble'
for men who had kept this a secret.[84] The trend to greater equality led
more to cohesion than division, however, reinforcing the value of the
plant to Linwood and neighbouring communities. The presence of
women 'brought more responsibility', according to another long-time
worker interviewed by Baddon. Males became more disciplined and less
dysfunctional in their behaviour.[85] Raised expectations had been challenged by pay disparity and redundancies, and the labour process was
enervating. But the position was not static: important improvements
were secured through union organisation, notably the achievement of

83 Moira McMillan, Interview with VW, Linwood, 13 December 2017; Reilly,
   Interview.
84 USASC, SOHC 001003, Baddon Interview with anonymised former Linwood
   worker.
85 USASC, SOHC 001012.

industry-standard wages; and the intensity of the line was at least mitigated through collective and individual acts of daily resistance. The
plant had proved its worth by the mid-1970s as a social resource that
was worth preserving.

SURVIVAL, 1975–8

The Labour government reinforced regional assistance to industry,
increasingly focused on the retention of established operations in
Scotland, especially in areas of rising unemployment. The defence of
jobs was politically expedient for Labour given the rising appeal of
the SNP, but industrial activity was also central to the realisation of a
range of policy goals, notably faster economic growth, minimisation of
unemployment and stabilisation of the balance of payments.[86] Labour's
distinct approach was demonstrated in a serious industrial crisis in the
early winter of 1975–6. Facing substantial market difficulties in the USA
and Europe, Chrysler advised the government and employees that it was
considering withdrawal from the UK unless it received substantial financial assistance. A total of 21,000 jobs in Scotland and the Midlands
were at stake.[87] Dialogue between Chrysler and the Labour government
began immediately with a private dinner in London between the Prime
Minister, Harold Wilson, and the firm's US President, Lynn Townsend,
and Chairman, John Riccardo.[88] The government's Central Policy Review Staff had been preparing a report that pointed to substantial over-
capacity in UK car manufacturing. Chrysler's UK market share was falling
from 7 to 5 per cent in the course of 1975. The loss of this relatively
minor player was therefore seen as tolerable and perhaps even desirable.
Government support could then be concentrated on other enterprises,
especially the quasi-nationalised BL.[89] Literature on the industry broadly
underscores this report's conclusion that rationalisation was required
for greater overall profitability, although higher capital investment than

---

86 Artis et al., 'Social democracy in hard times'.
87 NRS, SEP 4/3993, P. Bailey, Department of Industry to T. M. Band, Scottish
    Office, 30 July 1975; SEP 4/3995, Chrysler UK Ltd, note by John Riccardo,
    submitted to Secretary of State for Industry, 26 November 1975.
88 TNA, PREM 16/500, Note for the Record, Prime Minister's dinner with repre-
    sentatives of Chrysler Corporation, Stafford Hotel, St James's Place, London,
    21 January 1975.
89 TNA, PREM 16/500, John Hunt, memoranda for the Prime Minister, 31 October
    and 5 November 1975.

was ultimately achieved in 'under-performing' plants such as Linwood would have improved their production position.[90]

The threat of closure was vociferously opposed within Scotland by trade union representatives and Labour-led local authorities. Strathclyde Regional Council's intervention, noted earlier in the chapter, emphasised the relative youth of the Linwood workforce and the threat of abandonment to Renfrewshire and the West of Scotland more broadly.[91] Initially UK trade union leaders such as Jack Jones, TGWU General Secretary, as well as the Secretary of State for Industry, Eric Varley, opposed the rescue as corporate blackmailing. Jones wanted Chrysler to 'accept the odium' of abandoning the UK. He argued that the government should concentrate financial resources on the redundant Chrysler workers and other manufacturers, specifically BL.[92] A large group of Labour MPs with constituencies in the West Midlands took the same view according to the government's Chief Whip, Bob Mellish, reporting to Wilson.[93] Willie Ross, Secretary of State for Scotland, countered, arguing that rescuing Chrysler was 'politically unavoidable'. The damage would start with 5,700 jobs lost at Linwood. Employment would also fall at Ravenscraig steel works, provider of materials to the car plant, and Polkemmet colliery in West Lothian, which supplied coking coal to Ravenscraig. Both steelworks and colliery were seen as relatively modern production facilities that had received substantial public investment and thereby merited defending. Proposals for action included transfer of the Avenger model to Linwood from the West Midlands. Ross criticised UK union officials who opposed this on the grounds that jobs in England would be lost. A movement of employment from Scotland to England was far more common, usually without complaint from English trade unionists while generating 'considerable bitterness in Scotland'. In Chapter 2 it was noted that the SNP won eleven seats in the October 1974 general election and in thirty others came second to Labour. Fifteen of these

90 James Foreman-Peck, Sue Bowden and Alan McKinlay, *The British Motor Industry* (Manchester: Manchester University Press, 1995); Stephen Wilks, *Industrial Policy and the Motor Industry* (Manchester: Manchester University Press, 1984); Stephen Young and Neil Hood, *Chrysler UK: A Corporation in Transition* (New York: Praeger Publishers, 1977).

91 NRS, SEP 4/3996, N. J. Shanks, Scottish Office, Chrysler. Secretary of State for Scotland's meeting with representatives of Strathclyde Regional Council and Renfrew District Council, 3 December 1975; ML, Linwood, TD 758/1/1, Strathclyde Regional Council, Draft Report, Chrysler: Linwood, November 1975.

92 NRS, SEP 4/3995, note of a Meeting on 1 December 1975 – Chrysler.

93 TNA, PREM 16/502, K. R. S. to the Prime Minister, 14 December 1975.

were adjacent to Linwood. Ross told his Cabinet colleagues that nationalists would present closure as a 'symbol of UK mismanagement of the
Scottish economy'.[94]

Ross prevailed. Officially the case for supporting Chrysler rested on
economic benefits, notably the export of Linwood-produced cars to
Iran.[95] A projected £162 million in grants and loans to Chrysler over four
years was agreed. This would protect 5,000 jobs at Linwood. Joe Reilly
likened this rescue to the UCS victory in 1971–2, where 'responsible'
trade union leadership acted to enforce 'respectable' claims to economic
security through well-paid employment.[96] A future for the plant was
certainly obtained, but accompanied by 2,000 voluntary redundancies
in January 1976.[97] The plan was approved in the House of Commons by
a majority of twenty-one, and only with support from the eleven SNP
members because ten Labour members abstained.[98] Stewards at Linwood
argued for nationalisation as an alternative to both closure and financial
support for Chrysler, as did the STUC, restating its established criticism
that regional aid tended to stabilise corporate profitability with minimal
enhancement of employment security.[99] There was disquiet also within
Renfrewshire. 'The Chrysler "rescue" doesn't look quite such a piece of
benevolent charity when viewed from the Ponderosa Bar in the middle
of Linwood', wrote Pearson Phillips in *The Guardian*. 'To a production
work force which is to be cut in half, it seems a funny way to be rescued.'
Phillips anticipated future electoral problems for Norman Buchan.[100]

The government's intervention nevertheless reinvigorated confidence
and heightened expectations. The plant had not closed. Cars were still
being produced. Employment remained on a mass scale. The rescue's

94 NRS, SEP 4/3994, W. B. Fitzpatrick, File Note, Linwood, 10 November
   1975, and P. S. Hodge, SEPD/IDS, 'The Effect of the Chrysler Withdrawal
   from Linwood on West Central Scotland', 7 November 1975; SEP 4/3996,
   R. Williams, Note of a Meeting, 11 December 1975; TNA, CAB 129, Secretary
   of State for Scotland, Memo, Chrysler, 3 December 1975.
95 TNA, PREM 16/502, Sir Keith Berrill to the Prime Minister, 14 December
   1975; Edmund Dell, 'Lever (Norman) Harold, Baron Lever of Manchester
   (1914–1995)', *Oxford Dictionary of National Biography* (Oxford: Oxford
   University Press, 2004–16, online).
96 Reilly, Interview.
97 NRS, SEP 4/3996, Kirkpatrick, SEPD, The Chrysler Affair – A Chronology,
   1 October 1975 to 14 January 1976.
98 Adam Raphael, 'Chrysler aid approved by 21 majority', *The Guardian*,
   18 December 1975, p. 1.
99 STUC, *79th Annual Report*, p. 85.
100 Pearson Phillips, 'How it feels to the man in Linwood', *The Guardian*,
   21 December 1975, p. 2.

emphasis on partnership between management and workforce was a further hopeful innovation. Chrysler signed a Planning Agreement with the government in 1977 that aligned with Labour's high-profile industrial democracy agenda. The Bullock committee was examining worker directors in large manufacturing firms, seen as a mechanism by union advocates, including Jack Jones, for arresting disinvestment and protecting unionised jobs in manufacturing.[101] Multinational companies, the CBI and Conservative Party opposition combined to repel the Bullock majority report recommendation of union-channel worker directors.[102] Business representatives emphasised instead the value of other forms of employee participation. This could involve greater consultation, short of joint partnership, in workplaces rather than boardrooms, and focus on smaller-scope issues such as the speed of production rather than high-level strategic decisions like capital investment.[103] The terms of Chrysler's Employee Participation Programme were established in March 1976. Chrysler executives told union representatives and government officials that partnership would enable better decisions to be made and reduce shop-floor conflict.[104]

Chrysler produced a short film, *Building the New Chrysler*, to publicise Linwood's reinvigorated future. John Carty appeared, asserting that union and workforce ambition to improve production had secured the earlier-than-scheduled manufacture of the Avenger from August 1976.[105] The film was partly an attempt to rationalise public investment at the plant, which was scrutinised in 1976 by the cross-party House of Commons Expenditure Committee that visited Chrysler's UK sites and took evidence from 150 witnesses. The Scottish Office submission to this committee emphasised that Linwood's preservation had prevented a serious and potentially irreversible escalation of regional unemployment. The committee still concluded that the rescue was 'not an acceptable precedent for future action'. Sir Keith Joseph, the Conservative

---

101 Department of Trade, *Committee of Inquiry on Industrial Democracy* (Bullock), *Report*, Cmnd 6706 (London, 1977), pp. 20–2.
102 Jim Phillips, 'UK Business Power and Opposition to the Bullock Committee's 1977 Proposals for Worker Directors', *Historical Studies in Industrial Relations*, 31/32 (2011), pp. 1–30.
103 Paul Blyton and Peter Turnbull, *The Dynamics of Employee Relations* (Basingstoke: Palgrave, 2004), pp. 254–7.
104 NRS, SEP 4/1847, Chrysler UK note of presentation to Employee Participation and Communications meeting, Coventry Transport House, 31 March and 1 April 1976.
105 *Building the New Chrysler*, written and directed by John M. Mills (Formula One Films, 1976).

Party's Shadow Secretary of State for Industry, took the opportunity in the House of Commons to criticise the government's alleged 'habit of rescuing companies that are in trouble'. Joseph claimed that this approach diminished economic competitiveness and disincentivised business success.[106]

A remodelled Sunbeam was built along with the Avenger from September 1977. Chrysler's main commitment to Linwood, however, was a new model. The Planning Agreement of March 1977 showed that £11.7 million of Chrysler UK's proposed £75 million expenditure to 1980 would support production of the new car at Linwood from 1979.[107] Workers and union representatives told Bruce Millan, Secretary of State for Scotland, that this model was crucial when he visited Linwood in 1977. Delays in its introduction would compromise morale and possibly ignite serious unrest.[108] This hinted at important managerial opposition to both industrial partnership and the new car. Millan was therefore greatly 'disturbed' when one of the Linwood managers said it might be made at Ryton instead.[109] These difficulties had in fact been signalled as early as November 1976, when George Lacy, Chrysler UK's Managing Director and Chief Executive Officer, delivered a highly abrasive speech to Linwood management and workers. He claimed the company had suffered an 'embarrassing' loss of sales that was chiefly the result of workers not cooperating with the management. In place of partnership, he emphasised, there would be a 'return' to 'efficient "steady-state" management', with 'well-proven' company oversight of 'budget, output and quality'.[110]

The politically charged criticism of the workforce and assertion of managerial prerogative prefigured an industrial relations crisis in the autumn of 1977. At a company-wide meeting of the Planning Agreement Working Party in Coventry, Carty challenged management

106 *Eighth Report, Expenditure Committee, House of Commons, Session 1975–76*, 'Public Expenditure on Chrysler UK Ltd', Volume 1 – Report (London: HMSO, 22 July 1976); Parliamentary Debates, Fifth Series, Commons, 14 March 1977, Vol. 928, col. 118–67, with Joseph comment at 144; Young and Hood, *Chrysler UK*, p. 335.
107 TNA, T 390/237, Chrysler UK Limited, Planning Agreement, February 1977, Tables 5 and 6.
108 NRS, SEP 4/3999, SEPD, Brief for Secretary of State for Scotland visit to Linwood, September 1977.
109 NRS, SEP 4/3999, J. E. Cammell, Department of Industry, to George Lacy, Chrysler UK Managing Director and Chief Executive Officer, 12 September 1977.
110 ML, Linwood, TD 758/6/26, George Lacy speech to Management and Unions at Linwood, 5 November 1976.

representatives to refute the rumour that the new model, known as the Tango, was not coming to Linwood. Chrysler officials conceded only that design difficulties were delaying its introduction. Carty responded in moral-economy terms: the firm had a plain obligation to build the Tango at Linwood, to ensure stability for the plant's 7,000 workers who had supported the successful transfer of the Avenger and Sunbeam models.[111] A lengthy stoppage at Linwood commenced just two weeks later, which Chrysler later claimed as the trigger for building the Tango at Ryton.[112] The strike was provoked – perhaps exactly with this strategic outcome in mind – by management attempting to change the supervision of assembly workers in K block. The ostensible goal was identifying faults earlier on the line that could then be rectified more cheaply.[113] Existing consultation procedures were ignored: trouble was therefore inevitable.[114] The factory shut down within twenty-four hours as all other workers stopped in solidarity with inspectors who were sent home for refusing the new arrangements.[115] Management then broadened the argument, insisting that agreement be reached on a lengthy list of issues before a return to work could take place.[116] Jimmy Milne, STUC General Secretary, was advised by stewards that the company was prepared to close Linwood permanently rather than cede defeat. The factory remained closed for three weeks while Cabinet ministers and national trade union officers negotiated with Chrysler executives and the stewards.[117] Milne helped to achieve a resumption based on pre-dispute conditions, but before a week had passed Chrysler announced that the Tango would be produced at Ryton. This decision, taken without the Working Party, compounded the company's violation of the 1975 rescue plan, Millan advised Vardy.[118]

111 TNA, FV 22/172, Minutes of the Planning Agreement Working Party Meeting, Whitley, 6 October 1977. NRS, SEP 4/3996, Kirkpatrick, Scottish Economic Planning Department, The Chrysler Affair – A Chronology, 1 October 1975 to 14 January 1976; SEP 4/3999, Brief for Secretary of State for Scotland's Visit to Linwood, September 1977.
112 NRS, SEP 4/4000, A. G. Manzie, SEPD/IDS, note, Chrysler, 19 January 1978.
113 TNA, FV 22/96, J. E. Cammell, Chrysler Linwood – Industrial Disruption, 19 October 1077.
114 NRS, SEP 4/3999, W. R. C. Bell, Department of Industry, to M. Wake, Department of Employment, and A. G. Manzie, SEPD/IDS, to Department of Industry colleagues, 24 October 1977.
115 STUC, 81st Annual Report, 1978 (Glasgow, 1978), pp. 53–4.
116 ML, Linwood, TD 758/7/34, 'Observations in Plant', 27 October 1977.
117 TNA, FV 22/96, Chrysler Linwood Dispute – Note of Discussions at Department of Industry, 2 November -1977.
118 NRS, SEP 4/4000, Millan to Varley, 19 January 1978.

Industrial peace of sorts was obtained at Linwood in the winter that followed, owing to high-volume production of Avengers and Sunbeams. Total employment crested 9,000 in January 1978.[119] Milne wrote to Varley, concerned about the longer term. Without a new model, he argued, the plant offered limited employment stability and provided the SNP with major political capital. Chrysler had abandoned two cornerstones of the 1975 rescue deal: workforce consultation and economic security. Varley's response was that employment at Linwood was significantly higher than projected at the end of 1975, and a new model might still be forthcoming by the mid-1980s.[120] Varley visited Linwood in June 1978. The new model, the Horizon, was promised with a more specific start date of 1984.[121] Management then provoked a further lengthy strike after deciding to shorten hot environment relief time from fifteen to ten minutes, said to be the industry norm. The change was pushed through illegitimately, argued Livingstone of the TGUW, without adherence to established negotiating procedures. Around 500 TGWU members withdrew their labour and by increments production at the entire plant was totally halted in the final week of June.[122] Lacy told Varley that the shorter relief time would save £1 million per annum, a significant portion of recently announced annual losses at the plant of £5.6 million, itself the overwhelming majority of an overall Chrysler UK deficit of £6.7 million.[123] Former employees recalled the episode as an example of management's disingenuous tendency to provoke trouble so that unsold stock could be run down, but the issue could not be avoided for the relief time had been hard won through earlier collective action.[124] A compromise was again secured by national union officers and Chrysler UK executives, guided by Varley and his officials.[125]

As work resumed at Linwood on 7 August, John Riccardo told Varley that Chrysler's broad strategy of withdrawing from Europe and concentrating on larger units in the USA meant selling its UK operations

119 NRS, SEP 4/4001, Chrysler (UK) Ltd, Operating Plans for the Years 1978 and 1979.
120 NRS, SEP 4/4001, Milne to Varley, 31 January 1978, and Varley response, 8 February 1978.
121 NRS, SEP 4/4001, Peter Turner, Industrial Adviser, note to Varley, 15 March 1978, and J. Harrison, Secretary of State's Visit to Linwood, 16 June 1978.
122 TNA, FV 22/96, J. E. Cammell, Notes on Chrysler Linwood Dispute, 29 June and 14 July 1978.
123 TNA, FV 22/96, Note of Meeting at Department of Industry, 26 July 1978.
124 Reilly, Interview; Stobo, Interview.
125 TNA, FV 22/97, Note of a Meeting at the Department of Industry, 26 July 1978; Note, Linwood Back to Normal, 7 August 1978.

to the French-owned PSA. Varley was shocked by this sudden turn. He told the Prime Minister, James Callaghan, that the proposed sale represented the implied abandonment by Chrysler of its Planning Agreement obligations.[126] The transfer of ownership was nevertheless approved in September. Harold Lever, Chancellor of the Duchy of Lancaster and economic adviser to Wilson and then Callaghan, told Varley that this outcome vindicated the 1975 rescue. An existing operation with a large workforce, sufficiently viable to attract a major European purchaser, had successfully been maintained.[127] PSA agreed to manufacture cars at all Chrysler UK sites under the Talbot marque. It was compelled by the government to sign a Declaration of Intent with a commitment to maintaining Linwood, although this was 'not legally binding' and qualified by an important caveat: 'to the extent consistent with prevailing market conditions'.[128]

CLOSURE, 1979–81

The electoral events of 1979 were examined in Chapter 2. The referendum in March produced a majority of votes in favour of the Labour government's proposals for a Scottish Parliament, but short of the prescribed hurdle of 40 per cent of the electorate. The government was then defeated in a vote of confidence in the House of Commons and in the subsequent general election the Conservatives attained a majority in the UK, increasing its vote share in Scotland from 24.7 per cent in October 1974 to 31.4 per cent and number of seats won from sixteen to twenty-two. Labour 'won' the election in Scotland, its vote share rising from 36.3 per cent to 41.5 per cent, and number of MPs up from 41 to 44. Norman Buchan was re-elected in West Renfrewshire with increased vote share, from 38.5 per cent to 44.5 per cent. In his election address 'The man who works with you!' was 'WORKING with the men in Chrysler in Linwood to prevent closure of their factory', and attacking the alleged 'Stock Exchange morality' of the Tories, with their ambition to 'run a society in which a few companies control our wealth and in which fewer and fewer men and women are needed in employment'.

126 TNA, PREM 16/2121, Note of a Meeting held on Monday 7 August 1978; and Varley to James Callaghan, Prime Minister, 8 August 1978.
127 TNA, PREM 16/2121, Lever to Varley, 6 September 1978.
128 NRS, SEP 4/4003, Chrysler UK, Note of Meeting on 19 September 1978, between ministers and officials of Department of Industry and Scottish Office and Chrysler union officials and workplace representatives, including Carty and Livingstone.

His advocacy of collective action in pursuit of economic security for manual workers was plainly shared at Linwood. Endorsements came from the leading union convenors, Carty and Livingstone:

> At Chrysler the workforce have been impressed by the immediate accessibility and the grasp of the technicalities of modern industry. John Carty, convenor of the shop stewards at Chrysler stated: 'Norman has done a great deal over the past years to make sure that we still had jobs and the capacity to produce modern cars.' Jimmy Livingstone, TGWU convenor endorses this: 'He was the sort of MP we have needed at Linwood over these past years. I hope every Chrysler worker in West Renfrewshire will vote for him.'[129]

Buchan told reporters that 20,000 jobs in West Renfrewshire were at risk. He predicted that workers at Linwood, their jobs saved by a Labour government, would face the dole queue if a Conservative government was elected. Significant cuts to regional industrial aid were likely to follow.[130]

Buchan's warnings were borne out. During 1979 some 1,250 jobs were lost at Linwood and another 1,200 went in 1980. Talbot's market share in the UK contracted from 7 per cent to 6 per cent in 1980. The announcement of total closure with 4,800 redundancies followed in February 1981.[131] In Chapter 2 the unwillingness of the Conservative government to prevent industrial closures was emphasised. In the winter of 1980–1 the government's toleration of the crisis at Linwood contrasted vividly with the efforts made by the Labour government to keep the plant open in 1975–6. Prior to the closure announcement Sir Keith Joseph, now Secretary of State for Industry, agreed to a meeting with Talbot management along with MPs from affected constituencies, including Buchan. The official minutes baldly state that 'Sir Keith was extremely reluctant to agree to do anything at all'.[132] Gavin McCrone, economic adviser to government ministers in Scotland in the 1970s and 1980s, interviewed for this book, said that Scottish Office colleagues insulated their territorial interests from public expenditure cuts in the early 1980s.[133] George Younger, Secretary of State for Scotland, protested

129 UWS, NBA, Box 9, File 3. See also *The Press*, 27 April 1979.
130 *Paisley Daily Express*, 14 April 1979.
131 NRS, SEP 4/4005, R. Mountfield, Department of Industry, Note, 2 October 1980; SEP 4/4006, M. J. A. Cochlin, Department of Industry, Vehicle Division, Note on Linwood for Norman Tebbit, Under-Secretary of State, 16 February 1981.
132 NRS, SEP 4/4005, R. F. Butler, Talbot UK, January 1981.
133 Gavin McCrone, Interview with Jim Tomlinson, April 2018.

in a private meeting with Joseph, embarrassed because PSA was keeping open its Ryton plant while closing Linwood, the 'biggest loser'.[134] But Younger's concerns were dropped, and his officials provided the Prime Minister with a speaking note for the House of Commons arguing that closure would have limited wider implications. The multiplier effect, accentuated by the same department in 1975, was now said to be insignificant, with only 260 of 5,630 jobs at the Gartcosh and Ravenscraig steel mills affected, and perhaps 1,000 jobs in supply firms threatened.[135] Younger spoke in the House of Commons the day after the Prime Minister, armed with official notes detailing the market difficulties confronting Talbot. Younger endorsed the new moral economy of Thatcherism, arguing that PSA-Talbot 'have had to regroup to save themselves' in the UK. This had unfortunate results in Scotland but there was a chance that operations in the West Midlands could survive.[136]

Buchan had worried about territorial-cum-national divisions within the Chrysler UK workforce after the rescue in 1975–6, seeking to emphasise the value of solidarity between workers when facing a common enemy: 'It was not the lads in Coventry who were endangering Linwood, but the decision makers in Detroit', he wrote, in the *Scottish Daily News*, a labour movement-supporting paper published for a short time in Glasgow by journalists and print workers made redundant from the *Scottish Daily Express* in 1975.[137] Two cohorts of former Linwood workers, those who spoke to Lockyer and Baddon in the mid-1980s and those interviewed for this book in the late 2010s, nevertheless expressed a common view that the closure was Scottish national injustice. Both the employer and government were regarded as having valued workers in Scotland less than workers in England. One shop steward told Lockyer that this was highly political, contrasting the perceived militancy of Linwood with the compliance exhibited by his 'English colleagues'. Car manufacturing had grown in 'hard soil' at Linwood and 'ye'd tae be a hard man tae be a shop steward . . . Ah don't think the same thing

---

134 NRS, SEP 4/4005, R. G. L. McCrone, Talbot UK, Meeting between government ministers and PSA management, 16 January 1981; Joseph to Thatcher, 10 February 1981.

135 NRS, SEP 4/4006, I. P. Hetherington (SEPD), Additional Speaking Note for Prime Minister, Effect of Linwood Closure on Employment in Scotland, 16 February 1981.

136 TNA, FV 22/112, PSA Citroen, Closure of Talbot Linwood, Notes for Speech by the Secretary of State for Scotland, 17 February 1981.

137 *Scottish Daily News*, 18 June 1976.

existed in England'.[138] Looking back after nearly three decades of reflection, Ian Stobo could see that 'it probably made economic sense to close us down. We're two hundred miles away from the marketplace.' But he also retained the view that 'there was quiet celebrations in Coventry when they announced that Linwood was closing'.[139]

The isolation of the Linwood workers within the PSA-Talbot group made difficult the task of resisting closure, particularly given the escalation of unemployment since 1979. The STUC General Council met Linwood union representatives on Sunday 15 February 1981. George Bolton, Vice President of the NUM Scottish Area, urged the necessity of resistance. There was potential in mobilising opposition to closure within a broader campaign against the government's deflationary economic policy. Many of Bolton's members had been on unofficial strike for several days at this point, protesting against the threatened closure of pits across the British coalfields, including Cardowan in Lanarkshire and Sorn and Highhouse in Ayrshire. Bolton recognised the additional threat to mining jobs posed by Linwood's projected closure and argued that this should be resisted through 'concerted trade union action'.[140] Livingstone and other TGWU stewards organised an unsuccessful late defence, in language redolent of the UCS work-in: 'We demand the right to work, oppose redundancy and the closure of any one of the existing plants.'[141] There was little appetite, however, for this at Linwood. 'Open the box', many shouted during a mass meeting on whether to accept redundancy or fight for the plant. This was an ambiguous reference to the Thames Television gameshow, *Take Your Pick*, popular in the 1960s, where contestants gambled cash winnings by opening a box, hoping to scoop a star prize such as a foreign holiday. At Linwood 'open the box' had the opposite meaning: avoid gambling on an uncertain future in the plant by taking the redundancy money, which for many amounted to a year's wages.[142] 'There's nothing like a "Golden Handshake" to curb militancy', Torrington had one of his Centaur workers observing: 'A grand-in-the-hand's better than two feet in a picket line'.[143] Closure was

---

138 USASC, SOHC 001053, Lockyer interview with anonymised former Linwood worker.
139 Stobo, Interview.
140 GCUA, STUC General Council, Special Meeting to discuss Talbot/Linwood Car Plant, Congress Office, Sunday 15 February 1981.
141 Talbot Action Group, *The Case for the Maintenance of Full Employment and Not Closure: The Linwood Workers' Answer* (Linwood: TAG, 1981).
142 Reilly, Interview.
143 Torrington, *Devil's Carousel*, p. 224.

accepted by a reported ratio of 2:1. Linwood workers placed a mock coffin on top of the last car making its way along the assembly line.[144]

The loss of Linwood symbolised the end of large-scale industrial employment more broadly in Scotland, linked in historical memory and literature with the demise of other high-profile casualties in the 1980s such as Bathgate and Caterpillar, and, in the longer term, operations like the Ravenscraig steel mill that were demolished in the 1990s. Thatcher's governments and the Conservative Party were punished electorally in Scotland because they were careless of the effects of industrial job loss and made little effort – as Labour governments had done – to stimulate alternatives. Deindustrialisation came to sign-post the apparent failures of UK policy-making and constitutional structures more broadly, stimulating demands for Home Rule that were realised by the Labour government elected in 1997, and then for independence in the twenty-first century.[145] These were longer-run effects, but even in the short term the closure and its attendant economic and employment contexts contributed to the further political divergence of Scotland from England in the 1980s. The 1983 General Election was contested by the SDP–Liberal Alliance, which won almost a quarter of the popular vote in Scotland. As a result, Labour's vote share dropped to 35 per cent although the party lost only three of its seats. The Conservatives only lost one seat as its vote also fell, to 28 per cent, but this was well below its 46 per cent share in England. In Paisley South, a new constituency close to the site of Linwood that was contested for the first time, Norman Buchan was elected with 56.2 per cent of the vote.

Deindustrialisation, as Chapters 2 and 3 demonstrated, was a phenomenon of attrition. The peak of employment in firms that closed after 1979 had usually been passed ten or even fifteen years earlier.[146] The scale of job loss at Linwood in 1981 was therefore unusual, although it was only a little more than half of the 9,000 employed in 1977. By coincidence, in 1981 the Manpower Services Commission completed an analysis of those made redundant from Linwood between December 1975 and March 1976 within the Labour government's rescue of Chrysler UK. There were parallels with the experiences of those who left Fairfield and other shipyards during the previous Labour government's recapitalisation of UCS in 1969–70. Post-Linwood employment in the late 1970s typically involved lower wages and longer hours. As with UCS,

144 *Daily Record*, 26 January 2016.
145 Cameron, *Impaled upon a Thistle*, pp. 320–40.
146 Hood and Young, *Multinationals in Retreat*, pp. 106–13.

older men especially struggled to find work. Half the sample said that with hindsight they wished they had not volunteered for redundancy. A majority of those who were unemployed and looking for work, 59 per cent, had applied for a job back at Linwood. This unpromising local labour market situation was inevitably aggravated by the mass redundancy following the plant's closure.[147] Ian Stobo described 'suddenly discovering how the lower paid get on', working initially across three shift patterns as a baggage handler at Glasgow Airport. This was a passing phase, fortunately, in his working life, followed by a better paid and more secure position in logistics with a large retailer in Glasgow, but the experiences of others were different: he knew many men made redundant in their late forties and fifties in 1981 who 'never worked again'.[148]

The car plant was demolished in 1984. It lay vacant until the early 1990s when the Phoenix retail and leisure complex was developed. This included a twenty-four-hour supermarket, a multiplex cinema and a series of car showrooms, and expanded over time with additional retail outlets and adjacent private housing. The A761 from Paisley passes under a railway bridge a few hundred metres south of the Phoenix. The words 'TALBOT LINWOOD PLANT' were still visible on this bridge in the 2020s, a double curiosity, given the short life – not much more than two years – of the PSA marque in Renfrewshire. The memory of the car factory also lived on at the Phoenix multiplex cinema. When this was redeveloped in the 2010s, local high school students were asked to create a public mural conveying the site's history. The students focused on the early years of Rootes and the construction of the Hillman Imp. The 1981 plant closure was also prominently displayed, and its negative socio-economic consequences acknowledged. Former workers were pragmatic in their attitudes to the redevelopment. Ian Stobo and Joe Reilly retained no emotional attachment to the site where they had worked for years. Reilly was elected as a Labour councillor on the local authority a year before he left the plant and later served on the committee tasked with inducing companies to locate at the Pheonix. 'We were glad to grab anything, right?', he recalled, emphasising that his main objective was local employment.[149] Moira McMillan was on maternity leave when the plant closed in 1981. After redundancy she obtained comparable employment only briefly, on the Hillington industrial estate

147 D. Payne, Manpower Services Commission, Office for Scotland, *Closure at Linwood: A follow-up survey of redundant workers* (Edinburgh: Manpower Services Commission, November 1981), with details in Section 4.
148 Stobo, Interview.
149 Reilly, Interview.

in Glasgow, before further redundancy and employment in the care sector. Her husband, Pete, had been redundant from Linwood's assembly floor in 1979 and was unemployed for seven years before finding a job in the cleansing department of the local authority. Reflecting on the role that Linwood played in post-war regional policy and the impact of closure, McMillan highlighted the resilience of the local community:

> I think we accept the fact it was here but, er . . . er, we are all, kind of, philosophical saying, things change, it never stays the same. So get on with it, deal with it. Move on. You know, I think you will get that attitude. You can't turn the clock back. Just get . . . just get on with it.[150]

CONCLUSION

Linwood encapsulated the broad phenomenon of industrial change in Scotland from the 1950s to the 1980s. The car plant was established through UK regional policy to stimulate greater economic growth. It provided mass employment for manual workers, including those squeezed out of the staple industries, particularly shipbuilding and coal mining, contracting as these were from the late 1950s. New communities were built around the plant. The village of Linwood grew into a substantial town in less than a decade, as the young workforce was accommodated in local authority housing. There was large-scale migration from Glasgow and other older urban settlements. This was the working-class moral economy in operation: changes in employment and everyday life were significant but accepted on the promise of individual and communal improvement. The citizens of new Linwood brought with them the labour movement culture of Glasgow and Clydeside. Expectations of progress were compromised, however, by intermittent redundancies, short-time working and wages that were above local labour market levels but below national car manufacturing standards.

The plant was a contested space, in two related ways. First, there was a struggle for control in the sphere of production. There was a culture clash. Standardised and regimented production, overseen by management, was ranged against the Clydesider priorities of workforce autonomy and craft agency. This conflict was structural and could not be fully resolved. Industrial relations at Linwood were recurrently fractious, with frequent short stoppages in the 1960s and two large-scale strikes in the later 1970s. Clydesiderism, transmitted from the shipyards

150 McMillan, Interview.

and coal mines, nevertheless had a positive and valuable influence in the plant. Strong trade union organisation helped workers to gain substantial influence and control, even in the assembly block, and secured national pay standards. This organisation eased the adjustment from employment in the staple industries. Second, there were rival claims to ownership of the plant. The legal owner was Rootes, and then Chrysler UK, followed by PSA-Talbot. But the workforce and local community strongly asserted moral rights of ownership. Even in periods of flux and contraction the plant provided large-scale employment in an area of relatively high unemployment. Linwood was therefore defended vigorously against threatened closure and abandonment in 1975–6. The Labour government responded to pressure from trade unions, MPs and local authorities, keenly aware that closure would result in socially unacceptable levels of unemployment in Renfrewshire, with dangerous implications also for job security in steel production and coal mining.

The ending of Linwood reinforced Scottish nationalist criticisms of UK policy-making. The 1975–6 rescue cemented Linwood's apparent future as a large-scale employer, with Chrysler committed to the introduction of a new model and a new collaborative approach to production and industrial relations. This proved illusory, as Chrysler reneged on both promises: a decision to manufacture the new car in the Midlands was taken unilaterally by management, angering the Linwood workers and frustrating the Labour government. The 1979 General Election nevertheless showed that the Labour Party had drawn substantial political credit in Scotland from the rescue and the government's broader defence of industrial employment. Strengthened working-class moral-economy expectations were then mortally offended when the Conservative government refused to intervene to prevent Linwood's closure in 1981. The new turn in the morality of policy-making at UK level, beholden to the presumed logic of market forces and the sovereignty of private sector employers, caused major economic and social damage in industrial communities. The scale and suddenness of employment loss in Renfrewshire arising from the closure of Linwood, 4,800 redundancies with immediate effect, was a huge political shock, even by the standards of the early 1980s. The indifference exhibited by the Conservative government contributed significantly to Scotland's further political divergence from England.

6

Timex, Dundee:
Watches, Electronics and the Moral Economy

Timex was one of several US multinational firms attracted to Dundee by UK government regional policy after the Second World War. This corporate transplantation was central to the process of industrial diversification examined in Part I. The growth of Timex from its establishment in Dundee in 1946 was likewise shaped by government policy. A sharp expansion in production and employment in the 1960s was encouraged by the major expansion of regional policy incentives overseen by Harold Wilson's Labour administration. Employment at Timex peaked in 1974, a few years after the summit of manufacturing jobs across the UK. Timex in Dundee was a prominent example of the broader pattern of industrial restructuring experienced across Scotland, as older forms of employment in the staple industries gave way to work in new manufacturing sectors.[1] This amounted to an 'exchange', encouraging working-class moral-economy expectations that were later jolted by the withdrawal of US and other multinationals. Chapter 2 showed how the moral-economy framework influenced industrial restructuring in the coalfields of Scotland. In the 1960s coal industry employment in Scotland was more than halved, but substantial government intervention through regional assistance stabilised overall employment levels in coal communities. A similar pattern emerged in Dundee. The shrinkage of jute industry employment was accompanied by the increased employment of men and women in engineering factories on new industrial estates.

This chapter is organised in three parts. First, the arrival of Timex in Dundee is examined, along with the broad characteristics of work in its

---

1 Jim Tomlinson and Ewan Gibbs, 'Planning the new industrial nation: Scotland, 1931–1979', *Contemporary British History*, 30.4 (2016), pp. 584–606.

factories from the 1940s to the 1970s. The cultivation of moral-economy feeling is emphasised, as workers fought to express their voice in collective terms. The tightening of the local labour market helped them to impose their will on Timex, particularly in the 1960s. Second, the transition in Timex's history from watch-making to electronics is analysed. This was managed within the terms of the working-class moral economy until 1982–3, when management abandoned watch-making and sought to make 2,000 workers redundant, transgressing expectations of consultation and employment security. The workers' resistance and the long aftermath to this episode, with the departure of Timex from Dundee in 1993, forms the third part.

TIMEX IN DUNDEE

Timex was established in Waterbury, Connecticut, in 1944–5. The two central protagonists were Norwegian engineers, T. F. Olsen, Chairman, and J. Lemkuhl, President. Olsen is remembered in Dundee as the key financial and marketing strategist, and Lemkuhl as the engineering innovator who saw the possibility of producing mechanical wrist watches through adapting materials used in their wartime business producing armaments in the USA. The pair had moved to the USA to evade the German occupation, although there have been suggestions that politically they sympathised with the authoritarian right, at least in Norway.[2] UK representatives of the parent company opened negotiations with the Board of Trade in the spring of 1944. In November 1945 the same representatives indicated to Board of Trade officials an interest in making watches in an area of 'low humidity and clear atmosphere', with ambitions 'to set up a model industrial town on the line of their parent Coy [sic] in America'. They were also aware, however, that labour requirements would be met more easily through operating in an established town. Various sites in Scotland were identified – Kilmarnock, Dumbarton, Dundee, the Hillington industrial estate in Glasgow – plus several in northeast England, Northern Ireland and South Wales. Dundee was inspected on 21 November 1945. Eight days later, Lemkuhl told Cmdr Broadhead of the Board of Trade that he favoured Dundee.[3]

---

2 Timex History Group, Douglas Community Centre (THG), JP note, 21 June 2017.
3 TNA, BT 177/928B, R. J. W. Stacy, Board of Trade, to F. W. Farey-Jones, Waterbury (Britain) Ltd, 7 April 1944; BT Form For Interviews, UK Time, 8 November 1945; BT Interview Form, UK Time, 29 November 1945.

'The Timex' grew in Dundee incrementally.[4] In 1947 Board of Trade officials noted that 213 women and twenty-five men worked for the company in a premises on the Camperdown industrial estate.[5] By 1951 the number of women employed had more than doubled to 546, while the male labour force had increased to 355.[6] Growth in male employment is explained by the opening in 1948 of a large plant at Milton of Craigie, four miles east, where skilled engineers – attracted mainly from jute and shipbuilding – made tools and components to serve the assembly line at Camperdown. This investment, part-funded by the Board of Trade, was warranted because Camperdown had proved viable.[7] It also represented a saving on the cost of importing components from the USA. Milton was later extended in 1957 at a cost to the UK Treasury of £25,000, with further expansion in the 1960s. The Timex workforce across the city grew: to 1,549 women and 718 men in 1965; to 2,615 women and 1,216 men by 1967; and peaked eventually in 1974 at around 6,000, women and men combined.[8] Components from Milton were despatched to Timex facilities across the world. Tom Smith and Dave Howie, former engineers at Milton, remember also repairing machines sent from Timex units in the USA. Restored to order, these were returned to the US factories.[9]

Public investment was one pillar of the moral economy at Timex. Another was the investment by Dundee workers in the growth of the firm and the development of its products. Labour input was complicated by intersecting gradations of skill and gender. The division of labour that Timex established across its holdings in Dundee has been described by Bill Knox and Alan McKinlay as 'bifurcated'. There were employment opportunities for skilled engineers, mainly males, at Milton and in

---

4 Most former Timex employees use the definite article: Mona Bozdog, Robert Clark and the women of Timex, Generation ZX(X), at https://www.performing-play.co.uk/audio-1, accessed 20 January 2020.
5 TNA, BT 177/928B, Building Project, Scottish Region [Board of Trade stamped received 26 November 1947], erect factory to be occupied by UK Time branch of US Time Corporation, Camperdown.
6 *Census 1951: Scotland. Volume Four: Occupations and Industries. County Tables*, Table 13.
7 TNA, BT 177/1228, Agreement to build Milton of Craigie factory, copy sent to Board of Trade Directorate for Industrial Estates from Scottish Industrial Estates Ltd, Glasgow, 6 April 1948.
8 Jim Tomlinson, 'City of Discovery: Dundee since the 1980s', in Jim Tomlinson and Christopher A. Whatley, *Jute No More: Transforming Dundee* (Dundee: Dundee University Press, 2011), pp. 291–314, with detail at p. 293.
9 Tom Smith and Dave Howie, Interview with VW and JP, 3 July 2018.

the tool-making workshop at a third site, on the Dunsinane Industrial Estate. About 80 per cent of Camperdown workers were female, while 60 per cent of those at Milton were male. Across Dundee there were approximately two female employees per male in 1967.[10] Most of the supervisory staff at Camperdown were male too, indicating an important parallel with the jute industry, Dundee's predominant manufacturing sector prior to the Second World War.[11] Assembly-line work at Camperdown required high levels of manual dexterity and attention to detail. Involving substantial single task repetition, it was categorised as semi-skilled. Such gendered distinctions between women's and men's work, blurring objective dimensions of skill, have a long history, which was consolidated by the 'Fordist' practices of mass production firms like Timex.[12] The accuracy and speed with which the women assembled the watches contributed significantly to the consistently high overall quality of the Timex product in Dundee. The failure rate of Dundee-produced watches in quality inspections was negligible, according to male ex-workers, contributing to the firm's reputation as a reliable supplier.[13]

Timex operated in Dundee in a changing industrial labour market. Jute remained an important sector after the Second World War, but – as in the coalfield economies of Fife, West Lothian and Lanarkshire – textiles were gradually superseded in Dundee by engineering. Chapter 3 analysed the three phases of deindustrialisation from the mid-1950s to the mid-1990s. In the first phase, in the 'long' decade from 1955 to 1967, jute employment was relatively stable, with industry data showing that it fell from 19,000 in 1959 to 16,000 in 1969. In the second phase, from 1967 to 1979, and contra the experiences of relatively stable employment in coal and shipbuilding, jute then shrunk markedly, to 7,000. There was also an important re-composition of the workforce in gender terms, with women's share of jute jobs falling from 52.9 per cent in 1959 to 43.8 per cent in 1969 and 28.8 per cent in 1979 as the industry in Dundee shifted, broadly speaking, from packaging to linoleum

---

10 TNA, BT 177/1228, Applications for Treasury Financed Building on Industrial Estates or Site; Timex, Branch of US Time Corporation, 7 May 1965 and 11 October 1967.
11 William Walker Knox and Alan McKinlay, 'The Union Makes Us Strong? Work and Trade Unionism in Timex, 1946–83', in Tomlinson and Whatley, *Jute No More*, pp. 266–90.
12 Deborah Simonton, *A History of European Women's Work, 1700 to the present* (London: Taylor & Francis, 1998), p. 26.
13 THG, 21 June 2017.

underlay and carpet-backing.[14] Weaving was conducted on larger and heavier looms, and jute became much less attractive for women than new alternatives in engineering, where work was better paid, physically lighter, and undertaken in a much cleaner and less noisy environment. Many men also came to view jute as an employment sector of lesser value or even as last resort.[15] In the first half of the 1960s around 4,000 male jobs and 2,000 female jobs were established in Dundee in engineering and electrical trades.[16] Board of Trade officials compiled a list of firms employing 500 or more in Dundee in 1966. In first place was Jute Industries, with 4,066 employees. A very narrow second was NCR, with 4,048 employees, followed by Timex with 3,173. Four other large employers were also in engineering: Veeder Root, Morphy Richards, Bonar Long and Burndept. More than 12,000 workers were employed at these six firms, roughly half of whom were women.[17]

The expansion of engineering strengthened the collective position of workers in the local labour market. Men probably benefited from this more than women. There were opportunities for male engineers to move back and forward between Timex and NCR. Board of Trade data show that 'the Cash' had 3,289 male and 750 female employees in October 1965, a ratio of 4.3 to 1, with production governed much less by assembly line and more by the application of greater skill in assembly clusters.[18] There were other differences in labour regime at the two firms. NCR is remembered by ex-Timex workers in class terms as more benign, 'paternalistic' even, making provision for a range of welfare, sporting and other services for the workforce. In US labour history NCR is likewise characterised as exemplifying a tendency among manufacturing firms to use reward schemes, sports teams and hunting clubs to subvert and obstruct union organisation in the mid-twentieth century.[19] NCR was distinct in another way: after the decimalisation-geared peak

---

14 Jim Tomlinson, Carol Morelli and Valerie Wright, *The Decline of Jute: Managing Industrial Change* (London: Pickering & Chatto, 2011), p. 21.
15 Tom Smith, JP note of conversation, 26 February 2019.
16 A. D. Campbell, 'The Economic Structure of the Tayside Region', in S. J. Jones, ed., *Dundee and District* (Dundee: British Association for the Advancement of Science, 1968), pp. 337–46.
17 TNA, BT 177/2686, Miss McGhee (Office for Scotland) to Miss Hodkinson, 'Information for brief on Dundee', 29 November 1966.
18 TNA, BT 177/1222, Application for Treasury Financed Building on Industrial Estate, NCR 1 October 1965.
19 Elizabeth Faue, *Rethinking the American Labor Movement* (New York and London: Routledge, 2017), p. 84.

of production in 1971, noted in Chapter 2, the numbers employed fell through successive redundancies from just over 6,000 to under 2,000.[20]

At Timex the workforce tapered more slowly from its 1974 peak, illustrating the protracted and uneven pace of deindustrialisation in employment terms: in December 1982 the combined workforce was 4,200, still on par with 1967.[21] In this respect Timex illustrated a broader trend identified by Neil Hood and Stephen Young: the peak level of employment in multinationals that left Scotland after 1979 was usually passed ten or even fifteen years earlier.[22] Class tensions were more overt at Timex than at NCR. This was an additional element in the cultivation of moral-economy feeling. The firm focused resolutely on production matters, with limited social commitment. Like Caterpillar and other US firms established with state aid in Scotland, Timex was opposed to trade union recognition. This was an affront to the working-class moral economy and jarred with popular expectations of rewarding employment in regional-assistance multinational plants.[23] Union organisation was won through concerted collective action, by the engineers initially and then across Timex more broadly. By the late 1960s the closed shop was in operation, with union membership a precondition of employment in the Camperdown assembly plant as well as the engineering workshops at Dunsinane and Milton. Recognition did not bring harmony. Union voice was contested, relentlessly, by Timex managers. John Kydd, a leading shop steward, was dismissed during a strike over the introduction of new machinery in 1973, and only reinstated after a year-long protest.[24] 'Every day there was a crisis', Dave Howie recalls.[25] The AEU enjoyed an important social role in Timex, organising transport between the factories and housing estates. Timex had no role in providing this service, which was paid for by the workers, and supplied by the council, which ran the city's bus services.[26] Tom Smith, an AEU shop steward, states that he preferred this position, where workers enjoyed greater autonomy from their employer by controlling transport as well as a range of other

20 Stewart Ross, 'A rocky road for NCR but company still a major player in Dundee', *Evening Telegraph*, 27 August 2015, at https://www.eveningtelegraph. co.uk/2015/08/27/a-rocky-road-for-ncr-but-company-still-a-major-player-in-dundee/, accessed 27 August 2020.
21 Peter Hetherington and Stuart Mansell, 'Timex plant at risk', *The Guardian*, 11 January 1983.
22 Hood and Young, *Multinationals in Retreat*, pp. 5–8, 30–7.
23 Knox and McKinlay, 'Working for the Yankee Dollar'.
24 Knox and McKinlay, 'Union Makes Us Strong', pp. 273–7.
25 Howie, Interview.
26 Smith and Howie, Interview.

activities, including golf and tennis outings, and football and bowling teams.[27]

The closed shop helped union representatives to negotiate premium wages at the firm. Tom Smith doubled his earnings as an engineering apprentice in joining Timex from the jute industry in 1967. So did Dave Howie, who moved from marine engineering at around the same time.[28] Annual pay awards at NCR and Timex strengthened labour's position within collective bargaining, and extended the opportunity for improved wages, for they were six months apart. This meant a process of leap-frogging that some workers directly prospered from through switching between the firms periodically. High earnings are central to positive memories among male as well as female ex-Timex workers. Many stuck with Timex for long years and even decades: the firm always supplied high-quality equipment; the working environment along with the pay was radically superior to that which applied in jute mills; and there were opportunities for training and advancement.[29] More importantly, as Tom and Dave explain, the toolroom was a site of strong friendship:

JIM P: But you knew people who worked in the other factories who worked in NCR perhaps and similar jobs, or . . .? Have you much contact . . .? I mean . . .

TOM: Oh yeah, there was, there was quite a movement between the, the Timex and the Cash because, er, the wage negotiations were at different times. So if they went up, people moved back and forward then they moved up, they just kept climbing.

VALERIE: And was it similar work?

TOM: The very same.

VALERIE: Were you ever tempted to go over to NCR?

TOM: No, no because the company, I thought the company and the toolroom, you'd made friends then that I'm still friendly wi. I mean like, what is this? This is Tuesday? I'll meet them tomorrow afternoon for a couple of pints. So . . .

VALERIE: So that was more important to you than any extra money.

DAVE: Uh-huh.

27 THG, 21 June 2017.
28 Smith and Howie, Interview.
29 THG, 21 June 2017.

TOM: Yeah.

VALERIE: But you knew it'd be made up again, almost like
          your . . .

TOM: I mean you were maybe going for what . . .?

DAVE: A couple of pounds. Is it worth all the hassle? And,
          and you were settled.

TOM: Aye.

DAVE: You were in good company. The work was okay.
          It was, and you're looking at, erm, you're thinking
          you're going to be there for the foreseeable. And if you
          go into some place else, you're last in so if anything
          did happen . . .

TOM: You're first oot.

DAVE: . . . first oot. So . . . Right, well I'm, I'm here. I've been
          here for X number of years, so . . .

TOM: I mean, I'll be honest, if the Timex hadnae closed, I'd
          probably would have just stayed there till I retired.[30]

Long-term employees, especially those who served as union representatives, nevertheless emphasise that the regime of factory life was
difficult. In *Good Times, Bad Times*, a BBC Radio Scotland programme
first broadcast in December 2016, Charlie Malone, an AEU steward at
Timex in the 1980s and 1990s, remembered the firm as a prime target for
school-leavers seeking a secure apprenticeship in the late 1970s. Hoping
to follow his elder sister into higher education, Charlie was pushed by
working-class family circumstances to support the household by joining Timex. In his composed memory Charlie spoke about his entry to
the Milton plant in vivid terms, and against the grain of the Clydesider
memories of Chapter 4. These, to recap, framed their 'immersion' stories
in positive terms. Charlie, by contrast, experienced his initiation as 'like
going from colour to black and white'. After the freedoms of childhood,
and measured against the lost hope of university, Timex was a grim
and unrelenting confrontation with class inequality. Charlie repeated
this painful learning moment in conversation with two of the authors in
Dundee in 2019.[31]

---

30 Smith and Howie, Interview.
31 *Good Times, Bad Times*, presented by Ricky Ross, BBC Radio Scotland, first
    broadcast 3 December 2016; Jim Phillips and Valerie Wright, notes of meeting
    with Charlie Malone, Dundee, 19 March 2019.

Gender relations at Timex were complex, given the greater presence of female workers, especially at Camperdown. Tom Smith as well as Charlie Malone appeared in *Good Times, Bad Times* along with Kathleen McKinnon, Margaret Kydd and Wendy Cobb. The three women spoke about the control exerted by female assembly workers at Camperdown by 'managing' their male supervisors. This phenomenon is widely recognised in historical and sociological literature, seen as prevalent in manufacturing assembly where production depended on the compliance of labour.[32] Supervisors at Timex, mainly male, had production targets to meet. In the tight labour market conditions that applied in Dundee in the 1960s and 1970s, women assemblers were able to secure accommodation from their supervisors on a variety of issues, including the concession by management of an hour of pop music radio broadcasts each morning and afternoon. Dave Howie moved to a new role as a supervisor at Camperdown towards the end of the 1970s and remembers the subtleties of these intersectional gender and class encounters. Men who attempted to follow management's preferred approach by enforcing company regulations to the letter often encountered resistance from female workers. This disrupted the achievement of production goals. By seeking to accommodate the views and interests of the women under his supervision, and applying regulations flexibly, Dave felt he was in a stronger position in class terms, better able to attain the targets set by management.[33]

Kathleen McKinnon, Margaret Kydd and Wendy Cobb also spoke about the agency of women at Timex in organising a hidden economy where the female toilets operated as an unofficial market for a spectacular range of consumer goods, from groceries, including butchers' meat, to baby clothes. This can usefully be seen in ownership terms, an adjunct of the moral economy. The toilets were a female space, claimed by the women as their domain. The factory is recalled as central to their identity as producers as well as consumers, lifting them out of low-wage and no-wage poverty. In *Good Times, Bad Times* they remembered Friday nights out, spending their wages in pubs and clubs while still dressed in their Timex overalls.[34] These human elements feature prominently in three commemorative mosaics established in 2017 at former Timex locations by an arts project with links to Douglas Community Centre.

---

32 Ruth Cavendish, *Women on the Line* (London: Routledge & Kegan Paul, 1982), is a classic example.
33 Howie, Interview.
34 *Good Times, Bad Times.*

The mosaic on Harrison Road, adjacent to the former Camperdown plant, depicted women at the bus stop laughing and smiling at a shift's end; a few hundred metres away, near the original Timex location in 1946 on Coupar Angus Road, another mosaic picked out in capital letters the words 'nights out, totals, wages, laughs, fun', reinforcing the linkage between production ('totals') and consumption. The third mosaic, on Douglas Road behind the Asda supermarket that sits on the former engineering workshop at Milton, was a colourful abstract of cheerful faces. Jean Brown worked at Timex in the 1970s and 1980s, walking the short distance to Camperdown from her home in St Mary's. Interviewed in 2018, her dominant memory was the relatively high pay, which enabled her to support her young children and mother. She also recalled the agency that women had at Timex as workers, with the firm – through its male managers and supervisors – able to guide but not control the process of production at Camperdown.[35]

At Timex the AEU built on political links to the local authority in Dundee through the Labour Party, which had a factory branch at Timex, as did the Communist Party of Great Britain. The political influence of AEU members, many of them Timex employees, can be read in Dundee's Parliamentary elections and representation from the 1960s to the 1990s. Dundee West was represented by Peter Doig, former Labour group leader on the council, from 1963 to 1979, and then by Ernie Ross, another Labour member, and an AEU representative at Timex, until 2005. Dundee East was briefly represented from 1973 to 1974 by George Machin, an AEU official from Sheffield. Gordon Wilson took the seat for the SNP from 1974. He constructed and mobilised an anti-Labour vote in Dundee East, winning support from middle-class and owner-occupying working-class constituents.[36] In 1979 Wilson faced Jimmy Reid, AEU member and one of the UCS work-in leaders, who left the CPGB in 1976 before joining the Labour Party in 1977. Reid's candidacy divided the Labour Party locally in Dundee. George Galloway, then a prominent local activist in Dundee, anticipated that Reid's communist history would be gainfully exploited by anti-Labour forces, including the local and regional media, where D. C. Thomson's daily and evening newspapers articulated relentlessly anti-collectivist narratives. Reid's campaign strengthened the logic of Wilson's anti-Labour alliance, with

---

35 Jean Brown, Interview with VW, Dundee, May 2018.
36 Thomas A. W. Stewart, '"A disguised Liberal vote"? – Third-party voting and the SNP under Gordon Wilson in Dundee during the 1970s and 1980s', *Contemporary British History*, 33.3 (2019), pp. 357–82.

Conservative supporters, including prominent employers, publicly shifting allegiance to the SNP. Wilson won, although Labour's vote share as runner-up increased from 32.7 per cent to 36 per cent, in line with the national trend across Scotland.[37] Wilson's anti-labour coalition weakened in the 1980s. Thatcherism's undermining of the public sector as well as its reckless management of deindustrialisation was perceived in Scotland as a threat to their security by professional as well as manual workers.[38] Labour's fifty seats in Scotland in the 1987 general election included Dundee East, won by John McAllion with 42.3 per cent. His winning vote share then increased to 44.1 per cent in 1992 and 51.1 per cent in Tony Blair's Labour landslide across Scotland as well as the UK in 1997.

FROM WATCHES TO ELECTRONICS

Timex began production of Polaroid and then Nimslo 3D cameras in Dundee in the 1970s. By the early 1980s Timex had expanded this electronics remit by producing the ZX Spectrum, one of the first home computers, and tubes for early flat-screen pocket televisions, to fulfil contracts with Clive Sinclair, the inventor-entrepreneur. These new products and techniques were introduced in consultation with workers and their union representatives. This was consistent with the working-class moral economy operating in Timex, privileging joint-industrial dialogue and future employee security. Union culture and organisation helped Milton engineers exercise substantial control over the production of electronics as well as watches until the winter of 1982–3, when management made serious incursions on the moral economy. Union voice was challenged and employment security jeopardised. A change in personnel was important. Graeme Thompson, remembered locally as a benevolent figure who accepted trade unionism and collective workplace bargaining, was succeeded by a small team of electronic engineers, led by Barry Lawson, with experience in other multinationals, including Philips. Lawson courted disfavour among local union representatives and class-conscious workers by speaking openly about his experiences in Chile, where he had managed production after Augusto Pinochet's coup in 1973. This had ousted the socialist government of Salvador Allende,

37 Knox and McKinlay, *Jimmy Reid*, pp. 182–92.
38 Paterson, *Education and the Scottish Parliament*, pp. 21–7.

and oppressed labour activists along with other opponents in brutally murderous fashion.[39]

It was Lawson's express aim to establish Timex in Dundee as a 'successful electronics company'. This was a clear intimation that watch-making was unlikely to be retained in the longer term.[40] Lawson also attempted to marginalise union influence. Existing joint-industrial practices were subverted or ignored, and workplace tensions increased. A week-long strike at Milton in November 1982 was provoked by his suspension of five shop stewards for alleged 'poor performance'.[41] The stewards argued that this was part of an anti-union challenge, with management terminating various agreed procedures, notably overtime payments for cleaning machinery at the end of shifts.[42] Lawson was asserting his managerial sovereignty of the workplace, to paraphrase the industrial sociology of Alan Fox,[43] with the aim of establishing a new labour regime at Timex. Such was necessary, according to Martin and Dowling, to accelerate the transition from watches to contract electronics manufacturing. This was predicated on ever-tighter control of costs, to be achieved through more 'flexible' labour deployment, with lower wages and fringe benefits, and significantly less scope for autonomous and skilled engineering labour.[44] Management used the strike to rationalise the temporary redundancy of 1,200 component makers in December 1982.[45]

The dispute illuminated the changing political economy of industrial relations in Scotland after Thatcher's election. Lawson's approach was in line with the new government's ambition to extinguish union voice from workplaces and policy-making. The turn to electronics represented a closer fit with the government's ideological agenda, given the prominence of US-owned firms and the sector's anti-union, individualist culture.[46] Thatcher saw the 'right of management to manage' as a

39 Knox and McKinlay, 'Union Makes Us Strong'.
40 NRS, SEP 4/4064, J. Laydon, Scottish Economic Planning Department (SEPD), note of visit to Timex on 4 February 1983.
41 NRS, SEP 4/3574, clipping, *Courier & Advertiser* (hereafter *Courier*), 10 November 1982.
42 NRS, SEP 4/3574, clipping, John McKinlay, 'The time ticks away for Dundee', *Glasgow Herald*, 17 November 1982.
43 Alan Fox, 'Managerial Ideology and Labour Relations', *British Journal of Industrial Relations*, 4, 3 (1966), pp. 366–78.
44 Graeme Martin and Martin Dowling, 'Managing Change, Human Resource Management and Timex', *Journal of Strategic Change*, 4 (1995), pp. 77–94.
45 *The Scotsman*, 7 December 1982.
46 Knox and McKinlay, 'Working for the Yankee Dollar'.

prerequisite of economic innovation,[47] and, when addressing the Scottish Conservative Conference at the City Hall in Perth in May 1981, spoke warmly about Timex. The firm exemplified the alleged trend in industry to greater competitiveness under her governance, with mixed public–private investment enabling manufacture of the Nimslo 3D camera, plus the flat-screen tubes for 'the first genuinely pocket-sized TV'.[48] The company's strategic diversification included a telling collaboration with IBM,[49] one of the few US firms that successfully resisted union recognition at its Scottish base in Greenock.[50] The 3D camera was manufactured at the Dunsinane unit, fulfilling a contract signed in June 1980 with Nimslo Camera Ltd, a Bermuda-registered subsidiary of Nimslo Ltd.[51] Public money was involved: £1.8 million in grant funding. Production was projected at 250,000 units per annum.[52] The camera was for the 'amateur "point and shoot" market' and was priced at $200, with customers sending their films to Nimslo for processing. Alex Fletcher, Under-Secretary of State for Scotland with responsibility for industry, was advised by officials not to associate himself too closely with the 'ambitious' product, but to emphasise Timex's strong international reputation for quality, and the support provided by the UK government.[53]

The camera was produced for less than two years in Dundee. Late on a Friday afternoon, 7 January 1983, Nimslo issued a statement in London that it was ending its relationship with Timex. It was moving the 3D camera to Japan where production costs were an estimated 40 per cent lower. Worse news arrived on the following Monday, 10 January, when Timex informed the workforce and the government that it was ending watch-making and closing the Milton of Craigie plant. A total

47 Chris Howell, 'The British Variety of Capitalism: Institutional Change, Industrial Relations and British Politics', *British Politics*, 2 (2007), pp. 239–63.
48 MTFW, Speech to Scottish Conservative Party, 8 May 1981, www.margaret-thatcher.org/document/104644, accessed 16 January 2019.
49 TNA, PREM 19/1104, SEPD Brief for Prime Minister's Questions, 12 April 1983.
50 Dimitratos et al., 'The multinational enterprise'.
51 Kathleen McDermott, *Timex: A Company and its Community, 1854–1998* (Waterbury, CT: Timex Corporation, 1998), p. 184, copy with THG; THG, 16 August 2017.
52 NRS, SEP 4/5292, Leonard Seifert, Nimslo, to A. Davidson, SEPD, 24 September 1980; clipping, Nicholas Colchester, 'A £12 million gamble on make-believe', *Financial Times*, 2 December 1980.
53 NRS, SEP 4/5292, D. J. Bain, SEPD, Note for Under Secretary of State, 7 March 1980.

of 1,900 redundancies was projected.[54] This was a significant offence against working-class economic morality. Timex was not a branch-plant operation. The camera had been developed with the ingenuity of the workforce as well as public funding. Ernie Ross argued that Nimslo was 'stealing' the camera from Dundee. Timex was likewise guilty of abandoning responsibilities to the community and workforce acquired with the receipt of public money. Timex was compounding this villainy by transferring production to its Besançon operation in France.[55] Making workers redundant in this manner was more heinous than folding up production altogether in the face of competitive pressures. This is an important distinction, with job loss through capital flight acknowledged as a special category of injustice in the international literature on deindustrialisation.[56] The theft motif was common currency in working-class resistance to contractions and closures in Scotland in the early 1980s where capital was moving plant and products to lower-cost factories offshore.[57] The Timex case typified this trend. The illegitimacy of the management's strategy was repeatedly emphasised by the Milton stewards, led by their convenor, Gordon Samson.[58] Timex claimed that its French plant was simply fulfilling an existing production schedule, but the Milton engineers and their supporters insisted that their intellectual and moral property was being exported without due acknowledgement or compensation.[59] Workers in the affected departments were advised that their employment would cease on 20 April. In a published company history Timex related this major disinvestment to the alleged flaws of the Dundee operation: 'serious losses' were accruing because of 'high labour costs, restrictive work practices and low productivity'. But an international environment of rising competitive pressures and corporate retrenchment was also acknowledged. Timex closed other plants

---

54 NRS, SEP 4/3574, Copy of statement issued by Barry Lawson to Timex employees: Dundee Operations – Statement, 10 January 1983.
55 NRS, SEP 4/5292, miscellaneous SEPD official correspondence relating to questions raised by Ernie Ross about public subsidy of Nimslo, including SEPD note, 24 January 1983.
56 Cowie, *Capital Moves*.
57 Andy Clark, '"Stealing Our Identity and Taking It Over to Ireland": Deindustrialization, Resistance, and Gender in Scotland', in Steven High, Lachlan MacKinnon and Andrew Perchard, eds, The Deindustrialized World: Confronting Ruination in Postindustrial Places (Vancouver: University of British Columbia Press, 2017), pp. 331–47.
58 Elizabeth Bryce Lee, *The Timex Dispute Dundee 1983*, University of Edinburgh Honours Degree in Commerce Dissertation, 1984, pp. 30–4; copy with THG.
59 *Courier*, 9 April 1983.

between 1980 and 1984, in Puerto Rico, Mexico, Hong Kong and Taiwan, reducing its global workforce radically from 30,000 to 6,000.[60]

This was a moral-economy crisis in Dundee: workers' consultation rights had been ignored and their economic security jeopardised with dwindling alternatives to the lost jobs at Timex. The projected closure deepened the city's employment difficulties. At the start of 1982, Veeder Root still employed about 1,000 workers in Dundee. Of these, 295 were made redundant in increments from May to August in that year, and 400 more went in one wave in November, so that the firm retained just 300 workers. A. B. Dawson, the Dundee-based vice president of the firm, cited the pressure of falling demand in the UK and Europe more generally for the petrol pump computer equipment made in the city.[61] Jobs were also lost in older industries in the city, including the Robb Caledon shipyard, which closed in 1981. Scottish Office analysis indicated that factory closures and redundancies cost Dundee a total of 1,675 industrial jobs in the twelve months from 1 November 1981.[62] The government had sought to dispel the connection between macroeconomic policy and these employment losses. In November 1982, Alex Fletcher had told a civic delegation led by Ernie Ross that the real 'problem' was the refusal of Dundee workers to accept much-needed changes in industrial practices, to make the city more attractive to investors. The minister delivered the same message several days later to a group of Timex stewards, warning that Dundee's reputation had been damaged by industrial disputes arising from workforce intransigence. This was an expression of Thatcherite anti-working class and anti-trade union prejudice, without evidential foundation. Ken Fagan, Labour leader of Dundee District Council, responded in the civic meeting that his city's reputation for business-disrupting industrial militancy was almost entirely the creature of the local press, which sought to 'exaggerate trivial disputes from a vested dislike of trade unionism and the Labour Party'.[63] The generally pro-enterprise *Glasgow Herald* had, significantly, given space in its coverage of the strike at Milton in November 1982 to Scottish Development

60 McDermott, *Timex*, pp. 206–7, 214.
61 NRS, SEP 4/3574, J. S. Graham, SEPD, to Alex Fletcher, regarding Veeder-Root redundancies, 2 November 1982; clippings: MacDougall, SEPD, Redundancies and Closures – Dundee, 2 November 1982; *Evening Times*, 2 November 1982 and *The Scotsman*, 2 November 1982.
62 NRS, SEP 4/3574, William MacDougall, SEPD, Redundancies and Closures – Dundee, 1 November 1981 to 31 October 1982, 2 November 1982.
63 NRS, SEP 4/3574, Mr Fletcher's meeting with Ernie Ross MP and delegation, 10 November 1982.

Agency (SDA) research showing that Dundee's record for days lost to strike action was three times 'better' than the UK's as a whole.[64]

The crisis unfolding early in 1983 posed difficulty for the government. A general election was being planned for the early summer, where Conservatives would be defending several constituencies in Scotland affected by industrial closure and large-scale redundancy. Ross and Gordon Wilson sought to maximise the pressurise. Wilson wrote to the Prime Minister, criticising both Nimslo and Timex in moral-economy language borrowed from the Milton stewards. Nimslo had evaded direct communication with the workforce, and Wilson picked up on the suggestion in Dundee that Timex was shifting some of the watch-making business to Besançon, where the French government promised heavier subsidy than the UK government. This prefigured the outcome at Caterpillar four years later, examined in Chapter 2, where US multi-national rationalisation of European operations resulted in the closure of Scottish plant. Wilson told the Prime Minister this was 'unfair competition', but 'resolute action' from the UK government could retain some watch production, and 'stop this international conspiracy which is robbing Dundee of much needed employment'.[65] Government officials recognised privately that labour questions were 'not the key factor' in Timex's difficulties,[66] but Fletcher's public pronouncements generally reprised the anti-union narrative. He argued repeatedly that collective action to resist the ending of watch-making would be counter-productive, 'suicidal' even, threatening the continuation of the electronics operation at Camperdown.[67] In this he was supported by Clive Sinclair, who told journalists that he would abandon Dundee if a strike materialised.[68]

Union lobbying obtained a twenty-minute audience with the Prime Minister at the Holiday Inn in Glasgow on 28 January. The STUC's valuable role in mobilising broader support for workers in crisis arising from threatened closure and redundancy has been emphasised at various points in this book. Its officials were fully alive to the problems at Timex, and accompanied the stewards and Gavin Laird, AEU General Secretary, to this meeting. The union delegation told Thatcher that Timex was

---

64 NRS, SEP 4/3574, clipping, John McKinlay, 'The time ticks away for Dundee', *Glasgow Herald*, 17 November 1982.
65 TNA, PREM 19/1104, Gordon Wilson to the Prime Minister, 24 January 1983.
66 NRS, SEP 4/3574, I. S. Robertson to George Younger, Secretary of State for Scotland, and Alex Fletcher, 10 and 13 January 1983.
67 *The Guardian*, 11 January 1983.
68 NRS, SEP 4/3574, clipping, 'Sinclair threat to Timex: strike and we go', *The Scotsman*, 13 January 1983.

moving watch-making to Besançon because of superior subsidies from the French government. Fred Olsen, Timex owner and son of the firm's joint founder, had confirmed this in conversation with Laird. One of the stewards, N. Macintosh, emphasised that improved financial assistance to Timex in Dundee was not being sought to prop up an ailing concern, but to help in the development of a high-tech operation with growth potential, offering new products like the 3D camera and the Sinclair computer. Thatcher's response was curt. She asked whether the research and development for the watches and other products had been under-taken in Dundee or France. She may have known the answer before asking this question: in France.[69] Gordon Samson, part of the delega-tion, remembers her as being cold and unforgiving, and feeling that the meeting was unsuccessful.[70]

Scottish Office personnel were detailed to investigate the claims about the French government subsidies, thought to infringe European Economic Community regulations. European Commission advice, how-ever, was that Besançon was not in an EEC-assisted area, so was in receipt of lower regional aid from the Community than Dundee. The grants to Besançon came from the French government's national research and development budget, which was entirely legitimate. Company and government obligations were central to a union document issued on 1 February, 'The Future for Timex Dundee'. Without Timex in Dundee there would be no watch-making industry at all in Britain.[71] The Prime Minister wrote to Laird arguing that the subsidy question was largely irrelevant. In neoliberal terms familiar from her government's refusal to sustain manufacturing at Linwood car plant, examined in Chapter 5, she claimed there was declining market demand for mechanical watches. The Dundee redundancies were a simple reflection of over-capacity in supply.[72] George Younger, Secretary of State for Scotland, was more emollient than Fletcher. He persuaded Thatcher to support Timex's diversification with further public investment. He made a similar case to Geoffrey Howe, Chancellor of the Exchequer, emphasising that Timex still had a future in Dundee, and that the government should 'consoli-date the Company's strategy and provide the best prospect for secure

69 NRS, SEP 4/3575, Michael Scholar to Muir Russell, 31 January 1983.
70 THG, 21 June 2017.
71 THG, Green Box, AUEW, 'The Future for Timex Dundee', 1 February 1983.
72 TNA, PREM 19/1104, John S. Wilson, Private Secretary, Scottish Office, to Michael Scholar, Private Secretary, Downing Street, 4 February 1983, with draft letter to Gavin Laird from the Prime Minister; Prime Minister to Laird, 11 February 1983.

employment at the plant'.[73] The Secretary of State advised Olsen of the terms of this renewed offer: a grant for 22 per cent of the capital diversification costs, with a loan covering around 50 per cent of the balance.[74] Close contact between government and company continued. Fletcher informed Olsen that he and Younger had met a group of Timex union representatives and the two Dundee MPs on 3 February, telling them to forget about watch-making and concentrate on expanding the electronics business.[75] The same message was communicated by Thatcher and Fletcher to Gordon Wilson and Ernie Ross at a meeting in the House of Commons on 8 February.[76] The Prime Minister reinforced Fletcher's earlier warnings by saying that new investment would be 'jeopardised by strike action against the present redundancy programme'.[77] Wilson queried the emerging government-supported strategy at Timex. Without watches or an alternative Timex own-brand product, Dundee workers and the plants would be 'dangerously exposed to the fortunes of the contract engineering industry'. Ross concentrated on labour questions. Dundee's reputation for adversarial industrial relations was unwarranted, he argued, pointing to a favourable recent survey of seventy-one local employers showing that wages were one-third lower than the national average, and the Timex workers, who had met Olsen on 2 February, had 'not yet resorted to confrontation'. But they were concerned, having in their possession 'confidential documents' indicating that Olsen's commitment to Dundee would cease with the end of watch-making. The Prime Minister told Wilson and Ross that she understood the concern about the implications of the loss of watch-making and said that Fletcher would monitor Olsen's future production and employment plans closely.[78]

The meeting between Olsen and Timex workers was in Norway the previous week, his private jet carrying Dundee stewards over the North Sea from RAF Leuchars and back in a day. The stewards had received only limited details of the diversification plan,[79] and this secrecy

---

73 NRS, SEP 4/5292, Younger to Howe, 2 February 1983.
74 David Hencke, 'Timex owner may change attitude', *The Guardian*, 3 February 1983.
75 TNA, PREM 19/1104, Fletcher, draft letter to Olsen.
76 MTFW, Margaret Thatcher Engagement Diary, Tuesday 8 February 1983, at https://www.margaretthatcher.org.document147383.
77 TNA, PREM 19/1104, Muir Russell, Scottish Office, to Michael Scholar, 7 February 1983.
78 TNA, PREM 19/1104, Willie Rickett, Downing Street, to Muir Russell, 8 February 1983.
79 NRS, SEP 4/3575, clipping, *Courier*, 2 February 1983.

irked the government. More substantially, ministers were embarrassed by the broader features of the crisis. Thatcher, Younger and Fletcher had associated themselves and their government publicly with Timex in their speeches and actions since 1980. The firm had been presented as a winner in the new industrial situation, exemplifying a trend to product diversification and labour flexibility that the government sought to project as the viable future of manufacturing. Thatcher wrote to Olsen personally. Against Scottish Office advice,[80] she set out her concern that the ending of watch-making and the lost Nimslo contract would have a significantly detrimental impact on the welfare of the workforce and 'many other people in Dundee'. But there the criticism ended. The Prime Minister told Olsen that the government would continue to support the company's electronics strategy.[81] The Prime Minister's unusual intervention revealed the government's anxieties about the political consequences of large-scale redundancy in a Scottish city where deindustrialisation was rapidly accelerating. Olsen offered no ground on future Timex own-name products or research and development, acknowledging only his thanks that the government was 'supporting the new products vital to the Company's competitive future'.[82]

Union representatives in Dundee gathered further evidence of the employer's alleged bad faith. A dossier of confidential Timex documents, obtained in late March, was compiled; it was described in the press as a 'highly complex mass of invoices, purchase requisitions, internal memos and detailed plans'.[83] The dossier was used to support the moral-economy argument that Timex had misled the government as well as the Dundee workforce in denying that watch-making had been transferred to France. The union dossier purported to show that part of the repair and service section had already been moved, costing fifty Dundee jobs.[84] There was also evidence that watch cases scheduled to be produced at Camperdown were already being imported from France. Timex claims about the shrinking market for watches were contested too in the dossier, which carried company memos showing plans for four new analogue models as well as innovative digital products, to be bought from a Korean manufacturer and branded with the Timex logo. These watches could all be manufactured at Dundee, the union stated.[85] Timex

80 TNA PREM 19/1104, Fletcher to Thatcher, 10 February 1983.
81 TNA, PREM 19/1104, Thatcher to Olsen, 16 February 1983.
82 TNA, PREM 19/1104, Russell to Scholar, 4 March 1983.
83 *The Scotsman*, 30 March 1983.
84 *Courier*, 30 March 1983.
85 *Courier*, 30 March and 2 April 1983; *The Scotsman*, 30 March 1983.

ignored these claims. The Prime Minister's advisers sought advice on the dossier from Fletcher and his officials. They observed that Timex was acting within its rights to move plant and work to Besançon in running down the production of mechanical watches in response to falling global demand.[86] Timex was at liberty to continue its programme of voluntary redundancy, with 1,700 workers leaving between January and 20 March 1983. When the company then identified the remaining 200 for compulsory redundancy, the conflict grew more acute.[87]

THE MILTON OCCUPATION AND THE ENDING IN 1993

The compulsory redundancies, imposed without union agreement, were a further violation of the working-class moral economy. They were resisted in class terms by an occupation of the factory, which commenced on 8 April, led by the stewards. The occupiers reprised the language of the UCS work-in examined in Chapter 4. Banners were mounted on the exterior of the entrance: 'This Factory is Under New Management!' and 'We Will Fight for the Right to Work'.[88] The action was ambiguous: the occupiers did not attempt to keep the plant operating. In this respect their action differed from the UCS work-in. Two ambitions were nevertheless obvious: that the costs to Timex of closing Milton would be maximised, through improved redundancy terms; and that each of the workers facing redundancy should be offered redeployment to Camperdown. This reinforced the importance of protecting the security of other Timex workers in Dundee: the occupiers did not call for parallel action at Camperdown. Harry McLevy, AEU district secretary, told reporters in mid-March that it was important to isolate the assembly plant from the dispute. This was proving difficult, however, for Timex had instigated an important breach of the moral economy on this site also, threatening the closed shop. It emerged that a twenty-eight-year-old production technician, who started at Camperdown in October 1982, was not paying union subscriptions. Other technicians refused to work alongside him and went on strike in the second half of March. Managers responded by laying off 500 workers in total, a big portion of the factory's total labour force of 1,200. McLevy characterised the technician as 'a complete opportunist who cares nothing

86 TNA, PREM 19/1104, SEPD Brief for Prime Minister's Questions, 12 April 1983.
87 *Courier*, 21 March 1983.
88 Photograph captioned 'The scene at Milton works at 4pm yesterday', *Courier*, 20 April 1983.

about his colleagues and the company', and offered a pithy defence of the closed shop. 'He wants the wages, conditions and other benefits of the union. If you get on the bus you have to pay the fare.' McLevy also criticised Timex for abandoning established practice: where a worker refused union membership, he or she was sent home. In this instance the firm had done the opposite, retaining the non-union member while sending home the unionised workers. This moral-economy skirmish was won by the union. The technician was persuaded, perhaps by Timex management, 'to abide by union rules'. This was an important minor victory, preserving the closed shop at Camperdown until 1993.[89]

The Milton occupiers took their struggle to the STUC's annual conference at Rothesay in April, where Gordon Samson moved an Emergency Resolution that was passed unanimously. His short speech set out the occupation's moral-economy foundation: the importance of the watch-making industry; the future value of the 'high degree of engineering skills and technical knowledge'; the company's abandonment of Dundee after thirty-six years of profitable operations; the offence caused by capital flight; the indifference of the Tory government to the redundancies in a city of mass unemployment; and, above all, the 'right of every member of the working class, that is the right to work'.[90] The occupation was a setback for Timex and the government. The Sinclair contract included pilot work taking place at Milton on cathode ray tubes for flat-screen televisions. This activity was suspended for the duration of the occupation. Timex management communicated their unease on this matter to Fletcher and his officials, who in turn briefed Thatcher to say in the House of Commons that any 'significant delay in production of the cathode ray tube will not be tolerated'. The Prime Minister was also advised to threaten that a prolonged dispute would lead to the termination of all Sinclair and IBM contracts, and the total closure of Timex operations in Dundee.[91] Fletcher restated this intimidatory message in writing separately to Ernie Ross and James Tinney, secretary of the joint union committee at Timex: 'New attitudes are required for new industries', he asserted.[92]

89 Dundee Central Libraries, *Courier* clippings files, 17 and 31 March, and 1 and 2 April 1983.
90 STUC, *86th Annual Report*, Rothesay Pavilion, 18–22 April 1983 (Glasgow: STUC, 1983), pp. 486–9.
91 TNA, PREM 19/1104, SEPD Brief for Prime Minister's Questions, 12 April 1983.
92 TNA, PREM 19/1104, Fletcher to James Tinney, Secretary, Joint Union Committee, Timex Corporation Dundee, 29 April 1983, and Fletcher to Ross, 29 April 1983.

Delaying the Sinclair contract was not counter-productive and in fact enabled the occupiers to gain some traction with Timex, particularly as they came by information showing that Timex had already passed the 8,000 blueprints that detailed development work on the pocket TV tube to Besançon.[93] This further moral-economy injustice strengthened the occupation. Solidarity from the community in Dundee and support from the broader labour movement also helped. These were 'resources of hope', in the words of Raymond Williams.[94] Tom Smith remembers the practical assistance lent by the Labour-led local authority, the City of Dundee District Council. Housing rents were deferred, and 100 library books delivered to the occupation. Small businesses supplied food and entertainment, including videos and pool tables.[95] Management then announced 300 additional redundancies at Milton, affecting workers on the Sinclair contact, and an intention to take legal action to clear the occupiers from Milton.[96] This new attempt at intimidation involved those suspected of participating in the occupation receiving legal notices at their home addresses on 18 April. Workers willing to accept redundancy were instructed to attend the Block 1 Canteen at Milton of Craigie between 3pm and 4pm on 19 April. Otherwise, they would be judged in breach of contract and their employment immediately terminated.[97] Appealing to employees in this manner, over the heads of their trade union representatives, was a departure from existing practice and signalled a broader trend in the 1980s from collective bargaining to individualised employee–manager relations. Further letters were issued to home addresses on 27 and 29 April. When these were ignored the company issued written notices to home addresses on 5 May, indicating that legal action would be taken against the occupiers.[98] A petition was lodged in the High Court in Edinburgh on 6 May against 349 named individuals, demanding that they leave the Milton of Craigie premises.[99] Fletcher restated the threat that Timex would leave Dundee altogether

93 *Courier*, 15 April 1983.
94 Raymond Williams, 'Mining the Meaning: Key Words in the Miners' Strike', in Robin Gable, ed., *Resources of Hope: Culture, Democracy, Socialism* (London: Verso, 1989), pp. 120–7.
95 Tom Smith and Dave Howie, Interview.
96 University of Dundee Archive Services (DUA), MS 272, George Mason Collection, copy of all names and address of workers suspected of being involved in the occupation; Peter Hetherington, 'Legal action by Timex to end the factory sit-in', *The Guardian*, 7 May 1983.
97 DUA, MSS 272/3, J. Muir to George Mason, 18 April 1983.
98 THG, Green Box, J. Muir to H. Samson, 5 May 1983.
99 DUA, MSS 272/3, Timex Corporation against named employees, 6 May 1983.

because of the suspended Sinclair contract, this time in a meeting with STUC officials.[100]

The occupiers still did not yield. The company therefore held new talks with union officials on the terms of exit for the redundant workers. Held in London on Friday 13 May, these produced a draft agreement: all compulsory redundancies were to be withdrawn for a further ninety-day period; legal action by Timex to end the occupation would end; and for the redundant workers an interim short-term working arrangement would be instituted, restoring pension and redundancy rights, and first access to vacancies within the firm as these arose. McLevy of the AEU returned to Dundee but the provisional agreement was accepted by only fourteen of the 348 attending a mass meeting. Improved redundancy terms were then negotiated locally. These included an extension of the short-term working arrangement from thirteen to twenty-one days,[101] and payments for each year of reckonable service plus ex-gratia payments at least equivalent to twelve weeks' earnings.[102] Timex management also agreed to secure the desired 200 redundancies from Camperdown, where women workers had expressed a desire to leave, enabling transfers from Milton.[103] The engineering workshops had not been saved, but the occupiers had secured improved redundancy terms. More importantly, perhaps, they felt that their dignity as workers had been preserved, along with their collective voice as union members. Tom's words offer a powerful summation:

> We sat in. And while we kept it, you could argue that till the end of time . . . whether it did help or it didnae help. Everybody's got their own view of it. And I think at least it was something. Even if it was something fae yourself to say 'well at least I fought. I didnae just lie doon and get stamped on'.[104]

The occupiers left the plant at 8am on Friday 20 May. Scottish national and local themes were evident. A bagpiper, Billy Shields, son of a Milton worker, played the enduring local anthem, 'Bonnie Dundee'. Work recommenced immediately on the Sinclair contract.[105]

---

100 Roger Kerr, 'All Timex jobs "in jeopardy"', *The Guardian*, 8 May 1983.
101 TNA, PREM 19/1104, Timex Background note, 17 May 1983; and John S. Wilson to Michael Scholar, Downing Street, 18 May 1983.
102 DUA, MSS 272/3, J. Muir to George Mason, 23 May 1983.
103 Patrick Wintour, 'Timex workers claim victory over job cuts', *The Guardian*, 19 May 1983.
104 Smith and Howie, Interview.
105 *Evening Telegraph and Post*, 19 May 1983.

Timex now concentrated on low-cost production, competing with factories run by other multinational firms and its parent firm in Portugal. Some media assessments of the operation's future were upbeat, although its dependence on powerful customers in Sinclair and IBM, supplying circuit boards for its Scottish facility in Greenock, was identified as hazardous in 1984.[106] In October that year Timex proposed 370 further redundancies. These cuts were pushed through, reviving the expressions of workplace injustice in moral-economy language. The jettisoned jobs had been supported through publicly funded research and development. Sinclair was thinking about exporting some of his work to Japan.[107] Employment continued shrinking, to 1,000 in 1985 and 580 towards the end of 1990. Contract manufacturing for IBM by this point represented some 70 per cent of Timex business. The firm issued its staff with a *Fresh Start Program*. The US English feels significant, reinforcing the subaltern status of the Dundee operation.[108] This, according to Martin and Dowling, was the 'soft' human resource management face of the firm in the early 1990s, but there was also a 'hard' face, represented by a new chief at Camperdown, Peter Hall. Faced with a delay in orders from IBM, in late December 1992 Hall devised a series of radical labour cost-saving measures, including a programme of temporary lay-offs, a one-year wage freeze and reduced fringe benefits.[109]

The workforce examined Hall's plan with trade union representatives and resolved to resist it. A strike commenced on 29 January 1993.[110] Hall and two other Timex executives met Harry McLevy, now area officer of the Amalgamated Engineering and Electrical Union (AEEU), in the city's Invercarse Hotel on 10 February. McLevy was accompanied by Gordon Sampson and John Kydd junior, who concluded that Hall's objective was union derecognition. This came out in a hearing of the House of Commons Employment Committee, taking evidence from Timex management, including Hall, and union representatives in the

---

106 THG, Green Box, clipping, Alastair Balfour, 'How Timex stepped back from the brink', *Scottish Business Insider*, May 1984.
107 THG, Green Box, Jim Milne, TASS-AUEW Timex, to Ernie Ross, 10 October 1984.
108 THG, Green Box, Timex Electronics Corporation Dundee, Scotland, *Fresh Start Program: information booklet* (25 November 1990).
109 Martin and Dowling, 'Managing Change, Human Resource Management and Timex', pp. 84–5.
110 DUA, MSS 272/2, Peter W. Hall, President, Timex Electronics Corporation, to George Mason, 5 February 1993.

final week of April.[111] Samson's notes from the Invercarse negotiations tally with both union and Timex evidence to the House of Commons Employment Committee.[112] Stewards were willing to concede a six-month wage freeze but wanted a share in devising the lay-offs, favouring a work-sharing programme that would prevent compulsory redundancy. Hall refused, making plain his determination to exert complete control over the lay-offs, enforce a twelve-month wage freeze and a 15 per cent cut in fringe benefits.[113] Reluctantly, to avoid mass redundancy, the 340 workers affected accepted Hall's plan 'under protest', but they were dismissed anyway.[114]

Jimmy Airlie, the Fairfield engineer who led the UCS work-in, was elected to the AEU national executive in 1983. In this role he was drawn into a succession of punishing disputes relating to threatened and actual industrial closures in Scotland, including the Caterpillar occupation.[115] Airlie was interviewed in 1995 by the playwright John Carnegie, who was developing the script with Alan Spence for *On the Line*, staged later that year at the Rep Theatre in Dundee. Airlie told Carnegie that he viewed Hall, the Timex boss at Dundee, as 'completely untrustworthy', and felt that Olsen, still the principal owner-investor, was behind the dispute. The company had become even harder and more unrelenting since 1983: 'a dirty shower ae bastards'.[116] Airlie nevertheless believed, as a communist, in Lenin's maxim of 'one step back two steps forward'.[117] Greater willingness from the workforce to accept unpalatable concessions at the outset – in January 1993 – *might* have resulted in Timex remaining in Dundee. With this step back the union, still in position, *might* gradually have regained influence and voice in the workplace. But once Timex had recruited 'scab' labour Airlie realised that a negotiated return to work was highly unlikely, with the plant 'doomed'. Despite this reservation he threw himself into a series of secret talks with Hall

111 DUA, MSS 272/2, House of Commons, Session 1992–93, Employment Committee, *The Operation of Employment Legislation Governing Industrial Disputes: Minutes of Evidence*, Wednesday 28 April 1993, p. 15.
112 DUA, Commons Employment Committee, *Minutes of Evidence*, 28 April 1993, pp. 20–3, 33.
113 THG, Green Box, Gordon Samson's Note, Invercarse Hotel, Timex, 10 February 1993.
114 Peter Hetherington, 'Timex job fight turns clock back to 1980s', *The Guardian*, 3 March 1993.
115 Terry Pattinson, 'Obituary: Jimmy Airlie, 1936–1997', *The Independent*, 11 March 1997.
116 Jimmy Airlie, Transcript of interview with John Carnegie, 18 January 1995, at AEEU offices, Glasgow.
117 Pattinson, 'Obituary: Jimmy Airlie'.

and other Timex executives, seeking the reinstatement of the sacked workers. He was unsurprised that the proposals that emerged, including the retention of non-union labour, were completely unacceptable to those locked out.[118]

George Mason received his letter of dismissal on 17 February. A veteran of the 1983 occupation, Mason had worked at Timex for many years, and had served also as a Labour councillor, elected by his neighbours in Fintry.[119] Charlie Malone, a Timex steward and one of the AEEU representatives who gave evidence to the House of Commons Employment Committee, might have had Mason in mind when he spoke to MPs about 'people with upwards of 30/40 years' service'. Malone was emphasising the company's transgression of its moral-economy obligations to Dundee, accumulated since 1947. 'You have a community, people who have given their lives to Timex and they have a vested interest in Timex remaining in Dundee.' The union was fulfilling its responsibilities, he argued, and was seeking an agreement. 'But that must be done in the spirit of co-operation, not in the spirit of conflict.'[120] Malone was referring to the very angry and bitter lockout that had arisen from Hall's actions. The dismissed workers had been picketing daily – marshalling at the Harrison Road gates – as non-union replacement workers were bussed in, many of them from outwith Dundee. Memories of those locked out are punctuated with recrimination:

> Ah think that's why we're so bitter about people goin in and workin on our jobs, and people sayin 'well they've got families'. Well we had families too. And a lot of people that were out on strike didn't have men at thir backs to look after them. [. . .] A lot o them, young ones wae kids and everythin were maybe one parent family, they didn't have anything. I think that's why I'm . . . ay . . . I'm bitter. And it's never sorta eased. I'm still angry.[121]

Substantial pressure was placed on Hall and Timex management to reverse the dismissals and pay cuts by the STUC and Labour MPs from across Scotland, who helped to mobilise a campaign of solidarity in support of the sacked workers. In April and June there were major marches and rallies, with speeches and big crowds, in Camperdown Park. The campaign featured conventional male labour movement leaders, including George Bolton, President of the NUMSA, and then Arthur Scargill,

118 Airlie, Interview with Carnegie.
119 DUA, MSS 272/2, Hall to Mason, 17 February 1993.
120 DUA, Commons Employment Committee, *Minutes of Evidence*, 28 April 1993, p. 15.
121 Bozdog, *Generation ZX(X)*, Clip 30.

the NUM President himself, pictured marching through the streets of Dundee with Ernie Ross, John McAllion and Alex Salmond, leader of the SNP. But the campaign also included a feminist emphasis on the distinct position of women in Timex and Dundee more generally. The loss of relatively well-paid manual jobs was experienced in particularly negative terms by women less able to travel further distances for alternative industrial work.[122]

Some of the women involved asserted that their difficulties were partly the making of male shop stewards, including those transferred to Camperdown from Milton, who had 'moved in and [. . .] started tae take over'.[123] Jean Brown, an activist in the 1993 dispute, regretted the decision to strike. This placed the workforce outside the factory, reducing their capacity to defend their jobs or secure enhanced exit terms:

VALERIE: And you think it was a mistake to go out?

JEAN: Oh God, aye. That's what they were after. Aye, so we lost a lot of . . . we could have fought for a better redundancy. See even they would have done that, we could have . . . got a lot more than what we did get.[124]

The dispute attained UK-wide political and media attention. *The Guardian* claimed it was the biggest lockout since Rupert Murdoch had moved his News International titles from the Fleet Street quarter of central London to Wapping in the East End in 1986.[125] Murdoch had sacked 5,500 unionised print workers,[126] and in scale terms the comparison was a slight misdirection. The 340 dismissed by Hall amounted to a fraction of this. They also represented just one-eighteenth of those employed in Dundee by Timex in 1974 and one-sixth of the jobs lost at Milton in 1983. In Part I of this book it was shown that such misconception was commonplace in the chronicling of deindustrialisation: closures and opposition to closures were visible and attracted attention; but much greater job losses accumulated through attrition. The 1993

---

122 THG, Green Box, *Timex Workers' Bulletin*, No. 1, April 1993; *Scottish Socialist Movement*, Bulletin No. 9, June/July 1993; Maria Fyffe to Ernie Ross, 16 March 1993.
123 Bozdog, *Generation ZX(X)*, Clip 28.
124 Brown, Interview.
125 'Clocked Off', *The Guardian, Weekend Magazine*, 29 May 1993, 7–9.
126 Peter Bain, 'The 1986–7 News International Dispute: Was the Workers' Defeat Inevitable?' *Historical Studies in Industrial Relations*, 5 (Spring 1998), pp. 73–105.

dispute was still a transformative event for those involved. Workers with personal reservations, like Jean, accepted the collective decision and actively supported the strike. Hall resigned in June, triggering hopes of reinstatement, but Timex quickly moved to an announcement that the plant would close in August.[127] The personal and collective difficulty of this enforced departure was compounded for many by subsequent experience. Jean and other former Camperdown women who have been interviewed in life-course formats report that Timex provided them with their most satisfying and secure employment. The solidarity of the factory contrasted markedly with the precariousness and frequent isolation of the private sector service work that followed.[128] Symbolising the regretted transition was a story told by Jean about the demands of an affluent woman in her care who expressed demands for attention with an overbearing sense of middle-class entitlement.[129]

The severity of this loss, coupled with the high profile and acrimony of the Camperdown lockout, has conditioned an important curiosity of collective memory where 1993 is remembered and 1983 is not. *On the Line*, the play written by Spence and Carnegie, perhaps helped to cultivate this. It focused entirely on the 1993 strike and its immediate aftermath. The 1983 occupation was ignored. Milton appeared only in conjunction with the 'militants' who 'took over' at Camperdown and compelled the women to strike.[130] This was an ambiguous presentation of female agency, presenting 'strong' women as unwitting victims. Unsympathetic representations of male trade unionists as incompetents or chancers have continued to feature in testimonies of former Camperdown workers in the intervening years.[131] Media coverage in the 2010s included some acknowledgement of the longer history, noting the establishment and expansion of the factories in Dundee, but even this passed briefly over the occupation and concentrated on 1993.[132] This one-dimensional history was reprised in the *Rise and Fall of Timex in Dundee*, a television

---

127 Seamus Milne and Edward Pilkington, 'Timex workers vote for fight to continue', *The Guardian*, 4 June 1993; and Erlend Clouston, 'Timex closes dispute factory ahead of schedule', *The Guardian*, 30 August 1993.
128 Bozdog, *Generation ZX(X)*, Clip 5.
129 Brown, Interview.
130 Alan Spence and John Carnegie, 'On the Line', unpublished draft scripts, 1995; Rep Theatre, Dundee, *Programme*, 'On the Line, A Celebration of Timex in Dundee', Tuesday 9 – Saturday 27 April 1996, 'A Timex Chronology'.
131 Bozdog, *Generation ZX(X)*, Clip 8–38.
132 'The good, the bad and the Timex: A factory of the future . . . until tough times hit', *Evening Telegraph*, 28 August 2015; 'Remembering the Timex factory dispute', *The Scotsman*, 19 January 2013.

documentary first shown on BBC Scotland in October 2019. Dozens of former workers were interviewed in the making of the programme, including Tom Smith and other male engineers. About two-thirds of the one-hour programme were devoted to the 1993 dispute and Timex's departure from Dundee. The testimonies of the male engineers who had spoken to camera about the longer history of production and employment at Timex barely featured.[133]

The image of women on the assembly lines and then on strike fitted popular conceptions of Dundee as an intensive centre of female industrial employment. This is the legacy of Dundee's distinct history.[134] Women had a tradition of spirited protest in the late nineteenth and early twentieth centuries in the jute industry. This involved challenging the patriarchal authority of the mill owners as well as their male supervisors and workmates. Media narratives relating to Timex since the 1990s have routinely drawn on these representations of Dundee women workers and the city's presumed historical status as a 'women's town' or 'she town'.[135] The low profile of the 1983 occupation is nevertheless problematic. It was more important than the 1993 lockout in terms of scale and character. Skilled jobs were vital to families and communities in the city in the early 1980s as well as the men who confronted redundancy. The loss of 2,000 engineering jobs, in a union-regulated workplace, was sorely experienced. The fight for the 'right to work' in 1983 was a powerful restatement of the working-class moral economy that was under assault from employers and policy-makers.

CONCLUSION

Timex in Dundee illustrates one of this book's core themes: deindustrialisation in Scotland from the mid-1950s was gradual, by design, and phased. Multinational engineering acquired a major presence in Dundee after 1945 because policy-makers were making provision for

---

133 *The Rise and Fall of Timex Dundee*, BBC Scotland, first broadcast 19 October 2019; Tom Smith, conversation with JP.
134 Valerie Wright, 'Juteopolis and After: Women and Work in Twentieth-Century Dundee', in Tomlinson and Whatley, *Jute No More*, pp. 132–62.
135 Eleanor Gordon, *Women and the Labour Movement in Scotland, 1850–1914* (Oxford: Oxford University Press, 1991), p. 142; Emma Wainwright, 'Constructing Gendered Workplace "Types": The weaver–millworker distinction in Dundee's jute industry, c. 1880–1910', *Gender, Place & Culture*, 14.4 (2007), pp. 467–82.

the shrinkage of the staple trades in Scotland. Jute gave way to watches, along with cash registers and other engineering products. Timex grew with public as well as private investment, expanding in the relative affluence of the 1960s and early 1970s. Employment peaked across the company's Dundee factories in 1974. The acceleration of change in the 1980s, in Dundee as in Scotland, was advanced by strategic decisions, taken in the Timex case by business managers like Lawson, owner-investors such as Olsen, and policy-makers, namely Fletcher and Thatcher, who were ultimately careless with local feeling and circumstances. In 1983 the firm completed its gradual evolution, from mechanical watch-maker to contract electronics manufacturer.

Earlier steps in this transition had been made through dialogue with the workforce, in recognition of union voice and preserving economic security. The final conversion in 1983 was made without such agreement, and in this respect violated the working-class moral economy of deindustrialisation. The employment effects of this transition were powerful. From the 1950s to the 1970s Timex employed a substantial core of skilled and relatively autonomous engineering workers, mainly men, who in union terms were well-organised and influential within the firm and the city more broadly, along with larger numbers of less skilled and more closely supervised assembly workers, who were predominantly female. These workers asserted their right to shared authority across Timex operations in Dundee in moral-economy terms. The tight labour market situation of the 1960s helped workers to establish collective bargaining and a closed shop in all Timex factories. Class tensions were accompanied by complex gender relations, with the clear bifurcation of labour between skilled engineering at Milton of Craigie and assembly production at Camperdown. Women at Camperdown exerted significant influence within the plant, on the shop-floor, managing their male supervisors, and in social spaces, where they organised and pursued an alternative economy. After 1983 the position was transformed, with the company's Dundee workforce consisting largely of assembly workers with limited control over production. Union influence was substantially curtailed, although the closed shop was retained until the end of 1992. These developments were encouraged by the Conservative government, which breached the 'dual' moral-economy framework that had governed the earlier phase of deindustrialisation in Scotland. Social-democratic policy-makers had committed the state to the protection of economic security through manual employment. Workers had accepted the desirability of industrial restructuring on this promise of economic security but insisted that changes could only proceed through negotiation and agreement, and where employment opportunities were widened and expanding social expectations satisfied.

Product diversification and greater labour flexibility were pursued by Timex from the late 1970s onwards. The 1983 crisis showed that this was dangerous, with Nimslo leaving, and Sinclair and IBM threatening to follow. The government's response – embarrassed by the redundancies in an election year, and far from uncritical of Timex in private – was to assert the need for further changes in labour attitudes and practices. There was no accompanying effort, as had been the case from the 1950s to the 1970s, to stimulate employment and growth in manufacturing industry more broadly. The labour power of the Timex workforce was curtailed not only by the new regime within the firm, endorsed by the government's offer of financial support for subcontracted assembly production, but by the wider pattern of rising unemployment and job scarcity. The ending of production at Timex in 1993 was painful. The company's profitable production in the city had been enabled by significant public investment and the ingenuity of its employees. This underlined the character and strength of feeling within the workforce and the community which the Milton occupiers had articulated ten years earlier. The 1983 occupation and 1993 lockout each represented a brave and dignified defence of the moral economy which had raised the status of working-class people in Dundee and Scotland since the 1950s, improving living standards and social conditions. Those involved were not seeking to extend the life of declining industry or outdated employment practices, as Conservative policy-makers and Timex management claimed, but protecting their rights as workers to collective voice and economic security.

Part III

Legacy and Evaluation

Deindustrialisation since the 1990s

In the long economic expansion, the 'great complacency', which ran from the early 1990s to the Great Financial Crash (GFC) in 2007–8, Scotland shared with the rest of the Western world a marked but uneven prosperity. It then suffered from the GFC, the impact of austerity policies pursued by the London government, and thereafter a slow recovery, further weakened by the impact of the impending Brexit after the referendum of 2016. But throughout this period of macroeconomic fluctuations the trend of deindustrialisation continued, albeit with important variations in pace and character. The first part of this chapter summarises these broad patterns of economic change over the last three decades. Deindustrialisation was increasingly deployed as a term to understand what was happening in Scotland from the 1990s. Uses of the term were varied, sometimes inconsistent, and linked to broader ideological positions. To examine this evolving debate the second section of this chapter focuses on Glasgow. As stressed already in this book, deindustrialisation was general in Scotland, from the Borders to the Highlands, in all the big cities but also in small towns. Deindustrialisation was nevertheless especially prominent as a political as well as an economic phenomenon in Glasgow and its region, and this was where its effects were most analysed in Scotland.

From the late 1990s economic debate in Scotland was increasingly affected by the devolution of political power from London. In 2007 this involved the election of an SNP government at Holyrood. This sought to set a distinct national agenda, which was the focus of much debate during and after the 2014 independence referendum. Political divergence between Scotland and England, highly evident from the 1960s to the 1980s, and influenced strongly by the process of deindustrialisation in these decades, continued to widen from the 1990s to the 2010s. This is analysed in the third part of the chapter. By the time of the UK general election of 2019, notions of responding to these effects with policies aimed at 'reindustrialisation' were central to the Scottish political debate. The chapter's fourth part assesses the problematic nature of the reindustrialisation agenda before reflecting on the debate about the so-called 'half-life' of deindustrialisation: the manner in which industrial restructuring and then contraction from the 1950s to the 1980s continued to shape politics and society in the 2010s.

THE SCOTTISH ECONOMY SINCE THE 1990S

In common with the rest of the UK, Scotland's growth rate showed the impact of sharp cycles: continuous growth from 1997 to 2008, then a sharp contraction followed by slow recovery. After 2008 it is hard to disentangle cyclical and trend factors, but it seems likely that the GFC marked a transition to a newer lower trend rate of GDP growth, going from around 2.1 per cent per annum before the GFC to around 1.6 thereafter, up until the onset of the Covid-19 pandemic in 2020.[1] The GFC led to a 4 per cent fall in output in Scotland, with output *per head* falling by 4.8 per cent. Output eventually recovered more slowly than in previous recessions, reaching its pre-recession level only after five years from the previous peak. Output fell further in industry than in services (though financial services fell even more), with construction, always highly cyclically sensitive, shrinking by 23 per cent and not returning to its pre-recession volume until 2018. Though inflation never rose above 4.5 per cent (in 2011), money wage growth lagged behind, partly through pay freezes and caps in the public sector within the governing strategy of austerity. Median real wages therefore fell, not regaining their pre-recession level until 2019.[2]

Employment trends were broadly similarly to those in output. Expansion throughout the pre-GFC yeas was followed by decline, fluctua-

1 Stephen Boyle, 'Economic policy performance', in Kenneth Gibb, Duncan Maclennan, Des McNulty and Michael Comerford, eds, *The Scottish Economy* (Abingdon Routledge, 2018), pp. 78–81.
2 See https://fraserofallander.org/scottish-economy/scotlands-economy-ten-years-on-from-the-financial-crisis/; Annual Survey of Hours and Earnings, at https://www2.gov.scot/Topics/Statistics/Browse/Labour-Market/Earnings, both accessed 21 December 2020.

Table 7.1 Unemployment in Scotland (as percentage), 1997–2017

	Scotland: claimant count	Scotland: 'real level'*
1997	8.3	11.3
2002	4.6	10.3
2007	2.8	7.9
2012	4.2	9.8
2017	2.4	6.3

Source: C. Beatty, S. Fothergill and T. Gore, *The Real Level of Unemployment 2017* (Sheffield: Sheffield Hallam University, 2017).
Note: *Percentage of working–age population (16–64). This figure is adjusted to include those unemployed but not claiming benefit, and the hidden unemployed claiming incapacity benefit. The data are based on the methodology developed in various publications by Christina Beatty and her associates. We are very grateful to Christina Beatty for providing us with a consistent series, which differs slightly from the figures previously published.

tions and a return to 2009 levels only in 2014.[3] Unemployment followed a similar cyclical path, albeit with a return to long-term improvement during the slow recovery from the GFC. This is shown in Table 7.1, which compares those claiming out-of-work benefits with the 'real level' of unemployment. The real level, as noted in Chapter 3, encompassed 'all those who could reasonably be expected to have been in employment in a genuinely fully employed economy'. To those claiming benefit, it adds those available for work as measured by the Labour Force Survey and hidden unemployment among incapacity claimants, benchmarked against the fully employed parts of southeast England. The gap between the real level and the claimant count was consistently wider in Scotland as a whole than in England as a whole.[4]

Deindustrialisation continued throughout this period. It was especially evident in the years immediately after 2000 when, unlike in the economy as a whole, there was a recession in manufacturing output. This was driven largely by a sharp cycle in electronics, where output grew by 70 per cent between 1995 until 2000, but then fell by more than 40 per cent over the next three years.[5] This decline was driven

3 A. O'Connor, *Scotland's Employment by Industry and Geography* (Edinburgh: Scottish Parliament Information Centre, briefing SB17-71, 2017).
4 Christina Beatty, Steve Fothergill and Tony Gore, *The Real Level of Unemployment 2017* (Sheffield: Sheffield Hallam University, 2017).
5 Wendy Alexander, Jo Armstrong, Brian Ashcroft, Diane Coyle and John McLaren, 'The Political Economy of Scotland, Past and Present', in Diane Coyle, Wendy Alexander and Brian Ashcroft, eds, *New Wealth for Old Nations: Scotland's Economic Prospects* (Princeton, NJ: Princeton University Press, 2005), pp. 19–20.

by a major wave of lay-offs and plant consolidations, especially by US firms. Motorola terminated its two Scottish plants and NEC shut its factory at Livingston. These closures were immediately driven by a global downturn in demand for some electronics products such as mobile phones, combined with a wave of mergers and acquisitions in the industry. There was undoubtedly an underlying vulnerability to shifts of production to lower-cost locations in Eastern Europe and Asia, especially as most of the output was of a fairly 'traditional' character, rather than cutting-edge products. But as with the contraction of Timex in Dundee, it is too simple to ascribe the reduction in Scottish capacity wholly to 'globalisation' in the simple sense of an inability to compete with labour costs in developing economies. As Douglas Fraser, the BBC's business editor, noted when Texas Instruments closed its Greenock plant in 2016, production was being transferred 'to move to German, Japanese and American plants – not, you'll note, low wage economies'.[6] Globalisation in a different sense was nevertheless at work here, as many companies switched from regional to global strategies and structures, to the disadvantage of Scotland.[7] The result was that employment in Scotland in electronics halved between 1999 and 2003.[8]

Part I of this book showed that Scotland had a long history of attracting multinational investment. Despite the retreat in electronics, such investment continued in the twenty-first century. Foreign Direct Investment (FDI) was spread across most sectors of the economy and still highly significant in industry. Food, drink and tobacco were the largest manufacturing recipients of FDI, which created 11,658 jobs in the sector between 2003 and 2012.[9] This was valuable given the continued shrinkage of industrial employment overall in Scotland, with

6 'Whatever happened to Silicon Glen?' 28 January 2016, at https://www.bbc.co.uk/news/uk-scotland-scotland-business-35428124, accessed 21 December 2020.
7 Stephen Young, Duncan Ross and Brad MacKay, 'Inward foreign direct investment and constitutional change in Scotland', *Multinational Business Review*, 22.2 (2014), pp. 118–38, at p. 120.
8 Dimitratos et al., 'The multinational enterprise'; R. Brown, 'The Future of ICT industries in Scotland: towards a post-branch plant economy?', in N. Hood, J. Peat, E. Peters and S. Young, eds, *Scotland in a Global Economy: The 2020 Vision* (Basingstoke: Palgrave Macmillan, 2002), pp. 131–4; A. Young, *Forty Turbulent Years: How the Fraser Economic Commentary Recorded the Evolution of the Modern Scottish Economy* (Glasgow: Fraser of Allander Institute, 2015), pp. 23–4.
9 Young et al., 'Inward foreign direct investment', pp. 120–1, 138.

Table 7.2 Employees (full and part time) in major sectors of the Scottish economy, 2018 (as percentage)

Primary	1.6
Secondary	15.5
Mining, quarrying and utilities	2.7
Manufacturing	7.1
Construction	5.7
Tertiary	82.9
Health	15.5
Retail	9.0
Business administration and support	8.1
Accommodation and food services	7.7
Education	8.0
Professional, scientific and technical	7.0
Public administration	6.2
Transport	4.2
Sub-sectors with less than 100,000 employees	17.2

Source: Author calculations from ONS: *Business Register and Employment Survey*, 2019.
Total number of employees 2,508,600.

123,000 manufacturing jobs lost in the ten years before the GFC.[10] After 2009 decline continued, so that by 2018 manufacturing employed only 7.1 per cent of Scots, and 'industry' in total only 15.5 per cent. Note, by contrast, the striking scale of employment in health, detailed in Table 7.2, with over twice as many workers as in manufacturing. An important correlate of this continuing sectoral shift was the further overall weakening of trade unions and their greater concentration in the public sector. Union density among Scottish employees was 39 per cent in 1995 but only 30 per cent in 2005.[11] It is also important to note that these figures do not cover the self-employed, whose numbers in Scotland expanded to 15 per cent of working men and 9.1 per cent of working women by 2015. As many of these self-employed work shorter hours and get paid less than they had previously as employees, their status effectively disguises significant levels of under-employment.[12]

10 Paul S. Jones and Anne Green, 'The quantity and quality of jobs: changes in UK regions, 1997–2007', *Environment and Planning*, 41.10 (2009), pp. 2474–95, with detail at p. 2487.
11 David McCrone, *The New Sociology of Scotland* (London: Sage, 2017), p. 213.
12 J. Campbell and E. Thomson, 'Changing role of women in the Scottish economy', in Gibb et al., *The Scottish Economy*, pp. 13–139: McCrone, *New Sociology*, p. 210.

Deindustrialisation remained driven – as in the earlier period examined in Part I – by long-run patterns of technological change and trends in consumer demand. The process was reinforced from the mid-1990s by the expansion of manufacturing exports from China and other Asian economies. By 2019, China had become the biggest supplier of imports to Scotland in the 'office and automatic data-processing equipment' category, and dominated in the textiles and clothing category with others such as Vietnam and Hong Kong. This surge in produce from China since the 1990s has been the strongest trend overall in Scotland's global trading in goods. By 2019 China was the third biggest source of Scottish imported goods, almost at the same level as the USA, and lagging substantially behind only Norway, which was largely oil-related. This expansion of imported manufactures simultaneously improved the purchasing power of Scottish incomes, while further eroding the availability of industrial jobs. This was counterbalanced to some degree by expanding exports. Since 2010 China has been one of Scotland's fastest growing export markets.[13]

Changes in the gender composition of the workforce were characterised earlier in this book as central to the broader process of deindustrialisation. This reflected the broader shift away from a 'male-breadwinner' model of how society could or should work. Labour market changes after 1997 further entrenched the dual-income household as the Scottish norm. A clear measure of this is economic activity rates. In the twenty years after 1995 the female rate rose from 67.6 per cent to 75.4 per cent, while the male level fell from 83.7 to 82.6 per cent. This was a marked narrowing of the historic gap. This trend was driven in particular by the rise in activity rates among women with dependent children, especially those who were parents with a child below the age of five. Men remained hugely predominant in industrial sectors – energy and water, manufacturing and construction – although these sectors shrank in absolute terms. Women predominated in public administration, education and health. Over 70 per cent of all employees in these sectors were female. This reinforced in a Scottish context the well-established point that women workers have been the main gainers from the expansion of public sector employment, and the main losers when it is cut back. Women had particularly negative experiences of the 'contracting out' to the private sector of public services, with trade union recognition less prevalent and conditions of employment often significantly eroded.

13 See https://www.gov.scot/publications/export-stats-scotland-2018/, accessed 21 December 2020.

Gender pay gaps remained significant across the economy. This was partly because men gained a larger share of manufacturing jobs.[14]

These various gender inequalities were compounded by the unequal distribution between men and women of part-time employment. The phenomenon was 'sticky'. The STUC Women's Advisory Committee observed in 1988 that 43 per cent of female employees were part-time.[15] The erosion of manufacturing jobs appears to have worsened the position: 46 per cent of women worked part-time in 1996, compared with just 11.7 per cent of men.[16] This structural disadvantage compounded the inequalities encountered by women in the division of household labour and caring responsibilities as well as in occupational opportunity and workplace rights. It emerged in the 2000s that movement towards greater equality was also hindered by unjust and illegitimate employment structures where work chiefly performed by men was deemed more valuable than work chiefly performed by women, despite objective similarities in pre-entry skills and experience. Among the offending employers in Scotland were several local authorities, notably Glasgow City Council. Higher local authority pay for refuse collectors than care workers, sanctioned by trade union officialdom, was a particularly egregious example of this iniquitous pattern.[17]

DEINDUSTRIALISATION IN GLASGOW

Glasgow was a key location in the process of deindustrialisation in Scotland. This was partly because of the city's weight in the national economy and its prominent profile historically as a centre of industry. Its distinct chronology of deindustrialisation was also significant. Its most rapid contraction of industrial jobs mirrored the trend in Scotland from the mid-1950s onwards. But in some sectors, notably shipbuilding and heavy engineering, employment in Glasgow had been shrinking since the 1910s and 1920s. Glasgow was not only where deindustrialisation in Scotland most strikingly occurred, it was also where much of the Scottish debate on the genesis of deindustrialisation, along with its

---

14 Campbell and Thomson, 'Changing Role of Women in the Scottish Economy'.
15 GCUA, STUC Joint General Council/Women's Committee Seminar, October 1988.
16 The Scottish Office, *Scottish Abstract of Statistics*, 26 (Edinburgh: HMSO, 1998), Table 6B4.
17 Martin Beirne, Scott Hurrell and Fiona Wilson, 'Mobilising for equality? Understanding the impact of grass roots agency and third party representation', *Industrial Relations Journal*, 50.1 (2019), pp. 41–56.

effects and remedies, has focused. The city 'has captured the attention of a raft of researchers who have come to regard it as a model laboratory within which processes of deindustrialisation and urban regeneration might be illuminated'.[18]

The weight of Glasgow in the Scottish economy depends, of course, on the definition of Glasgow. The current claim in the Clyde Plan of the 'City region', covering a third of Scotland's population and generating a third of its wealth, seems broadly in line with a long-standing historical pattern.[19] It is a well-established narrative that this city region's industrial peak was before 1914, when the Clyde dominated world shipbuilding to an extraordinary extent. Glasgow was also important in a range of other heavy engineering products, such as locomotives. This focus on capital goods exposed the city to punishing contraction after 1920, when these industries suffered especially from global deflationary pressure and increased international competition, problems exacerbated in the great depression of the early 1930s. Economic policy-makers by this point tended to take the view that Glasgow was condemned to stagnation because of its narrow and hence outdated industrial structure. But the urgency of action was offset in the late 1930s by the rearmament boom, followed by the Second World War itself and then the decade or so of post-1945 reconstruction. Contraction re-emerged in earnest in the mid-1950s. Shipbuilding suffered a spectacular decline. By 1971 employment in the various yards had shrunk to around 11,000, little more than 10 per cent of the industry's Edwardian peak.[20]

The work-in of 1971–2, examined in Chapter 4, prevented the total disappearance of shipbuilding from Glasgow, but despite the subsequent nationalisation of the industry across the UK further losses followed. By 2020 there were only two yards still open in the city, both survivors of the UCS era, Fairfield and Scotstoun. Owned by BAE Systems, they employed a relatively small number of workers engaged in military contracts, mainly for the UK Royal Navy. While the decline of shipbuilding rightly has a central role in the narrative of Glasgow's modern history, it is important to remember – reflecting on the analysis presented in Chapters 2 and 3 – that losses in the yards along with those in engineering plants were only a small component in the more general contraction

18 Martin Boyle, Christopher McWilliams and Gareth Rice, 'The spatialities of actually existing neo-liberalism, 1977 to present', *Geografiska Annaler Series B: Human Geography*, 90 (2008), p. 314.
19 See https://www.clydeplan-sdpa.gov.uk/, accessed 21 December 2020.
20 A. Pike, 'Structural Transformation, Adaptability and City Economic Evolutions', Working Paper 8, *Case Study Report: Glasgow* (2017), p. 22.

of industrial employment. The gender politics of deindustrialisation are glaring in this respect. By comparison with the well-known Upper Clyde struggles, where men were built along with the ships, to paraphrase Jimmy Reid, little attention was paid to the disappearance of female jobs in textiles, the sector marked by the largest absolute loss of employment in Glasgow, from around 36,000 in 1971 to 2,500 in 2015. This included the incremental shrinkage of Templeton's, the carpet manufacturer, which moved production from its idiosyncratically beautiful factory beside Glasgow Green to a dwindling number of smaller sites in the city, before ceasing production altogether in 1981.[21] The second biggest declining sector, the manufacture of electrical equipment, was likewise a heavy employer of women.[22] These losses across categories meant that by the early 1990s manufacturing employment in Glasgow in absolute terms was less than a quarter of the level of the early 1950s.[23]

This more recent pattern, with a range of manufacturing sectors disrupted by deindustrialisation, should be underlined. It suggests an unwarranted over-emphasis in historical interpretation to the demise of the heavy industries. Sydney Checkland's account was framed in a highly negative register by the upas tree imagery used for both title and central theme. He claimed that 'the upas tree of heavy engineering killed anything that sought to grow beneath its branches.'[24] As a long-term perspective this was exaggerated, ignoring the range of other industries that were allowed by circumstances to flourish in the city, including food, drink and tobacco, another substantial employer of women. These contracted less steeply than textiles from the 1970 to the 1990s, stabilising at around 10,000 for a while in the 2000s. The relative health of the food, drink and tobacco sector was admittedly atypical for manufacturing as a whole. In electrical and machinery industries job numbers approximately halved from around 11,000 in the two decades after 1995. A further sharp decline of textiles in these decades, down from around 12,000 to 2,000 workers, was probably in quantitative terms the most important effect on Glasgow's labour market of the rise of Asian competition noted in the first section of this chapter. This aspect of the

21 Rory Stride, 'Women, Work and Deindustrialisation: The case of James Templeton & Company, Glasgow, c. 1960–1981', *Scottish Labour History*, 54 (2019), pp. 154–80.
22 Pike, 'Structural Transformation', p. 22.
23 John MacInnes, 'The deindustrialisation of Glasgow', *Scottish Affairs*, 11 (1995), pp. 73–95, at 73.
24 Sydney Checkland, *The Upas Tree: Glasgow 1875–1975 . . . and after 1975–80* (2nd edn; Glasgow: Glasgow University Press, 1981).

Glasgow story is congruent with the broader Scottish experience, noted above: the 'second wave' of multinational enterprise investment, focused on electronic and digital production associated with 'Silicon glen', was reversed from the mid-1990s.[25]

Responses to deindustrialisation in Glasgow were complicated by the focus of policy-makers in the 1950s and 1960s on the city's housing problems. An extraordinarily ambitious project of population resettlement was planned. This aimed to rehouse half the city's population, a quarter of them in 'overspill' new towns outwith the city boundary.[26] This plan, though never pursued to the extent originally envisaged, has been the subject of much subsequent policy and historical contention. From the point of view of those who moved, the experience was clearly mixed. The phenomenon of the high-rise flats is illustrative in this respect. The broader amenity of the new flats themselves was widely initially appreciated, but high-rise living was often linked to serious problems of social isolation.[27] Economic and employment strategy were intimately connected to this rehousing programme. The cases of Linwood, Caterpillar and Bathgate showed how housing often followed the establishment of new industrial projects. New local authority homes were major incentives for workers considering migration from Glasgow to these and other plants. The effort made by policy-makers to transplant manufacturing into the new towns and suburbs was successful. American multinationals especially moved in significant numbers to the 'greenfield' sites of Cumbernauld and East Kilbride. Job turnover in these towns seems to have been high, but in the 1960s there was a continuing influx of new employment to offset closures.[28] These towns were nevertheless exposed to especial vulnerability when the corporations that owned the 'branch plants' changed course, often involving abandonment of Scottish operations. Glasgow was gradually denuded of employment as a result of this mass migration. Its remaining workforce was also characterised by decreasing levels of skill and educational qualification.[29]

The movement of population exacerbated what came to be constructed as the 'inner-city' problem, where Glasgow was regarded as

25 Pike, 'Structural Transformation', p. 22.
26 MacInnes, 'The deindustrialisation of Glasgow', p. 81.
27 Abrams et al., *Glasgow*.
28 MacInnes, 'The deindustrialisation of Glasgow', p. 81.
29 Chik Collins and Ian Levitt, 'The "modernization" of Scotland and its impact on Glasgow, 1955–79: "unwanted side effects" and vulnerabilities', *Scottish Affairs*, 25 (2016), pp. 277–93.

a particularly serious example of a much wider malaise.[30] Only slowly from the early 1980s was this aspect of development reversed. As in other urban centres that experienced deindustrialisation, the population of the inner city stabilised and then gradually increased, partly owing to the growth of higher-skilled positions being filled by highly educated workers. By the 2000s Glasgow exhibited the standard pattern of a combination of 'lovely' and 'lousy' jobs common in Scottish and British cities, although with an especially heavy incidence of most of the negative features of such a labour market.[31] The city's condition in this respect was consistent with Beynon's reflections on living with and within capitalism in the twenty-first century, forty years after he had analysed the 'Fordist' division of labour in an ICI factory at Avonmouth with Theo Nichols. Fordism had survived the transition to service-based employment: the division of labour observable in the chemicals plant in the 1970s between 'donkey' and 'science' work prefigured the divergence in services of 'lousy' and 'lovely' jobs. The lousy jobs have become lousier, of course, without the protections of collective bargaining and social-democratic policy that existed in the 1970s, and as capitalism has more fully penetrated social, household and family relations.[32]

As a pioneer of the historical process of deindustrialisation, Glasgow was also a city where that term was applied early, widely and systematically to try and understand its problems. Analysts used the term explicitly from the early 1990s to explain the city's distinct economic and urban history: 'Glasgow can be regarded as a classic case of deindustrialisation and disurbanisation. It was one of the first major conurbations to industrialise: it seems inevitable that it should have been amongst the first to deindustrialise.'[33] This led to the identification and examination of the 'Glasgow effect', the city's disproportionately severe problems of poor health, addictive behaviour and economic deprivation. In many accounts the Glasgow effect was seen as product of the character and pace of the city's deindustrialisation. This was strikingly evident in the research undertaken by the Glasgow Centre for Population Health

---

30 Aaron Andrews, 'Multiple Deprivation, the Inner City and the Fracturing of the Welfare State: Glasgow, c.1968–78', *Twentieth Century British History*, 29 (2018), pp. 605–24.
31 Goos and Manning, 'Lousy and Lovely Jobs'.
32 Beynon, 'After the Long Boom'.
33 W. Lever, 'Deindustrialisation and the reality of the post-industrial city', *Urban Studies*, 28 (1991), pp. 983–99.

(GCPH),[34] positioning deindustrialisation as a key cause of poor health via its cultivation of deprivation and poverty.[35] There was detailed investigation of a particular puzzle: why there were 'extra' levels of ill-health in Glasgow, compared with similar post-industrial cities subject to broadly similar policy regimes in the UK, notably Manchester and Liverpool. The central if contentious claim was that 'the city, over time, was made more vulnerable than the comparator cities to the particular socio-economic and political exposures (poverty, deprivation, widening income inequality), resulting in worse health outcomes'. This vulnerability was attributed to a series of historical factors, including high levels of overcrowding before the Second World War, then the rehousing and depopulation of the 1950s to the 1970s, followed last but not least by the city's prioritisation of inner-city gentrification and commercial development from 1979 onwards.[36]

This discussion of health pointed to the widening inequalities of the deindustrialising labour market, with poor health outcomes exacerbated for those without the skills or educational qualifications required to access especially non-manual jobs.[37] While the 'gentrification' of Glasgow may have been a problem as well as a solution, it was nevertheless accompanied by a growth of employment. From 1970 to the mid-1990s both inner Glasgow and the outer ring of the city showed significantly worse performance on employment growth than Scotland as a whole. But in the second half of the 1990s employment grew rapidly, especially in the centre.[38] This expansion included many 'lovely' jobs, with a significantly faster growth of financial services than in Edinburgh although from a lower base.[39] The data in Table 7.3 indicate that while this trend continued in the 2000s, there were not enough 'lovely' jobs

34 D. Walsh, G. McCartney, C. Collins, M. Taulbut and G. Batty, 'History, politics and vulnerability: explaining excess mortality in Scotland and Glasgow', *Public Health*, 151 (2017), pp. 1–12.
35 There is a very extensive literature on Glasgow's poor health, see for example, P. Norman, P. Boyle, D. Exeter, Z. Feng and F. Popham, 'Rising premature mortality in the UK's persistently deprived areas: Only a Scottish phenomenon?' *Social Science Medicine*, 73 (2011), pp. 1575–84.
36 Walsh et al., 'History', p. 6.
37 D. Webster, J. Brown, E. Macdonald and I. Turok, 'The interaction of health, labour market conditions and long-term sickness benefit claims in a post-industrial city: A Glasgow case study', in C. Lindsay and D. Houston, eds, *Disability Benefits, Welfare Reform and Employment Policy* (Basingstoke: Palgrave Macmillan, 2013), pp. 111–33.
38 Ivan Turok and Nick Bailey, 'Twin track cities? Competitiveness and cohesion in Glasgow and Edinburgh', *Progress in Planning*, 62 (2004), pp. 168–9.
39 Turok and Bailey, 'Twin track cities?' p. 159.

Table 7.3 Employment by sector in Glasgow, 2016–17 (percentage of employed population)

Agriculture and fishing	1.7
Manufacturing	6.6
Construction	6.8
Energy and water	1.7
Transport and communication	8.0
Banking, finance and insurance	18.1
Distribution, hotels and restaurants	18.4
Public administration and health	34.1
Other services	6.1

Source: Scottish Cities: The Glasgow Indicators Project, at https://www. understandingglasgow.com/indicators/economic_participation/comparisons/with_ other_places/employment_by_industry/scottish_citi, accessed 6 January 2020.

by the early 2000s to match the number of graduates. The rise of graduates in 'non-graduate' work was a new form of 'under-employment' that became much more common as the University system expanded.[40]

The ambiguous consequences of this turnaround were spelt out by Turok and Bailey. The growth of inner-city, non-manual jobs 'created a narrower range of job opportunities compared with the skills of core city residents, resulting in greater in-commuting from surrounding areas and a smaller reduction in local worklessness than might have been the case with broader-based growth'.[41] This important observation raises two further questions: what happened to unemployment in Glasgow, and is employment still a key factor in shaping economic welfare in the 'new' labour market?

Table 7.4 shows that the trend 'real' level of unemployment fell in the city and an adjacent local authority area, Inverclyde, which incorporates the former industrial towns of Greenock and Port Glasgow. It also shows, however, that were was a large but narrowing gap between the claimant count and that 'real' level. This was not a new phenomenon. It appeared in Chapter 3 as an important feature of the labour market in the 1980s and early 1990s. As in this earlier period, in the 2000s and 2010s there were many within the non-working population who were reliant on Incapacity Benefit (Employment and Support Allowance from 2008). The evidence was strong that many of these claimants were 'hidden unemployed', who in a stronger labour market would be

40 University of Strathclyde Careers Service, 'Survey of Graduate destinations' (2003).
41 Turok and Bailey, 'Twin track cities?' p. 171.

Table 7.4 Unemployment in Glasgow, 2002–17 (as percentage)

	Glasgow city: claimant count	Glasgow: 'real level'	Inverclyde: claimant count	Inverclyde: 'real level'
1997	8.5	20.8	5.6	13.0
2002	6.9	18.0	4.1	12.8
2007	6.3	13.7	4.5	12.3
2012	6.0	14.8	5.8	14.4
2017	3.3	9.3	4.5	10.6

Sources and derivation: See Table 7.1.

in paid jobs. Detailed work on Glasgow in the expansionary years preceding the GFC showed a fall in claimants from roughly three times to twice the national average. This reflected a rising demand for workers rather than the impact of changes made to the benefit system.[42] Annual data for the period since the onset of the GFC suggested that the trend fall in Employment and Support Allowance claimants to 2007 then ended in 2011, and the figure remained stable thereafter.[43]

How meaningful in welfare terms was the expansion of numbers in work until 2011? As in the rest of Scotland, part-time work for men and especially women expanded after the GFC. Many of these women wanted part-time employment to fit with their domestic responsibilities, but would have welcomed longer hours, so can be defined as 'underemployed'.[44] The rise of part-time work was an indicator of overall labour market change in Glasgow since the 1980s. Complete absence of employment over a long period became less prevalent, although it was still significant, giving way to much more 'churning' where individuals fluctuated between low-paid and short-run jobs and unemployment. Because such individuals were likely to live in households where others had similar labour market experiences, work provided limited

42 D. Webster, J. Arnott, J. Brown, I. Turok, R. Mitchell and E. Macdonald, 'Falling incapacity benefit claims in a former industrial city: Policy impacts or labour market improvement?' *Policy Studies*, 31 (2010), pp. 163–85.
43 Scottish Cities: The Glasgow Indicators Project, 'ESA AND Incapacity benefit rates in selected Scottish cities and Scotland, 2000–2016', at https://www.understandingglasgow.com/, accessed 21 December 2020.
44 C. Harkins and J. Egan, *The Rise of In-work Poverty and the Changing Nature of Poverty and Work in Scotland: What are the Implications for Population Health?* (Glasgow: GCPH, 2013) pp. 19–21; Campbell and Thomson, 'Changing role of women in the Scottish economy', pp. 137–40; Scottish Cities: The Glasgow Indicators Project, 'Underemployment rates in selected Scottish cities and Scotland, 2000–2016', at https://www.understandingglasgow.com/, accessed 6 January 2020.

respite from poverty. In Glasgow as well as across Scotland and parts of the UK there was an increasing incidence of poverty in households where at least one member was in work.[45] The polarisation of the deindustrialised labour market can be further elaborated. In Glasgow, and Scotland more generally, this was most evident in the stagnation of earnings at the lowest percentile (the bottom 10 per cent of the distribution) compared with the growth for the top percentile. This was how rising earnings inequalities in the city were largely driven in the years after 1997, though the process seems to have halted at the time of the GFC, since when top earnings have stagnated.[46] At the bottom end of the distribution, this meant that in 2016

> half a million jobs in Scotland – 20 per cent of all employee jobs, and almost 40 per cent of part-time jobs – were paid below the level of the 'real' living wage (RLW). Approximately 65,000 of those jobs were in Glasgow. The figures had improved slightly by 2017 (and to a greater extent in some parts of Scotland) but remained high.[47]

Deindustrialisation in Glasgow was accompanied by an important strengthened reliance on public sector employment. This initially contracted in the early years of the Conservative-Liberal Democrat austerity period from 2010, then stabilised and even grew slightly.[48] In Glasgow around 26 per cent of all workers, with 33 per cent of women, were in the public sector in the late 2010s. This was significant on two counts: employment in the public sector is generally more stable than the private sector; and the public sector earnings structure in the last twenty-five years has favoured bigger increases at the bottom than the top end of the distribution.[49] More broadly, the long-run expansion of public sector employment in cities like Glasgow emphasises how we must be

45 Harkins and Egan, *The Rise of In-work Poverty*, pp. 13–16; Nick Bailey and Des McNulty, 'Inequality and poverty in Scotland', in Gibb et al., *Scottish Economy*, pp. 202–4.
46 D. Walsh and B. Whyte, 'Trends in earnings and income inequalities in Scotland and the UK 1997–2016' (2018), pp. 12–3, 21, at https://www.gcph.co.uk/assets/0000/7144/Trends_in_earnings_and_income_inequalities.pdf, accessed 21 December 2020.
47 Walsh and Whyte, 'Trends', p. 5. In 2016 the RLW was set by the Living Wage Foundation at £8.25 per hour outside London.
48 The Scottish Government, *Public sector employment in Scotland*, at https://www.gov.scot/publications/public-sector-employment-scotland-statistics-3rd-quarter-2019/, accessed 21 December 2020.
49 See Walsh and Whyte, 'Trends', pp. 29–34, at https://www.gcph.co.uk/assets/0000/7144/Trends_in_earnings_and_income_inequalities.pdf, accessed 4 January 2021.

careful in characterising what happened to labour markets from the 1990s onwards. Some analysts mistakenly conflated globalisation with deindustrialisation. One author claimed that: 'Glasgow, like other older industrial cities, has experienced the effects of the emergence of a global economy, and the de-industrialisation of the UK economy.'[50] Such comments mirrored claims about the whole of Scotland, said to be a country that 'operates and competes in a global market place, and globalisation has been a central driver of changes within labour markets, economies and the very nature of employment'.[51] But as Turok and Bailey pointed out in relation to both Glasgow and Edinburgh, 'external demand in both cities is dominated by regional (Scotland) and national (UK) markets, not European or other foreign markets. The situation is symptomatic of a more service-oriented economy and has changed since the heyday of manufacturing, when steel, ships and engineering products were very significant'.[52] So if we are focusing on recent decades it is important to note that the trend rise of employment in the public sector was part of an overall rise in the service sector that in broad terms reflected a process of *de-globalisation*. Glasgow and other cities were in truth *much more globalised* when heavily industrialised than they were in the 2000s and 2010s. Later deindustrialisation was driven more by technical change and shifting patterns of demand than globalisation in the sense of international competition.[53] After 1997, competition from Asia continued the long-running decline of employment in textiles and clothing, and also reduced the size of electronics, but in the longer and bigger picture of Glasgow's deindustrialisation, these were small elements.

DEVOLUTION AND INDEPENDENCE

The election of the New Labour government in May 1997 marked a watershed in Scotland's history. The government's proposals for devolved Parliaments in Scotland and Wales reflected the deep impact on UK politics of the working-class moral economy of deindustrialisation examined in this book. There was recognition that unreconstructed UK policy-making and constitutional structures had failed to accommodate

---

50 Michael Pacione, 'The view from the tower: Geographies of urban transformation in Glasgow', *Scottish Geographical Journal*, 125 (2009), pp. 127–81, p. 148.
51 Harkins and Egan, *The Rise of In-work Poverty*, p. 17.
52 Turok and Bailey, 'Twin track cities?' p. 155.
53 Jim Tomlinson, 'The Deglobalization of Dundee, circa 1900–2000', *Journal of Scottish Historical Studies*, 29 (2009), pp. 123–40.

popular and distinct demands, particularly in Scotland, for stronger protection of economic and social security.[54] Gordon Brown, Labour's Chancellor of the Exchequer, had been an early Labour advocate of devolution from the early 1970s onwards, influenced strongly by STUC thinking on the matter. In numerous speeches, articles and other public interventions Brown positioned Home Rule as enabling more sensitive management of deindustrialisation's effects. He was intimately familiar with these from his hometown in Kirkcaldy, and as MP for an economically disadvantaged coalfield constituency in Fife from 1983 onwards.[55] A two-question referendum was held in September 1997 on the Labour government's proposals: on whether a Parliament should be established; and whether it should have tax-varying powers. The national vote across Scotland was affirmative by a margin of three to one on the first question, and almost two to one on the second. In local authority areas adversely affected by industrial job losses in the 1980s the victory margins were slightly wider. In Glasgow, East Ayrshire, North Lanarkshire and West Dunbartonshire more than 80 per cent of votes cast were in favour of establishing the Parliament and more than 70 per cent supported the tax-varying powers. The first Parliament was elected and the first devolved administration formed, a Labour–Liberal Democrat coalition, with Donald Dewar as First Minister, in 1999.

The question of whether enhanced national sovereignty or self-determination could unlock greater economic success had frequently dominated the political agenda since the 1960s. Scotland's devolution from 1999, and especially the election of a first nationalist government in 2007, therefore shifted the terms of argument, even before the impact of the GFC. The SNP government, operating without a majority at Holyrood from 2007 until 2011, pursued significant changes to the structure of policy-making, which had previously remained little altered from the departmental framework inherited by the devolved administration in 1999. The use of the term 'Scottish Government' was an important symbolic as well as practical point of departure, distinct from the term 'Scottish Executive' utilised by Labour–Liberal Democrat coalitions.[56] The government's policy agenda shifted slowly and then accelerated after the SNP's remarkable victory in the Scottish Parliament election in May 2011. The SNP increased its share of constituency votes by

54 The Scottish Office, *Scotland's Parliament*, Cm 3658 (Edinburgh: HMSO, 1997).
55 Adam McInnes, 'Deindustrialisation and Gordon Brown's Approach to Devolution in Scotland', *Scottish Labour History*, 54 (2019), pp. 126–53.
56 John Elvidge, 'Government in Scotland', in Gibb et al., *The Scottish Economy*, pp. 311–22.

12.4 per cent to 45.4 per cent and additional-member regional votes by 13 per cent to 44 per cent. It won an overall majority in the Parliament, an eventuality, it was widely held, that the UK government had believed impossible when designing the devolved electoral system in 1997–8. The Scottish Government's distinctive policy-making stance was further developed in the run-up to the September 2014 referendum on independence. The Scottish Government summarised its key economic argument in *Scotland's Future*, the independence manifesto published in November 2013: 'The gap between rich and poor, the increasing concentration of economic activity in one part of the UK and the imbalances in the structure and composition of the UK economic model all suggest that continuing as a regional economy will hamper job creation in Scotland and reduce economic resilience and security in the long-term.'[57]

In focusing on the growth of inequality, especially evidenced by disproportionate income gains at the top end of the distribution, the Scottish Government drew on longer-running moral-economy narratives. The linkage of economic disparity, social justice and policy-making was further underscored by the austerity policies pursued after the GFC by the Conservative–Liberal Democrat Coalition government established in London in 2010. The Scottish Government articulated a broad-based revulsion in Scotland arising from the UK government's benefit cuts and contentious reform of welfare, Universal Credit. This was further 'rolled out' after the election of a Conservative UK government in 2015. The Scottish Government used its limited powers under devolution to mitigate the negative impact on claimants of this benefit, enabling fortnightly rather than monthly payments, and for housing elements of the entitlement to go directly to landlords.[58] Political divergence between Scotland and England was also clear in the tone used by the Scottish Government in matters relating to employment and trade unionism. Partnership with the STUC and its affiliates was emphasised in the 2013 independence manifesto,[59] and in 2015 the government established the Fair Work Convention, an advisory and research body that endorsed the value of workplace union voice.[60]

57 Scottish Government, *Scotland's Future: Your Guide to an Independent Scotland* (Edinburgh: Scottish Government, 2013), p. 6.
58 Scottish Government, 'Offering flexibility to Universal Credit recipients', 31 October 2018, at https://www.gov.scot/news/offering-flexibility-to-universal-credit-recipients/, accessed 24 April 2019.
59 Scottish Government, *Scotland's Future*, pp. 103–9.
60 Fair Work Convention, 'Effective Voice', at https://www.fairworkconvention.scot/the-fair-work-framework/effective-voice/, accessed 24 April 2019.

The widening distance between policy-making in Scotland and England was reflected in the increasing salience of nationalist critiques of the 'failed Westminster model' of economic governance. Deindustrialisation was presented as a key consequence of this 'failure'. With its impact on the labour market, the shrinkage of industrial employment was presented as a key source of widening inequality, as well as causing macroeconomic concern because of its perceived impact on the growth rate of the Scottish economy. Hence deindustrialisation was taken up in Scotland more than anywhere else in Britain as a key term of analysis in policy-making circles. The SNP strategy, outlined in the 2013 manifesto for independence, was to give a higher priority to manufacturing. The manifesto published data showing that median salaries in manufacturing in Scotland in 2011 were 26 per cent higher than in services. The term 'reindustrialisation' was explicitly used. A new industrial strategy would be devised, organised around investment and 'indigenous companies and ownership', with various hazily defined aspirations: 'boosting high-value jobs', 'promoting innovation', 'addressing geographical disparities' within Scotland and 'boosting exports'.[61] The reindustrialisation argument was supported by reference to American literature emphasising the comparatively high value of industrial employment and production,[62] and buttressed by the claim that manufacturing could make a 'disproportionate contribution to environmental sustainability'.[63] The issue of reindustrialisation assumed greater urgency after the referendum and is discussed further in the final section of this chapter.

The impact of deindustrialisation on the labour market can also be seen as underpinning new policy initiatives in the area of income maintenance. With the loss of industrial jobs, the polarisation of the labour market, and the rise of precarious incomes, there was a surge of interest in forms of universal basic income (UBI). This would guarantee every individual a minimum income independent of employment status. Such policy ideas were not themselves new, nor confined to Scotland, but had come to be seen as much more pertinent in a deindustrialised country.[64] In September 2017 the Scottish Government announced funding for local authority trials, with Citizen's Basic Income schemes supported in

61 Scottish Government, *Scotland's Future*, pp. 93, 97–8.
62 Susan Helper, Timothy Krueger and Howard Wial, 'Why Does Manufacturing Matter? Which Manufacturing Matters? A Policy Framework' (Washington, DC: Brookings Metropolitan Policy Programme, 2012).
63 Scottish Government, *Scotland's Future*, pp. 95–6.
64 Guy Standing, *Basic Income: And How We Can Make It Happen* (London: Penguin, 2017).

Fife, Edinburgh, Glasgow and North Ayrshire.[65] These were monitored by a cross-party group in the Scottish Parliament.[66] A working group involving Public Health Scotland and local authority officials published a Draft Final Report in the summer of 2020. This recommended a broader three-year pilot, with emphasis on universality, unconditionality and periodic cash payment to individuals rather than households. The pilot would test various assumptions about incentives and costs by providing a Joseph Rowntree Foundation-derived Minimum Income Standard payment in one defined territorial area with a population of about 2,500, and an existing Benefits-level payment in another defined territorial area with a population of about 14,600. For an adult aged twenty-five years to pension age this would mean £213.59 per week in the Minimum Income Standard area and £73.10 per week in the Benefits-level area.[67] Implementation of basic income policies, it should be noted, would mark a historic shift away from fundamental features of the political assumptions of many decades. It would require a recognition that the mantra 'work is the best route out of poverty' no longer applied, and that the left's long-sustained focus on 'the right to work' no longer had the same salience. During the Covid-19 emergency of 2020, the First Minister, Nicola Sturgeon, and SNP MPs pressed the UK government to introduce UBI at least on a temporary basis to relieve the financial pressures encountered by workers cut off from employment.[68]

The distinct approach in Scotland to the management of deindustrialisation, congruent with working-class moral economy traditions, extended to the question of historical justice for the casualties of industrial job loss. In October 2016 the UK Home Secretary, Amber Rudd, refused to establish an inquiry into policing at the 'Battle of Orgreave', where South Yorkshire Constabulary initiated a violent confrontation

65 Basic Income Scotland, at https://basicincome.scot/, accessed 24 April 2020.
66 Scottish Parliament Cross-Party Group, Basic Income, at https://www.parliament.scot/msps/basic-income.aspx, accessed 16 April 2019.
67 *Assessing the Feasibility of Citizens' Basic Income Pilots in Scotland: Final Report*, prepared by the Citizens' Basic Income Feasibility Study Steering Group, June 2020, at https://basicincome.scot/2020/06/10/draft-final-report-cbi-feasibility-study, pp. 7–19, accessed 12 August 2020.
68 Ashley Cowburn, 'Case for universal basic income "strengthened immeasurably" by coronavirus pandemic, says Nicola Sturgeon', *The Independent*, 10 April 2020, at https://www.independent.co.uk/news/uk/politics/coronavirus-universal-basic-income-uk-ubi-nicola-sturgeon-a9459156.html. accessed 21 December; 'PMQs: Blackford and Raab on universal basic income call', BBC News Scotland Politics, 22 April 2020, at https://www.bbc.co.uk/news/av/uk-politics-52384856/pmqs-blackford-and-raab-on-universal-basic-income-call; both accessed 24 April 2020.

with striking miners at the BSC coking plant near Rotherham.[69] In June 2018, by contrast, Michael Matheson, the Scottish Government's Cabinet Secretary for Justice, established an independent review of the impact of policing on affected communities in the strike in Scotland. The review, chaired by John Scott QC, began collecting evidence in August 2018. Public consultation meetings were held across the ex-coalfields in mining welfare institutes between October and December 2018. Former strikers provided vivid testimony of police harassment, intimidation and physical violence. The unusually vindictive punishments in sheriff courts were also emphasised, along with the suspected collusion between police and the NCB to secure the dismissals from employment of strike activists.[70] An interim report was submitted to Matheson's successor as Secretary for Justice after a Scottish Cabinet reshuffle, Humza Yousaf, early in 2019. The final report was delayed by various external pressures, notably the complications arising from the UK government's preparations for departure from the European Union in 2019, and then the Covid-19 emergency.[71] It was published in October 2020, recommending collective pardon for 500-plus miners convicted in Scotland for public order offences in 1984–5. The Scottish Government accepted this recommendation, with Humza Yousaf promising that the necessary legislation would follow the 2021 Holyrood election.

While deindustrialisation continued after 1997, it was not accompanied by the high-profile battles over closures that had marked the preceding quarter of a century. The final closure of the Caledonian Railway works in Glasgow in the summer of 2019 followed, like so many such cases, long years of erosion of employment. A centre for locomotive construction from the middle of the nineteenth century, the facility employed 2,800 in 1966, but numbers were cut by 1,200 in 1988 when it shifted to a purely maintenance role, and numbers were down to 200 by 2019. The decline of activity and employment was accompanied by frequent shifts in ownership and restructurings once the plant had been sold into private ownership in 1988, again a common pattern.[72] At Grangemouth,

---

69 David Conn, 'Absent Amber Rudd accused of "bitter betrayal" over Orgreave', *The Guardian*, 1 November 2016.

70 Author notes of Public Consultation Meeting, Fallin Miners Welfare Society and Social Club, 5 December 2018.

71 Scottish Government, 'Policing during miners' strike: independent review', at https://www.gov.scot/groups/independent-review-policing-miners-strike/, accessed 9 May 2019.

72 See https://twsmedia.co.uk/2019/07/31/st-rollox-gone-but-not-forgotten/, accessed 21 December; *The Scotsman*, 27 July 2019.

the privatisation of British Petroleum opened the way to the eventual sale of the chemical complex, which sits alongside the refinery, to INEOS in 2005. There followed years of reorganisations, contracting out and pressure on the workforce to accept poorer conditions, at the same time as the company was receiving substantial government support for what was and is regarded as one of Scotland's key industrial assets. Working-class moral economy reasoning was consequently evident in local and indeed Scottish national responses in 2013, when INEOS threatened closure with the loss of 800 jobs. The company successfully forced through a further major package of measures to worsen pay and pensions, accompanied by the targeted removal of trade union activists.[73]

The Scottish Government did intervene in a number of cases of threatened closure. The SNP manifesto for the 2019 UK general election claimed that 'Unlike successive Westminster governments, we will never turn our back on Scottish industry. We have stepped in to secure a future for Scottish Steel, Pinney's, BiFab and more recently, Ferguson's shipyard – taking it into public control.'[74] The intervention in Scottish Steel was to find a buyer for the Dalzell and Clydebridge plants when they were mothballed by Tata Steel.[75] In the case of Pinney's BiFab, with three fabrication yards, the government brokered a takeover from the Canadian JV Driver Group. The government assumed a minority stake in the reconstructed firm.[76] Ferguson shipyard, employing around 300 workers in Port Glasgow, was nationalised in 2019. This intervention was linked to the fact that the shipyard's key products – also the chief source of its problems – were two ferries for Caledonian MacBrayne, Scotland's main ferry company, and hence an important supplier of Scottish transport infrastructure.[77]

The limits of what the Scottish Government was able or willing to do was illustrated by the biggest single industrial closure in recent years in Scotland, the Michelin plant in Dundee. In the autumn of 2018 Michelin announced that this would close in 2020. In rationalising this decision Michelin cited a slowdown in the car market, partly linked to Brexit,

73 Mark Lyon, *The Battle of Grangemouth: A Worker's Story* (Chadwell Heath: Lawrence & Wishart, 2017); *Guardian* 9 November 2013.
74 SNP, *Stronger for Scotland* (Glasgow: SNP, 2019), p. 22.
75 Lucy Christie, 'Deal is close to save stricken plants', *Daily Record*, 24 March 2016.
76 'BiFab deal is first step on a long road' (Leader comment), *Scotsman*, 17 April, 2018.
77 Newsroom staff, 'SNP defends Caledonian MacBrayne NI payments to 1,000 seafaring staff', *Scotsman*, 19 August 2019.

and Asian competition.[78] The factory employed 845 workers. It was the largest manufacturing facility by far in Dundee, with a lengthy pedigree, having opened in 1971. The Scottish Government offered Michelin financial support if it retained production in Dundee, but to no avail.[79] In contrast to the contested shrinkage of Timex in 1983 and then departure from Dundee in 1993, the closure of Michelin was not resisted by the redundant workers. The site was earmarked in the autumn of 2019 for a new government-industry partnership, the Michelin Scotland Innovation Parc, with plans for up to 500 workers in renewable energy and other high technology activities. The Parc was jointly funded by Dundee City Council, the Scottish Government and Michelin. The end of tyre production was brought forward from June 2020 by three months when operations were suspended by the Covid-19 emergency.[80] Pessimism surrounded the closure, although the relative longevity of Michelin's presence in Dundee was noteworthy, forty-nine years to Timex's forty-six.[81]

The SNP government did not evidently become less popular in electoral terms as a result of the continued loss of industrial activity and employment. This may have reflected the positive impact of the SNP's reindustrialisation strategy and rhetoric. More probably it was because deindustrialisation was still framed in popular understanding as a UK policy failure. In the 2014 independence referendum and the 2016 EU membership referendum the SNP was able to mobilise, among others, a constituency of the economically marginalised. These were the people who had experienced most strongly the negative employment effects of deindustrialisation. In England this constituency was pulled to the political right, drawn towards the UK Independence Party and then the

---

78 Douglas Fraser, 'Dundee Michelin tyre factory closes with loss of 850 jobs', BBC News, 6 November 2018, https://www.bbc.co.uk/news/uk-scotland-tayside-central-46097215, accessed 21 January 2021._

79 Scott Milne, 'Michelin confirms end of tyre production in Dundee but will support plan for new skills and training centre', *The Courier*, 30 November 2018.

80 Scottish Government, '£60m. for Michelin Scotland Innovation Parc', at https://www.gov.scot/news/gbp-60m-for-michelin-scotland-innovation-parc/, accessed 21 December; the Scottish Government's role in creating the Parc was highlighted in the SNP manifesto for the 2019 general election, where it was contrasted with the UK government's lack of financial input: *Stronger for Scotland*, p. 22; Rob McLaren, 'Coronavirus: Tyre production will not restart at Michelin Dundee', *The Courier*, 27 March 2020.

81 Brian Taylor, 'Michelin closure: a dark day in Dundee', BBC News Scotland, 6 November 2018, at https://www.bbc.co.uk/news/uk-scotland-scotland-politics-46112216, accessed 24 April 2020.

Brexit Party.[82] In the 2014 referendum there was 44.7 per cent support for independence. This share was exceeded in several ex-coalfield local authority areas: East Ayrshire, North Lanarkshire, where there was an independence majority, South Lanarkshire, Clackmannan and Fife. There were independence majorities also in Dundee and Glasgow, the cities where deindustrialisation's impact had been most pronounced in Scotland.[83] The 2016 referendum produced a Remain vote of 62 per cent in Scotland. The lowest ex-industry local authority Remain vote was in Ayrshire, with 58.3 per cent, with others slightly ahead of the Scottish national trend, notably, again, North Lanarkshire at 63.1 per cent.[84]

The UK General Election of December 2019 confirmed the widening of political divergence between Scotland and England. Table 7.5 shows that the combined vote share of Conservative and Brexit parties was twice as large in England as in Scotland, 49.2 per cent to 25.6 per cent, and that the combined vote share of Labour and Conservative was almost twice as large in England as in Scotland, 81.3 per cent to 43.7 per cent.

Tables 7.6 and 7.7 indicate that deindustrialisation was a major contributor to the consolidation of this historical trend. Table 7.6 highlights the very low level of support for Conservative and Brexit candidates in ex-industrial constituencies in Scotland, well below even the modest Scottish national average. SNP candidates won in Glasgow Central, home to the Fairfield shipyard that featured in Chapter 4 of this book, in Paisley and Renfrewshire South, location of the Linwood car manufacturing plant analysed in Chapter 5, and in Dundee West, site of the Timex Camperdown factory examined in Chapter 6. The high combined vote shares of Labour and SNP in these constituencies amounted to a significant rejection of right-wing populism in ex-industrial constituencies.

Table 7.7 offers a comparative reading of ex-coalfield constituencies in Scotland and England. The English constituencies selected have distinct political and industrial traditions but in each case there was substantial

---

82 Which is not to suggest that the 'yes' vote was largely a protest of the 'left-behind'. A more accurate summary recognises the male middle-class leadership of the campaign, leading to significant success amongst working-class men, but with notably less support amongst women of all classes. Lindsay Paterson, 'Utopian pragmatism: Scotland's choice', *Scottish Affairs*, 24 (2015), pp. 22–46.

83 Roderick McInnes, Steven Ayres and Oliver Hawkins, *Scottish Independence Referendum 2014: Analysis of results* (London: House of Commons Library, 2014), p. 4.

84 Matthew Goodwin, 'Labour's core voters no longer share its progressive values', *The Guardian*, 24 June 2016; Ian Jack, 'First the elite ignored the estates. Now the estates have turned on the elite', *The Guardian*, 25 June 2016.

Table 7.5 Vote share of four political parties in England and Scotland (as percentage), December 2019

	Conservative	Brexit	Labour	SNP
England	47.2	2.0	34.1	–
Scotland	25.1	0.5	18.6	45.0

Source: https://www.bbc.co.uk/news/election/2019/results, accessed 13 December 2019.

Table 7.6 Vote share of four political parties in selected Scottish ex-industrial constituencies (as percentage), December 2019

	Conservative	Brexit	Labour	SNP	Labour and SNP combined
Dundee West	12.4	3.1	24.3	53.8	78.1
Glasgow Central	9.2	–	33.1	49.2	82.3
Paisley and Renfrewshire South	17.6	–	25.4	50.2	76.6

Source: As Table 7.5.

Table 7.7 Vote share of four political parties in selected Scottish and English ex-coalfield constituencies (as percentage), December 2019

	Conservative	Brexit	Labour	SNP
Kirkcaldy and Cowdenbeath*	20.1	2.4	32.6	35.2***
Midlothian*	21.7	–	29.7	41.5
Coatbridge, Chryston and Bellshill*	12.7	–	35.4	47.0
Barnsley Central**	21.4	30.4	40.1	–
Bolsover**	47.4	9.0	35.9	–
Mansfield**	63.9	–	30.8	–

Source: As Table 7.5.
* Scottish ex-coalfield constituencies.
** English ex-coalfield constituencies.
*** SNP candidate suspended from party membership during campaign and elected as independent, apparently with support from local party activists.

support for Conservative and/or Brexit candidates. In Bolsover the defeated Labour candidate, Dennis Skinner, had been MP since 1970, with personal and family connections to the coal industry and the NUM. In the Lanarkshire constituency of Coatbridge, Chryston and Bellshill the combined vote share for Labour and SNP, 87.4 per cent, represents in exaggerated form the general trend across ex-industrial constituencies shown in Table 7.6, and evident to a lesser extent in Central Fife and Midlothian. It confirms the much higher level of popular support in Scotland than in England at the end of the 2010s for social-democratic responses to the continuing problems of deindustrialisation.

REINDUSTRIALISATION AND THE 'HALF-LIFE' OF DEINDUSTRIALISATION

'Reindustrialisation' was a logical aim in the 2010s for those who believed that deindustrialisation could and should be reversed. The term had been used to describe industrial modernisation in Scotland in the 1960s and 1970s, with the growth – stalled though this became – of new manufacturing enterprises. It also appeared in discussion of processes in the northeast USA, and was extensively deployed in analyses of post-Soviet Russia.[85] The issue was widely discussed across Europe in the 2010s.[86] Interest was closely associated with recognition of the significance of the world-historic rise of Chinese industry, not only as a supplier of manufactured imports previously produced domestically in the West, but also as a strategic challenger to the West's global industrial hegemony.[87]

In Scotland it was continually deployed by the SNP government within its broader vision for post-independence national renewal. A detailed strategy was published in 2014 with the explicit title *Reindustrialising Scotland for the 21st Century*. This focused on manufacturing rather than other parts of industry, which was a commonplace in literature on reindustrialisation as well as deindustrialisation. In this connection it is worth emphasising that the data in Table 7.2 indicate that it will not be long, extending trends forward from the early 2020s, that employment in construction matches that in manufacturing. Echoing the 2013

---

85 E. Westkamper, *Towards the Re-industrialization of Europe: A Concept for Manufacturing for 2030* (Berlin: Springer, 2014).
86 'Reindustrialisation is essential for relaunching the EU economy', *The Parliament*, 24 October 2017, at https://www.theparliamentmagazine.eu/articles/opinion/reindustrialisation-essential-relaunching-eu-economy, accessed 21 December 2020.
87 See https://www.robert-schuman.eu/en/european-issues/0256-reindustrialising-europe-the-issues-at-stake-in-a-european-innovation-and-industry-policy; K. Cowling and P. Tomlinson, 'Post the "Washington Consensus": economic governance and industrial strategies for the twenty-first century', Cambridge Journal of Economics, 35 (2011), pp. 831–52.

independence manifesto, *Reindustrialising Scotland* made this assertion: 'A stronger manufacturing sector can increase innovation, tackle geographic inequalities, support internationalisation and create high-value and well-paid jobs.' An additional claim was that reindustrialisation would advance the desired transition to a low carbon economy,[88] constituting a forward-looking agenda and not aiming to revive 'old' industrial employments but to expand job numbers in 'new' sectors such as renewable energy.[89] This positioning involved a clear rebuke to those who believed that the 'key impulse behind reindustrialisation is nostalgia'.[90] The 2014 document built on both an earlier commitment from the Labour–Liberal Democrat Scottish Executive to a 'Green Jobs Strategy' in 2005, and the SNP's identification in 2011 of the 'transition to a low carbon economy' as one of its 'strategic priorities' in government.[91] It also mirrored, and indeed anticipated, an argument advanced in 2019 by the European Commission about the mutuality of interest between industry and environmental protection.[92]

In 2017 Scottish Labour's *Industrial Strategy* called for a more committed approach to reindustrialisation, arguing that the SNP government had managed only a few defensive interventions. These preserved employment in a number of specific instances, but did not amount to the development of an effective strategy.[93] By the 2019 UK general election Scottish Labour was aiming for a 'green industrial revolution' that would create a million jobs across the UK. The centrality of industry

88 Scottish Government, *Reindustrialising Scotland for the 21st Century: A Sustainable Industrial Strategy for a Modern, Independent Nation* (Edinburgh: Scottish Government, 2014), pp. 1, 51.

89 G. Allan, P. MacGregor and K. Swales, 'Greening regional development: employment in low-carbon and renewable energy activities', *Regional Studies*, 51 (2017), pp. 1270–80.

90 A. Grant, 'For goodness sake, forget about reindustrialisation', at https://www.huffingtonpost.co.uk/entry/for-goodness-sake-forget-about-re-industrialisation_uk_5b7dc5e9e4b03067348d99db, accessed 21 December 2020.

91 Scottish Executive, *Going for Green Growth: A Green Jobs Strategy for Scotland* (Edinburgh: Scottish Executive, 2005), p. 6; Scottish Government, 'Government Economic Strategy', 2011, http://www.apse.org.uk/apse/index.cfm/members-area/briefings/2011/11-63-scottish-government-economic-strategypdf/, accessed 21 January 2021.

92 European Commission, *The European Green Deal*, COM (2019) 640 final, at https://ec.europa.eu/info/sites/info/files/european-green-deal-communication_en.pdf, accessed 21 December 2020.

93 Scottish Labour, *An Industrial Strategy for Scotland* (Glasgow: Scottish Labour, 2017).

to the attainment of greater economic security and social justice was strongly emphasised:

> Just as the original Industrial Revolution brought industry, jobs and pride to our towns, Labour's world-leading Green Industrial Revolution will rebuild them, with more rewarding well-paid, unionised jobs, lower energy bills that will reduce fuel poverty, and support whole new industries to revive parts of our country that have been neglected for too long.[94]

The STUC also endorsed this agenda.[95] Unsurprisingly, the strongest advocates and pioneers of this policy were the Scottish Greens, who framed reindustrialisation as part of a 'Green New Deal'.[96] By the summer of 2020 this framing was widely used, with Richard Leonard, leader of the Scottish Labour party, calling for a post-Covid investment in infrastructure and renewables, which he suggested could create 131,000 'good quality jobs'.[97] Outside Scotland, the Conservative UK government elected in 2015 moved more slowly. Its 2017 paper was tentatively entitled *Building our Industrial Strategy*, and eschewed the term 'reindustrialisation'.[98]

Reindustrialisation was therefore a policy-making issue within the UK, the European Union and even globally. The debate nevertheless had distinctly Scottish features, and arguably reinforced Scotland's political divergence from England. The urgency of reindustrialisation in Scotland was related to explicit projections about the number of jobs that could be created. The basis of such projections was complex and controversial. The extent of new employment arising from green energy production was not clear. Much of the manufacturing associated with 'greening' the economy is dominated by China (for example, in solar panels and batteries) or other countries (for example, in wind turbines), and building domestic capacity to compete would be an arduous task. Clearly some jobs would be created, but whether this

---

94 Scottish Labour, *Real Change: For the Many not the Few* (Glasgow: Scottish Labour, 2019), p. 13.
95 'STUC responds to launch of re-industrialising Scotland', 13 June 2014, www.stuc.org.uk/media-centre/news/1090/stuc-responds-to-the-first-minister-s-launch-of-reindustrialising-scotland; broader support at https://commonweal.scot/policy-library/renew-six-policies-can-refresh-scottish-governments-domestic-agenda, accessed 21 December 2020.
96 See https://greens.scot/scottish-green-new-deal, accessed 21 December 2020.
97 *The Scotsman*, 24 August 2020.
98 HM Government, *Industrial Strategy: Building a Britain Fit for the Future* (London: BEIS, 2017).

would have a transformative impact on the labour market was doubtful.[99] In a broader historical context the bigger question was how far
and in what sense any expansion of such employment would reverse
the impact of the deindustrialisation experienced in Scotland since the
1950s. Contemporary Scottish proponents of 'green' reindustrialisation
were clear that the aim was to expand *skilled* jobs, improving the prospect of sustainable economic growth and individual prosperity. The
SNP strategy rightly noted how manufacturing was 'up-skilling' and
employing more and more educated people.[100] This point was emphasised in sociological terms by David McCrone:

> the old mainstream industries of manufacturing and construction . . . have
> undergone fundamental change. The image of masses of semi-and unskilled
> workers is also a redundant one. Both industries are still 'manual', but man-
> ufacturing is now evenly split between skilled trades and process plant and
> machine operatives (roughly 25 per cent each), and only one in ten are in
> unskilled . . . occupations. The majority of construction workers are now
> 'skilled' (56 per cent), and less than one in ten are defined as unskilled. There
> are few 'navvies' left in the construction trades.[101]

It was this long-run 'up-skilling' that made manufacturing jobs relatively more rewarding than most service occupations. But this trend also
meant that successful reindustrialisation would have little to *directly*
offer those with limited education and skills, though it would incentivise the acquisition of such skills. It was clearly not going to remedy the
central problem of deindustrialisation identified in this book, namely
the loss of relatively well-paid jobs that could be undertaken by citizens with rudimentary entry-level skills and qualifications. This point
could be extended to the other sectors of manufacturing that the Scottish
Government was seeking to expand in the 2010s. In promoting the case
for such expansion, the rhetorical emphasis was that 'manufacturing
companies are at the heart of our high skill–high wage economy'. This
reinforced the sense that new jobs would not be created for 'factory
hands' and would not directly redress the longer-term problem of labour
market polarisation.[102]

---

99 Allan et al., 'Greening regional development'; M. Minio-Paluello, 'Jobs in
Scotland's New Economy' (Glasgow: Scottish Green Party, 2015).
100 Scottish Government, *Reindustrialising Scotland*, pp. 37, 40–1.
101 McCrone, *New Sociology of Scotland*, p. 206.
102 Sarah Jardine, Chair of the Scottish Manufacturing Advisory Board, in Scottish
Government, *A Manufacturing Future for Scotland*, p. 2: see https://www.
skillsdevelopmentscotland.co.uk/media/41516/a-manufacturing-future-for-
scotland-1.pdf, accessed 21 December 2020.

The debate still underlined the continued value in Scotland of industrial activity and employment, which remained strongly associated with economic security and social justice. Historical memory was important in generating – and regenerating – this association. In the 2010s the Bathgate commercial vehicle plant and the Caterpillar earthmoving equipment factory, both closed for almost thirty years, gave rise to community-based legacy groups. These collected interviews and a range of perspectives on the social history of the respective plants. There was an emphasis on the role of the factories in building communal solidarity through intergenerational learning as well as economic resilience.[103] Similar initiatives took hold among former Linwood workers in Renfrewshire and Timex workers in Dundee, in the same decade. Key protagonists in all four cases were men and women born in the 1940s and 1950s, retired in the 2010s, who remembered their working lives in positive terms. They exhibited 'critical nostalgia' in their memories of industrial employment, noting points of conflict and tension but also stressing the security and stability that they enjoyed.[104] Younger people were involved too. The Caterpillar Legacy Group included school visits, where ex-occupiers spoke to primary and secondary school pupils about their experiences of industrial employment and their campaigning for workplace rights and economic security. These encounters reinforced the sense that deindustrialisation was not complete. Indeed, with various social problems in the 2010s in the USA as well as the UK related to the ending of mass industrial employment in the 1980s, a 'half-life' of deindustrialisation was hypothesised.[105]

The half-life concept is persuasive, although it tends to be applied largely to the negative effects of deindustrialisation, notably population decline in ex-industrial localities, along with a decaying built environment and heavy unemployment, plus poor mental and physical health. These disfigured Scottish society too, still, in the 2010s. But in the Scottish case it also seems apt to extend the half-life concept in a more affirmative manner, to encompass the continuing presence and influence of the working-class moral economy of deindustrialisation that has been

---

103 Ewan Gibbs, Susan Henderson and Victoria Bianchi, 'Intergenerational Learning and Place-Making in a Deindustrialized Locality: "Tracks of the Past" in Uddingston, Scotland', *International Labor and Working Class History*, forthcoming, 2021.

104 Bonnett, *Left in the Past*, pp. 1–3.

105 Sherry Lee Linkon, *The Half-life of Deindustrialisation: Working-Class Writing about Economic Restructuring* (Ann Arbor: University of Michigan Press, 2018).

identified and examined in this book. In other words, the set of expectations and rules that accompanied working-class adjustment to industrial and employment changes from the 1950s to the 1980s still had traction in shaping popular responses to economic and social conditions in the late 2010s and early 2020s. This was evident in the results of successive UK general elections in the 2010s and the referendum on UK's membership of the European Union. Borrowing from Raymond Williams, Strangleman argues that the 'half-life' encompassed powerful 'residual structures of feeling'.[106] In Scotland the 'half-life' of the working-class moral economy was still applied by citizens of different generations in Scotland to understand the fairness of their economic and social condition, using norms and structures that had developed within the gradual reordering of industrial society. The formative experiences in youth of older citizens who attained adulthood in the 1960s or 1970s were important in constructing a common 'intelligible moral order', and the outlook of younger citizens socialised in ex-industrial communities since the 1980s was also shaped by industrial-era norms. The working-class moral economy survived this acceleration of deindustrialisation, even as economic security was reduced in industrial or, more accurately, former industrial, communities. It lingered long into the twenty first century, continuing to shape Scotland's distinct politics. The expectations of communal security and voice in the making and taking of strategic decisions – in workplaces and society more generally – remained important influences in policy-making.

The 'half-life' frame of analysis can shape highly pessimistic conclusions. There is frequent discussion of existential as well as material loss.[107] Walkerdine's discussion of damaged working-class self-confidence in a South Wales steelmaking community identified corrosive disengagement from economic life as the central consequence of deindustrialisation. Gendered male expectations were prominent, as younger men especially rejected 'women's employment' in service sectors.[108] Such emphasis on social dysfunction in South Wales jarred, however, with the findings of two other studies. Robert MacKenzie and his colleagues found that redundant steelworkers in the early 2000s coped with new employment situations and labour market conditions because they retained a strong occupational and collective class identity. Work in other sectors was

106 Strangleman, 'Deindustrialisation and the Historical Sociological Imagination', pp. 471–2.
107 Linkon, *Half-life*, p. 58.
108 Walkerdine, Valerie, 'Transmitting class across generations', *Theory & Psychology*, 25 (2015), pp. 167–83.

informally benchmarked against the unionised environment of steel; exploitative conditions were recognised and resisted as a result.[109] Huw Beynon and his colleagues developed this theme, arguing that working-class traditions in South Wales developed in the world of industry have shaped economic life beneficially for manual and non-manual employees in the long age of deindustrialisation. A strong culture of trade union organisation and activism passed from one generation to the next, so that collective bargaining in service occupations in the early 2010s was more robust in South Wales than in many regions of England.[110] Empirical evidence indicates that historical tradition also had lasting effects in Scotland. In Strathclyde in 2017 collective bargaining coverage was significantly higher than in regions of England with similar employment structures.[111] Here was a different kind of 'Glasgow effect': the enduring employment culture of Clydeside bridged the incomplete passage from industrial to post-industrial society. This was clear in the testimonies of the former Fairfield shipyard workers examined in Chapter 4 of this book. The particular 'structure of feeling' on Clydeside, privileging collective action in pursuit of economic security, remained a valuable resource in the 2010s, enabling workers to mitigate such negative effects of deindustrialisation as low pay and authoritarian employers.[112]

CONCLUSION

Deindustrialisation remained a prominent economic, social and political phenomenon in Scotland from the 1990s to the 2010s. It did not end in the 1980s. It was a process, not an event. Employment structures were nevertheless still dynamic. There was a continued if slower movement of workers from industrial sectors to services. Within industry there were gradual and further shifts, particularly out of textiles. Food and drink retained its robust profile from the 1980s and construction was resilient, particularly during the long period of economic growth from the

109 Robert MacKenzie, Mark Stuart, Chris Forde, Ian Greenwood, Jean Gardiner and Robert Perrett, 'All that is Solid? Class Identity and the Maintenance of a Collective Orientation amongst Redundant Steelworkers', *Sociology*, 40.5 (2006), pp. 833–52.
110 Huw Beynon, Rhys Davies and Steve Davies, 'Sources of variation in trade union membership across the UK: the case of Wales', *Industrial Relations Journal*, 43.3 (2012), pp. 200–21.
111 Gregor Gall, 'Still brothers and sisters in arms? A note on trends in union membership and statistics', *Scottish Labour History*, 53 (2018), pp. 73–83.
112 Strangleman, 'Deindustrialisation', p. 472.

mid-1990s to the Great Financial Crash of 2007–8. Globalisation had some important effects on employment, although in terms of the erosion of manufacturing jobs in Scotland this was exaggerated. There was, in any case, a substantial phenomenon of deglobalisation, as working-class economic welfare particularly was influenced by spending decisions made by central governments at Westminster and in Edinburgh, and the public sector remained an important employer, especially of women. Gender inequalities in employment were not eradicated, however. In the later decades of deindustrialisation, female share of manufacturing employment fell. Women were more likely than men to be in part-time employment and to experience under-employment, and gender pay inequalities were not eradicated. Some trade union negotiators and employers, including local authorities, were apparently complicit in this. The case of Glasgow illustrated each of these national trends, although the key employment problems of deindustrialisation – unemployment and under-employment – were especially acute here, as were various indicators of deprivation, including the relatively poor health of the population. The Glasgow 'effect' reflected the long-running influences of deindustrialisation as a slow historical process.

Deindustrialisation was a big factor in Scotland's political divergence from the 1960s to the 1980s. This trend continued and if anything widened further after devolution, most visibly in the lengthy imbroglio over Brexit in the late 2010s and renewed debates about Scottish independence, an issue plainly not resolved by the 2014 referendum. SNP governments in Edinburgh were apparently more willing defenders of industrial enterprises and employment than Conservative UK governments. The SNP's reindustrialisation strategy reflected the deep influence of the working-class moral economy of deindustrialisation, offering prospects of stable and better paid jobs. With much of this work in renewable energies, the strategy also connected with moral-economy ambitions for sustainable industry and social justice. The strategy was problematic, admittedly, in that it was unlikely to correct fully the central employment problem of deindustrialisation, namely the loss of large numbers of relatively well-paid jobs for citizens with limited skills and qualifications. It nevertheless was a positive attempt to build greater economic resilience generally and provide more meaningful incentives in the world of employment. In its dialogue with trade unions, its promotion of 'fair work' and financial support for manufacturing enterprises, the Scottish Government both acknowledged and reinforced the enduring value in Scotland of industrial employment.

Conclusion:
Deindustrialisation and the Moral Economy

This book has intervened in three related areas of historical debate: on the character and chronology of deindustrialisation, through detailed analysis of its employment effects; on the moral economy, focusing on working-class understanding of the legitimacy and fairness of industrial change; and on Scotland's distinct political trajectory from the 1950s onwards.

Economists in the UK became concerned about deindustrialisation in the 1970s. Some viewed the stagnation of industrial output as problematic, likely to result in lower overseas earnings and slower economic growth, because productivity gains would be harder to achieve in services. In the 1980s, as deindustrialisation intensified, some economists were more sanguine, rationalising the phenomenon in terms of Britain's comparative advantage in services, especially financial services. Deindustrialisation had damaging employment effects across much of Britain, with especially large concentrations in parts of London and pockets of the English Midlands, Northern England, South Wales, Northern Ireland, and Central Scotland. The acceleration and depth of job losses contributed to a shift in the predominant understanding of deindustrialisation. Seen in the 1970s as a relatively abstract macroeconomic issue, it was now interpreted as an engrained social problem. An important misapprehension was formed: that deindustrialisation was a sudden and catastrophic shock. It was in fact a much longer-running phenomenon. In the UK industrial employment peaked in the 1960s and tapered slowly in the 1970s before contracting rapidly in the 1980s. Nor was experience in the UK unique. The loss of industry employment and output share was common to all mature economies in the late twentieth century, and in the twenty-first century became observable in more recent industrialisers, including China.

What was distinct about deindustrialisation in the UK, however, was its phased manner. Three distinct periods were evident in the detailed case of Scotland following post-Second World War employment peaks in the staples of coal, metals, shipbuilding and textiles. The shrinkage of these sectors was encouraged by government policy in the first phase identified, in the decade or so to around 1967. Lost jobs in the staples were offset by new employment in manufacturing enterprises. In Scotland the path towards more rapid economic growth involved a partnership of sorts between the state and multinational firms, including many from the USA, which were persuaded through regional policy grants and loans to locate their production in areas formerly reliant on the staples. The Labour governments from 1964 to 1970 were particularly active in this endeavour. The changing coalfield economies of Lanarkshire, West Lothian and Fife, examined in Chapter 3, illustrate the general trend. Restructuring was both rapid and remarkably successful in sustaining employment stability and economic security. In Scotland as a whole mining jobs more than halved in the decade from 1961. Coal's share of male employment in Fife fell from nearly a quarter in 1961 to a tenth in 1971, with similar patterns in West Lothian and Lanarkshire. Yet the intensity of industrial employment across the three counties was broadly sustained. Major engineering initiatives offset coal's decline, with large-scale employment in various factories in Fife's New Town of Glenrothes, at Caterpillar in Uddingston, Lanarkshire, and BMC in Bathgate, West Lothian. These changes brought opportunities for women as well as men that more than compensated for the substantial losses in textiles. In Lanarkshire in 1961 the employment share of textiles and engineering among women was approximately equal. By 1971 the share of engineering was six times greater than textiles. Economic security was strengthened from another direction, with job prospects for women further enriched by the growth of public services. From 1951 to 1971 female employment in West Lothian doubled in health services, trebled in education and quadrupled in local government.

The second phase of deindustrialisation in Scotland began in the late 1960s, with the stagnation of new manufacturing growth and early signs of the 'retreat' of multinational investment. Economic security was stabilised by the UK government, responding to trade union activism and lobbying. The STUC played a vital role in coordinating this mobilisation, although pressure from below was vital, most visibly in the case of shipbuilding, with the work-in on the Upper Clyde in 1971–2 examined in Chapter 4. Employment in three of the staples – shipbuilding, steel and coal – was protected, particularly by the Labour government elected in 1974.

The incremental shrinkage of employment in industry overall never-theless continued. This reflected the retreat of the multinationals that had been established in Scotland through regional policy. Employment in these firms generally peaked between the late 1960s and mid-1970s, often a decade or more before they left Scotland altogether. The case of Timex in Dundee in Chapter 6 demonstrated this amply, qualifying two important misapprehensions in deindustrialisation literature: the vast majority of industrial jobs were not lost as a result of plant closures but through attrition; and the shrinkage of employment in industrial sectors was severely aggravated but not initiated by Margaret Thatcher's Conservative governments in the 1980s. This acceleration reflected a major change in the political management of deindustrialisation from 1979. During this third distinct phase of deindustrialisation – which lasted into the 1990s – there was no meaningful effort to encourage job alternatives in the areas where economic security was drained by the heavy contraction of employment.

The book's moral-economy framework, influenced by the writings of Karl Polanyi and E. P. Thompson, helped to refine the analysis of this shift in the management of deindustrialisation from 1979. Economic security was maintained in Scotland from the 1950s to the 1970s through the interaction of a social-democratic policy-making moral economy and a working-class moral economy. Both Conservative and Labour governments accepted an obligation to maintain high levels of employment. Using Polanyi's schema, this meant re-embedding eco-nomic activity in a richer and more secure pattern of social relationships and obligations. Rising living standards were promised to workers, pro-vided they showed a willingness to move into higher-growth manufac-turing sectors. This was the essence of the 1944 *Employment Policy* White Paper, reiterated in the Labour government's 1965 *National Plan* and 1966 Scottish *Plan For Expansion*, examined in Chapter 2. Dialogue between the state and the political and trade union represen-tatives of workers was strengthened. STUC and other union officials enjoyed access to policy-makers, especially although not only under Labour governments. Increased regional policy expenditure was a tan-gible product of this interaction in the first phase of deindustrialisation, underpinning the diversification of the coalfield economies. The move-ment out of coal, metals, ships and textiles was managed through this moral-economy bargaining. Adapting Thompson's moral economy of the eighteenth-century English plebeian crowd, which emphasised cus-toms and expectations, the book showed that Scottish workers in these staples tolerated the transition of the 1950s and 1960s on two grounds.

First, their voices were heard, through political and trade union representatives, as part of the dialogue and consultation that usually preceded major changes in industrial employment at local level. Second, the changes broadly offered material improvement: economic security was preserved in the short run and hopes of improving living standards were realistically projected forward. It was significant that most of the industrial initiatives examined in this book were accompanied by major exercises in housing construction and community renewal. Bathgate, Caterpillar and the Linwood car plant in Renfrewshire, examined in Chapter 5, each demonstrated this. Purpose-built local authority housing was an important and even decisive attraction for younger workers who formed these new communities, many of them leaving older habitats – especially in Glasgow – to do so.

Such public investment in social as well as industrial infrastructure was key to the development of working-class moral-economy feeling. There was tension at times in the multinational plants, with a culture clash between management and workers, arising in part from mismatched expectations. Workers acquired a sense of communal ownership: the factories 'belonged' to the communities that were built around them with public money. The legal owners, the multinationals, expected compliant employees, and were taken aback by workforce demands for trade union recognition and greater control over production, which was predominantly semi-skilled and as such a further layer in the culture clash. Skilled workers – coming from craft orientations in shipbuilding and heavy engineering as well as mining – were discomfited and even offended by standardised mass production and the close managerial supervision of their labour. This was particularly evident at Linwood and at Bathgate, where the motor industry tendency also to short-time working and redundancy in periods of cyclical recession was strongly resented, offending moral-economy expectation of regular hours and steady income. Trade union voice was also contested, especially in the multinational plants. At Caterpillar and Timex workers had to fight for union recognition. These victories reinforced the workforce sense of ownership, which extended to products – the earthmoving equipment, the watches – that were developed and manufactured to a high level of precision through the expertise of labour as well as management. Ownership consciousness contributed significantly to workforce and community anger when the multinationals moved these products out of Scotland, to plants elsewhere. Corporate theft was apprehended by the workers, an important element in their attempts to resist deindustrialisation by occupying 'their' factories, in Dundee in 1983 and Uddingston in 1987.

Working-class moral economy feeling was recurrently articulated during employment crises in the second phase of deindustrialisation. The 'bargain' that workers had been offered by policy-makers, full employment in exchange for their flexibility in accepting industrial restructuring, was compromised by multinational disinvestment and rising unemployment, particularly marked after the election of Edward Heath's Conservative government in the summer of 1970. Workers confronting redundancy from the staples now had recourse to a dwindling stock of labour market alternatives. This explains the refusal by shipyard workers to accept the closure of their yards on the Upper Clyde in 1971–2. The work-in, compelling Heath's government into a major policy reversal, was a working-class moral economy victory. As was the miners' improved pay position, obtained through strike action in 1972 and 1974 by workers frustrated by the impact of deindustrialisation on their job security as well as their wage levels. Stabilisation of employment and remuneration in these sectors – along with steel – under the 1974–9 Labour governments illustrated further the impact of moral-economy activism. Expectations could no longer be met through employment in multinationals and other private sector manufacturing firms, so Labour reinvested in the older staples. Labour ministers also intervened in select cases where projected private sector disinvestment threatened major socio-economic damage. The 'rescue' of Chrysler UK, explored in Chapter 5, was a key episode. Willie Ross, Secretary of State for Scotland, persuaded the Cabinet that the closure of Linwood would exert unacceptable social pain on Renfrewshire, with dangerous economic ripples that would jeopardise employment in steel and coal in Lanarkshire and West Lothian.

The working-class moral economy was grossly offended by the intensification of deindustrialisation after 1979. Thatcherism represented a different kind of moral economy from the social-democratic policy-making variant that it superseded. The liberalisation of markets was characterised as a moral as well as material question. Collective organisation and action, especially trade unionism but also public ownership, were regarded as unacceptable barriers to the freedom of markets and individuals. Trade unions were ostracised, their meaningful influence removed from policy-making, and their rights in workplaces incrementally dismantled. Conservative governments after 1979 did not intervene to prevent large-scale industrial closures, as the Labour government had done. In Thatcherite terms it was illegitimate as well as inefficient for the government to deny private corporations the right to make decisions on these matters. Nor did the Conservative governments, to restate an important point, seek to stimulate alternatives to the 250,000 industrial jobs that were lost in Scotland in the decade from 1979. Employment loss on this scale, and the related growth of unemployment, massaged as this was in official measures, transgressed working-class moral-economy sentiment in Scotland. Like members of Thompson's eighteenth-century English crowd, these Scottish working-class citizens were influenced in their thinking by cultural as well as material understanding. They experienced their common condition as profound unfairness.

Scotland's distinct political trajectory was shaped by this working-class reading of deindustrialisation. Non-manual workers also identified with the broad aims of economic security and social justice. A close correlation followed between declining industry share of employment in Scotland and sinking electoral support for Conservatism and Unionism. The Conservative and Unionist Party outpolled Labour in Scotland in the UK general elections of 1951, 1955 and 1959. It did not do so again until 2017, but still trailed a distant second to Scotland's new dominant force from the late 2000s, the SNP. Labour's post-1959 ascendancy was briefly threatened by the SNP in the general elections of 1974. But the Labour government elected that year gained support in Scotland through its economic agenda, which plainly sought to protect the security of manual workers by safeguarding industrial employment. Labour's share of the vote increased in Scotland by more than 5 per cent from 1974 to 1979. Jobs in industry were valued in part because of their intrinsic qualities: the class solidarity of the mine, the mill and the factory were important, as was the shared endeavour of production. But what was also valued, perhaps more so, were the extrinsic properties: relatively good wages for workers with limited entry-level skills and qualifications, and with rights protected through strong trade union voice and organisation. These job properties – both intrinsic and extrinsic – were diminished in the post-1979 economic and political environment. The Conservative and Unionist Party had already squandered much political capital in urban and industrial Scotland, presiding over the escalation of unemployment in the early 1970s. Thatcher's adventurism – widely rated as materially dangerous and morally repugnant in Scotland – made her party unelectable. Middle-class professionals and manual workers alike were alienated by the erosion of economic security and the government's rhetorical attacks on the value of public service. Hints of a Conservative revival in the late 2010s were over-played, ignoring the political hegemony of social democracy in Scotland. Roughly two-thirds of votes cast in the 2017 and 2019 UK general elections were for the SNP and Labour combined. These two parties were at times bitter opponents, but they drew on similar socio-economic constituencies, particularly in urban Scotland. Both emphasised a mix of public and private enterprise, a focus on partnership between employers and workers, the value of union membership, and the importance of industrial activity and work.

The SNP's ascendancy in the 2000s and 2010s – and the centrality of social democracy in Scotland – was connected to the longer history of deindustrialisation examined in this book. Deindustrialisation was the single most important issue influencing the emergence of support for political devolution for Scotland within the UK in the 1960s. The STUC was a key player, channelling demands for Home Rule initiated by coal miners and others who experienced deindustrialisation as an external imposition from Westminster and Whitehall. The UCS crisis intensified the arguments about 'faceless men' in London, remote from communities that were ruined by impersonal and immoral disinvestment decisions. Labour attempted to legislate for devolution in 1979 and did so again, successfully, in 1997. The influence of the STUC was still felt in the Scottish Constitutional Convention, which drafted the proposals for a Scottish Parliament in the late 1980s that became Labour policy. Political differences between Scotland and England widened further after the Parliament's establishment. Scottish independence became a live possibility, and remained so despite the outcome of the 2014 referendum. Majority public opinion in Scotland in the late 2010s was clearly resistant to the insular and backward-looking dead-end of Brexit that took a remarkable cross-class grip in England, straddling ex-coal villages, former engineering heartlands, struggling seaside towns and plush yet resentful southern suburbs. Public support for collective action in pursuit of common economic security clearly influenced Scotland's continuing political divergence from England. This reinforced the enduring presence in Scotland of the working-class moral economy of deindustrialisation.

Bibliography

INTERVIEWS

Unless otherwise indicated, these were conducted in the homes of interviewees, with place of work of interviewee or family members where appropriate in parenthesis.

Tam Brady (Fairfield), Interview with Valerie Wright, Paisley, 20 September 2017.

John Brannan (Caterpillar), Interview with Ewan Gibbs at University of the West of Scotland Hamilton campus, 21 February 2017.

Barry Brown (Linwood), Interview with Valerie Wright, Paisley, 22 November 2017.

Jean Brown (Timex), Interview with Valerie Wright, Dundee, 8 May 2018.

Janet Burrows (Caterpillar), Interview with Ewan Gibbs, Tannochside Miners' Welfare, 20 January 2017.

John Cooper (Linwood), Interview with Valerie Wright, Glasgow, 11 June 2018.

John Gillen Interview with Ewan Gibbs, University of the West of Scotland Hamilton campus, 21 February 2017.

Brian Glen (Fairfield), Interview with Valerie Wright, Fairfield Heritage, 12 October 2017.

Alan Glover (Fairfield), Interview with Valerie Wright, East Kilbride, 23 September 2017.

Bobby Gordon (Fairfield), Interview with Valerie Wright, Fairfield Heritage, 5 October 2017.

John Hume, Interview with Valerie Wright and Jim Phillips, Lilybank House, University of Glasgow, 23 November 2017.

Helen Knight (Caterpillar), Interview with Ewan Gibbs, Tannochside Miners' Welfare, 20 January 2017.

Bill McCabe (Caterpillar), Interview with Ewan Gibbs, Tannochside Miners' Welfare, 20 January 2017.

Jim McRobbie, Interview with Ewan Gibbs, Viewpark Community Centre, 12 December 2016.

Gavin McCrone, Interview with Jim Tomlinson, Glasgow, March 2018.

Benny McGoogan (Fairfield), Interview with Valerie Wright, Fairfield Heritage, 25 October 2017.

Moira McMillan (Linwood), Interview with Valerie Wright, Linwood, 13 December 2017.

Iain Murray (Fairfield), Interview with Valerie Wright, Johnstone Local History Museum, 7 December 2017.

Alex Neill (Linwood), Interview with Valerie Wright, Glasgow, 18 September 2017.

John O'Neill (Linwood), Interview with Valerie Wright, West Kilbride, 26 February 2019.

Joe Reilly (Linwood), Interview with Valerie Wright, Johnstone Local History Museum, 7 December 2017.

John Sharp (Linwood), Interview with Valerie Wright, Johnstone Local History Museum, 14 December 2017.

John Slaven (Caterpillar), Interview with Ewan Gibbs, Scottish Trades Union Congress Offices, Woodlands, Glasgow, 5 June 2014.

Tom Smith and Dave Howie (Timex), Interview with Valerie Wright and Jim Phillips, Dundee, 3 July 2018.

Ian Stobo (Linwood), Interview with Valerie Wright, Paisley, 15 November 2017.

David Torrance (Fairfield), Interview with Valerie Wright, Old Kilpatrick, 4 October 2017.

Timex History Group, Interview with Jim Phillips, Dundee, 16 August 2017.

Alex Wright (Fairfield), Interview with Valerie Wright, Paisley, 29 August 2017.

OTHER INTERVIEWS

Mona Bozdog generously provided recordings of interviews she conducted with 11 former Timex workers in 2018. Mona Bozdog, Robert Clark and the women of Timex, *Generation ZX(X)*, all audio can be found at https://www.perform-ingplay.co.uk/audio-1, accessed 20 January 2020.

ARCHIVE MATERIALS

Dundee Central Libraries
Courier & Advertiser, clippings files, various dates.
Dundee Rep Theatre, 'A Timex Chronology' in Programme entitled 'On the Line, A Celebration of Timex in Dundee', Tuesday 9 April–Saturday 27 April 1996.

Glasgow Caledonian University Archives
Scottish Trades Union Congress, General Council Papers.
Scottish Trades Union Congress, Economic Committee Papers.
Scottish Trades Union Congress, Women's Advisory Committee.

Mitchell Library, Glasgow
TD 758   Linwood (deposited by the Scottish Archive Council in 1982).
UCS 2   Fairfield.

National Records of Scotland, Edinburgh
CB 360   National Coal Board, Scottish Division, Michael Colliery.
DD 10   Scottish Home Department, Papers.
SEP 2   Industry Department of Scotland, Papers.
SEP 4   Board of Trade Office for Scotland and Successors, Papers.
SEP 10   Ministry of Labour, Reports.
SEP 14   Scottish Development Department, Papers.
SEP 17   Secretary of State for Scotland, Correspondence.

The National Archives, Kew
BT 177   Board of Trade and successors.
BT 291   Admiralty and successors: Shipbuilding and Repair.
CAB 129   Cabinet: Memoranda (CP and C Series).
CAB 130   Cabinet: Miscellaneous Committees: Minutes and Papers (General Series).
CAB 134   Cabinet: Miscellaneous Committees: Minutes and Papers (General Series).
EW 7   Department of Economic Affairs: Regional Policy.
EW 8   Department of Economic Affairs: Growth, Incomes and Prices Policy Division.
EW 27   Department of Economic Affairs: Industrial Division and Industrial Policy Division.
FV 22   Ministry of Technology and successors: Vehicles and Mechanical Engineering Products Division and successors.
FV 36   Ministry of Technology and successors: Electrical Engineering, Chemical and Shipbuilding Industries.
FV 44   Industrial Reorganisation Corporation.
LAB 10   Department of Employment and Predecessors: Industrial Relations.
LAB 28   Royal Commission on Trade Unions and Employers' Associations (1965–8).
LAB 108   Department of Employment: Economic Policy (Manpower) Division.

LAB 110   Department of Employment: Research and Planning
                           Division.
PREM 15   Prime Minister's Office: Correspondence and Papers,
                           1970–4.
PREM 16   Prime Minister's Office: Correspondence and Papers,
                           1974–9.
PREM 19   Prime Minister's Office: Correspondence and Papers,
                           1979–97.
T 224   Treasury: Agriculture, Transport and Trade Division.
T 369   Treasury: Domestic Economy Sector, Industry and
                           Agriculture.
T 390   Treasury: Domestic Economy Sector, Industrial Policy.

Timex History Group, Douglas Community Centre, Dundee (DCC)
Miscellaneous Amalgamated Engineering Union materials on Timex.

University of Dundee Archive Services
MSS 272   George Mason Collection.

University of Glasgow Archives and Special Collections
GB 248, ACCN 3613 Papers of Sir Robert Smith, UCS Liquidator.
DC 65   Department of Economic & Social Research.
UCS 5   Upper Clyde Shipbuilders.

University of Strathclyde Archives and Special Collections (USASC)
GB 249, SOHC   Conversations with workers at the former Linwood car
                           plant, conducted by Cliff Lockyer and Leslie Baddon,
                           1981–5.

University of the West of Scotland Special Collections
GB 0605 DC014   Norman Buchan Parliamentary Papers.

OFFICIAL PUBLICATIONS

Assessing the Feasibility of Citizens' Basic Income Pilots in Scotland: Final Report, Prepared by the Citizens' Basic Income Feasibility Study Steering Group, June 2020, at https://basicincome.scot/2020/06/10/draft-final-report-cbi-feasibility-study, accessed 21 December 2020.
British Steel Corporation: The Road to Viability, Cmnd 7149 (London: HMSO, 1978).
Department of Economic Affairs, *The National Plan*, Cmnd 2764 (London: HMSO, 1965).
Department of Employment, *Employment in the Ports: The Dock Labour Scheme*, Cm. 664 (London: HMSO, 1989).

Department of Trade, *Committee of Inquiry on Industrial Democracy (Bullock)*, *Report*, Cmnd 6706 (London, 1977).

Employment: The Challenge for the Nation, Cmnd 9474 (London: HMSO, 1985).

Employment Policy, Cmd 6527 (London: HMSO, 1944).

Eighth Report, Expenditure Committee, House of Commons, Session 1975–76, 'Public Expenditure on Chrysler UK Ltd', Volume 1 – Report (HMSO, London, 22 July 1976).

European Commission, *The European Green Deal*, COM (2019) 640 final, at https://ec.europa.eu/info/sites/info/files/european-green-deal-communication_en.pdf, accessed 21 December 2020.

General Register Office for Scotland, *1991 Census. Report for Scotland. Part Two, Fife Region* (Edinburgh: HMSO, 1993).

General Register Office for Scotland, *Scotland's Census 2001: Key Statistics for Council Areas and Health Boards across Scotland* (Edinburgh: HMSO, 2003).

General Register Office (Scotland), *Census 1951: Scotland. Volume Four: Occupations and Industries. County Tables* (Edinburgh: HMSO, 1956).

General Register Office (Scotland), *Census 1961: Scotland. Country Reports* (Edinburgh: HMSO, 1963–4).

General Register Office (Scotland), *Census 1961: Scotland. Volume Six: Occupation, Industry and Workplace* (Edinburgh: HMSO, 1966).

General Register Office (Scotland), *Census 1971: Scotland. Economic Activity* (Edinburgh: HMSO, 1975).

General Register Office (Scotland), *Census 1981: Scotland. Regional Reports* (Edinburgh: HMSO, 1982).

General Register Office (Scotland), *Census 1981: Scottish Summary* (Edinburgh: HMSO, 1983).

House of Lords, *Report from the Select Committee on Overseas Trade* (London: HMSO, 1985).

HM Government, *Industrial Strategy: Building a Britain Fit for the Future* (London: BEIS, 2017).

McInnes, Roderick, Steven Ayres and Oliver Hawkins, *Scottish Independence Referendum 2014: Analysis of results* (London: House of Commons Library, 2014).

Manpower Services Commission, Office for Scotland, *Closure at Linwood: A follow-up survey of redundant workers* (Edinburgh: Manpower Services Commission, November 1981).

Ministry of Power, *Fuel Policy*, Cmnd 3428 (London: HMSO, 1967).

Monopolies and Mergers Commission, *National Coal Board: A Report on the efficiency and costs in the development, production and supply of coal by the National Coal Board, Volume One* and *Volume Two*, Cmnd 8920 (London: HMSO, 1983).

National Coal Board, *Report and Accounts, 1983/4* (London: NCB, 1984).

National Dock Labour Board, Reports and Accounts, 1947 to 1989 (London: NDLB).

O'Connor, A., *Scotland's Employment by Industry and Geography* (Edinburgh: Scottish Parliament Information Centre, briefing SB17-71, 2017).

Office for National Statistics, Long-term trends in UK employment: 1861 to 2018 (London: ONS, 2019).

Office for National Statistics, *Business Register and Employment Survey, 2019*, at https://www.ons.gov.uk/employmentandlabourmarket, accessed 20 January 2021.

Parliamentary Debates, Fifth and Sixth Series, Commons and Lords (London: HMSO).

Scottish Development Department, *Central Scotland: Programme for Development and Growth*, Cmnd 2188 (London: HMSO, 1963).

Scottish Executive, *Going for Green Growth: A Green Jobs Strategy for Scotland* (Edinburgh: Scottish Executive, 2005).

Scottish Government, 'Government Economic Strategy', 2011, www.scotland.gov.uk/Resource/Doc/357756/0120893.pdf.

Scottish Government, *Scotland's Future: Your Guide to an Independent Scotland* (Edinburgh: Scottish Government, 2013).

Scottish Government, *Reindustrialising Scotland for the 21st Century: A Sustainable Industrial Strategy for a Modern, Independent Nation* (Edinburgh: Scottish Government, 2014).

Scottish Government, 'Offering flexibility to Universal Credit recipients', 31 October 2018, at https://www.gov.scot/news/offering-flexibility-to-universal-credit-recipients/, accessed 21 December 2020.

Scottish Government, *Public sector employment in Scotland*, at https://www.gov.scot/publications/public-sector-employment-scotland-statistics-3rd-quarter-2019/, accessed 21 December 2020.

Scottish Office, *Scottish Abstract of Statistics*, 1 (Edinburgh: HMSO, 1970).

Scottish Office, *Scottish Abstract of Statistics*, 4 (Edinburgh: HMSO, 1974).

Scottish Office, *Scottish Abstract of Statistics*, 9 (Edinburgh: HMSO, 1980).

Scottish Office, *Scottish Abstract of Statistics*, 10 (Edinburgh: HMSO, 1981).

Scottish Office, *Scottish Abstract of Statistics*, 12 (Edinburgh: HMSO, 1983).

Scottish Office, *Scottish Abstract of Statistics*, 18 (Edinburgh: HMSO, 1989).

Scottish Office, *Scottish Abstract of Statistics*, 26 (Edinburgh: HMSO, 1998).

Scottish Office, *Scotland's Parliament*, Cm 3658 (Edinburgh: HMSO, 1997).

Scottish Office, *The Scottish Economy, 1965 to 1970: A Plan For Expansion*, Cmnd 2864 (Edinburgh: HMSO, 1966).

Scottish Statistical Office, *Digest of Scottish Statistics*, 16 (Edinburgh: HMSO, 1960).

Scottish Statistical Office, *Digest of Scottish Statistics*, 21 (Edinburgh: HMSO, 1963).

Scottish Statistical Office, *Digest of Scottish Statistics*, 27 (Edinburgh: HMSO, 1966).

Scottish Statistical Office, *Digest of Scottish Statistics*, 34 (Edinburgh: HMSO, 1969).

Shipbuilding Inquiry Committee, 1965–77, Report, Cmnd 2937 (London: HMSO, 1966).

INDUSTRY, LABOUR AND POLITICAL PARTY PUBLICATIONS

Committee of Inquiry appointed by the Scottish Council (Development and Industry) under the Chairmanship of J. N. Toothill, *Report on the Scottish Economy* (Edinburgh: Scottish Council, 1961).

Cowan, James R., 'National Coal Board: Scottish Area in the 1980s', *Mining Technology*, 62, No. 711 (January 1980), pp. 20–1.

Labour Party, *Twelve Wasted Years* (London: Labour Party, 1963).

Scottish Labour, *An Industrial Strategy for Scotland* (Glasgow: Scottish Labour, 2017).

Scottish Labour, *Real Change: For the Many not the Few* (Glasgow: Scottish Labour, 2019).

SNP, *Stronger for Scotland* (Glasgow: SNP, 2019).

STUC, *62nd Annual Report*, Dunoon, 20-24 April 1959 (STUC: Glasgow, 1959).

STUC, *71st Annual Report*, The Beach Ballroom, Aberdeen, 16–19 April 1968 (Glasgow: STUC, 1968).

STUC, *79th Annual Report*, The City Hall, Perth, 19–23 April 1976 (STUC, Glasgow, 1976).

STUC, *80th Annual Report*, The Pavilion, Rothesay, 18–22 April 1977 (Glasgow: STUC, 1977).

STUC, *81st Annual Report*, The Music Hall, Aberdeen, 17–21 April 1978 (Glasgow: STUC, 1978).

STUC, *86th Annual Report*, Rothesay Pavilion, 18–22 April 1983 (Glasgow: STUC, 1983).

STUC Glasgow, *91st Annual Report*, Ayr, 19–23 April 1988 (Glasgow, 1988).

Talbot Action Group, *The Case for the Maintenance of Full Employment and Not Closure: The Linwood Workers' Answer* (Linwood: TAG, 1981).

West Lothian Trade Union Council, *Unity Is Strength: West Lothian Memories of the Miners' Strike, 1984–85* (West Lothian TUC, 2015).

ONLINE COLLECTIONS

Basic Income Scotland, at https://basicincome.scot/, accessed 21 December 2020.

Corporate Welfare Watch, Corporate-welfare-watch.org.uk, accessed 21 December 2020.

Fair Work Convention, at https://www.fairworkconvention.scot/, accessed 21 December 2020.
Margaret Thatcher Foundation, at https://www.margaretthatcher.org/, accessed 21 December 2020.
Scottish Cities: The Glasgow Indicators Project, at https://www.understanding-glasgow.com/, accessed 21 December 2020.

NEWSPAPERS

The Courier & Advertiser.
The Daily Record.
Evening Telegraph and Post.
The Financial Times.
The Guardian and *Manchester Guardian.*
The Independent.
Paisley Daily Express.
The Scotsman.
Scottish Daily News.
The Sunday Times.
The Times.

TELEVISION, FILM AND DVDS

The Bowler and the Bunnet, written and researched by Clifford Hanley, directed and presented by Sean Connery (Sean Connery, Scottish Television, 1967), 36 minutes, black and white; available on *Tales From the Shipyard: Britain's Shipbuilding Heritage on Film* (British Film Institute, 2011).
Building the New Chrysler, written and directed by John M. Mills (Formula One Films, 1976).
Cinema Action, *UCS 1* (1971); available on *Tales From the Shipyard: Britain's Shipbuilding Heritage on Film* (British Film Institute, 2011).
Nae Pasaran!, produced and directed by Felipe Bustos Sierra (Debasers Fillums, 2018), at https://naepasaran.com/, accessed 21 December 2020.
The Rootes Group (*Films of Scotland and the Rootes Group, 1963*) produced by Glasgow Films, available on National Library of Scotland, Moving Image Archive, at https://movingimage.nls.uk/film/0085, accessed 4 January 2021.
Timex Westclox (STV, 1971) available on National Library of Scotland, Moving Image Archive, at https://movingimage.nls.uk/film/T0989, accessed 4 January 2021.
Young in Heart (Films of Scotland and the Rootes Group, 1963), producer David Welsh, available from National Library of Scotland, Moving Image Archive, at https://movingimage.nls.uk/film/1480, accessed 4 January 2021.

SECONDARY LITERATURE

Abrams, Lynn and Callum Brown, 'Introduction: Conceiving the Everyday in the Twentieth Century', in Lynn Abrams and Callum Brown, eds, *A History of Everyday Life in Twentieth-Century Scotland* (Edinburgh: Edinburgh University Press, 2010), pp. 1–12.

Abrams, Lynn, Barry Hazley, Valerie Wright, and Ade Kearns, 'Aspiration, Agency, and the Production of New Selves in a Scottish New Town, c.1947–c.2016', *Twentieth Century British History*, 29.4 (2018), pp. 576–604.

Abrams, Lynn, Ade Kearns, Barry Hazley and Valerie Wright, *High-Rise Homes, Estates and Communities in the Post-War Period* (London: Routledge, 2020).

Alberti, Gabriella, Ioulia Bessa, Kate Hardy, Vera Trappman, Charles Umney, 'In, Against and Beyond Precarity', *Work, Employment and Society*, 32.3 (2018), pp. 447–57.

Alexander, K. J. W. and C. L. Jenkins, *Fairfield: A Study of Industrial Change* (London: Allen Lane, 1970).

Alexander, Wendy, Jo Armstrong, Brian Ashcroft, Diane Coyle and John McLaren, 'The Political Economy of Scotland, Past and Present', in Diane Coyle, Wendy Alexander and Brian Ashcroft, eds, *New Wealth for Old Nations: Scotland's Economic Prospects* (Princeton, NJ: Princeton University Press, 2005), pp. 11–32.

Allan, G., P. MacGregor and K. Swales, 'Greening regional development: employment in low-carbon and renewable energy activities', *Regional Studies* 51 (2017), pp. 1270–80.

Amiapu, A. and A. Subramanian, 'Manufacturing or services? An Indian illustration of a development dilemma', Working Paper 409 (Washington, DC: Centre for Global Development, 2015).

Andrews, Aaron, 'Multiple Deprivation, the Inner City and the Fracturing of the Welfare State: Glasgow, c.1968–78', *Twentieth Century British History*, 29 (2018), pp. 605–24.

Appleby, J., *Economic Thought and Ideology in Seventeenth-Century England* (Princeton: Princeton University Press,1978).

Artis, M., D. Cobham and M. Wickham-Jones, 'Social democracy in hard times: the economic record of the Labour government 1974–79', *Twentieth Century British History*, 3 (1992), pp. 39–53.

Atkinson, Anthony and John Micklewright, 'Turning the screw: benefits for the unemployed, 1979–1988', in Anthony Atkinson, ed., *Poverty and Social Security* (London: Harvester Wheatsheaf, 1989), pp. 125–57.

Autor, D., D. David and G. Hanson, 'The China syndrome: labor market effects of import competition in the United States', *American Economic Review*, 103 (2013), pp. 2121–68.

Bacon, R. and W. Eltis, *Britain's Economic Problem: Too Few Producers* (London: Macmillan, 1976).

Bailey, Michael, 'Changing Tides of Industrial Democracy: Red Clydeside and the UCS Work-In as Political Heritage', *International Journal of Heritage Studies*, 25.12 (2019), pp. 1319–88.

Bailey, Nick and Des McNulty, 'Inequality and poverty in Scotland', in Kenneth Gibb, Duncan Maclennan, Des McNulty and Michael Comerford, eds, *The Scottish Economy* (Abingdon: Routledge, 2018), pp. 194–214.

Bain, Peter, 'The 1986–7 News International Dispute: Was the Workers' Defeat Inevitable?' *Historical Studies in Industrial Relations*, 5 (Spring 1998), pp. 73–105.

Barnett, Corelli, *The Collapse of British Power* (London: Eyre Methuen, 1971).

Barnett, Corelli, *Audit of War* (London: Macmillan, 1986).

Bathgate Once More: The Story of the BMC/Leyland Truck and Tractor Plant, 1961–86, compiled and edited by Elizabeth Bryan (Edinburgh: Workers' Educational Association, 2012).

Baumol, W., 'Macroeconomics of Unbalanced Growth: The Anatomy of Urban Crisis', *American Economic Review*, 57 (1967), pp. 415–26.

Baumol, W., 'Health Care, Education and the Cost Disease: A Looming Crisis for Public Choice', *Public Choice*, 77 (1993), pp. 17–28.

Beatty, Christina and Stephen Fothergill, 'The diversion from "unemployment" to "sickness" across British regions and districts', *Regional Studies*, 39 (2005), pp. 837–54.

Beatty, Christina and Stephen Fothergill, 'Labour Market Adjustment in Areas of Chronic Industrial Decline: The Case of the UK Coalfields', *Regional Studies*, 30 (1996), pp. 627–40.

Beatty, Christina, Stephen Fothergill and Tony Gore, *The Real Level of Unemployment 2017* (Sheffield: Sheffield Hallam University, 2017).

Beatty, Christina, Stephen Fothergill and Tony Gore, *The State of the Coalfields 2019* (Sheffield Hallam University and the Coalfields Regeneration Trust, 2019), at https://www.coalfields-regen.org.uk/research-and-reports, accessed 21 October 2019.

Beckett, Andy, *When The Lights Went Out: What Really Happened to Britain in the Seventies* (London: Faber & Faber, 2009).

Beirne, Martin, Scott Hurrell and Fiona Wilson, 'Mobilising for equality? Understanding the impact of grass roots agency and third party representation', *Industrial Relations Journal*, 50.1 (2019), pp. 41–56.

Bell, D., *The Coming of Post-industrial Society: A Venture in Social Forecasting* (London: Heinemann, 1974).

Ben-Atar, D., 'Alexander Hamilton's Alternative: technology policy and the report on manufactures', *William and Mary Quarterly*, 52 (1995), pp. 389–414.

Beynon, Huw, 'After the Long Boom: Living with Capitalism in the Twenty-First Century', *Historical Studies in Industrial Relations*, 40 (2019), pp. 187–221.

Beynon, Huw, *Working for Ford: Men, Masculinity, Mass Production and Militancy* (Harmondsworth: Penguin, 1973).

Beynon, Huw, Rhys Davies and Steve Davies, 'Sources of variation in trade union membership across the UK: the case of Wales', *Industrial Relations Journal*, 43.3 (2012), pp. 200–21.

Black, Lawrence, *The Political Culture of the Left in Affluent Britain, 1951–64* (Basingstoke: Palgrave Macmillan, 2003).

Blackaby, Frank, ed., *De-industrialisation* (London: Heinemann, 1979).

Bluestone, Barry, 'Foreword', in Jefferson Cowie and Joseph Heathcott, eds, *Beyond the Ruins: The Meanings of Deindustrialisation* (Ithaca, NY: Cornell University Press, 2003).

Bluestone, Barry and Bennett Harrison, *The Deindustrialisation of America: Plant Closings, Community Abandonment, and the Dismantling of Basic Industry* (New York: Basic Books, 1982).

Blyton, Paul and Peter Turnbull, *The Dynamics of Employee Relations* (Basingstoke: Palgrave, 2004).

Bogdanor, Vernon, *Devolution in the United Kingdom* (Oxford: Oxford University Press, 1999).

Bonnett, Alastair, *Left in the Past: Radicalism and the Politics of Nostalgia* (London and New York: Bloomsbury Press, 2010).

Borland, J. and M. Coelli, 'Labour market inequality in Australia', *Economic Record*, 92 (2016), pp. 517–47.

Bosworth, B. and S. Collins, 'Accounting for growth: comparing China and India', *Journal of Economic Perspectives*, 22 (2008), pp. 45–66.

Boyle, Martin, Christopher McWilliams and Gareth Rice, 'The spatialities of actually existing neo-liberalism, 1977 to present', *Geografiska Annaler Series B: Human Geography*, 90 (2008), pp. 313–25.

Boyle, Stephen, 'Economic policy performance', in Kenneth Gibb, Duncan Maclennan, Des McNulty and Michael Comerford, eds, *The Scottish Economy* (Abingdon: Routledge, 2018), pp. 73–87.

Brittan, Samuel, 'How British is the British sickness?' *Journal of Law and Economics*, 21 (1978), pp. 245–68.

Broadberry, Stephen, *Market Services and the Productivity Race, 1850–2000: British Performance in International Perspective* (Cambridge: Cambridge University Press, 2006).

Broadberry, Stephen, 'The rise of the service sector', in Roderick Floud, Jane Humphries and Paul Johnson, eds, *The Cambridge Economic History of Modern Britain: Vol. II, 1870 to the Present* (Cambridge: Cambridge University Press, 2014), pp. 330–61.

Broadberry, Stephen and Bishnupriya Gupta, 'The historical roots of India's service-led development: a sectoral analysis of Anglo-Indian productivity differences, 1870–2000', *Explorations in Economic History*, 47.3 (2010), pp. 264–78.

Broeze, F., *The Globalization of the Oceans: Containerization from the 1950s to the Present* (St Johns, Newfoundland: International Maritime History Association, 2002).

Brown, R., 'The Future of ICT industries in Scotland: towards a post-branch plant economy?', in N. Hood, J. Peat, E. Peters and S. Young, eds, *Scotland in a Global Economy: The 2020 Vision* (Basingstoke: Palgrave Macmillan, 2002), pp. 130–45.

Brown, Richard and Peter Brannen, 'Social Relations and Social Perspectives amongst Shipbuilding Workers – A Preliminary Statement: Part One', *Sociology*, 4.1 (1970), pp. 71–84; and 'Part Two', *Sociology*, 4.2 (1970), pp. 197–211.

Brown, R. K., P. Brannen, J. M. Cousins and M. L. Samphier, 'The Contours of Solidarity: Social Stratification and Industrial Relations in Shipbuilding', *British Journal of Industrial Relations*, 10 (1972), pp. 12–41.

Callaghan, John, Steven Fielding and Steve Ludlum, *Interpreting the Labour Party: Approaches to Labour Politics and History* (Manchester: Manchester University Press, 2003).

Cameron, Ewen A., *Impaled upon a Thistle: Scotland since 1880* (Edinburgh: Edinburgh University Press, 2010).

Campbell, A. D., 'The Economic Structure of the Tayside Region', in Jones, S. J., ed., *Dundee and District* (Dundee: British Association for the Advancement of Science, 1968), pp. 337–46.

Campbell, J. and E. Thomson, 'Changing Role of Women in the Scottish Economy', in Kenneth Gibb, Duncan Maclennan, Des McNulty and Michael Comerford, eds, *The Scottish Economy* (Abingdon: Routledge, 2018), pp. 135–51.

Cavendish, Ruth, *Women on the Line* (London: Routledge & Kegan Paul, 1982).

Chang, Ha-Joon, *Kicking Away the Ladder: Development Strategy in Historical Perspective* (London: Anthem, 2003).

Checkland, Olive and Sydney Checkland, *Industry and Ethos: Scotland 1832– 1914* (2nd edn; Edinburgh: Edinburgh University Press, 1989).

Checkland, Sydney, *The Upas Tree: Glasgow 1875–1975 . . . and after 1975–80* (2nd edn; Glasgow: Glasgow University Press, 1981).

Chick, Martin, *Changing Times: Economics, Policies, and Resource Allocation in Britain since 1951* (Oxford: Oxford University Press, 2020).

Clark, Andy, '"There is nothing here for us and nothing for the future": Deindustrialisation and the dynamics of workplace occupation, 1981–1982', *Labour History Review*, forthcoming, 2021.

Clark, Andy, '"Stealing Our Identity and Taking It Over to Ireland": De-industrialization, Resistance, and Gender in Scotland', in Steven High, Lachlan MacInnon and Andy Perchard, eds, *The Deindustrialized World: Confronting Ruination in Postindustrial Places* (Vancouver: University of British Columbia Press, 2017), pp. 331–47.

Clark, C., *The Conditions of Economic Progress* (2nd edn; London: Macmillan, 1953).

Collini, Stefan, 'The Literary Critic and the Village Labourer: "Culture" in Twentieth-Century Britain: The Prothero Lecture', *Transactions of the Royal Historical Society*, 14 (2004), pp. 93–116.

Collini, Stefan, 'Moral mind: R. H. Tawney', in *English Pasts: Essays in History and Culture* (Oxford: Oxford University Press, 1999), pp. 177–94.

Collins, Chik and Ian Levitt, 'The "modernization" of Scotland and its impact on Glasgow, 1955–79: "unwanted side effects" and vulnerabilities', *Scottish Affairs*, 25 (2016), pp. 277–93.

Cowie, Jefferson, *Capital Moves: RCA's Seventy-Year Quest for Cheap Labor* (New York: New Press, 2001).

Cowling, David, *An Essay For Today: Scottish New Towns, 1947–97* (Edinburgh: Rutland Press, 1997).

Cowling. K. and P. Tomlinson, 'Post the "Washington Consensus": economic governance and industrial strategies for the twenty-first century', *Cambridge Journal of Economics*, 35 (2011), pp. 831–52.

Crafts, N., *Can De-industrialisation Seriously Damage Your Wealth?* (London: Institute of Economic Affairs, 1993).

Crafts, N., 'Deindustrialisation and economic growth', *Economic Journal*, 106 (1996), pp. 172–83.

Crewe, I., 'Labour force changes, working class decline and the Labour vote: social and electoral trends in postwar Britain', in F. Piven, ed., *Labor Parties in Postindustrial Societies* (Oxford: Oxford University Press, 1991), pp. 20–46.

Damer, Seán, 'Life after Linwood? The Loss of the Cash Nexus, or, De-industrialisation in the Periphery', British Sociological Association Conference, University College Cardiff, 5–8 April 1983.

Davis-Smith, Justin, *The Attlee and Churchill Administrations and Industrial Unrest, 1945–55: a study in consensus* (London: Pinter, 1990).

Delaunay, J.-C. and J. Gadrey, *Services in Economic Thought: Three Centuries of Debate* (2nd edn; Boston: Kluwer, 1992).

Deane, P. and W. Cole, *British Economic Growth, 1688–1959* (Cambridge: Cambridge University Press, 1962).

Dell, Edmund, 'Lever (Norman) Harold, Baron Lever of Manchester (1914–95), *Oxford Dictionary of National Biography* (Oxford: Oxford University Press, 2004–16, online).

Dennis, Norman, Fernando Henriques and Clifford Slaughter, *Coal Is Our Life: An Analysis of a Yorkshire Mining Community* (London: Tavistock, 1969).

Devine, T. M., *The Scottish Nation, 1700–2000* (London: Penguin, 1999).

Dickson, Tony and David Judge, eds, *The Politics of Industrial Closure* (London: Palgrave Macmillan, 1987).

Dimitratos, Pavlos, Ioanna Liouka, Duncan Ross and Stephen Young, 'The multinational enterprise and subsidiary evolution', *Business History*, 51 (2009), pp. 401–25.

Drucker, Henry and Gordon Brown, *The Politics of Nationalism and Devolution* (London: Longman, 1980).

Edgerton, David, 'The prophet militant and industrial: The peculiarities of Corelli Barnett', *Twentieth Century British History*, 2 (1991), pp. 360–79.

Edgerton, David, *The Rise and Fall of the British Nation* (London: Allen Lane, 2018).

Elvidge, John, 'Government in Scotland', in Kenneth Gibb, Duncan Maclennan, Des McNulty and Michael Comerford, eds, *The Scottish Economy* (Abingdon: Routledge, 2018), pp. 311–22.

Farmer, Elspeth and Roger Smith, 'Overspill Theory: A Metropolitan Case Study', *Urban Studies*, 12 (1975), pp. 151–68.

Faue, Elizabeth, *Rethinking the American Labor Movement* (New York and London: Routledge, 2017).

Feinstein, C., 'Structural change in the developed countries in the twentieth century', *Oxford Review of Economic Policy*, 15 (1999), pp. 35–55.

Field, Geoffrey G., *Blood, Sweat and Toil: The Remaking of the British Working Class, 1939–45* (Oxford: Oxford University Press, 2011).

Findlay, Patricia, 'Resistance, Restructuring and Gender: The Plessey Occupation', in Tony Dickson and David Judge, eds, *The Politics of Industrial Closure* (Basingstoke: Macmillan, 1987), pp. 70–96.

Fisher, A. G. B., *Clash of Progress and Security* (London: Macmillan, 1935).

Foden, Mike, Steve Fothergill and Tony Gore, *The State of the Coalfields: Economic and social conditions in the former mining communities of England, Scotland and Wales* (Sheffield: Coalfields Regeneration Trust and Sheffield Hallam University, 2014).

Foreman-Peck, James, Sue Bowden and Alan McKinlay, *The British Motor Industry* (Manchester: Manchester University Press, 1995).

Foster, John, 'A Proletarian Nation?', in Tony Dickson and John Treble, eds, *People and Society in Scotland, Vol. III, 1914–90* (Edinburgh: John Donald, 1992), pp. 201–41.

Foster, John, 'The Twentieth Century, 1914–1979', in R. A. Houston and W. W. J. Knox, eds, *The New Penguin History of Scotland* (London: Penguin, 2001), pp. 417–93.

Foster, John and Charles Woolfson, 'How Workers on the Clyde Gained the Capacity for Class Struggle: the Upper Clyde Shipbuilders' Work-In, 1971–2', in John McIlroy, Nina Fishman and Alan Campbell, eds, *British Trade Unions and Industrial Politics: Volume Two: The High Tide of Trade Unionism, 1964–79* (Aldershot: Ashgate, 1999), pp. 297–325.

Foster, John and Charles Woolfson, *The Politics of the UCS Work-in: Class Alliances and the Right to Work* (London: Lawrence & Wishart, 1986).

Fox, Alan, 'Managerial Ideology and Labour Relations', *British Journal of Industrial Relations*, 4.3 (1966), pp. 366–78.

Franklin, Stephen, *Three Strikes: Labor's Heartland Losses and What They Mean for Working Americans* (New York: Guilford Press, 2001).

Fuchs, V., *The Service Economy* (New York: NBER, 1968).

Gall, Gregor, 'Still brothers and sisters in arms? A note on trends in union membership and statistics', *Scottish Labour History*, 53 (2018), pp. 73–83.

Gamble, Andrew, *The Free Economy and the Strong State: the Politics of Thatcherism* (Basingstoke: Macmillan, 1994).

Gareau, F., 'Morgenthau's Plan for Industrial Disarmament in Germany', *Western Political Quarterly*, 14 (1961), pp. 517–34.

Gellner, E., *Nations and Nationalism* (Oxford: Basil Blackwell, 1983).

Gerschenkron, A., *Economic Backwardness in Historical Perspective* (Cambridge, MA: Harvard University Press, 1962).

Gibbs, Ewan, '"Civic Scotland" vs Communities on Clydeside: Poll Tax Non-Payment c. 1987–1990', *Scottish Labour History*, 49 (2015), pp. 86–106.

Gibbs, Ewan, *Coal Country: The Meaning and Memory of Deindustrialisation in Post-war Scotland* (London: University of London, 2021).

Gibbs, Ewan, 'The Moral Economy of the Scottish Coalfields: Managing Deindustrialization under Nationalization, c. 1947–1983', *Enterprise and Society*, 19.1 (2018), pp. 124–52.

Gibbs, Ewan and Jim Phillips, 'Who Owns a Factory? Caterpillar Tractors in Uddingston', *Historical Studies in Industrial Relations*, 39 (2018), pp. 111–37.

Gibbs, Ewan, Susan Henderson and Victoria Bianchi, 'Intergenerational Learning and Place-Making in a Deindustrialized Locality: "Tracks of the Past" in Uddingston, Scotland', *International Labor and Working Class History*, forthcoming, 2021.

Gilmour, Alison, 'The Trouble with Linwood: Compliance and Coercion in the Car Plant, 1963–1981', *Journal of Scottish Historical Studies*, 27 (2007), pp. 75–93.

Goldthorpe, John, David Lockwood, Frank Bechhofer and Jennifer Platt, *The Affluent Worker: Industrial Attitudes and Behaviour* (Cambridge: Cambridge University Press, 1968).

Goldthorpe, John, David Lockwood, Frank Bechhofer and Jennifer Platt, *The Affluent Worker: Political Attitudes and Behaviour* (Cambridge: Cambridge University Press, 1968).

Goldthorpe, John, David Lockwood, Frank Bechhofer and Jennifer Platt, *The Affluent Worker in the Class Structure* (Cambridge: Cambridge University Press, 1969).

Goodman, J. F. B. and P. J. Samuel, 'The Motor Industry in a Development District', *British Journal of Industrial Relations*, 4 (1966), pp. 336–65.

Goodrich, Carter, *The Frontier of Control* (London: Pluto Press, 1975; first published 1920).

Goos, M. and A. Manning, 'Lousy and Lovely Jobs: The rising polarisation of work in Britain', *Review of Economics and Statistics*, 89 (2007), pp. 118–33.

Gordon, Eleanor, *Women and the Labour Movement in Scotland, 1850–1914* (Oxford: Oxford University Press, 1991).

Gordon, R., *The Rise and Fall of American Growth: The US Standard of living since the Civil War* (Princeton, NJ: Princeton University Press, 2016).

Green, E. H. H., *Thatcher* (London: Bloomsbury, 2006).

Halliday, Robert S., *The Disappearing Scottish Colliery* (Edinburgh: Scottish Academic Press, 1990).

Hames, Scott, *The Literary Politics of Scottish Devolution – Voice, Class, Nation* (Edinburgh: Edinburgh University Press, 2019).

Haraguchi, N., C. Cheng and E. Smeets, 'The importance of manufacturing in economic development: has this changed?' *World Development* 93 (2017), pp. 293–315.

Harkins, C. and J. Egan, *The Rise of In-work Poverty and the Changing Nature of Poverty and Work in Scotland: What are the Implications for Population Health?* (Glasgow: GCPH, 2013).

Hartwell, R., 'The service revolution: The growth of services in the modern economy', in C. Cipolla, ed., *The Fontana Economic History of Europe, III: The Industrial Revolution* (London: Fontana, 1973), pp. 358–96.

Harvie, Christopher, *Fool's Gold: the Story of North Sea Oil* (Harmondsworth: Penguin, 2004).

Harvie, Christopher, *No Gods and Precious Few Heroes: Scotland since 1914* (Edinburgh: Edinburgh University Press, 1993).

Hayter, Dianne, *Fightback! Labour's traditional right in the 1970s and 1980s* (Manchester: Manchester University Press, 2005).

Henderson, W. O., *The Rise of German Industrial Power 1834–1914* (London: Temple Smith, 1975).

Helper, Susan, Timothy Krueger and Howard Wial, 'Why Does Manufacturing Matter? Which Manufacturing Matters? A Policy Framework' (Washington, DC: Brookings Metropolitan Policy Programme, 2012).

Herron, Frank, 'Redundancy and Redeployment from UCS, 1969–1971', *Scottish Journal of Political Economy*, 19.3 (1972), pp. 231–51.

Herron, Frank, *Labour Market in Crisis: Redundancy at Upper Clyde Ship-builders* (London: Macmillan, 1975).

Hobsbawm, Eric, 'The Forward March of Labour Halted?' in Martin Jacques and Francis Mulhern, eds, *The Forward March of Labour Halted?* (London: Verso, 1981), pp. 1–19.

Hobsbawm, Eric J., *Industry and Empire* (London: Weidenfeld & Nicolson, 1968).

Hood, Neil and Stephen Young, *Multinationals in Retreat: the Scottish Experience* (Edinburgh: Edinburgh University Press, 1982).

Horrell, Sara, 'Living standards in Britain 1900–2000: Women's century?' *National Institute Economic Review* (2000), pp. 62–77.

Howell, Chris, *Trade Unions and the State: the Construction of Industrial Relations Institutions in Britain, 1890–2000* (Princeton, NJ: Princeton University Press, 2005).

Howell, Chris, 'The British Variety of Capitalism: Institutional Change, Industrial Relations and British Politics', *British Politics*, 2 (2007), pp. 239–63.

Hull, C., ed., *The Economic Writings of Sir William Petty* (Cambridge: Cambridge University Press, 1899).

Iversen, T. and A. Wren, 'Equality, employment and budgetary restraint: the trilemma of the service economy', *World Politics*, 50 (1998), pp. 507–46.

Jackson, Alvin, *The Two Unions: Ireland, Scotland, and the Survival of the United Kingdom, 1707–2007* (Oxford: Oxford University Press, 2012).

Jackson, Ben, 'Neo-liberalism and the trade unions, c. 1930–1979', in Clare Griffiths, James Nott and William Whyte, eds, *Classes, Cultures and Politics: Essays on British History for Ross McKibbin* (Oxford: Oxford University Press, 2011), pp. 263–81.

Johnman, Lewis and Hugh Murphy, *British Shipbuilding and the State: A political economy of decline* (Exeter: University of Exeter Press, 2002).

Jones, Paul S. and Anne Green, 'The quantity and quality of jobs: changes in UK regions, 1997–2007', *Environment and Planning*, 41.10 (2009), pp. 2474–95.

Kaldor, Nikolas, *Causes of the Slow Rate of Growth of the United Kingdom* (Cambridge: Cambridge University Press, 1966).

Keegan, William, *Britain without Oil* (Harmondsworth: Penguin, 1985).

Kendrick, Steven and David McCrone, 'Politics in a Cold Climate: The Conservative Decline in Scotland', *Political Studies*, 37 (1989), pp. 589–603.

Keynes, John Maynard, 'National self-sufficiency', in John Maynard Keynes, ed., *Collected Writings*, Vol. XXI (London: Macmillan, 1971).

Kitson, Michael and Jonathan Michie, 'Britain's industrial performance since 1960: Underinvestment and relative decline', *Economic Journal*, 106 (1996), pp. 196–212.

Kitson, Michael and Jonathan Michie, 'The De-industrial Revolution: The rise and fall of UK manufacturing, 1870–2010', in R. Floud, J. Humphries and P. Johnson, eds, *Cambridge Economic History of Modern Britain: Vol. II, 1870 to the Present* (Cambridge: Cambridge University Press, 2014), pp. 302–29.

Knox, Bill and Alan McKinlay, 'Working for the Yankee Dollar: US Inward Investment and Scottish Labour, 1945–1970', *Historical Studies in Industrial Relations*, 7 (1999), pp. 1–26.

Knox, W. W., *Industrial Nation: Work, Culture and Society in Scotland, 1800–Present* (Edinburgh: Edinburgh University Press, 1999).

Knox, W. W. and A. McKinlay, '"Organizing the unorganized": union recruitment strategies in American transnationals, c. 1945–1977', in Gregor Gall, *Union Organizing: Campaigning for trade union recognition* (London: Routledge, 2003), pp. 19–38.

Knox, W. W. and A. McKinlay, 'American Multinationals and British Trade Unions', *Labor History*, 51.2 (2010), pp. 211–29.

Knox, William Walker and Alan McKinlay, 'The Union Makes Us Strong? Work and Trade Unionism in Timex, 1946–83', in Jim Tomlinson and Christopher

A. Whatley, eds, *Jute No More: Transforming Dundee* (Dundee: Dundee University Press, 2011), pp. 266–90.

Knox, W. W. J. and A. McKinlay, *Jimmy Reid: A Clyde-built Man* (Liverpool: Liverpool University Press, 2019).

Kuznets, S., *Modern Economic Growth* (New Haven, CT: Yale University Press, 1966).

Lawrence, Jon, *Me, Me, Me? The Search for Community in Post-War England* (Oxford: Oxford University Press, 2019).

Lawrence, R. and L. Edwards, 'US Employment Deindustrialisation: Insights from history and international experience', Petersen Institute for International Economics, Policy Brief (Washington, DC: Petersen Institute, October 2013).

Lengelle, M., *The Growing Importance of the Service Sector in Member Countries* (Paris: OECD, 1966).

Lever, W., 'Deindustrialisation and the reality of the post-industrial city', *Urban Studies*, 28 (1991), pp. 983–99.

Levie, H., D. Gregory and N. Lorentzen, eds, *Fighting Closures: Deindustrialisation and the Trade Union* (Nottingham: Spokesman, 1984).

Levi-Faur, D., 'List and the political economy of the nation state', *Review of International Political Economy*, 4 (1997), pp. 154–78.

Levinson, Marc, *The Box: How the Shipping Container Made the World Smaller and the World Economy Bigger* (Princeton, NJ: Princeton University Press, 2008).

Levitas, Ruth, 'Fiddling while Britain burns? The "Measurement" of unemployment', in Ruth Levitas and Will Guy, eds, *Interpreting Official Statistics* (London: Routledge, 1996), pp. 45–65.

Linkon, Sherry Lee, *The Half-life of Deindustrialisation: Working-Class Writing about Economic Restructuring* (Ann Arbor: University of Michigan Press, 2018).

Lyon, Mark, *The Battle of Grangemouth: A Worker's Story* (Chadwell Heath: Lawrence & Wishart, 2017).

McCrone, David, *The New Sociology of Scotland* (London: Sage, 2017).

McDermott, Kathleen, *Timex: A Company and its Community, 1854–1998* (Waterbury, CT: Timex Corporation, 1998).

MacDonald, Catriona L., 'Scotland's Affluent Workers? Pay, Stability and the Struggle for Parity at the Bathgate Motor Plant', *Scottish Labour History*, 48 (2013), pp. 95–115.

Macdonald, Catriona M. M., *Whaur Extremes Meet: Scotland's Twentieth Century* (Edinburgh: John Donald, 2009).

MacDougall, Ian, *Voices From Home and Work* (Edinburgh: Mercat Press, 2000).

MacDougall, Ian, *Voices of Leith Dockers: Personal Recollections of Working Lives* (Edinburgh: Mercat Press, 2001).

McGill, Jack, *Crisis on the Clyde* (London: Harper Collins, 1973).

McGuire, Charlie, '"Going for the Jugular": The Steelworkers' Banner and the 1980 National Steelworkers' Strike in Britain', *Historical Studies in Industrial Relations*, 38 (2017), pp. 97–128.

McInnes, Adam, 'Deindustrialisation and Gordon Brown's Approach to Devolution in Scotland', *Scottish Labour History*, 54 (2019), pp. 126–53.

MacInnes, John, 'The deindustrialisation of Glasgow', *Scottish Affairs*, 11 (1995), pp. 73–95.

MacKenzie, Robert, Mark Stuart, Chris Forde, Ian Greenwood, Jean Gardiner and Robert Perrett, 'All that is Solid? Class Identity and the Maintenance of a Collective Orientation amongst Redundant Steelworkers', *Sociology*, 40.5 (2006), pp. 833–52.

McKinlay, Alan, John Boyle and William Knox, '"A Sort of Fear-Run Place": Unionising BSR, East Kilbride, 1969', *Scottish Labour History*, 54 (2019), pp. 103–25.

McKinlay, Alan and Philip Taylor, 'Privatisation and Industrial Relations in British Shipbuilding', *Industrial Relations Journal*, 25.4 (1994), pp. 293–304.

Mannheim, Karl, 'The Problem of Generations', in Karl Mannheim, *Essays on the Sociology of Knowledge* (London: Routledge & Kegan Paul, 1952), pp. 276–322.

Marquand, David, *Mammon's Kingdom: An Essay on Britain, Now* (London: Allen Lane, 2014).

Marshall, Alfred, *Industry and Trade: A study of industrial technique and business organisation; and of their influences on the conditions of various classes and nations* (London: Macmillan, 1919).

Martin, Graeme and Martin Dowling, 'Managing Change, Human Resource Management and Timex', *Journal of Strategic Change*, 4 (1995), pp. 77–94.

Martin, R. and R. Rowthorn, eds, *The Geography of Deindustrialisation* (London: Macmillan, 1986).

Matthews, R. C. O., C. Feinstein and J. Odling-Smee, *British Economic Growth, 1856–1973* (Oxford: Oxford University Press, 1982).

Maver, Irene, *Glasgow* (Edinburgh: Edinburgh University Press, 2000).

Miliband, Ralph, *Divided Societies: Class Struggle in Contemporary Capitalism* (Oxford: Clarendon, 1989).

Mill, John Stuart, *Principles of Political Economy, People's Edition* (London: Longmans Green, 1896).

Minio-Paluello, M., 'Jobs in Scotland's New Economy' (Glasgow: Scottish Green Party, 2015).

Mitchell, James, *The Scottish Question* (Oxford: Oxford Scholarship Online, 2014).

Murden, Jon, 'Demands for Fair Wages and Pay Parity in the British Motor Industry in the 1960s and 1970s', *Historical Studies in Industrial Relations*, 20 (2005), pp. 1–27.

Murphy, Hugh, '"From the Crinoline to the Boilersuit": Women Workers in British Shipbuilding during the Second World War', *Contemporary British History*, 13.2 (1999), pp. 82–104.

Needham, D., *Monetary Policy from Devaluation to Thatcher, 1967–82* (Basingstoke: Palgrave, 2014).

Norman, P., P. Boyle, D. Exeter, Z. Feng and F. Popham, 'Rising premature mortality in the UK's persistently deprived areas: Only a Scottish phenomenon?' *Social Science Medicine*, 73 (2011), pp. 1575–84.

Oglethorpe, Miles K., *Scottish Collieries: An Inventory of the Scottish Coal Industry in the Nationalised Era* (Edinburgh: Royal Commission on the Ancient and Historical Monuments of Scotland, 2006).

O'Rourke, Kevin and Jeffrey Williamson, eds, *The Spread of Modern Industry to the Periphery since 1871* (Oxford: Oxford University Press, 2017).

Pacione, Michael, 'The view from the tower: Geographies of urban transformation in Glasgow', *Scottish Geographical Journal*, 125 (2009), pp. 127–81.

Paterson, Lindsay, *Scottish Education in the Twentieth Century* (Edinburgh: Edinburgh University Press, 2003).

Paterson, Lindsay, *Education and the Scottish Parliament* (Edinburgh: Dunedin Academic Press, 2005).

Paterson, Lindsay, 'Utopian pragmatism: Scotland's choice', *Scottish Affairs*, 24 (2015), pp. 22–46.

Paulden, Sydney and Bill Hawkins, *Whatever Happened at Fairfield?* (London: Gower Press, 1969).

Payne, Peter L., 'The Scottish Council (Development and Industry)', in Michael Lynch, ed., *The Oxford Companion to Scottish History* (Oxford: Oxford University Press, 2001), pp. 574–5.

Payne, Peter, 'Scottish Development Agency', in Michael Lynch, ed., *The Oxford Companion to Scottish History* (Oxford: Oxford University Press, 2001), pp. 575–6.

Perchard, Andrew, '"Broken Men" and "Thatcher's Children": Memory and Legacy in Scotland's Coalfields', *International Labor and Working Class History*, 84 (2013), pp. 78–98.

Petrie, Malcolm, 'Anti-socialism, liberalism and individualism: Rethinking the alignment of Scottish politics, 1945–1970', *Transactions of the Royal Historical Society*, 28 (2018), pp. 187–217.

Phillips, Gordon and Noel Whiteside, *Casual Labour: The Unemployment Question and the Port Transport Industry* (Oxford: Oxford University Press, 1985).

Phillips, Jim, 'Class and Industrial Relations in Britain: The "long" mid-century and the case of port transport, 1920–1970', *Twentieth Century British History*, 16.1 (2005), pp. 52–73.

Phillips, Jim, 'Oceanspan: Deindustrialisation and Devolution in Scotland', *Scottish Historical Review*, 84 (2005), pp. 63–84.

Phillips, Jim, *The Industrial Politics of Devolution: Scotland in the 1960s and 1970s* (Manchester: Manchester University Press, 2008).

Phillips, Jim, 'UK Business Power and Opposition to the Bullock Committee's 1977 Proposals for Worker Directors', *Historical Studies in Industrial Relations*, 31/32 (2011), pp. 1–30.

Phillips, Jim, *Collieries, Communities and the Miners' Strike in Scotland, 1984–85* (Manchester: Manchester University Press, 2012).

Phillips, Jim, 'Containing, Isolating and Defeating the Miners: The UK Cabinet Ministerial Group on Coal and the Three Phases of the 1984–5 Strike', *Historical Studies in Industrial Relations*, 35 (2014), pp. 117–41.

Phillips, Jim, 'The Closure of Michael Colliery in 1967 and the Politics of Deindustrialization in Scotland', *Twentieth Century British History*, 26.4 (2015), pp. 551–72.

Phillips, Jim, 'Economic Direction and Generational Change in Twentieth Century Britain: The Case of the Scottish Coalfields', *English Historical Review*, 132 (2017), pp. 885–911.

Phillips, Jim, 'The Meanings of Coal Community in Britain since 1947', *Contemporary British History*, 32.1 (2018), pp. 39–59.

Phillips, Jim, *Scottish Coal Miners in the Twentieth Century* (Edinburgh: Edinburgh University Press, 2019).

Pike, A., 'Structural Transformation, Adaptability and City Economic Evolutions', Working Paper 8, *Case Study Report: Glasgow* (2017).

Polanyi, Karl, *The Great Transformation: The political and economic origins of our time* (Boston, MA: Beacon Press, 1944).

Redwood, John, *Going for Broke: Gambling with Taxpayers' Money* (Oxford: Basil Blackwell, 1984).

Robinson, Emily, Camilla Schofield, Florence Sutcliffe-Braithwaite and Natalie Thomlinson, 'Telling Stories about Post-war Britain: Popular Individualism and the "Crisis" of the 1970s', *Twentieth Century British History*, 28.2 (2017), pp. 268–304.

Rodrik, D., 'Premature deindustrialisation', *Journal of Economic Growth*, 21 (2016), pp. 1–33.

Rogan, Tim, *The Moral Economists: R. H. Tawney, Karl Polanyi, E. P. Thompson, and the Critique of Capitalism* (Princeton, NJ: Princeton University Press, 2017).

Rose, D., C. Vogler, G. Marshall and H. Newby, 'Economic restructuring: the British experience', *Annals of the American Academy of Political and Social Science*, 475 (1984), pp. 137–57.

Rowthorn, R. and J. Wells, *Deindustrialisation and Foreign Trade* (Cambridge: Cambridge University Press, 1987).

Rubinstein, W., *Capitalism Culture and Decline in Britain, 1750–1990* (London: Routledge, 1993).

Savage, Mike, 'Working Class Identities in the 1960s: revisiting the Affluent Worker Studies', *Sociology*, 34 (2005), pp. 929–46.

Schama, S., *The Embarrassment of Riches: An Interpretation of Dutch Culture in the Golden Age* (London: Collins, 1987).

Scott, Peter, 'Regional development and policy', in Roderick Floud and Paul Johnson, eds, *The Cambridge Economic History of Modern Britain: Volume III, Structural Change and Growth, 1939–2000* (Cambridge: Cambridge University Press, 2004), pp. 332–67.

Simonton, Deborah, *A History of European Women's Work, 1700 to the present* (London: Taylor & Francis, 1998).

Sherif, T., *A De-industrialized Britain* (London: Fabian Society, 1979).

Singh, A., 'UK industry and the world economy: a case of deindustrialisation?' *Cambridge Journal of Economics*, 1 (1977), pp. 113–36.

Smith, Adam, *The Wealth of Nations* (Oxford: Oxford University Press, 1976).

Standing, Guy, *Work after Globalization: Building Occupational Citizenship* (London: Edward Elgar, 2009).

Standing, Guy, *The Precariat: The New Dangerous Class* (London: Bloomsbury, 2011).

Standing, Guy, *Basic Income: And How We Can Make It Happen* (London: Penguin, 2017).

Stewart, Thomas A. W., 'A disguised Liberal vote'? – Third-party voting and the SNP under Gordon Wilson in Dundee during the 1970s and 1980s', *Contemporary British History*, 33.3 (2019), pp. 357–82.

Strangleman, Tim, 'Deindustrialisation and the Historical Sociological Imagination: making sense of work and industrial change', *Sociology*, 51 (2017), pp. 466–82.

Streeck, Wolfgang, 'Through Unending Halls', *London Review of Books*, 7 February 2019, pp. 29–31.

Stride, Rory, 'Women, Work and Deindustrialisation: The case of James Templeton & Company, Glasgow, c. 1960–1981', *Scottish Labour History*, 54 (2019), pp. 154–80.

Sutcliffe-Braithwaite, Florence and Natalie Thomlinson, 'Women's Activism during the Miners' Strike: Memories and Legacies', *Contemporary British History*, 32.1 (2018), pp. 78–100.

Thompson, E. P., *The Making of the English Working Class* (London: Gollancz, 1963).

Thompson, E. P., 'The Moral Economy of the English Crowd in the Eighteenth Century', *Past and Present*, 50 (1971), pp. 76–136.

Thomson, Alistair, 'Anzac Memories: Putting popular memory theory into practice in Australia', in Robert Perks and Alistair Thomson, eds, *The Oral History Reader* (London: Routledge, 1998), pp. 300–10.

Thorpe, Andrew, 'The Labour Party and the Trade Unions', in John McIllroy, Nina Fishman and Alan Campbell, eds, *British Trade Unions and Industrial Politics: Volume Two: The High Tide of Trade Unionism, 1964–79* (Aldershot: Ashgate, 1999), pp. 133–49.

Tomlinson, Jim, *Monetarism: Is There an Alternative?* (Oxford: Basil Blackwell, 1986).

Tomlinson, Jim, *Hayek and the Market* (London: Pluto Press, 1990).

Tomlinson, Jim, 'Correlli Barnett's History: the Case of Marshall Aid', *Twentieth Century British History*, 8 (1997), pp. 222–38.

Tomlinson, Jim, *The Labour Governments, 1964–70: Volume 3: Economic policy* (Manchester: Manchester University Press, 2004).

Tomlinson, Jim, 'Mrs Thatcher's Macroeconomic Adventurism, 1979–81, and its Political Consequences', *British Politics*, 2 (2007), pp. 3–19.

Tomlinson, Jim, 'The Deglobalization of Dundee, circa 1900–2000', *Journal of Scottish Historical Studies*, 29 (2009), pp. 123–40.

Tomlinson, Jim, 'City of Discovery: Dundee since the 1980s', in Jim Tomlinson and Christopher A. Whatley (eds), *Jute No More: Transforming Dundee* (Dundee: Dundee University Press, 2011), pp. 291–314.

Tomlinson, Jim, 'De-Industrialization not Decline: A New Meta-Narrative for Post-War British History', *Twentieth Century British History* 27.1 (2016), pp. 76–99.

Tomlinson, Jim, *Managing the Economy, Managing the People: Narratives of Economic Life in Britain from Beveridge to Brexit* (Oxford: Oxford University Press, 2017).

Tomlinson, Jim and Ewan Gibbs, 'Planning the new industrial nation: Scotland, 1931–1979', *Contemporary British History*, 30.4 (2016), pp. 584–606.

Tomlinson, Jim, Carol Morelli and Valerie Wright, *The Decline of Jute: Managing Industrial Change* (London: Pickering & Chatto, 2011).

Torrance, David, *'We in Scotland': Thatcherism in a Cold Climate* (Edinburgh: Birlinn, 2009).

Torrington, Jeff, *The Devil's Carousel* (London: Mandarin, 1997).

Touraine, A., *The Post-Industrial Society: Tomorrow's Social History: Classes, Conflict and Culture in the Programmed Society* (London: Wildwood House, 1974).

Tregenna, F., 'Deindustrialisation: An issue for both developed and developing countries', in J. Weiss and M. Tribe, eds, *The Routledge Handbook of Industry and Development* (New York: Routledge, 2015), pp. 97–113.

Tribe, K., *The Economy of the Word: Language, History and Economics* (Oxford: Oxford University Press, 2015).

Tuckett, Angela, *Scottish Trades Union Congress: The first 80 years* (Edinburgh: Mainstream, 1986).

Turnbull, Peter and Victoria Wass, 'The Greatest Game No More – Redundant Dockers and the Demise of "Dock Work"', *Work, Employment and Society,* 8.4 (1994), pp. 487–506.

Turnbull, Peter, Charles Woolfson and John Kelly, *Dock Strike: Conflict and Restructuring in Britain's Ports* (Aldershot: Avebury, 1992).

Turok, Ivan and Nick Bailey, 'Twin track cities? Competitiveness and cohesion in Glasgow and Edinburgh', *Progress in Planning*, 62 (2004), pp. 135–204.

Wainwright, Emma, 'Constructing Gendered Workplace "Types": The weaver-millworker distinction in Dundee's jute industry, c. 1880–1910', *Gender, Place & Culture*, 14.4 (2007) pp. 467–82.

Walkerdine, Valerie, 'Transmitting class across generations', *Theory & Psychology* 25 (2015), pp. 167–83.

Walsh, D. and B. Whyte, 'Trends in earnings and income inequalities in Scotland and the UK 1997–2016' (2018), pp. 12–13, 21, at https://www.gcph.co.uk/assets/0000/7144/Trends_in_earnings_and_income_inequalities.pdf, accessed 4 January 2021.

Walsh, D., G. McCartney, C. Collins, M. Taulbut and G. Batty, 'History, politics and vulnerability: explaining excess mortality in Scotland and Glasgow', *Public Health*, 151 (2017), pp. 1–12.

Webster, D., J. Arnott, J. Brown, I. Turok, R. Mitchell and E. Macdonald, 'Falling incapacity benefit claims in a former industrial city: Policy impacts or labour market improvement?' *Policy Studies*, 31 (2010), pp. 163–85.

Webster, D., J. Brown, E. Macdonald and I. Turok, 'The interaction of health, labour market conditions and long-term sickness benefit claims in a post-industrial city: A Glasgow case study', in C. Lindsay and D. Houston, eds, *Disability Benefits, Welfare Reform and Employment Policy* (Basingstoke: Palgrave Macmillan, 2013), pp. 111–33.

Westkamper, E., *Towards the Re-industrialization of Europe: A Concept for Manufacturing for 2030* (Berlin: Springer, 2014).

Whiteside, Noel, 'Casual Employment and Its Consequences: A Historical Appraisal of Recent Labour Market Trends', *Historical Studies in Industrial Relations*, 40 (2019), pp. 1–26.

Wiener, Martin, *English Culture and the Decline of the Industrial Spirit 1850–1980* (Cambridge: Cambridge University Press, 1981).

Wilks, Stephen, *Industrial Policy and the Motor Industry* (Manchester: Manchester University Press, 1984).

Williams, Raymond, 'Mining the Meaning: Key Words in the Miners' Strike', in Robin Gable, ed., *Resources of Hope: Culture, Democracy, Socialism* (London: Verso, 1989), pp. 120–7.

Wilmott, Peter, 'East Kilbride and Stevenage: Some Social Characteristics of a Scottish and an English New Town', *Town Planning Review*, 34.4 (1964), pp. 307–16.

Wilson, David F., *Dockers: The impact of industrial change* (London: Collins, 1972).

Winch, Donald, 'Mr Gradgrind and Jerusalem', in Stefan Collini, Richard Whatmore and Brian Young, eds, *Economy, Polity and Society: British Intellectual History 1750–1950* (Cambridge: Cambridge University Press, 2000), pp. 243–66.

Wood, A. and J. Mayer, 'Has China deindustrialised other developing countries?' *Review of the World Economy*, 147 (2011), pp. 325–50.

Woolfson, Charles and John Foster, *Track Record: The story of the Caterpillar Occupation* (London: Verso, 1988).

Wren, A., ed., *The Political Economy of the Service Transition* (Oxford: Oxford University Press, 2013).

Wright, Valerie, 'Juteopolis and After: Women and Work in Twentieth-Century Dundee', in Jim Tomlinson and Christopher A. Whatley, eds, *Jute No More: Transforming Dundee* (Dundee: Dundee University Press, 2011), pp. 132–62.

Wrigley, Chris, *British Trade Unions Since 1933* (Cambridge: Cambridge University Press, 2002).

Wrigley, E. A., *The Path to Sustained Growth: England's Transition from an Organic Economy to an Industrial Revolution* (Cambridge: Cambridge University Press, 2016).

Wrigley, E. A., 'The PST System for Classifying Occupations', Cambridge Group for the History of population and Social Structure, paper 20, at <www.geog.cam.ac.uk/research/projects/occupations/abstracts/> accessed 25 April 2019.

Young, Alf, *Forty Turbulent Years: How the Fraser Economic Commentary Recorded the Evolution of the Modern Scottish Economy* (Glasgow: Fraser of Allander Institute, 2015).

Young, Stephen and Neil Hood, *Chrysler UK: A Corporation in Transition* (New York: Praeger Publishers, 1977).

Young, Stephen, Duncan Ross and Brad MacKay, 'Inward foreign direct investment and constitutional change in Scotland', *Multinational Business Review*, 22.2 (2014), pp. 118–38.

Zheng, J., 'The 'Entrepreneurial State' in "Creative Industry Cluster" Development in Shanghai', *Journal of Urban Affairs*, 32 (2010), pp. 143–70.

DISSERTATIONS AND THESES

Bryce Lee, Elizabeth, *The Timex Dispute Dundee 1983*, University of Edinburgh, Honours Degree in Commerce Dissertation, 1984.

Gibbs, Ewan, *Deindustrialisation and Industrial Communities: The Lanarkshire Coalfields c.1947–1983*, University of Glasgow PhD, 2016.

Gilmour, Alison, *Examining the 'Hard-boiled Bunch': Work Culture and Industrial Relations at the Linwood Car Plant,* University of Glasgow PhD thesis, 2009.

MacDonald, Catriona L., *The Shopfloor Experience of Regional Policy: Work and Industrial Relations at the Bathgate motor plant, c.1961–86*, University of Glasgow, PhD, 2013.

Index

EU representative:
Easy Access System Europe
Mustamäe tee 50, 10621 Tallinn, Estonia
Gpsr.requests@easproject.com

www.ingramcontent.com/pod-product-compliance
Lightning Source LLC
Chambersburg PA
CBHW051954270326
41929CB00015B/2656